User Interface Design

ACM PRESS

Editor-in-Chief:

Peter Wegner, *Brown University*

ACM Press books represent a collaboration between the Association for Computing machinery (ACM) and Addison-Wesley Publishing Company to develop and publish a broad range of new works. These works generally fall into one of four series.

Frontier Series.   Books focused on novel and exploratory material at the leading edge of computer science and practice.

Anthology Series.   Collected works of general interest to computer professionals and/or society at large.

Tutorial Series.   Introductory books to help nonspecialists quickly grasp either the general concepts or the needed details of some specific topic.

History Series.   Books documenting past developments in the field and linking them to the present.

In addition, ACM Press books include selected conference and workshop proceedings.

User Interface Design

Harold Thimbleby

University of Stirling

ACM Press
New York, New York

Addison-Wesley Publishing Company
Wokingham, England • Reading, Massachusetts • Menlo Park, California
New York • Don Mills, Ontario • Amsterdam • Bonn
Sydney • Singapore • Tokyo • Madrid • San Juan

ACM Press Frontier Series

Copyright ©1990 by the ACM Press, A Division of the Association for Computing Machinery, Inc. (ACM).

Cover designed by Hybert Design and Type, Maidenhead
and printed by The Riverside Printing Co. (Reading) Ltd.
Printed in Great Britain by T J Press (Padstow) Ltd, Cornwall.

First printed 1990.

British Library Cataloguing in Publication Data
Thimbleby, Harold, *1955–*
   User interface design. – (ACM press frontier series)
   1. Man. Interactions with computer systems
   I. Title
   004.019

   ISBN 0–201–41618–2

Library of Congress Cataloging in Publication Data
Thimbleby, Harold.
      User interface design / Harold Thimbleby.
         p.   cm. – (ACM Press frontier series)
      Includes bibliographical references.
      1. User interfaces (Computer systems)   I. Title.   II. Series.
   QA76.9.U83T48   1990
   005.1–dc20   90–320
   ISBN 0–201–41618–2   CIP

Preface

How not to get lost in the complexities of our own making is
still computing's core challenge.   *Edsger Dijkstra*

User interfaces are those parts of computing systems that allow the person
using the computer access to the facilities offered by the computer. Put
bluntly, without user interfaces computers would be useless. User interfaces
are often not as good as they could be: very often they are an afterthought
and in themselves may be difficult to understand, causing the user to make
unnecessary mistakes. Human–computer interfaces are not even as carefully
designed as computer–computer interfaces. They could be much better.

This book will help user interface designers to think more clearly
about interactive computer systems; it will help them appreciate some of
the latent variety and possibilities in interface design; it will help them avoid
some of the limiting traps; above all it will provide a critical framework
within which poor design can be recognized and attacked.

Computer science is necessary in user interface design. Computer
science should not just provide the programs that implement user interfaces,
but it has a definite role in design, which will be developed in this book. The
standards of computer science can be applied to user interface design. In
particular, it has a creative role—a role that is underplayed. Bad computer
science in the past has meant that the 'solutions' have generally been sought
in human sciences: studying users, their tasks and how they actually use
computers. Computer scientists have been deskilled. Computer science

is far more than the merely technical activity of knowing algorithms and writing programs for given designs.

To date, when computer science plays a role in Human–Computer Interaction (HCI) it has been seen as playing a support role: to program particular designs and to make systems work. From that perspective, this book will broaden the scope of computer science to play an active role in design. For instance, users differ radically—and some of these differences may be expressed as preferences for particular computational strategies; we shall also see that many purely technical devices to improve computer performance can be carried over into user interfaces to improve the human–computer system performance. Conversely, this book will expose some non-computer science readers to some of the exciting possibilities that can be suggested and realized by formal ideas. User interface design is also, fundamentally, a creative exercise: creativity in design is addressed throughout the book, and especially in the later chapters.

I have presented user interface design guided by, but not overwhelmed by, a formal motivation. By means of formality, and abstraction in particular, we can focus on and reason about the subtleties and details of using computers. Without formality it would be far too easy to get lost in the intricacies of particular applications. Thus in the chapter about undo (Chapter 12) we are not talking about undo in an airline reservation system, nor about undo in a circuit design system, but we are talking about undo *in general*, for whatever system it might be provided by. We can discern design possibilities and principles about undo that apply to *all* systems.

One of the main problems of working in user interface design is that by the time some idea is understood and we have a good idea how to do it, computers have moved on. We now have a very good idea how to design word processors, but now users are into desktop publishing: word processors are *passé*. By being abstract we very effectively side-step this problem. As we shall see, the formal structures of word processors, desktop publishing (and whatever comes next) can all be reasoned about equally when we refuse to get carried away by concrete details.

Some people might worry when formal methods are applied to user interfaces. Somehow formal methods are supposed to reduce the humanity and free choice of the user, and this would be worrying. In fact, *any* description of people runs the risk of being held up as a standard and deployed for repression. Where this book uses formality the intention is to expose issues, to formulate questions and hence allow you to analyse better and choose between the possibilities. This book is to enable you to act creatively, thoughtfully and effectively in user interface design.

Although documentation (manual writing, training, and so on) is not addressed as an issue in itself, the advantages of good documentation, both for users and designers, are emphasized. Documentation helps everyone to understand complex systems, and one suspects that designers sometimes need that understanding more than users. A recurring theme in this book will be the effectiveness of clarifying accurate documentation—a difficult process of first truthfully admitting idiosyncrasies, then improving the design to eliminate them. Being truthful about interactive systems—saying what is implemented, and implementing what is said—assumes that we have certain standards and a certain degree of discernment to perceive the salient issues.

The quest for truth in the face of the complexity of user interface design and the limitations of humans, whether as users or designers, motivates the book, which falls into two major parts:

▷ The first part, up to Chapter 9, describes user interfaces, various complicating factors, views on interacting with computers, and views on designing systems. Novel connections between users and computers are explored. Chapter 9 is a watershed: it is about science and explores the approach of science and justifies the application of scientific standards to user interface design.

Having embraced scientific standards the aim of the second part of the book is to explore their potential in user interface design.

▷ For a scientific approach to have merit in user interface design there needs to be a way, first, of taking an abstract view of interactive systems. This will be a source for the formative ideas underlying scientific theories for design. This abstract view must be 'binocular': for both designer and psychologist—for both computer and user. Secondly, theories must be substantial: they must be sufficient to appraise interesting aspects of typical interactive systems design. Furthermore, merely being critical is insufficient: criticism must also lead on to creative design. And even creativity is not sufficient: it must be successful often enough! Showing that this is possible is the task undertaken in the second part of the book.

The organization of the book is described more fully in Section 1.4.

I hope that you will find the way I have structured the material is in itself interesting, and that you will dig into the pile and find little treasures here and there for yourself. You will, no doubt, find skeletons that *you* can flesh out much better than I ever could. The point of the book is to get you productively involved.

Some vogue notions (for example, visual programming) get scant coverage. As the field of user interface design matures and becomes more systematic the 'important' things that can be said—and the important things we want to say—about various areas will change. There is no need to give a complete treatment of *everything* presently in user interface design: such a treatment would anyway be encyclopedic in scope and would hardly be read. In any case, the more abstract treatment undergirding this book makes such detail largely unnecessary. Many specific details would go out of date alarmingly fast—amazingly, for such a modern field, the study of its *history* is already a subject in its own right!

Readership

Although I have not discussed the technology of computer systems at all, it will certainly help if you have had some experience with some of the more recent examples of interactive systems, and know about things like: windows, menus, spreadsheets, editors, compilers, and the now ubiquitous mouse. To follow the discussion in some places, you will find knowledge of a programming language like Pascal essential; I also mention LISP, Prolog and Smalltalk, but assume less background in these languages. The book is at the level of second-year computer science undergraduates, though most of the material is new or used in new ways. The material, then, will also appeal to research workers as well as practitioners.

Teaching

I have used all of the material in this book for university and industrial courses and seminars over a period of years. Each chapter provides enough material for a one-hour presentation, with material to spare. The lecturer can be selective or flexible: the extra material often makes it easier to pursue students' comments as they arise, yet retain an overall structure. Depending on their past experience, students will find it useful to have a hands-on, practical component to their course. Working in small groups, they should certainly try set tasks on proprietary software (for example, write an essay using an idea outliner; use a drawing package; try a flight simulator; control a robot arm) and, depending on their level, criticize, formally evaluate or experimentally evaluate some suitable system. Videos are a useful supplement and are readily available from manufacturers (for example, product demonstrations) and research laboratories. Whatever their background, practicals give students common ground to criticize the various systems they have experienced; this can be very useful in follow-up seminars. Programming as an end in itself is generally too slow to give students the wide-ranging experience they would more quickly obtain by attempting various small tasks on proprietary programs—but programming environments and prototyping tools can still usefully be covered in practicals. Of course, there is a place for substantial projects, done individually or in groups. (Chapter 19 gives some project ideas and suggested background reading.)

Harold Thimbleby
Stirling University, Scotland 1990.

Acknowledgements

The University of York generously provided me with a sabbatical term at the Knowledge Sciences Institute, University of Calgary in 1986, which was sufficient encouragement to *really* start the book. Computers make writing and rewriting too easy—they encourage the consumption of many trees; the Department of Computer Science at York and later the Department of Computing Science at Stirling provided all the printing facilities I could require. I hope that improved user interfaces will soon save paper.

I am indebted to the Human Computer Interaction Group and colleagues at the University of York, particularly Alan Dix, Michael Harrison, David Lau-Kee, Andrew Monk and Colin Runciman. Michael originally challenged us to think formally, a view that his group has now developed substantially, and which underpins much of this book. Chapter 15 is based on a paper written with Colin Runciman which was published separately (Runciman and Thimbleby, 1986). Elsewhere, Bruce Anderson, Richard Bornat, Tom Carey, George Coulouris, Brian Gaines, Saul Greenberg, John Long, Bruce MacDonald, William Newman and Ian Witten have all made helpful and extensive suggestions. Anonymous reviewers at Addison-Wesley made devastating criticisms which helped remove many errors!

It is invidious to make a full list of the people who helped me in the task of writing this book. Some people lent ideas, some people lent encouragement when I was flagging. Some people may be relieved that I have not suggested their responsibility for errors; others may unfortunately be upset that I have apparently ignored their contribution to some good ideas.

Anyway all such contributions pale into insignificance against the sacrifices my wife Prue and all my family made continually for several years. I am very grateful for their love and support, for their perseverance and unfailing encouragement when I would often rather have packed up—especially early in the morning.

Isaac, my youngest son, contributed a few characters here and there; he also crashed my word processor. *What* does '`FATAL ERROR: stack overflow system halted`' mean to a one-year-old? What was so fatal about it? Anyway, he carried on typing, no doubt happy enough that the computer had put something on the screen. And my eldest, William, wondered why I should want to write about computers using a computer. It's worth knowing: I was often sustained in my effort to write because the word processors I used were so incredibly nasty that I *knew* there had to be some designers who ought to read my book.

Copyright acknowledgements

Acknowledgement is due to the following for permission to reproduce their material:

The Trustees of the Pooh Properties, Methuen Children's Books, Curtis Brown & John Farquharson, E. P. Dutton and the Canadian publishers McClelland & Stewart, Toronto for a quotation from Milne A. A. (1927). *Now We Are Six*. (Used in Chapter 1.)

W. H. Freeman and Company for an extract from Weizenbaum J. (1976). *Computer Power and Human Reason*. Copyright © 1976 by W. H. Freeman and Company. Reprinted with permission. (Used in Chapter 5.)

Kluwer Academic Publishers for a diagram from *Man-Computer Interaction: Human Factors Aspects of Computers and People*. (Used in Chapter 5.)

I should also like to thank the following copyright holders for giving their permission to reproduce updated extracts from some of my previously published papers:

Academic Press Inc. (London) Ltd for 'Dialogue Determination', *International Journal of Man-Machine Studies*, **13**, 295–304 (1980). (Used in Chapter 8.) 'Equal Opportunity Interactive Systems', co-authored with Colin Runciman, *International Journal of Man-Machine Studies*, **25**, 439–51 (1987). (Used in Chapter 15.)

Cambridge University Press for 'Ease of Use—The Ultimate Deception' and 'The Design of Two Innovative User Interfaces', both in *Proceedings British Computer Society Conference on Human Computer Interaction* (1986). (Used in Chapters 6 and 16 respectively.)

The Institute of Electrical and Electronics Engineers, Inc. for 'Delaying Commitment', *Software*, **5**, 78–86, May 1988 (© 1988 IEEE). (Used in Chapters 8 and 17.)

Pergamon Press plc for 'Failure in the Technical User Interface Design Process', *Computers and Graphics*, **9**, 187–93 (1986). (Used in Chapter 7.)

Van Nostrand Reinhold for 'Literate Programming', in Ralston A. and Reilly E. D. (editors) *The Encyclopaedia of Computer Science and Engineering* 2nd edition. (Used in Chapter 17.)

Butterworth-Heinemann Ltd for 'You're right about the cure: don't do that', *Interacting with Computers*, **2**(1), 8–25 (1990). (Used in Chapter 18.)

Contents

Boxes

Chapter 1

Introduction

Well, this bit which I am writing, called Introduction, is really
the *er-h'r'm* of the book, and I have put it in, partly so as not
to take you by surprise, and partly because I can't do without
it now. There are some very clever writers who say that it is
quite easy not to have an *er-h'r'm*, but I don't agree with them.
I think it is much easier not to have all the rest of the book.

A. A. Milne

The invention of writing about 5 000 years ago was a significant step in the
history of mankind as it enabled man to make records of his laws, stories,
civilization and calculations. Ideas could also be permanently recorded
and so started to have an authority of their own: ever since, the written
word has been held in awe—exploited first by diviners now by lawyers.
But about 1 500 years ago, when paper was invented by the Chinese, it
was no longer necessary to revere existing ideas nor dispose of them by
scrubbing the palimpsest clean. It was a cheap writing medium, which made
recording the thought process, rather than just its end result, economical.
Philosophy, art, commerce, mathematics, creative expression, law making
and just about everything blossomed. Later, the invention of movable-type
printing facilitated mass dissemination of information and hence changed
politics. More recently, about 40 years ago, the electronic computer came on
the scene, and we discovered we could do all this—think outside our heads—
without making any manifest records at all. The consequences of this last
development are just starting to be explored: How should copyright laws
work? What about invasion of privacy? How complex can rules get before
they become inhuman? What about information rights? Is the computer

always right? Who is responsible for computer error? What, indeed, are computers for, and who really benefits?

The purpose of computers is to benefit people. The view taken as the starting point for this book is that the people who should be benefiting from computers are the users, and the people best able to help them to benefit are designers. By 'users', we mean the people who have to sit down in front of computers and actually use them. By 'designers' we mean, for the moment, the people who design computer systems.

User interfaces are employed because they benefit somebody, but apart from the cynical benefits, such as commissions to the salesman, what are these benefits?

▷ *Enjoyment*: The user may wish to enjoy himself through using the interactive system. Obvious examples are playing games, hacking programs, exploring interesting problems and using the computer as a medium to communicate with others. Less obvious examples are creative systems for musical and artistic design, or word processors for easy verbal expression. Users may obtain enjoyment by using an acquired skill with a complex interactive system. Paradoxically, the 'worse' the system design, the more it may be enjoyed *after* getting used to it: users may find satisfaction by being repositories of detailed information about a system! However, such users would not have had status if the system had been so easy to use that there was no need for experts. Enjoyment may be quite subtle; for instance, if some users have certain special skills, they may prefer to be in a position where an organization relies on their goodwill.

▷ *Enabling new skills*: Computers enable users to do things never before possible. It is useful to distinguish between mere **augmentation** (increasing speed, quality and complexity) and **enabling** (that is, empowering users to perform totally new skills). Modern power stations and supersonic aircraft might not be run *at all* without computer assistance, and users with disabilities may break free from their constraints. Of course, some of the new skills that computers augment and enable are only necessary because of the system complexity made possible by the existence of the computers themselves.

▷ *Delegation*: The interface permits the user to abstract from task details; that is, the computer attends to details and lets the user concentrate on higher-level issues. People may use computers to delegate responsibility—with positive or negative results. For instance, the user may have to tell his clients, 'You can't do that because the computer can't do it.' Delegation may mean the user is not responsible for the machine he has to use! Usually, though, delegation is useful, especially when the computer system is designed to take responsibility for checking or handling potentially dangerous or simply tedious situations.

▷ *Safety*: The user need not work in dangerous or inhospitable conditions if a computer can control and monitor the system. Examples range from remote-controlled submersibles, coal mining and nuclear plant control to space exploration.

▷ *Development*: The user may wish (or be required) to learn something by using an interactive system. For some topics, such as arithmetic drill, the computer can verbalize information (such as the arithmetic rules the user seems to be using) which otherwise would not have been explicitly or clearly known to the user. User development may be **reflexive**; for instance, where the user can learn about himself, perhaps by using a careers advice or counselling system. The user has to know how to use the system itself, and educational tools for that purpose may be a major concern of the designer.

▷ *Doing things at once*: Before the days of computers, most tasks had to be done in stages, one step at a time in the right order, and often only one person (or a highly coordinated group) could do each stage. The result was that jobs took the sum of the times of their component stages, and if problems were noted at later stages, compromises were forced since going back to revise earlier stages was often impractical or too costly. For example, if you were going to give an illustrated talk, you would prepare your talk, design your slides, then prepare notes for students and your own speaker's notes. Each stage would be separate. As you prepared your speaker notes you might notice a spelling mistake in a slide, but it is now too late— it has already been prepared. However, if you did the work with a suitable computer system (a presentation manager) you could make this and other changes, at *whatever* stage you noticed them, and the changes would automatically appear on slides, student notes, and in the talk itself, as if you were doing all the stages of the job 'at once'. Another example: in conventional publishing, you first decide what you want to write, then you get it made up into pages. But in a desktop publishing system, you can enter text and concurrently arrange it to look nice—the system lets you do the tasks 'at once' so you can do them in any order you choose, sometimes worrying about layout, sometimes about what you are writing.

▷ *Computing*: Lest we forget, the most obvious benefit of computers is that they can compute! They can manage a company payroll, integrate $\sin^{100}\theta \, d\theta$, prove the four-colour theorem, construct or enhance pictures of objects that we cannot see with our eyes, compute the trajectory of a spacecraft, and so on.

All of these benefits are available when using well-designed computing systems, but they are particularly evident when using interactive computer systems. The interactive computer most directly benefits its immediate user—and these benefits are most readily squandered if the system is not designed well enough. However, the conventional, more organizational, reasons for using computers should not be forgotten:

▷ *Productivity*: The interface may permit the user to perform certain tasks faster and over longer periods without rest; for instance, many production-line tasks are routine, and a single user may be able to supervise robots, replacing the jobs of several people.

▷ *Managing complexity*: The computer permits or aids users to perform more complex tasks than they would otherwise be able to undertake. Obvious examples are controlling complex processes that would otherwise take several people or controlling real-time systems, such as 'fly-by-wire' aircraft.

▷ *Reliability*: Computer systems work more reliably than humans. The computer does not get tired or distracted: once programmed, it can perform routine operations any number of times, at great speed, and each operation exactly the same. Of course, 'reliability' is a great simplification—for some tasks, computers are much more reliable than humans, but for others they are totally unsuitable because they are too inflexible.

▷ *Quality*: Computer systems permit the user to achieve greater quality, accuracy and reproducibility (such as in computer aided manufacture or desktop publishing). Strictly speaking, these benefits result from the computer technology rather than the user interface itself. Computers can be 'trained' or programmed by experts, so that untrained users can take advantage of the expertise; for instance, an expert welder might train a robot to do a complex sequence of spot welds, then unskilled workers can simply position components to be welded.

▷ *Security*: The interface may check a user's authority to perform certain tasks, or it may require confirmation before performing potentially costly or irrevocable actions. Computers can keep records of everything that they do and who asks them to do what. This sort of information is essential for many tasks, particularly for financial matters ranging from inventory control and accounting to more mundane matters such as billing users for computer or other machine time.

We can summarize the benefits as communication and control.

Man invented writing to make communication with himself (at a later time) and with others more reliable and less prone to error. The computer, then, can be seen as a new development in *communication*. Computers mediate communication between people. They enable a single user to record his thoughts for examination later; they enable a single user to share information with others on international networks; they enable groups of users to form interest groups; they make shared thinking possible. Computers extend the horizons of everyone. If the computer is a new medium for communication, what sort of communication takes place, or might take place, between designers and users?

The computer can also be seen as a new development in *control*. Computers mediate control. A computer can control physical devices (by robot remote control, for instance) or participate in vehicle control using servomechanisms; computers can also control people—by storing and manipulating personal data. If the computer is a new medium for control, what sort of control is imposed, or might be imposed, by designers on users? Ultimately, the designer is in control, or mediates it for his clients—he has a hegemony. Once a system has been designed and delivered, it has to be used accordingly. The designer should take this hegemony seriously.

Before embarking on this book, it is well to remember that the communication and information we shall talk about is not just what passes each way at the user interface; it also includes the information of control—the political information. For some users, especially those that are handicapped with respect to their human potential, the computer can be liberating, providing them with autonomy; for some users—whether 'ordinary' computer users just doing their job or people exploited by organizations knowing something (correctly or incorrectly) about them— it can be devastating and remove all hope of self-respect and autonomy. Indeed, *every* benefit mentioned earlier can be inverted: computers may remove enjoyment; they may disable people and reduce job satisfaction; they may force the user to make difficult decisions (for instance, consider a surgeon's medical advice system); they can make life unsafe (are missiles programmed correctly?); they may hinder personal development; they can reduce productivity. Or, for instance, consider the point that computers aid the user's development, and consider the fact that many people are now unable to find work because the computer tends to make work more sophisticated. Users—and computer users will soon be the 'normal' members of society—require longer, more advanced and more risky training.

User interface design is about interacting with complex computer systems. The problems encountered in this interaction are very similar to those of politics in interacting with the populace, although, of course, in politics the emphasis is more on infrequent consultation (voting) and more on control (legislation). User interface design might give some insight into parallel issues, but it may also be used as a new tool in democracy. What would happen if every individual of voting age had computerized access to consultative systems used by government?

Until the industrial revolution, animals and workers were no more than machines. Industrialization did not bring exploitation of workers, as that was already happening and had been going on for millennia. No, industrialization gave us a sensibility for humanity that until then had never been feasible; it enabled us to see more clearly the enslavement and exploitation that had been going on all along. Interactive computers will certainly intrude into everyone's life, perhaps in ways more subtle and disturbing than the machinery of the past, but maybe they herald a new appreciation of what it means to be human. Already the intrusion of computers into our lives has highlighted the relevance of human factors.

Most early computers could only add; some could subtract as well. Now that computers can do much more, user interface design is not only a technical issue but we also have to be concerned with the people, as people, who use computers. Consider a few examples of how computers extend our appreciation of what it means to be human: handicapped users can use computer-controlled speech synthesizers—and suddenly they are back in the community; musicians can use computer controlled music synthesizers—when otherwise they would never be able to afford the services of an orchestra; children can use word processors—and enjoy developing stories, when otherwise they would be hindered by the mechanics of writing; students can run educational systems on their home computers in their own time—when otherwise they would need to attend daytime classes and pay tuition fees; computer simulations can be used for training—when otherwise there would be the costs and dangers of involving real systems (essential for training for disaster management—like how to prevent a nuclear reactor meltdown).

1.1   User interfaces

User interfaces to complex systems now abound: washing machines, video recorders, cameras, cars, handheld calculators, telephone systems, sewing machines and personal organizers are all examples where the interface enables a flexible system to be tuned to particular applications. Thus, old washing machines were simple and had few options; different washing needs had to be met with different washing machines (mangle, scrubbing board, hand). Today, a washing machine is designed to be general purpose, and it employs a user interface to specialize it to particular sorts of washing loads. Similarly, early computers could only add and subtract, and the idea of a user interface hardly merited consideration. Today, computers are capable of a vast range of activities, and they require user interfaces to specialize them to the particular tasks that their users have in mind.

User interface design is a very difficult business. It combines two awkward disciplines: psychology and computer science. These disciplines have very different cultural backgrounds: psychology is concerned with people; computer science with computer machinery. Psychologists are supposedly sympathetic and understanding; computer scientists are supposedly mathematical and precise. Psychologists have enough trouble understanding people even when they are not using computers; computer scientists have enough trouble getting programs to work even when they are not being used by people. Good user interface design requires these two perspectives to be united.

The problem this book addresses is two-faced. Life is too *short* to rely on psychology and time-consuming empirical studies of the system to be designed. Yet, life is too *long* to rely on computer science: we can surely do better than live with merely technically acceptable solutions. The dilemma is that computer scientists are becoming more formal, trying to get programs 'right first time', yet practitioners in user interface design are increasingly advocating iterative design, because it never seems possible to design an interactive system that is good enough first time. How do we reconcile formal methods, trying to implement systems correctly to specifications worked out in advance, with the apparent need for after-the-fact experimentation? To cope with the problem, we need to broaden the scope of computer science to have an active and creative role in design.

There was a time when the expert programmer was the one who knew the computer being used in great detail. Now, with the increasing use of high level languages and abstraction, the expert programmer is the one who knows the application, what to program, and the needs of the user in great detail. This is some change, and a very desirable change in perspective. Even so, the computer continues to fare better than the user. Why is it a 'bug' to 'divide by zero', but not a 'bug' to delete the user's data? Why is it good style to write a neat program, but not so neat to enable the user to express himself clearly and concisely? Why are complaining users always told that if only they did things this way or that way that their problems would not arise, whereas programmers are not allowed to debug programs by telling computers to work differently? Just look at a manual for any interactive system: if it is honest, it will have disclaimers and bug warnings. One manual for a standard word processor writes, 'You cannot delete more than 100 paragraphs.' That statement in the manual means the designers must have known about this bug *before* the program was sold; they must have been content to leave the bug alone. Any user who wanted to delete around 100 paragraphs could easily lose count. If they were deleting 99— fine! If they were deleting 101—tough! Why can't this word processor have a piece of program that converts an attempt to delete, say, 170 paragraphs into two steps of 100 and 70 paragraphs, each of which it could delete? After all, that is what it is expecting the user to do. What are computers for? Not only are there bugs in user interfaces, but too many designers are content to let them stay that way.

Many user interfaces, if they were to be used not by a person but instead by a computer, would simply not be 'usable' by the computer at all. Bugs in user interfaces are difficult to discover and 'unnecessary' to fix, because human users are very adept at finding ways to cope even with the most ridiculously designed interfaces. Current practice in designing interactive computer systems treats users as less than computers.

Computers get away with a lot of nonsense with their human users that other computers could not even tolerate.

When computer–computer communication fails, the computers are incompatible; the computers simply do not 'talk to each other'. If your word processor and your printer are incompatible, there is nothing much that can be done. But whoever heard of user and computer being incompatible? Users perhaps try too hard to use computers in the face of difficulty. If they were less forgiving of their idiosyncrasies, user interfaces would soon have to be drastically improved. Ask yourself which interactive programs had anything in their user interface design that aimed them specifically at humans, rather than, say, at martians? In contrast, every computer–computer interface devotes much attention to the limitations and features of the corresponding computers.

> Computers keep you honest. When human beings reason
> verbally they can convince themselves of a lot of fallacious
> things because it's really hard to be aware of the premises
> they're sticking in. So thinking is very loose. But with a
> computer if you say such and such processes will produce such
> and such phenomena, and you write the program, and they
> don't—well, bad luck. You'd better find out what to do about
> it. You have no way of fooling yourself.   *Herbert Simon*

There are two ways we can take these observations:

▷ First, here is a basis that can be used to criticize bad design. Whenever you are using a computer, you might ask, if I was a computer, could I have been 'programmed' to know what would happen now, or what I should do next? The chances are that the system you are using is too complex or just does not give you enough information to understand it properly. Too much is guesswork and relies on hidden assumptions. Is the documentation clear enough? Most systems have bugs: does the documentation admit them and give the user enough information to circumvent the problems? (See Box 1.1.)

▷ Secondly, if so much attention is paid to the problems of computer–computer communication, because computers as a rule cannot cope with ambiguity, errors, deadlock, and so on, what can we learn from the techniques used to help them? For example, computers use various techniques, such as handshaking, to ensure that messages are not misunderstood when transmitted from computer to computer, so can we use handshaking in human–computer communication?

So, a modest step in the right direction is to assume that the users are at least computers. We shall work through the consequences of this view, although, of course, we know that people are much more complex and are

Box 1.1 What's so good about display editors?

Try writing a program to use a text editor. In other words, the program you are to write should behave like a human user of a text editor. The first task for your program should be something simple, like finding all lines containing a certain word. First try controlling a line-oriented text editor for this task. Then repeat the exercise with a display-oriented text editor. Remember, your program should issue exactly the same commands as a user performing that same task, and it should base its actions on the contents of the screen.

Suppose you want to change the fourth character of a file to an **x**. For a programmer, using any normal programming language, this task should be trivial. In an interactive editor, however, the position of the fourth character depends on what the first three characters are. Even for such a simple task, what the user has to do depends very much on the context of the task. And very often, not all of that context is available to the user. To emphasize the point, imagine writing a computer program that generates the actions the user would have to make in order to change the character. It would be a much more complex program than the one that worked in a conventional way, directly inside the computer! If you write the program, you *must* take into account the possibility that the first three characters may be, for example, space, newline, tab. The program has to establish such facts (leaving the first three characters unchanged), then it has to find the fourth character to change appropriately. The task only appears simple until the demands on the user are spelt out in the sort of detail that would be normal to spell out for a computer!

When you have finished this project, use your skill and judgement to complete the following sentence in not more than 20 words: 'Display editors are easier to use than line editors because ...' My own answer is something to the effect that: 'Display editors are *not necessarily* easier to use. They just camouflage their problems with some rather attractive features; it is these features that make display-based text editors preferable, not easier to use.'

Your exercise, if you were to carry it out, should have shown that user interfaces are surprisingly difficult to use. Paradoxically then, some 'easier' interfaces, like display editors, are even harder to understand. There is a lot of tacit knowledge in using any program: display editors are successful to the extent that this assumed knowledge coincides with the user's knowledge. Certainly, very little of the knowledge required to write your programs will be found in the user's manual! This is why designers like their own programs so much (see Section 7.2).

embedded in complex situations. The intention is to treat people using computer systems at least as well as we already treat computers.

It is very easy to ignore important design issues. The problem is that it is possible to build working computer systems far too easily, without much thinking at all. For instance, if the program does not work when **n** is 100, we just add a line that says if n = 100 then fixit! The cheaper computing technology becomes, the easier it is to use it in a piecemeal fashion. Consequently, systems become vast, with a multitude of *ad hoc* features accreted over a long period (a process exacerbated by the fallacy of composition, see Section 7.6). If computers were slower or smaller, designers would have to deliberate over their designs. Can this feature be traded for that? Can a more powerful concept do both? Should there be so many features anyway—the user might need the memory for his data?

1.2   Abstraction: The players

Any profession forms a view as to its chosen subject of enquiry. A psychologist will see psychological issues in human–computer interaction; a sociologist, social phenomena; a graphic artist, opportunities for artistic design. Most computer scientists see user interface design as, at best, a technical issue of programming—programming is where the issues that concern *them* lie. This book extends the computer scientist's view to the wider concerns of interaction, and the interplay between users, computers and designers.

Every situation in which computers are used differs, so it is wise to start by defining some terminology that lets us get to the main issues without having to worry about circumstantial details. Abstractions will make the style of the book more direct, but at the cost of, at times, giving a false impression of integration, everything supposedly going on inside one computer and the heads of abstracted individuals.

User interface design involves three participants: user, computer, designer—and perhaps more than one of each. Normally, it is quite obvious which is which, but we shall define the roles of these participants carefully.

We define **user** as the participant *with choice*. The exercise of this choice may be limited in many ways—for instance, by job description, by handicap, even by having to use a computer—but the essential criterion is that the user has choice and can exercise this choice in working with a computer. There are many more specific terms than 'user', such as casual-users, discretionary-users, naïve-users, expert-users, handicapped-users, young-users, average-users, and so on, but in the main it will be preferable to remain non-specific about their personal attributes. Sometimes, the plain term 'user' is used to include those people who make decisions on behalf of the actual user—managers, governments and employers, for instance.

We define **computer** as the participant *with a program*; that is, the computer obeys instructions. And whose instructions? We define **designer** as the participant *who anticipates* the possible choices of the user and who somehow encodes these possibilities as a computer program.

Everything that a computer obeys can be called **program**, irrespective of whether a programmer actually supplied it. Sometimes we shall see that it is very useful to think of the user as supplying programs—even though we call them commands, mouse clicks, and so on. The user too must be 'programmed', in the widest sense. In this book, we shall mainly use the word **documentation**, but sometimes **explanation** or **manual**, to mean the knowledge given to the user to help him use the system. So, in any sentence, the occurrence of the word *document* does not exclusively mean written documentation, on-line documentation or a person-to-person training session. It means *any* of those, and perhaps even ways that have not yet been devised.

Note that these definitions are deliberately abstract. Thus, the designer may be the user's manager: a manager would typically recruit a software company (that is, an organized group of so-called designers) who would convert the manager's anticipations of the requirements into programs. For our purposes, the essential point is the politics of the situation, not the technological expertise. In this case, the manager effectively designs the system and makes the anticipatory commitments which are then transformed into a program.

From a pragmatic stand, we must therefore admit that many other people apart from 'computer scientists' are involved in computer system design. There are also the analysts who help prospective users (or users' employers) determine the design requirements; there are the technical authors who devise and write documentation; there are the evaluators who establish how well a design suits its users' requirements or various other criteria, such as how marketable or profitable the design might be. Sometimes these people will work together as a team; sometimes they will be in separate departments and have very little interaction; they may even be antagonistic to each other.

The computer need not be an electronic computer; it could be any mechanized process, such as a bureaucratic form-filling system. The point is that, by using the term 'computer', we are not automatically assuming a total and exclusively electronic computer solution for whatever tasks the user is undertaking.

The term 'user' is being used in an unconventional sense, for the same reason. Sometimes there will be one user, sometimes several; sometimes all users will be in one location, sometimes they will be dispersed. By defining 'user' as an abstract formal term, we are not worrying about such details.

It is even possible for user and designer roles to be carried out by a single person. Such situations arise very frequently when programmers use computers: they write programs for their own use and therefore have to design for themselves. It is even possible for a programmer to imagine what a computer would do when programmed in a certain way: in this case, even the computer role is implemented by the imagination of that person.

The important point is that the use of computers implies a division of people into two groups: those who are in control and anticipate, and those who are under control, however weak, and choose. The computer mediates the communication between these people.

In summary, it is pedantic to make distinctions between designers, programmers and all the other types of role involved. In this book, we shall mainly use the term **designer**, and occasionally the more specific terms 'programmer', 'implementer', 'evaluator', and so on, for precision and stylistic relief. Similarly for the terms **user** (some users are programmers or dancers) and **computer** (some computers are people).

Likewise, the pronoun 'he' is used to relate to both male and female throughout the book (except where the sex is specifically known). This is an abstraction, like the others described above, that results in a clearer style. Incidentally, 'he' as used in this book should be taken to relate to people, not just of arbitrary sex, but of any race, age, social class, or whatever. In interactive systems themselves, great care must be taken to avoid prejudice; this is not easy since merely trying to find out what to do can itself be troubling.

1.3   Abstraction: The machinery

Just as we abstract from the specific details of users, designers and computers, so it is also convenient to abstract from the specific details of the machinery used in any particular interaction. The notation this book uses is that everything the user submits to the computer is written like *this*, whereas everything the computer produces is written thus (see Box 1.2). From the use of these typefaces, you are to understand that the user and computer are speaking—they may be using typewritten text, buttons or anything really. For example, if the user can press a button marked 'stop', we can represent that by saying that the user submits *stop*. On some user interfaces there may be no button marked 'stop', so the same action may have to be effected by typing each letter individually, as in *h a l t* (it might be a German system).

Obviously, a general-purpose system will have a full alphabetic keyboard, and a calculator or cash dispenser will have numerical buttons. The disadvantage of this type of keyboard for the user is that the ability to submit anything to the computer makes it harder to decide exactly what to say. Thus, a keyboard with only two buttons marked yes and no is easier to use than one with five buttons e n o s y, even though the latter can be used to say some other things that might make other tasks faster than answering a long series of mind-numbing yes/no questions. An alternative is for the computer to reconfigure the 'keyboard' as each part of the interaction suggests. When a yes/no response is appropriate, yes and no are the buttons; when a choice between stop/start/repeat must be made, then stop, start, repeat are the buttons. This **menu-based** style of

Box 1.2 Summary of notation.

In order to present the user interface effectively in black and white in the static medium of paper, different styles of typeface have been adopted. Computer input and output—that is, what the user submits or reads— is generally shown throughout in typewriter style, not that interactive computer systems use typewriters very much nowadays. To help clarify conversational dialogues, the computer's contribution is shown in `standard typewriter`, while the user's is in *`slanted typewriter`*. When necessary, a cursor is printed as a symbol *between* the indicated characters, thus 'a◊b', although many interactive systems would display it *over* the right character. In many systems, the cursor flashes, it is therefore more readily located by the interactive user than by the book reader!

When the user has to type a special key to initiate the computer, it is written as '↩', sometimes spelt out as `enter`; it is a carriage-return key on many systems. `enter` need not mean that the user types out the five letters `e n t e r`, merely that the user has submitted a command called Enter, which might, for example, be the name engraved on a single button, or could even be a word spoken to the computer. A space, where necessary to distinguish it from nothing, is shown as '␣'.

Many interactive systems do not use text; instead, the user interacts with drawing tools and produces pictures, or maybe the system uses speech or some other non-textual technique. A simple textual interaction, such as `print file3`, may in fact be constructed from a sequence of movements and pictures. For some users and some applications, this may be much easier than typing in some artificial language. Some pictures (so-called icons) take up less space than the idea they represent; on the other hand, speech or sound may be much better. The possibilities are endless. But from our point of view, in a book, a pictorial interface for each example would take a few pages of pictures to describe adequately, whereas the textual interface takes a line. So the preponderance of textual examples in this book is not because text is generally better for user interfaces, but because text is almost always better for adult books.

interaction is clearly one extreme of keyboard interaction. (Section 16.9.4 gives a real example of where a menu might be extended at least to every key normally available on a keyboard.) Often, textual menus are inappropriate, as words may be too long, and so pictures (**icons**) may be used instead.

Keyboards are normally operated by the user's fingers (although some users hold a stick in their teeth), but if the keyboard—or menu—is displayed on the screen, then other means can used. The most popular pointing device is the mouse, although it is quite possible for screens to be equipped with touch-sensitive devices so fingers can still be used. Common alternatives are trackballs and joysticks, sometimes with interesting mathematical input transforms (for example, being rate controlled or non-linear). The user can be given greater freedom using a 'dataglove': a hand glove with sensors to track where the user is pointing, whether he is gripping, and so on. Even the direction of eye gaze, the user's controlled breathing, sucking and puffing may be used to control a mechanical pointing device.

And for output, the computer need not only present data as text on a black and white screen. It might be green! It might be a graph, or a picture, or a sound, music or speech. The output device might be something small, like a digital watch, or it might be something big that the user climbs into, like a flight simulator. It might be electrical impulses that move the user's paralysed hand. The possibilities are endless.

The problem, then, for this book is that there are many concrete alternatives for user input and output, yet we do not always want to spell out the various alternatives and their relative merits, nor always explore the circumstances under which such merits can be most effectively realized— *even though such issues are crucial*. What about direct computer–brain links, say? We will conveniently assume that the user has a keyboard, a mouse and a display capable of showing both text and graphics—as representative of any of the possible devices. Since, for us, these devices are abstract, concrete issues (such as the layout and design of keyboards; the design of special interfaces for the handicapped; the design of interfaces for special tasks, such as musical composition, flying aircraft or for doing architectural design) can be glossed over. Even with these simplifications we will be kept happily occupied for the rest of the book!

Interesting and important things can be said about human–computer interaction when we *do* abstract away from the endless representational details. Often, the designer's quite understandable preoccupation with representation means that the underlying meaning and structure of interaction gets lost. We can *reason* about user interface design and know the limits of our reasoning—and the limits and possibilities of our interactive systems.

1.4   Structure of the book

Having sketched the book's point of view on user interface design, how does the argument develop through the chapters?

▷   *Chapters 2–5*: Chapter 2 [*Interaction*] raises the fundamental issues in interaction and design. The central role of models is made clear. The next three chapters, 3 [*From the user*], 4 [*Through the interface*] and 5 [*To the computer*], look first at the user, then the interface, then the computer. Each topic is covered abstractly; thus, we do not have to worry whether users have red or green hair, whether interfaces use French or Spanish, or whether computers are electronic or extraterrestrial.

▷ *Chapter 6*: The purpose of this book is to make systems easier to use—certainly to help designers make their systems better. But 'easier to use' is a rather vague slogan. Chapter 6 [*Easy to use?*] explores several issues to do with ease of use. There are many systems that would be better if they were *harder* to use, but the main argument is that there are some things that cannot be easy to use in principle. Chapter 6 makes an important analogy between the use of computers and the use of any formal notation, such as mathematics. This analogy is behind many of the book's later insights.

▷ *Chapters 7–8*: If 'easy to use' is simplistic, then 'design' glosses over many deep problems. The purpose of Chapter 7 [*Basic design problems*] is to raise some of the systemic design issues; for instance, users change their mind, so no matter how well a system is designed, something else would have been better! There may be systemic problems in design, but the designer's attitudes are often more important. Design is difficult, and there are different ways to react to its difficulties. For example, we might make the user interface very restrictive, so that its design is easy to analyse; or we might build prototype systems, try them out and have several goes at developing the best system. Chapter 8 [*Attitudes to design*] explores these issues. Interestingly, there are connections between the way humans habitually tackle complex problems like design and the ways in which computers may be programmed. Exploring such traits is interesting, not least because designers can now consciously choose appropriate design strategies, rather than merely doing whatever comes naturally.

▷ *Chapter 9*: The chapters so far have reviewed the present state of user interface design. They have made a large number of novel connections between design and computing: between designers, computers and users. One theme is the complexity of user interface design. Science is, of course, a highly developed intellectual approach for understanding the complexities of nature: we now argue that user interface design is synthetic science and discuss the consequences. Hence Chapter 9 [*Science*] discusses science and the role of science in user interface design.

▷ *Chapters 10–11*: Science in theory is quite different from science in use. Chapter 10 [*Principles for principles*] develops an approach for applying scientific standards to user interface design. We introduce generative user-engineering principles which have a status for user interfaces similar to that of scientific theories. Next, we must show that there are such theories! This is the task of Chapter 11 [*Modes and WYSIWYG*], which discusses modes, WYSIWYG and some other crucial issues. Of particular interest is the development of principles that are domain independent; that is, ready-made, pre-tested principles that can be used in new applications.

▷   *Chapters 12–13*: Modes may make user interfaces more powerful, but they increase the probability of accidental errors. Chapter 12 [*Undo*] examines mechanisms for undoing operations, such as those made after a mode error. Undo allows the user to 'talk about' the past with the computer, and so we explore ideas that make 'the history' part of the interaction rather than an afterthought. The behaviour of an interactive system can be expressed as a mathematical function of its history of interaction with the user: this is an ideal that lends itself to formalization. Thus Chapter 13 [*A formal model for interactive systems*], next, develops a simple model of interactive systems. Although simple, this model can readily express various important user interface principles.

▷   *Chapter 14*: Rather than develop the model with increasing formality, or apply it to a concrete example of an interactive system with all the nasty details, we go on to discuss the use of mathematics more generally in design. Chapter 14 [*Mathematics*] shows that mathematics, even very simple mathematics, can be used creatively and critically in design.

▷   *Chapters 15–17*: The next three chapters look at design more generally. Chapter 15 [*Equal opportunity*] introduces a powerful new design principle and gives copious examples. Indeed, we can now see how to design our own principles. Next, Chapter 16 [*An example design*] applies our insights to developing a small application. We deliberately choose the boring old handheld calculator, since the chances of innovative design here would seem to be remote in such a heavily explored area! Innovation however turns out to be easy. Chapter 17 [*Good by design*] discusses design in general, drawing out steps that were merely implicit in the previous chapter and, indeed, throughout the book. There are very powerful and general ways to develop high-quality, innovative user interfaces. Anyone can use such methods to improve the design of systems.

▷   *Chapters 18–19*: The penultimate chapter is an epilogue and takes a look into the future of interactive systems design. The final chapter [*Carrying on*] contains a bibliography and suggestions to follow up and practise the ideas in this book. You can help make that future.

Chapter 2

Interaction

A curious analogy could be based on the fact that even the hugest telescope has to have an eye-piece no larger than the human eye.

Ludwig Wittgenstein

A potential computer user needs to understand how to use it to carry out work. Of course, there are different ways to understand and people will have different abilities for doing so. One user may want to know how to get the computer to perform some task such as printing a shopping list; another might want to play a better game of chess by understanding the machine's strategy; another might be a programmer who wants to express some command in a particularly elegant way and to do so it is necessary to understand the system in considerable detail.

Humans have a natural propensity for understanding, for **modelling** their environment: both to control it and to be able to think about it, perhaps to 'control' it in their imagination. Because we can balance on one leg, recognize a bird call and hold conversations, shows that we have an innate capacity for modelling: we depend on it for our everyday survival. In an everyday conversation, when someone says 'I know exactly what you mean'—when perhaps that is not so—the listener is letting his model of the situation you are describing fill in various details you have not yet divulged.

Users of computers form models of the computer systems. These models may be quite specific and analytic (for instance, 'if I do this, then it will do that' or 'it works like *this* ...'); they may be metaphorical (for example, 'it works something like a typewriter'); they may be teleological or anthropomorphic (for example, 'it does not *want* to do that'). Models

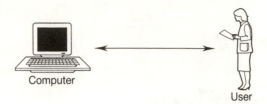

Figure 2.1   Computer–user interaction.

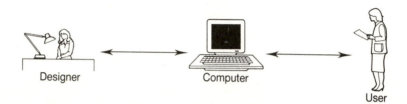

Figure 2.2   Bringing in the designer.

are necessary to use a system. The style and veracity of the model depends very much on the user's training and previous experience, and indeed on the design of the computer system itself, and how much the designer was in tune with the user's needs. Computers can be designed to suggest more complex models of themselves than they really warrant.

The simplest view of human–computer interaction is shown in Figure 2.1. The arrow represents the **user interface**. The user interface is an information channel that conveys information between user and computer. Figure 2.1 is a departure from tradition: traditional definitions of the user interface suppose that it is 'interactive'. Our diagram makes no mention of temporal issues, and emphasizes that the user interface exists for both non-interactive and interactive modes of computer use. The design of programming languages is as much part of user interface design as the design of arcade games.

From our perspective, however, the diagram is deficient for it omits the *designer*. Figure 2.2 rectifies this problem.

The most interesting thing about Figure 2.2 is that the apparently equal status of the two arrows is misleading. *First* the designer implements a computer system (generally a software system, but sometimes the designer will be in a position to choose, if not influence, hardware aspects of the system): this is generally the result of a bout of intense work. *Then* the user interacts with the system, perhaps very intensely, over a much longer period. Also, the bandwidth available in each direction between the user and computer is not equal. Thus the identical arrows in Figure 2.2 are

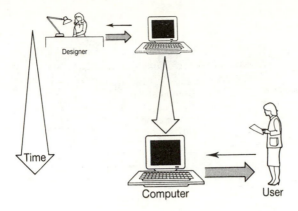

Figure 2.3   Allowing for time.

somewhat misleading; they represent very different styles of interaction. Figure 2.3 makes both the time and the quantity of interaction more explicit. The limited bandwidth for communication between designer and user is effectively reduced further by the difficulties of modifying designs: the user might communicate, but it often has no result! Inevitably the computer becomes a scapegoat for the designer. How often have you been told, 'it is done like this *for* the computer' or 'the *computer* can't do *that*!'

The information flowing through the user interface is not sufficient to use the computer. There are information flows in addition to those shown that enable the user to operate. For instance, over the years, the user has acquired information about how the world and things in it operate and some of that knowledge *must* (of course!) be drawn upon to use a computer. More specifically, the user will have information about the tasks he wants to undertake in conjunction with the computer system: these tasks will not be fully represented in just the information flowing through the user interface, so a more realistic information-flow diagram is shown in Figure 2.4.

For example, the user has a task to undertake (it may be a particular user with a task specified in his job description or an imaginary user with a typical task to perform); the designer knows something about that task. The designer and user may also cooperate, to varying degrees, to help ensure that the designer has the right information about the user's task.

We might continue to refine the diagram. For instance, the user does not work in isolation, but is part of a social system; or we might note that the computer is probably part of a distributed system. The interface may be **open**; that is, used to control external devices (as in industrial process control) or equivalently to control simulated devices (for example, simulating aircraft controls for pilot training). In these cases there are real-time requirements and physical **compatibility** requirements.

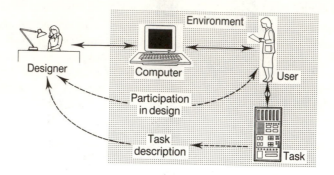

Figure 2.4   More information flow.

Directions of movement that are expected by most people are **population stereotypes** (see Section 3.2); and systems that correspond to such stereotypes are compatible. Note that what is compatible in one culture is not necessarily compatible in another. For example, if a joystick is used, when it is pulled back the plane should *soon* (real-time requirement) *increase* (compatibility requirement) in altitude. In a **closed** system the user is operating on more abstract objects within a freer time scale. For example, the user may be preparing a spreadsheet. Any feedback that may come from the outside world will occur after this particular phase of the interactive session with closed tasks. The external compatibility requirements are minimal and the designer has correspondingly greater freedom of choice. The relevance of compatibility to user interface design will be taken up again in Chapter 15.

But we are taxonomizing and not introducing *powerful* new concepts into the discussion. Let's emphasize the central concepts raised so far:

▷ The designer's information about the user and his tasks is *mostly imagination*. What the designer thinks he knows will inevitably be based heavily on his own personal world experience. It is therefore rather too easy to underestimate the effects of individual differences, particularly to misjudge the differences between the designer and the user.

▷ The user interface information flow alone is *too low* to make interaction satisfactory if that is the only channel of information. Almost all techniques for improving user interfaces can be interpreted as increasing the information bandwidth of the user interface. The 'fallback' is to tell the user more about how the system works—write better documentation or training manuals, or send the user on courses . . . all of which provide the user with more information before setting hands on the interface.

So how are systems really used, if there is not enough information in the interface itself?

> ▷ The most important source of additional information to make systems usable comes from, on the user's side, **mental models**, and, on the computer's side, **programs**. The mental models and programs are run simultaneously by user and computer: they provide the additional information essential for the user interface to operate.

And why are there any problems?

> ▷ The models/programs are *not equivalent*. It would be rather remarkable if user models and computer programs were equivalent, even if the computer was a biological twin of the user. User interfaces are difficult to use because these models/programs provide different information. They are certainly not isomorphic, they are not synchronized, they use different logical systems, they have different bugs and limitations, and so forth.

There is ample opportunity for the user *and* computer to get confused. We defined user, computer and designer in the last chapter as abstract roles: what distinguishes these roles is their models, and the models are clearly of very different natures.

It is useful to introduce a term to help remind us that *all* computer systems have models of their users. Some interactive systems may have explicit models of the user: a teaching system might, for instance, keep a score of a student's correct answers, and repeat exercises or vary the difficulty of questions appropriately. Other systems will have no explicit model, not even a scalar score or 'verbosity' settings to permit users to have chatty or quiet dialogues. However, even these systems have an implicit model of the user, namely the assumptions built into the program by its designer. Many assumptions are 'trivial': for instance, the program may make implicit assumptions that the user will *never* try to word-process a document over a megabyte in length. Others will be much more subtle. The **canonical model** is this predetermined, generally implicit, model of the user (or other system)—canonical simply means 'according to a formula', that is, according to the program as devised by the system designer.

Human–computer interaction can be improved by:

> ▷ Increasing the coherence between the mental model and the canonical model. But if the user's and the system's model were *exactly* equivalent, there would be little point using the computer for it could all be done in the head—the canonical model has to have certain 'advantages', such as speed or resolution as we described in Chapter 1.

> ▷ Decreasing reliance on that coherence, typically by increasing the information capacity of the user interface. But making the user interface bandwidth indefinitely large would have consequent problems of its own. Would it involve brain surgery and special prostheses?

I find it amusing that when display-based systems are demonstrated the demonstration often ends up with a bewildering amount of data on the screen. It is almost as if the purpose of the demonstration is to show off the capabilities of the hardware—just how much can be packed on a big screen—rather than how easy the system might be to use. Perhaps, in the eyes of its designers, the ability to make the display look like a disorganized desk so demonstrates the bandwidth of the system that one is supposed to infer it is easy to use. The problem is that the user needs high bandwidth *and* constraint to know how to run the models. With no structure, a high bandwidth can be used as a palliative for a poor design, and is sometimes used as a substitute for good structure; with little bandwidth, a sophisticated structure makes the system hard to learn to use effectively. In summary, a high bandwidth provides lots of information, but it is not necessarily informative.

2.1 Bottlenecks

Information is not some etheric concept that can be transferred from point to point instantly and without cost; none of the concepts above would have any significance if information could always be readily available in the right form where it was needed. For our present purposes we need not consider 'mind transfer' that would somehow sidestep all known bandwidth limitations and known limitations about people's stamina for new knowledge. Information takes up space for memory to store it, requires space and time to transfer it from point to point (for example, along wires or nerves), can be changed by computation or thought and, unfortunately, is also subject to error. Circumventing errors itself takes up space, time and computational resources.

Enough information must be transferred between user, designer and computer for an effective design to result. Once a system has been implemented, enough information must be transferred between user and computer for the user to be able to make effective use of the system. And, prior to use, the designer (or his representatives) must give the user adequate information to start using the system (for instance, by providing documentation or relying more on shared world knowledge). For many reasons, none of these information channels is as wide as one might wish.

For simplicity, let's concentrate on the user–computer interface (the other two interfaces raise similar issues) and assume that the pressing problem is for the user to obtain information from the computer. The discussion could be made twice as long by exchanging the words 'computer' and 'user' in each example—there is no need to think *exclusively* of the user trying to obtain information from the computer; sometimes the computer needs information from the user—and then three times longer again by examining each of the three bottlenecks of Figure 2.5 separately.

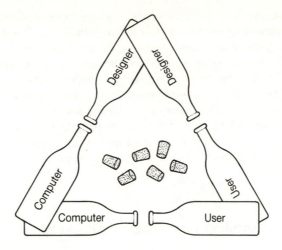

Figure 2.5 External bottlenecks.

Computer, user and designer are abstractions of the real thing. Unfortunately, information has to be got to and from the right place at each end of the interface, and there are hidden bottlenecks *within* both computer and user. Starting from inside the computer and ending inside the human mind, the bottlenecks are:

(1) The von Neumann bottleneck (see Chapter 4 for further details). Information must be transferred from the computer memory, processed and then output. The information to be transferred may run to millions of bits, but it must be processed in steps, each step operating on only tens of bits.

(2) The interface bottleneck itself:

  (a) The computer input/output bottleneck. For instance, the screen is not big enough or of high enough resolution or the keyboard can only be used to enter one byte every tenth of a second.

  (b) The user input/output bottleneck. The user's eyes, fingers, and so on are physiologically limited.

(3) The mental bottleneck. Once the user 'has' the information impinging on his senses, either it must be stored for later use, or the user must think about it there and then. Either way, the user is limited by the way the human mind works: memorization is difficult; thinking is difficult; and doing both at once is nearly impossible.

For clarity it is useful to distinguish information *transfer* bottlenecks (2a, computer input/output; 2b, human input/output) and information *processing* bottlenecks (1, von Neumann; 3, mental).

'Bottleneck' is a nice, emotively laden term that rather suggests difficulty in conveying information, amassing backlogs, maybe with things overflowing. A more moderate term is **filter**. Using this term, instead of bottleneck, we can see how effective *exploitation* of filters, rather than *avoidance* of bottlenecks, can improve the user interface. For example, suppose that the computer has a very large database of facts and the user wishes to know the details of just one of them: the computer can first of all filter the database so that relatively little useless information is actually transmitted to the user. Various techniques are available for widening bottlenecks, to meliorate information transfer, which we will look at in Chapter 4.

2.2 Testing models and magical thinking

Users construct internal models of the systems they use. These models will be constrained by the architecture of the mind (and the social context in which the users find themselves)—and by information and experience available to them. The models that users construct are not static but evolve over time as new information is accumulated and assessed.

Models are precious things and users are generally reluctant to perform experiments from which they can learn things that may invalidate their models. Instead, when evidence accumulates that a model is inadequate, a user will often elaborate the model rather than discard it and search for a simpler one. **Magical thinking**, as it is called, occurs when a user employs spurious information to help reconcile his inadequate model with actual system behaviour. An extreme example is that when a user had a lucky rabbit's foot in his pocket, he may have managed to get the system to print a file properly. The rabbit's foot becomes an accredited part of the model, and the user is reluctant to find out whether he can use the system *without* the foot. Further success with the system, with the rabbit's foot accessible, will reinforce the user's behaviour. Once the user has 'discovered' the magical effect of the rabbit's foot, if it should fail, he will search for other similar elaborations. For instance, the rabbit's foot 'only works in the *left* pocket'—which the user realizes just happens to be where it was last time he was successful. I myself don't use a rabbit's foot, but I do think that if I change the baud rate on my terminal link it somehow 'resets' the system: this *may* be right, or it may be my imagination, my techno-rabbit.

Superstitious thinking is quite sensible if a person only has a limited time to experiment with the system. Superstitious thinking is very similar to the phenomenon known to all programmers: when a program gets large and cumbersome, but it still needs changes, it reaches a stage of complexity that Brian Kernighan calls 'write only'. The only way to develop the program is to *add* more to it: what is there is already too complex to understand

and rationalize. The problem with programs, and possibly also with mental models, is that the program only shows the final ideas of its writers: all the rest, its history and development, the testing and debugging, the refining route from the original simple program to the now complex program, is lost. What the programmer wants to help him modify a complex program is the *reason* why the program is as it is; and that has been lost. Similarly people think superstitiously, 'write only', when they don't know the teleology of the system they are trying to 'understand'.

2.3 Criticisms of the model view

Models are alternative ways of describing things. Generally a model is more abstract than the thing it describes. A model car looks sufficiently like a car to entertain a child, but it may contain no engine or rear-window de-mister. Mathematical models have additionally a well-defined relation with the thing being modelled. The advantage of a model is that it permits someone to reason more effectively about *certain* aspects of the thing modelled.

There are various criticisms of the model view, and although they are 'philosophical', many are serious attacks on our endeavour to understand user interfaces.

> ▷ The **metacircular model** criticism, or **Hume's Problem**. Unfortunately, at some stage you have to understand the model itself, and that generally requires *another* model. Therein lies a danger of infinite regress—a problem that has been recognized for a long time. For instance, if you explain how the human mind works by positing an homunculus living in the pineal gland, how do you explain the homunculus itself? Ultimately a metacircular model is hit, which is explained in terms of itself or in terms of an earlier model. We will see in Chapter 4 that metacircular models *do not* explain lots of crucial things, and that this feature can be turned to advantage.

> ▷ Loss of **representation**. The main point of a model is to have something simpler to reason with, and generally this means abstracting and glossing over various representational details. We trade abstracting out the rear-window de-mister with having a better grasp of other (or more critical) aspects of the design. This is valid if our concern is with correctness, efficiency or any such readily defined properties. But if we are concerned with vague properties, like ease of use, more issues will be lost beyond the focus of the modelling. In this book, we have deliberately chosen to use keyboard, mouse and display as canonical interaction devices, and we have thereby lost representation detail and choices inherent in their alternatives.

> ▷ The **holist** criticism. Loss of representation is a 'simple', or at least conscious, tradeoff. The holist view is more radical: it claims that

modelling unavoidably loses issues of *essential* significance. The whole of a system has properties that are nowhere present in any of the parts that are being modelled. For instance, a system may have purposes and goals that no parts of it separately exhibit.

Douglas Hofstadter mentions that he was once in a conversation about a computer system that became unusably slow when more than 35 people were using it. He suggested finding the 35 in the program and increasing it ... the point is that there is no such variable. You could not deduce 35 from a model unless it was purpose built to discover that figure, in which case there will always be something else, perhaps more important, that cannot be deduced.

▷ The **Turing Hierarchy** criticism. A model powerful enough to describe an interesting interactive system is likely to be Turing Complete (see Chapter 5): it could therefore model everything a Turing Machine could model. It is therefore not clear what such a model says about the *particular* system.

▷ Given that modelling does happen—and it must be admitted that our brain's neurons or our computer's electronic gates model thinking or computing respectively *in some sense*—and despite its problems, maybe the issue is not what is modelled, which is a variable factor, but *how* things are modelled and how models are used. This is the **phenomenalist** alternative (described in more detail in Box 2.1). Even if we are thinking about or with a model, we are engaged in activity. Thus, there is an alternative perspective to modelling: life is not based on theories or models but on actions, that is, on phenomena.

2.4 Projection and transference

User models are rarely fully conscious and known to the user. People ride bicycles and perform all sorts of activities without really knowing how they do it. Careful observation of the user's behaviour may however expose the model. One common route for a model to be revealed is through **projection**, when the user interacts with a system (another person or a computer system) as if that system was itself using part of the user's model. The user assumes the system will do, or wants to do, something, implicitly because the user himself wants to (or would want to in those circumstances). Projection, then, is a sophisticated phenomenon; it is generally subtle, often ascribing motives that users may not even recognize in themselves. Projection saves time: it is easier to project rather than first check that the model is accurate. (Chapter 11 makes clear that there are occasions where it is impossible to check that a model is accurate anyway.)

Box 2.1   Phenomenology.

Whatever models users may have of interactive systems, the reason why they use computers is because they have purposes, they want to perform activities with other people and with themselves. These are all so-called **phenomenological** issues (Winograd and Flores, 1986). The main issues from the phenomenological, rather than modelling perspective, are:

▷ **Agency** is more fundamental than modelling. If we want to comprehend how to use a system, we indeed employ a model. But even using a model to understand the system, we are necessarily engaged in the activity of *using* that model. The argument is that it is not the modelling but the phenomenon of use that is central. In particular, agency involves transferring information from one agent to another (for instance, to and from user and computer) in order to make or alter **commitments**. In fact we will discuss commitments and attitudes towards commitments many times throughout this book—for example, that designers and users have differing styles of commitment to interactive systems.

▷ We can only be engaged in a limited number of phenomena—possibly only one phenomenon namely 'us'. We are therefore **blind** to all other phenomena. Blindness, then, is analogous to the loss of representation caused by abstraction in a model.

▷ We cannot avoid being in phenomena. Even if the user stops submitting commands, the computer may draw conclusions from the slowed reaction times. For example, interacting with an arcade game: *whatever* the user does, the computer is still playing it. The user is **thrown**; he is engaged in interaction, or whatever phenomenon, even when he wants to 'step back' and reflect on it.

▷ Normally the user will be performing tasks with the computer, for instance writing a letter. The computer is **ready to hand**, for it is acting as an extension of the user, the computer as such is transparent. That is, the task the user is thrown in is writing as such, the computer only becomes apparent when it intrudes. This brings us to the next point.

▷ Systems do not stay ready to hand indefinitely, they may **break down**. So when the user has typed a megabyte-long letter, suddenly the system imposes itself on the user and interrupts the activity. The user can no longer continue writing his letter, readiness to hand is lost: the phenomenon of letter writing has broken down, and now the user must solve problems of quite a different nature.

Under the phenomenological stance, 'ease of use' must be thought of as a disposition. Systems are not easy to use—ease of use is not a property 'had' by a system—but systems have a disposition to be easy (or difficult) *when* used.

The transition from the standard reductionist view of modelling (models are the answer) to phenomenalism (agency is the answer) will be mirrored in Section 8.1 when we consider personal intellectual sophistication.

Clearly, the more complex a system, the more likely the user is to project. In the context of user interface design, projection is generally unfortunate since it occurs when the user's knowledge of the system is sufficiently vague and when the user is not fully aware of the model.

Transference is a psychological mechanism related to projection, but instead the user projects not his own model but one from some other personality (such as one of his parents). This means that the user may 'lock' the interface into some pattern of discourse that in real life has been frequently rehearsed with the other person. Of course, transference is an important phenomenon in counselling, but it happens in a more mundane way with computer systems. The user may transfer models learnt with other systems on to the present system.

2.5   Non-determinism

Systems may not provide the user with enough information for him to perform his tasks. This may be because the user does not have a good enough model (his fault?), or it may be because the system is intrinsically unpredictable (the system's fault?).

ERNIE (the Electronic Random Number Indicator Equipment) excepted, very few computer systems are completely or deliberately random and fundamentally non-deterministic. Most sources of randomness (for example, real-time races) are considered to be bugs: computer programs should (at least in principle) be predictable or fully determined. In these cases, the only source of non-determinism is in the unpredictable interactions with the real world—such as actions of other users or other resources not under the control of the programmer (for example, a chemical plant). Of course, many games rely on randomness: to help provide surprises, and to reduce the amount of precise information known to the user.

A situation may *appear* to be random if the user does not have an adequate model of it, though we have already seen that the user is likely to develop a complex or magical model of its behaviour if he, for one reason or another, does not explicitly classify it as 'random'. However, many systems are known by their users to interact with the real world, that is, with other users or with industrial processes. It is generally not possible for the user to model these events adequately, so system behaviour that results from real-world interactions is accepted as non-deterministic.

A special case of interference from the real world is dependence on time when the user is unable to discriminate the intervals. 'Real-time races' occur when system decisions are made depending on which information arrives first: the system can easily discriminate intervals of nanoseconds that the user perceives as simultaneous. Alternatively, intervals may be so long that the user cannot discriminate modest differences. A system may have a precise schedule for erasing old information, say files unused for more than 28 days. It may be that users do not have such a precise conception of 'month': they may underestimate the age of data in which they have a special interest—and then be surprised when the system erases it. That is, they have not modelled it.

Non-determinism may arise through simple lack of knowledge. This may be because of poor explanation in the first place, or it may arise due to poor memory. A designer should consciously take account of these factors and provide features to restore and supply information. Such features may be very general, such as note-takers, diaries, transcripts (that is, automated note-takers); they may be passive (such as user manuals); they may be active (such as guidance and help systems).

2.6 Conclusions

This chapter explored interaction. We saw that successful interaction relies on models; it goes without saying that computers run programs in order to interact with humans, but it needs emphasizing that humans run programs—called models—to enable them to interact with computers or indeed anything else. Although there are interesting philosophical problems which we briefly touched on, the practical issue is that computer programs and user models are not equivalent. This causes problems that are exacerbated by the limitations (communications bottlenecks) of the user interface.

The analogy of humans running programs has its dangers; it has advantages too. Straight away we see that the user needs suitably formed data to 'run his program'—meaning that the output from the computer should be suitably defined. Then, of course, the user needs a program! Thus, the system must be documented (quite how the user converts the documentation into a program in his head is another matter, but he certainly needs the information). Intriguingly the idea that the user runs a program step by step, fragment of input, fragment of output, is not the only way we can take the program analogy. There are other programming paradigms, and we will shortly explore the impact of these alternatives on user interface design.

To help towards designing good user interfaces, the next three chapters lay the foundations for understanding the user, the interface and the computer. Understanding design and designers comes later!

Chapter 3

From the user

Man is still the most extraordinary computer of all.
John F. Kennedy

Whether we act as users or designers, our reasoning processes are unreliable. Consider playing a game like chess (or some other board game with no element of chance apart from making mistakes). Both players have all the information about the positions of the pieces in front of them: there is no unknown information. In principle, the outcome of the game should be a foregone conclusion. But the players simply cannot think clearly enough about the choices open to them, nor the full consequences of their next move on the state of play many moves later. These problems are not simply because players think slowly. Even if chess players could take as long as they wished between moves, they would still make mistakes. So human thought processes are limited; if human thought were not limited, playing chess would be far less interesting.

A simple (and widely known) experiment you can try will illustrate the point nicely (Johnson-Laird and Wason, 1977). Suppose there is a pack of cards and you are told,

each card with a vowel on one side has an even number on the other side

Four cards are then placed on a table surface, and show 'A', 'B', '1' and '2' on their upper faces (Figure 3.1). Which cards would you have to turn over to check what you had been told about the cards was true? Try working this out now—though if you have met this problem before, you are partly testing your memory rather than your reasoning processes.

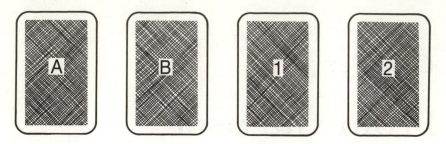

Figure 3.1   A problem with four cards.

Many people when asked this question say that looking to see the other side of the 'A' card is sufficient (there should be an even number on the other side). But you would have to turn over the '1' too, since there might be a vowel on the other side of it. Actually, you must also turn over the card with 'B' on it: perhaps you were assuming that cards could not have letters on both sides. To show that the property is true (of the four cards on the table), you have to turn them all over except the '2'. So this is a trivial problem, and most people make silly slips. Dual lessons can be drawn out, however.

First, a designer may assert that a system he has designed (and it will be much more complex than a four-card quiz) has some property P. He is unlikely to claim seriously as a system property that it is 'easy to use', but whatever properties are actually claimed for the system *it is highly probable that the system does not maintain the stated properties*, because ensuring it really does will surely be harder than in the example of the cards where it was already easy to make mistakes.

The second lesson, the dual of the first, is that a technical view of a system gives conceptual power. And, furthermore, such *conceptual power often comes so cheaply with good notations that it is too easy for the designer to dismiss other people's problems along with the problems themselves*. The designer knows a notation to solve other people's problems—but that does not stop them being real problems for people, unlike the designer, without the conceptual aids. An example of this might be, 'of course it doesn't do that because the buffer is only so big'—no problem for the designer, but what can the user think who does not know what a buffer is? We shall see later (in Section 6.2.1) that mathematics is not the only way to facilitate clear thinking.

Humans have limited cognitive resources, as do computers (an issue we shall explore in Chapter 5). If it takes a long time for a human to examine a problem, it may be that a human will not bother to examine it: besides, some things take so long that death might intervene before the problem is solved. So it is quite possible for someone to maintain inconsistent beliefs. I may believe both P and not P at the same time (P

could be some complex predicate—say, a political belief), simply because I have neither the time nor inclination to discover that these beliefs are inconsistent. If I, as a typical user, am inconsistent, what hope is there of designing a formal computer system that I can use easily? Or, again, if you ask me what interactive system features I like, you may well find that my preferences are non-transitive. Normally, preferences should be transitive. If A is preferred to B, and B to C, then A should be preferred to C. But it is quite possible that users may prefer a menu interface to the command-based interface; they may prefer the knowledge-based direct manipulation to the menu; and they may choose the command-based interface to the knowledge-based direct manipulation interface. Such non-transitivity can arise not just because of complicating factors, such as the sequence the users are shown the features and how much they have learnt in the meantime, and how their expectations have changed, but because the users simply do not examine the consequences of their beliefs. Their beliefs are sufficiently consistent, so long as they are never faced with all three options at the same time.

3.1 Short-term memory and attention

People cannot play chess perfectly, or take perfect part in practically any non-trivial activity, because of information processing limitations. But, can we obtain some more detailed insight into how people think? We can use the chess example again as a simple illustration, but the principles seem quite general—and are particularly relevant to user interface design (you need only consider designing a program to play chess to see that there is *some* relevance).

Suppose we ask people to memorize the positions of chess pieces on a board. It turns out, not surprisingly, that chess experts are much better than novices at remembering board positions. But, what is surprising, is that most experts are no better than novices at remembering *random* board positions. The chess masters' expertise does not necessarily extend to non-chess configurations. What masters recall is structured: they recall that a bishop was attacking a certain piece, that a pawn was pinned, and other such technical details. Of course, the novices do not have such sophistication; they may simply remember arbitrary components of a position—such as the men in the first row—which may or may not be relevant to the game.

If you are asked whether two chess boards are the same, you can very easily tell if you see them in rapid succession. Incoming information to the mind is buffered for about a quarter of a second in five sensory memories, one memory for each of the five senses (touch, smell, sight, hearing, taste). The sensory memory has a large capacity, but there is no way to refresh the information except by repeating the external stimulus (for example, by looking at the chess board again). To remember something for longer, the mind must **attend** to a particular sense. Shifting attention takes about 50 ms, though the eye generally shifts attention by actually moving, so a shift of visual attention takes longer, about 200 ms.

An example of selective attention is the cocktail party phenomenon; despite the noise and interfering conversations, we are able to attend to a single conversation at a noisy party. Generally, we only follow one conversation at a time, and we can choose which one. The different senses have different attentional priorities (though the actual priorities depend on circumstances and on the person's **expectancy**). It is generally faster to get a person's attention by using an audible stimulus rather than a visual one; olfactory stimuli are slower still. Good interactive systems will take advantage of the user's various senses, particularly by using audible stimuli if rapid attention is required—for instance, making a suitable noise on detecting an error.[1]

Once selected, information is processed and copied to a small **short term memory** or STM (also called **working memory**). STM appears to be where consciousness resides; it is where we do our thinking. The STM has a capacity of around seven things. Unused information in STM decays after about 20 seconds, we'll soon see that *using* your mind may mean that STM loses information much faster! However we can refresh the memory indefinitely by a process called **rehearsal**. Data is not stored in memory literally, but is processed into abstractions, called **chunks**. Essentially, a chunk is a name that can be evaluated to the data it represents. Obviously, the more capacious chunks are, the more effective use may be made of memory, especially STM which has a small capacity. Chunks, like abstractions, are hierarchical and can contain sub-chunks. It seems that words are frequently used for chunking: most people's STM is predominantly verbal.

A simple example is that at some time your STM may be storing seven, six, or eight words. You may describe the spelling, etymology and other features of these words: you have clearly stored far more than 10 units of information in STM. Of course, the act of turning attention to details like the spelling of one of these words will generate more information to be retained in STM. This will interfere with your retention of the other words.

Suppose you want to telephone a company. First you look up the number: the eye scans the number and it enters sensory memory. You attend to the number—rather than other features of the telephone directory—and enter the number into STM. You either have to dial the

---

[1] Sound can be heard all over the place. Some thought must be given to problems such as whether *only* errors are notified to the user by a specific sound which everyone else can hear too. Prompts could beep as well; then other users would not know your errors from your prompts. There is no reason why sound transducers could not be highly directional; alternatively, perhaps vibrating keyboards that only individual users can notice could be tried out. Physically locking the keyboard is probably too disruptive for most tasks, though it might be a useful precaution in some circumstances.

number rapidly or have to repeat the number to yourself (rehearse it) to ensure that you do not lose it from STM. A few minutes later you may have forgotten the number altogether. Or again, if you ask somebody the time, he may look at his watch and then tell you the time. The chances are that he will not rehearse the time to himself, the whole process is too fast for this to be necessary. If you then ask again a little later, he will have to look at his watch once more.

Information is processed into chunks; the more a chunk abstracts the more efficient the use of memory becomes. People, not surprisingly, find it satisfying to form chunks. The experience of forming a chunk is called **closure**, but is actually a somewhat more general phenomenon. The anxious feeling of not quite being able to recall a word that is apparently on 'the tip of your tongue' derives from being unable to form a closure, and, as it were 'wrap up' the word in a chunk. We can infer that when people are inhibited from forming a closure (for example, the interactive system they are using interrupts their thought processes, telling them of some implementation error, perhaps), they will make inefficient use of STM and run the risk of losing information from it as they attend to the interruption.

We can view STM as a stack. When the user wants to do something, he pushes the goal on to his STM–stack; when he has done it he pops it off the STM–stack, then closure is the act of popping or clearing the stack. We see from this analogy that closure is necessary from time to time, otherwise the user will lose track of what he is doing, as goals get lost off 'the bottom' of the stack.

It is possible for different uses of STM to **interfere** when there is some conflict. For example, if we have to do some arithmetic sums at the same time as memorizing something we may exceed the capacity of STM and something will get lost. It is interesting that a master chess player does not do more thinking in STM than a novice: his STM is no larger. Indeed, he possibly thinks no further ahead into the game than the novice, but his chunks are more powerful, and he can therefore think more deeply and selectively than the novice before overflowing his STM. Players sometimes beat much better chess players by adopting a lunatic strategy: this reduces the effectiveness of the expert's chunking, which is generally limited to more sensible chess positions (the so-called **enough rope** strategy).

The sense of closure may be sufficient to eclipse other goals the person has outstanding, still awaiting closure. For example, consider going up to a ticket machine and buying a ticket. You drop your money in, and take your ticket. You walk away leaving your due change behind. The major closure of obtaining your ticket interfered with the other, secondary, intention of obtaining your money's worth. This is a particular example of a **termination error**, caused by 'too effective' closure. The closure obtained when taking your ticket is incorrectly taken as a sign to terminate *all* interaction with the ticket machine.

Another, similar, example will show how careful design of an interactive system can reduce termination errors. Suppose you wish to obtain some money from an automatic cash dispenser. You insert a cash card in a slot; then the system requires you to submit some secret codes; then how much you want; and then the system presents you with the money you wanted. You walk away. But you left your card in the machine. This is a termination error which could easily have been avoided by a different design, requiring the user to take the card back, *then* dispensing the money. With this alternative design, the user does not reach closure until he has 'tidied up', in this case taken the cash card back.

STM is limited not just by its capacity but also by the information available to it. In general, whatever mental processes we are discussing, it is useful to distinguish between processing that is primarily **resource limited** and that which is primarily **data limited**. If we consider eyesight: vision is data limited when it gets too dark, but is resource limited when too much is happening in the visual field for the individual to process it all. Note that poor eyesight means that more resources are used to try and process what can be seen; this explains why wearing spectacles improves your hearing as the optical correction to the eyesight releases resources for improved hearing. Unfortunately, if some task is data limited, the brain will tend to devote extra resources to try and compensate for the missing or corrupt data; this can cause a detriment in concurrent operations. Thus when users do not know what to do, that is, they are lacking help information, their performance may drop significantly and they may miss cues that the designer thought were 'obvious'. That red warning message! Of course, the designer is very rarely data limited with respect to the use of the interactive system he is designing!

3.2 Long-term memory

As material is rehearsed in STM, somehow it gets transferred to **long term memory** (LTM) after about five seconds. Unlike the other memories, LTM records information indefinitely. The more you play chess, the more chess positions are remembered. LTM has a very large capacity and a very slow decay (if any). All our general knowledge, knowledge of language and so on is in LTM; all personal knowledge of episodes in our lives is recorded in LTM. There is some evidence that LTM is in principle perfect, but that memory access becomes increasingly difficult without rehearsal because of interference from other memories. Recall from LTM takes at least one-tenth of a second. The efficiency of recall is improved by so-called **elaboration techniques**, for instance, using mnemonics or mental imagery, to associate whatever you want to remember with a known picture. Some elaboration techniques rely in part on the extra rehearsal in STM that is required, this seems to store the information more coherently into LTM.

An interesting view is that human memory is not worse than computer memory (as commonly thought) but that human *forgetting* is worse than computers (computers can forget totally—by assignment: after x := 2; a computer has irrevocably forgotten the old value of x). Many problems with user interfaces arise from the user failing to forget now obsolete information.

Elaboration techniques may be thought of as methods for constructing hash functions. In the same way that few hash functions are perfect, LTM and STM suffer from an effect also called **interference**, as if different items in memory have the same hash values. It then becomes hard to recall one thing because you have learnt another related thing. Interference in LTM can have disadvantages and advantages: it means, for instance, that learning a new interactive system will be influenced by what the user has learnt from previous systems. Depending on the similarity between the two interactive systems, this may help or hinder. The designer has more control over the interference that will happen between memorizing different parts of a single system. Sometimes it will be best to make a new interactive system design as *different* as possible to minimize untoward effects of interference. Evidence from studies of bilingualism suggests that most interference when learning two languages occurs when one language is minor and the other elaborate: perhaps users will have most problems when one interactive system is complex and heavily used, and the other of minor interest. In interactive systems use, actual occurrences of interference (irrespective of their origins in STM, LTM or other psychological interference) are termed **carry-overs** (or, alternatively, **conceptual captures**).

Interference in STM is closely related to **priming**: putting an idea into someone's head (as it were) makes it easier for the person to use that idea—rightly or wrongly. The following experiment can be tried out on a friend: Ask your friend how to spell the word shop. They will reply s-h-o-p, or treat the experiment as a trick. Now, quickly ask them what to do at a green light. Most likely, you will get the answer, 'stop'. Wrong! Some people are not even aware that they have made a mistake.

For an example of carry-over, consider a user who frequently uses a text editor. The user can move a cursor (with commands like up and down) around the screen, and add and delete text at will. In another context, the user runs a command to list the files he has. The screen therefore fills with lines of text, representing files (and their sizes, ages and other such information). If the user wants to delete one of these files, he should run the delete command and specify which file he wants deleted. Instead, he types up up up delete-line, submitting commands carried over from the text editor, where he would have deleted the right line. The old story of the person who went upstairs to find his glasses, but then went to bed is a good illustration. The act of going upstairs is more frequently associated with going to bed; presumably the person failed to rehearse the original reason for going upstairs (collecting glasses) and for this person the going-to-bed concept was the most frequent way of forming closure after going upstairs.

On the other hand, when people panic or are put under considerable pressure, they often revert to **stereotyped** behaviour—as if they use a quick-and-nasty hash function. Older, even instinctive, or more rehearsed memories are recalled instead of possibly more appropriate memories. If my computer starts smoking, I shall switch it off. I am likely to do this by flicking the switch *up*, even though I know that the computer is American, and American switches switch things off by being flicked *down*.

Stereotypes mean that although systems may be made differently in order to reduce interference for *normal* use, under stress the users may make many more mistakes (and, furthermore, be less able to recover from the mistakes). It might have been better for there to be a greater similarity: at least the user would then have had a chance to make interference mistakes under normal conditions and have been able to learn appropriate strategies for recovering from them.

For example, imagine that a word processor is being used, and the user answers the telephone. Unknown to him, he rests something on the space bar, which autorepeats and the screen is filled with blanks. When the telephone call is over, the user looks at the screen which is by now completely blank. All his work has gone! If the user has the obvious model of the system, from which he too-rapidly infers that a blank screen signifies a fault, then he may decide to reboot it, or start again ... a remedy that is guaranteed to really destroy his work! If the user was not panicking, he might pause to think: for instance, there might be a status line on the screen that shows the word processor is still running, but the cursor is in column 2 000 and this may help him to find where he was before the phone call.

Chess players often make their games more exciting by putting themselves under stress, or by undertaking several activities at once; this certainly causes interference in STM, and (given the pressures to win) may bring up stereotyped moves. In a sense, you are playing not against your opponent's STM and LTM recall, but against his whole personality.

3.3   People are far more complex than that

I have presented an almost simple-minded description of mind. The human and his mind are far more complex; there is not room here to explore more profound models of thinking and performance (though the book will introduce further concepts later). In particular, I have not greatly emphasized the following:

> ▷ *Individual differences*: People are different; they work in different ways with different efficiencies. Different people will tend to have different styles of thinking that they bring to problems such as interacting with computers: some may rely on learnt knowledge, principles, and so on, others may work things out dynamically. (See

Chapter 8 which emphasizes individual differences at a more general level.)

▷ *Parallel processing*: People can do more than one thing at once (this is obvious: you can cross a road and hold a conversation; you can hum a tune and write a letter). The brain works by massively parallel processing, the mind being full of little independent specialized devices, all 'thinking' at the same time (this, too, is obvious: the brain is full of independent neurons). However, the practical consequences of this view, except for stimulating research, are not clear.

▷ *The expert systems view*: It is productive to view the mind as an expert system. For instance, we may view LTM as a body of rules, and STM as the blackboard or workspace. The cognitive limitations of the brain impose certain properties on the expert system engine: for instance, that the number of goals in STM is limited; that access to rules in LTM increases their probability of future access. This is a powerful analogy for advancing both artificial intelligence (AI) and cognitive science.

▷ *Wider issues*: The user may be fatigued, or anxious because he is working in a public place, badly paid and unmotivated. His answers to the computer may affect his legal status. All these environmental issues greatly affect the user.

The point that has been made is that people are not simple machines, they have curious limitations and curious skills, and, by implication, computers can go some way to meliorating these limitations. For instance, STM is very small in comparison with the amount of information that can be crammed on to a typical display screen: the display can be used as a cache or external memory for the human mind. More detailed modelling will show that the information on the screen has to be organized in an appropriate way and must be sufficiently static, if search times are not to increase so much as to offset the gains (see Section 11.7.5).

An excuse for the shallow treatment might be as follows. There are all sorts of more sophisticated models of mind (and different models work at different levels). However, the models—being more faithful—are more complex, and they start to look like programming languages. To understand these more powerful theories requires understanding an architecture of mind and a scheme for programming and manipulating it. On the whole, the real power of these theories can only be realized if you have a computer simulation handy.

At a more abstract level, we can say some pertinent things about users. The next four subsections explore users and how their attitudes and general complexity make user interface design more interesting.

3.3.1   Cognitive dissonance

People have ideas, opinions, attitudes, values and knowledge and these may or may not be consonant with each other. Immediately after a decision between two alternatives, for instance, there will be dissonance between the ideas supporting the choice made and the ideas around the choice that might have been made instead. Thus arises **cognitive dissonance**. The theory of cognitive dissonance (Festinger, 1957) suggests that cognitive dissonance is uncomfortable, and reducing it is a basic human drive like satisfying hunger.

Cognitive dissonance can be reduced by various means. First, the person may change his circumstances (for instance, by changing the computer he is using but does not like); second, he may choose to decrease the importance of the conflicting elements (for instance, by saying that doing his job is more important than worrying about the user interface); third, he can add further consonant, supporting, ideas (for instance, deciding that he made the right decision after all); and last, he may selectively expose himself to supporting ideas (for instance, only reading adverts for the system he has bought).

In brief, cognitive dissonance is disparagement of something that has proved unattainable—sour grapes. What you can't have, you don't like, and what you have, you do like. One of Descartes's maxims in his *Discourse on the method of properly conducting one's reason and of seeking the truth in the sciences* was if you can't change something, change your mind. Make a virtue out of necessity. The system I use is much better than the one you use, and, indeed, I will be increasingly adamant the more trouble I took learning and using my system.

The effects of cognitive dissonance are perhaps most apparent when people have to pay for something: they have to justify the cost of their decisions. The rewards from most arcade games are ephemeral, yet the user has to pay for the game. In the case of addiction, the cost of playing may become significant: but, counter-intuitively, the cost of playing itself may not deter the user. This is an example of the effect of cognitive dissonance: the more the user pays to play a game, the harder he convinces himself that he really does enjoy it—which conviction further fuels his addiction.

Not all users pay for the pleasure of using computers, but cognitive dissonance still has a significant role in forming users' opinions about systems. If a system is difficult to use (or a game is costly to play), the user may convince himself that it is really worth using. If the user fails to resolve the dissonance, he would have to explain why he wasted time learning the system, and why he continues to use it. Cognitive dissonance sometimes results in intellectual sacrifice.

Cognitive dissonance makes it extremely hard to judge other people's opinions about interactive systems. For instance, there is a large group of people who claim that object-oriented programming is 'the solution' to user interface problems. Most, however, are quite ignorant of object-oriented programming, so by default they may accept these claims or at least envy the sophisticated computer systems normally needed to run object-oriented systems! But suppose you set out to check the claim for yourself. This will entail, let's say, six months of getting to grips with a real object-oriented system (like Smalltalk), and a further six months spent acquiring deeper knowledge. After which time, you make an objective judgement? Of course not! If you have persevered, each day deciding that perseverance was not a waste of time, you are hardly likely to end up claiming object-oriented programming is not the answer, and your investment of time therefore misguided.

3.3.2 Users adapt

Users are becoming more sophisticated, they are going on computer appreciation courses ... so the designer might claim his system is so advanced it has a 'next generation' interface, by which he means that in order to use it one has to have been on these courses, imbued by the computer culture. There is some truth in this argument, but it remains the case that the next generation of users is being trained in an environment which has grown accustomed to irrational and mostly petty user interfaces; the argument in its clearest form is actually: 'soon users will be able to cope with this system because they will have already used equally bad systems (like I have)'.

Presented with even a manifestly bad system, users invest a lot of themselves in learning how to handle it just in order to use it at all (perhaps by using so-called **satisficing strategies**—non-optimal but adequate strategies, see Section 3.3.4) and then they justifiably resent any so-called 'improvements'.

A simple scenario suggests itself. Imagine that a user complains about a small inconsistency that has become apparent in a user interface. It is a detail which was too small to have been mentioned in the user's original documentation, but the designer was probably aware of the decision which led to the feature. At the time the designer had probably decided that, in the absence of obvious user interface principles, the decision could be made on purely technical grounds—a euphemism for implementing whatever is easiest. Now, when the user complains, it does not appear to be worth while to change the system as there are other users who might actually rely on it in its present form. Inertial reasoning takes over and the system is left unchanged. This user, like all others before him, then learns to live with the feature as it is. Later, when designing another system, the designer is faced with a similar type of choice, and again he decides on a least-effort implementation basis; but now he can also argue that from his 'user interface design experience' the choice is otherwise arbitrary: whatever had been chosen last time, the users would have adapted to and later come to rely upon.

An example from everyday life—how we treat spelling—will illustrate the issue quite simply. Everybody agrees that we would be better off rationalizing the way English is spelt, but nobody will do it. We persist in spelling words like 'though', 'psalm', 'right', in an irregular and inexplicable way, rather than contrive a simpler system.[2] Making things easy to use is not the problem. The problem is: things might have been easier to use than they are, but by the time you've found out, it is too late. Typewriter (or computer) keyboards are a case in point: there are no end of suggestions for improving them and good reasons for doing so, but the QWERTY keyboard is here to stay because so many people have got used to it. It is easier to stay with nonsense than face the cost of changing over to something that would almost certainly be better. And with computers, the 'nonsense' is often so much better than anything that went before, that we are all prepared to put up with it—a word processor, for instance, almost however badly designed, does a wonderful job.

3.3.3   Homeostasis

People generally maintain equilibrium with their environment by making self-regulating adjustments. The standard example is how we maintain our body temperature: if the ambient temperature falls, we raise our metabolic rate and thereby maintain our temperature, even though we radiate more energy. It is easy to imagine all sorts of homeostatically maintained potentials which are relevant to user interface design.

Users take risks, and the risks they are prepared to take depend on their assessment of the consequences of their actions. If an interactive system provides safety features (for example, an undo command, Chapter 12), then they will simply make more mistakes. Under the assumption of homeostasis, whether a user is better off depends on changes in the *perceived* level of risk and of the personal homeostatic level that is being maintained.

So, if a system is made easy to use, it will only be used to do more difficult things. If a system is made safer to use, it will only be used in more extreme circumstances. On balance, life for the user is no easier or safer. Homeostasis, then, is an important design issue because it emphasizes that

---

[2] Some educators might argue that the 'problem' lies in our lack of appreciation of our rich etymological heritage. If we but knew Greek and Latin, for instance, things would seem more rational. This view has some truth in it—corresponding to 'improve training and documentation' to make interactive systems easier to use—but it begs the question why Greek and Latin themselves work the way they do. If you trouble to learn Greek and Latin it may be a comforting thought that the structure of those languages helps to explain why we cannot sort out English spelling (see Section 3.3.1).

whether users benefit from a system depends as much on the users' attitudes as it does on the concrete design of the system. And, of course, the users' attitudes are formed in part by documentation and other training.

We will see in Section 7.2 how homeostasis affects designers, and causes them to make systems far more complex than they need be.

3.3.4   Satisficing

Satisficing is a form of local optimization where awareness or avoidance of the cost of establishing an overall best-choice leads to the acceptance of a good-enough choice. Thus users may adopt a **satisficing strategy**, for instance failing to exploit the power of the system by preferring to use combinations of well-known operations. They would rather not learn, or acquire skills with, additional (though more efficient) commands for the present task. Learning the new skills, although it might save time in the long run, would delay the user when he already knows he can do what he wants in a reasonable time. Clearly a flexible system will permit users to adopt theoretically non-optimal strategies for particular tasks, and different users will be able to make their tradeoffs at different levels.

3.3.5   The Hawthorne Effect

If people were merely physical objects, doing experiments to see how they worked under certain circumstances would be relatively simple, and as likely to bring forth results as any other physical experiment. Unfortunately for the experimenters (and fortunately for people), people are not so simple. Doing the experiment may itself cause people's behaviour to alter. The **Hawthorne Effect** is that people tend to work harder when they sense that they are participating in something new, or in something in which they have more control (Mayo, 1933).

The Hawthorne Effect is similar to the medical placebo effect, where medical interest alone, demonstrated by prescribing placebos, obtains a positive therapeutic effect; both are **experimental effects**, where an experiment ends up creating its own effect rather than testing the object of the experiment.

A simple experiment in the 1920s was conducted to find out the relationship between workplace illumination and productivity. Obviously if the lights are off, the workers will not be able to see; and somewhere before the lighting is blinding, there should be an optimum level of illumination. However, the experiments in the relay assembly room at Western Electric's Hawthorne plant led to quite different conclusions.

The first experiments were inconclusive; further experiments were designed using more careful experimental procedures. In one experiment, the intensity was reduced to that of moonlight and workers maintained their production and reported less fatigue. In another experiment, lighting was brilliant: and workers reported that they liked bright lights. In fact, the experiment was not revealing the effects of lighting conditions so much as showing the effect of being involved in an experiment.

It will not be necessary to draw out the parallels between the low bandwidth communication between management and workforce and the user interface bottleneck—except to point out that the computer often mediates between the two and frequently restricts communication further. Suffice it to say that as a result of his involvement with these experiments, Elton Mayo became the founding father of the Human Relations movement.

3.4   Skill/rule/knowledge

Different sorts of knowledge are encoded in the mind in different ways, for different purposes and as a result of different levels of practice. It is most practical to make a three-way distinction, which we now consider (Rassmussen, 1983).

When we come to a new task, such as typing, we first have to think about typing and finding keys, and so on. Later, with more practice, the typing skill becomes autonomous, that is, we no longer have to think consciously about it. Clearly, skilled performance, such as typing or riding a bicycle, requires considerable amounts of processing somewhere in the mind, but that processing occurs independently of conscious thought.

The simplest explanation is that conscious thinking using STM decides what to do (for example, to type a phrase). This phrase may be represented as a chunk in STM. The chunk is then directed to the motor system, which converts the chunk to finger movements. The motor system runs independently of the STM. The usual terminology is to call the output chunks **routines**, and to imagine the motor system as a buffering device. The cognitive system fills the motor system buffers with routines that are then flushed in **bursts** of autonomous activity. Perhaps few of us are skilled enough at typing to imagine how typing can be autonomous. Another example will help. Suppose I decide to cycle to a road junction, which I do by filling the motor buffer with the appropriate routines. While cycling to the junction, the motor system executes the cycle-to-junction routine (which involves many subroutines for pushing the pedals around, balancing the bike, and so on). This leaves the rest of my cognitive system free to plan more of the route or whatever. The same phenomena occur when using interactive systems.

But, when I started to learn to ride a bicycle, I certainly could not plan a route as well as managing to stay upright. STM was used for balancing, and rather like rehearsal transfers information to LTM, practice transfers skill to the motor system. And with further practice at a particular task, the level of abstraction used in the motor routines increases: the motor system can run autonomously for longer and longer periods performing more and more complex parts of a task. The rate of improvement, called the **law of practice**, follows a logarithmic form for many tasks. Improvement is most noticeable in early practice sessions and then drops off, but rarely ceases altogether.

Note that cognitive skills also follow a logarithmic law, but that there is more scope for learning new abstractions. New abstractions change the base of the logarithms and permit further improvements. This is one reason why teaching is so difficult: the teacher is so well practised that he no longer uses abstractions that make any sense to the learner. The driving instructor may say 'change down' (gears) but the learner has to manipulate the clutch, accelerator, move the gear stick and continue steering. The documentation writer should remember this!

A similar effect occurs with the abstractions used for programming the motor system. With practice, as we have seen, these abstractions become more sophisticated. But also, the cognitive system may no longer be able to recall their representation. Thus the beginner user expends considerable conscious mental effort learning a system. Gradually, through practice, routine skills transfer to the motor system. The STM can instruct the motor system to submit single commands, then, as more skill is acquired, longer and longer sequences of commands.

It is interesting that as the motor system runs autonomously, there needs to be less conscious rehearsal. So it is quite possible for people to become skilled at some operation and forget how they do it. Indeed, once rudimentary routines are in place, increments to the skill can occur unconsciously. I get better at typing without thinking about it. And when that sort of skill level has been acquired, a typist may no longer be able to recall where certain keys are. If a skilled typist wants to know where the r key is, he might have to imagine which finger would be moved to hit it, that is, by running a motor routine but suppressing any actual output. This is very important, for it means that with very complex skills we may no longer be able to describe in words what or how we are doing things.

Skill-based performance runs without conscious attention or control; once the user has decided on a goal, the activities to reach it take place smoothly in a continuous series of actions. Skilled performance is often based on feedforward control: the human acts as a control system synchronizing movements with the behaviour of the system but mostly ignoring feedback (which, if anything, is internalized by the user). This will only work, of course, if the user's control model is an adequate representation of the interface. With varied and frequent practice, the user's control model will be adequate whatever the interface design details (or so a designer might argue), but when the user is under stress (as in an emergency or error-recovery situation, or sometimes, even when the user does not know what to do) he will revert to preferred, stereotyped actions which may be contradictory to the ones he has learnt, with unfortunate consequences.

The boundary between skill and rule-based performance depends on the user's training, experience and attention. A rule is a collection of skilled behaviour patterns; feedback from the system triggers a rule, and the user then follows the associated skilled routine.

Knowledge-based behaviour has to be used when an interaction has not been rehearsed frequently enough for rules to have been developed by the user. In this case the user will formulate goals explicitly and will try to make a plan of action prior to further interaction: the user *decides* what to do. Since the user's goals are determined by the successful step-by-step pursuit of his task, they can be largely independent of detailed feedback from the system. Imagine a user wishes to request a hardcopy of a document he has just written. He uses his knowledge to decide which command is appropriate, say, `print file1`. He then activates the rule to type the corresponding letters. If he is a skilled user of the system, even if he makes typing mistakes, he can correct them at a skill-based level. Notice that knowledge-based operation interferes with STM: if users have to think about how to use the interface, they may easily lose track of where they are and what they wanted to do.

As a user gains experience, behaviour moves towards skilled performance making, in turn, greater use of feedforward control, and making greater assumptions of the coherence of the user interface. The user will be better motivated if a system encourages the steady transition from knowledge to skill-based interaction with it.

3.5   Symbolic/atomic/continuous

User operation can be characterized at three levels of abstraction: knowledge, rule and skill (Section 3.4). To each of these human modes of behaviour there corresponds the symbolic, atomic or continuous styles of interface, or the linguistic categories, semantic, syntactic and lexical. The information exchanged across the user interface is not just a stream of bits all with the same significance: it is structured, different parts are used for different purposes and in different ways. User interface input, then, can be partitioned into three styles: symbolic (composite coding), atomic (discrete coding) and continuous (analogue coding). Output, too, may be classified as symbolic, atomic or continuous.

▷ **Symbolic**:   Commands can be arbitrarily sophisticated and composed out of other commands before they are executed. Symbolic commands are generally textual and have a non-trivial syntax. For example, a command such as `delete *.txt` is a symbolic command; the syntax is ⟨*operation*⟩ ⟨*expression*⟩ and the expression ('`*.txt`' in the example) evaluates to a list of file names ending in .txt. While the user types the characters, d, e, ... x, t, the system does nothing (other than record the characters submitted); only when the user submits some symbol enter or ↩, does the system evaluate *.txt and delete. Symbolic interfaces are often **extensible** (the user may be able to define new commands), such interfaces may permit the user to define new command abstractions.

▷ **Atomic**: Commands are based on special-purpose keys and are perceived to be executed immediately. Any syntax is trivial. Atomic actions either succeed completely or have no effect (other than a possible diagnostic effect), that is, they are 'quantized'. There is no opportunity for the user to compose atomic commands except sequentially, one after another. Menu interfaces are atomic, and the complaints that menu interfaces are not powerful enough stems from the inherent inability to construct composite menu commands from basic menu-selection commands. (Note that there is nothing to stop an atomic interface being used to construct a program, which is subsequently processed by a symbolic class interface; nor is there anything to stop a symbolic interface being employed to define new atomic commands.)

▷ **Continuous**: A continuous interface is based on continuous input devices such as light pen, mouse, joystick, cursor wheels, trackball: input is non-quantized. Continuous input generally relies on very rapid (usually visual) feedback for effective use. With perceptible feedback delays, the user may **hunt**—over-shooting targets. There is even less ability to compose commands, instead interaction is continuous and relies entirely on the user's motor (eye, finger, hand, arm movement) skill rather than on his cognitive, measuring or structuring skills. Continuous devices can be used for selection (from menus or from geometric objects), and are then used to support an atomic style of input; they can also be used to supply parameters to a symbolic interface (to specify a numeric value, for instance). Continuous devices are also quite appropriate for selecting keys from a 'soft keyboard' which enables the user to construct symbolic input in an extended character set.

So, on the one hand, there is a clear distinction between styles of interaction: symbolic, atomic and continuous, and with different advantages. On the other hand, each style is sufficient to emulate the others, so the distinction is easily blurred—and of course, a real interactive system will mix all styles, using each as appropriate for different facets of its interface. Since incremental interaction is superior to batch communication (Chapter 4, next), atomic interfaces are generally used to help the user break down symbolic interactions into manageable fragments. Without incremental

---

Box 3.1   Direct manipulation.

Many tasks involve moving things around: from turning knobs and setting switches to collecting pictures and putting them in folders. Such tasks can be represented on the computer screen by a simulation of the real world. Accurate pictures, or symbolic pictures (**icons**), represent objects which the user can manipulate by operations such as selecting and moving. Quite a few not so natural tasks, like using a calculator, can also be simulated: the screen can show a picture of the calculator with working buttons that the user can 'press' by moving the cursor over and clicking a button.

Typical direct manipulation interfaces add other facilities. There will be various operations, such as deleting, duplicating, printing, editing, that can be applied to any selected object. Generally objects are typed and 'know' what operations they can submit to, and they may automatically invoke one of these operations if they are selected in a certain way (for example, if a single click on the mouse selects them, a rapid double click might activate them).

Direct manipulation, DM, is so called because it manipulates objects in a very direct way. Two major advantages are: objects are visible, and therefore help remind users how to operate the system; manipulating objects uses real-world skills (moving, pointing). The user interface is improved, then, the more directly objects can be manipulated. Note that many real-world operations, such as moving an object from one place to another, are continuous and reversible: these are considered central properties of direct manipulation systems. Conversely, where tasks involve abstract processing, logical reasoning, composition and so forth, direct manipulation has less clear advantages. Nevertheless, a direct manipulation style can often be factored out and hence simplify a large part of an interface.

The success of direct manipulation arises from the fact that it forces designers to solve interface design problems simply, without adding the sort of gratuitous complexity that is so easy in textual languages. Screens get *obviously* cluttered if direct manipulation interfaces get too complex; in textual languages the complexity of a feature is hidden until it is used. In direct manipulation, if something is hidden it simply cannot be used.

---

atomic interfacing, the user would be very unlikely (in fact, exponentially unlikely) to compose a correct symbolic submission of any length.

An entirely symbolic interface can easily be supported using a conventional timesharing system: the user builds up command lines, hits **enter** and only then does the timeshared computer processor have to do something for that user. Symbolic interfaces are ideal for mainframes; once entered, the symbolic command may entail an arbitrary amount of 'number crunching', but while the user is typing it the feedback is so simple it can be handled entirely by a multiplexer. The mainframe need not provide feedback for several seconds, or exceptionally some minutes (hopefully it will tell the user how long it is going to take first). Such a style is appropriate to the economics of large computer installations: where the capital investment in computers exceeds 'human costs'.

An atomic interface requires some sort of feedback for each function issued by the user, which may be on every keystroke, that is at a rate of about 10 per second: this can only be sustained by processing power more dedicated to the user and which is not so easily timeshared. However there is still relative freedom in the feedback timing, and atomic interfaces are often well supported by minicomputers timesharing no more than about a dozen or so users.

A continuous interface requires a guaranteed real-time response; for example, the cursor must keep up with a pointing device (for example, a mouse) however fast the user moves it. If not, the user hunts. The pointing device may be used to move complex displayed objects, so quite powerful local processing power is often required just for screen updates.[3] A continuous interface can only be supported effectively on a workstation or personal computer.

It is interesting to compare the tradeoffs of the three styles of interaction under assumptions of error and whether the styles allow a previous submission to be reused. For instance, any error in a symbolic interaction results in the submission being lost; whether it can be recovered depends on the user's LTM. A system may provide **naming** as a way of expediting chunking: the user can commit a name to LTM far more easily than what the name denotes. Let's say the user has to tell the system that one of his printers has 66 lines and 80 columns: it is far easier, once this has been found out, to call it `details`, and then use the name `details` instead of the actual numbers—if the system allows this.

In an atomic interface, an error causes a single action to be lost— perhaps more if there is a 'roll on' effect from the error. How the user recovers from an atomic error is limited by STM: for instance, if the error is not reported rapidly enough, the thoughts that led to the user making the error may have been lost for good from STM.

Finally with a continuous interface, errors as such do not arise: or, rather, they arise all the time and the user's actions serve to minimize discrepancies between where an object is and where it ought to be. Continuous systems must be reversible, since over-shoot and under-shoot are equally likely errors.

The term **reactive** is often used to describe systems which are atomic or continuous (or capable of supporting atomic or continuous styles), to emphasize the fast, per-action, feedback.

---

[3] Hence the techniques where only an abstract indication is provided of proposed screen updates. Instead of moving a window and its detailed contents around on the screen following the user's gestures, it is faster to move a transparent outline box with no content.

3.6   Distinguishing lexical, syntactic and semantic levels

For reasons that are largely to do with the exigencies of writing programs, it is popular to distinguish between lexical, syntactic and semantic levels in user interfaces. The lexical level has to do with the form of individual commands (and, conversely, the form of symbols output to the user from the system). Next, the syntactic level is to do with the rules of combination of commands or symbols. Lastly, the semantic level determines what valid combinations of symbols mean. Lexical, syntactic and semantic distinctions in the computer system correspond to the skill, rule and knowledge distinctions in the user.

Programs (and programming language compilers in particular) are conveniently divided into phases, each performing analysis at one of these levels. First, a compiler performs lexical analysis to see what the symbols are, then it performs syntactic analysis to see if the symbols have been put together sensibly, then it performs semantic analysis, which will generally result in it 'understanding' the program, and therefore being able to compile it to machine code. In user interface design, the lexical level is associated with presentation; there are many guidelines here to guide the designer (what symbols to use, what colours, and so on). At the syntactic level, there are fewer guidelines, but more methods and techniques the designer can draw on. He may be helped by **UIMS**, User Interface Management Systems. The application component of the user interface, 'what it does', is the domain of semantics. It would be pointless to lay down rules for semantics: this is the most general level, constrained only by the task to be undertaken by the system. The semantics must be fixed by the requirements of the task, rather than by more general human factors.

Unfortunately, these levels are interwoven, and any distinction between them is pragmatic rather than fundamental. For instance, suppose I say 'hello woyuwert computer'. It would be easy to say this utterance consists of three lexical symbols, hello, woyuwert and computer. Syntactic analysis would require that woyuwert was an adjective perhaps, and semantic analysis would no doubt reject the whole utterance as nonsense.

Yet we could consider the symbols h, e, l, o, w, and so on to be the lexical elements, and the syntax level then applying the rules of spelling. Thus woyuwert is a syntactic error, rather than a semantic error. But it would be equally valid to treat hello and computer as lexical symbols, but reject woyuwert lexically, for there is no such word (just as we would reject compuℵer because ℵ is not lexically an acceptable letter in the context).

Nevertheless, the distinction is useful (it helps separate concerns when designing programs), but only when *given a particular view of the language*.

Now it would be sad if the best view was in all cases determined by how the designer wanted to construct his program! Instead, I propose that lexical, syntactic and semantic levels are best distinguished by how they *fail* to work, rather than how they work (for example, in a program).

There are two perspectives: how long it takes to detect an error, and what the consequences of the error are.

A lexical error can be detected immediately, and certainly before the next fragment or whole symbol is processed. (Obviously we could have some discussion about what 'immediately' means: it is sufficient to say, 'perceived as instantaneous'.) A syntactic error cannot be detected immediately, for syntax is about rules of combining symbols—and in general detecting a syntax error requires looking ahead. A semantic error is generally detected much later.

A lexical error can be reported directly, and is easy to recover from. The user simply submits a correct lexeme (symbol). A syntactic error is much harder to recover from (for its consequences may spread far into the past and future), but there is no need for the system to do anything other than report the error. Finally, a semantic error has severe consequences: something is done, but not what was intended. For example, if we attempt to compile and run a program containing syntax errors, nothing (except getting diagnostics) happens. But if we try a semantically incorrect program, then *anything* might happen.

3.7   Conclusions

A remarkable thing about humans is that they can think very ably despite all the limitations that beset their thinking. These limitations are normally hidden and only revealed in somewhat artificial experiments. This is not too surprising as the introspection that might have revealed the limitations is working within the very same limitations. In fact, we may not think very ably at all, we just think we do because we know no better!

Over millennia humans have no doubt evolved ways of keeping these limitations hidden. Thus the way English or any natural language is normally used means that it is intelligible. Similarly other social conventions keep people within their normal operating limits. But computers do not necessarily adhere to these complex and apparently arbitrary conventions: like the psychological experiments, computers often expose limitations in human abilities. The difference is that psychologists want to expose and study the boundaries of mind, but computers discover such boundaries by accident. Designers will avoid such accidents only when they acknowledge the sorts of psychological issues this chapter has touched on.

When a designer decides how to make a system to help fly an aircraft, many differences between the designer's environment of cosy office and the pilot's environment of high speeds and G forces are fairly obvious. The designer can take a few hours over a design decision: but the pilot must react very fast when he handles the corresponding part of the system. Design errors where such differences are forgotten are comparatively rare. But a much less obvious difference between the designer and user is their cognitive load under the different conditions.

During design, the designer mostly uses LTM to make decisions, say, about screen layout. And where LTM fails him, he can always browse through the system specification or a program listing to see what should happen. The user does not have this privilege. If something appears briefly on the screen, or many new things appear, the user's STM may suffer. Perhaps at the next step in interaction the user has no idea what to do. Of course, the designer would know exactly what to do, because the way he has been able to think about interaction has exploited quite different cognitive resources under different conditions.

This chapter has only briefly looked at a small part of mental issues, but it emphasizes that the way people think must be taken into account in the design of interactive systems. And then there are all the social, motivational and other issues. We shall take up this topic again in Section 7.2 and call it the **ergonomics issue**.

Chapter 4

Through the interface

To live effectively is to live with adequate information.

Norbert Wiener

Consider playing the game Twenty Questions, which is normally played interactively between people. Played between user and computer, the user tries to discover what the other player, the computer, is thinking of by asking no more than twenty questions. At each step the user asks a question, and from the answer decides on the next question to ask. The computer is allowed to reply **yes** or **no**.

Now consider the game played not interactively but in batch: the user would have to prepare all twenty questions beforehand, and *then* obtain twenty answers. The user would have to be ingenious to prepare twenty questions in advance that gave him useful information. If he chose the questions well he could select from about 2^{19} objects, which is quite big enough; he would also have to be very motivated, so as not to get bored preparing the questions. If the user made a mistake he would have little chance to recover. But in the normal interactive game, the user could simply start playing Nineteen Questions after making a mistake, an only marginally harder game.

In Twenty Questions, each answer fixes a component of the 'thing thought about' by the opponent; interactive feedback, with an answer to each question as it is asked, enables each answer to fix an independent component. The point is that each experiment—each question/answer—is manageable in the interactive case.

Hence it is easy to see that, as a general strategy, user interfaces are used more effectively if the user can select or fix components of an interaction with immediate feedback. Conversely, and symmetrically, the computer will find interaction easier if *it* can get immediate feedback from the user—though the questions computers ask users are usually more routine, and could more easily have been prepared beforehand.

Such arguments assume that Twenty Questions is a representative example. In the Twenty Questions couldn't a better user interface simply tell the user what the object was, without all the questions? We must examine some responses to this objection. First, there are some tasks where asking questions will actually help or assess the user—useful in a teaching environment, where the student may be learning about the set of objects, or learning how to formulate questions. Secondly, subtly, there is no need for the computer to know what the object is until the last question is asked: it is possible to play an adversarial form of Twenty Questions, where the adversary (the computer) gives any reply so as to prolong the game as long as possible. The only restriction is that all answers must be consistent. This appears to be a very different game—we can imagine that the user is interacting with the computer to compute some particular result (the 'object')—but if it is played well, it is impossible to distinguish it from the conventional game. Thirdly, there are lots of other examples that we could have used instead of Twenty Questions. A game of chess would make a good example. A game of chess played in batch ('Here are *all* of my moves; what are yours?') is a quick way of losing, even to a mediocre opponent.

We have seen that interaction improves communication; what other techniques are available?

▷ Often information can be communicated effectively by communicating **abstractions** that can be used to reconstruct the actual information. For instance, if I want to give you some information about the *Oxford English Dictionary*, it is much easier to refer you to it than to give it to you! The OED as a concept is an abstraction of a vast amount of text. On the other hand there is a danger that we agree on the abstract terms but not on the *meanings* of the abstractions: it is often difficult to tell. If my version of the dictionary differs from yours, we may well get confused: for instance, one of us may think OED refers to any Oxford dictionary, the other may think OED refers specifically to a particular edition of that massive multivolume work. Distinguishing abstractions requires explanation; this introduces an overhead that reduces the immediate advantage.

▷ Information may be transferred **interactively**. Rather than transfer the entire *Oxford English Dictionary* to a user, the user could request the definition of 'hysterosis' [*sic*] and get just that meaning. Interaction breaks up information transfer, and is the main way to reduce the cost of errors: little time and few resources are wasted before an error can be detected and remedied. Non-interactive communication has periods of **batched** communication and periods of quiescence. During the periods of quiescence the interface is not being used, but at times of information transfer the limited communications capacity may retard communication. The advantages of non-interactive communication are clearly not in effective information transfer, but must be found elsewhere, for instance in the organizational economics of providing information processing.

Since batch communication is after all a form of interaction, albeit slow and disastrous under error conditions, it is useful to employ the term **incremental interaction** to mean step-by-step interaction in distinction to batch interaction. Asking 20 questions in one go is batch interaction; asking them one at a time is incremental.

▷ The user may obtain information by **experiments**. Twenty Questions was a good example, but we will leave a full discussion of experiments to Chapter 9. Often, once getting an answer, you wish you had not asked the question and wasted a go. Forgiving opponents may let you have an extra turn: a well-designed user interface may allow the user to 'take back' actions that later seem to have been ill-considered. Being able to undo actions—to encourage the user to experiment without worry of penalty—is such an important technique that all of Chapter 12 is devoted to the topic.

▷ Information often has an underlying pattern that can be **induced**: if the pattern can be inferred correctly, then it may be possible to avoid transferring the bulk of it, since the user can compute it for himself. Much information is obviously data, some is also functional (for example, how the computer works). This information cannot be transferred directly, instead the user infers how it works in the course of using it. The user interacts with the computer and infers enough for his needs. Hopefully, it is not necessary to infer *all* of the computer's model.

▷ A special case of induction is where the user can correct the computer: this is called **adaptive modelling**. Basically, the computer does its best to anticipate what the user is going to do next, and tells the user. The user then corrects the computer's prediction. When the computer is right, or nearly right, the user has less to do. Adaptive modelling can be disconcerting, since the computer may make 'mechanical' predictions based on too little information; yet the user still has to concentrate to catch the computer's bad predictions. Sometimes it is better to use a fixed, preprogrammed, modelling technique, where all the adaption has gone on before the user interacts: this makes the user's induction easier and more reliable.

A good adaptive interface can be very efficient at the expense of making the user do more thinking, and being vigilant to detect incorrect predictions; sometimes, then, a user will actually be more efficient with a simpler interface that does less adaption. In which case, the designer has to build in all the necessary adaption when the system is designed; this may be harder than leaving it up to the computer.

▷ Information need not be transferred at all. It might be best for the computer to retain the information if it is to be used again (this is often called **caching**—see Section 4.2, below). The user may be reassured that the information exists (and that it can be checked in principle): but the user can choose to ignore the detailed information. Given that the system is interactive, information may be **browsed**: the user can choose what information he sees and in what order, but he need not see all of it.

▷ Some information may be computed faster by the computer, and some information, especially for tasks involving pattern recognition, faster by the user. Processing speed is the main reason why computers are used for closed tasks (tasks not depending on or affecting external events). For instance, establishing $31 \times 52 = 1\,612$ with a calculator gives *no* information, for the equation is a tautology. However, it does provide information if the user is unable to process as fast, for with slow information processing powers one cannot know that there is no information contained in the response![1]

▷ Computers are very good at reconstructing information by running programs; this facility can be used to compensate somewhat for the narrow bandwidth input channel for providing information *to* the computer. It serves to emphasize the differences between man/man and man/computer interaction since people so rarely follow instructions precisely—and it also serves to emphasize the differences between the ordinary user and the designer, who is particularly skilled at programming computers.

If these very general techniques improve interaction, we next ought to find out if we can discover any more. Indeed we can, and we will see that what we can call the **von Neumann correspondence** is a rich source of ideas.

4.1   The von Neumann correspondence

A problem arises in the internal design of computers: information is not always where we would like it, and a general method that always ensures information is available in the right place would be costly. The problem

---

[1] Kant made a distinction between analytic statements, which are tautologous, and synthetic statements that provide new facts. When we allow for processing limitations, all statements can be viewed to varying degrees as synthetic.

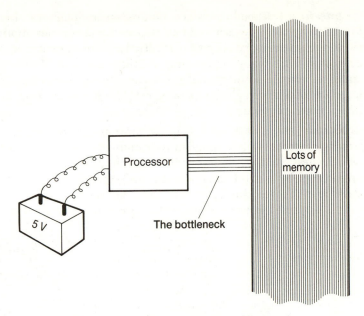

Figure 4.1   The von Neumann bottleneck.

in computers is called the **von Neumann bottleneck**, after John von Neumann, one of the founders of computing science.

It is interesting that the term 'von Neumann bottleneck' honours von Neumann's essential contributions to computer system design, yet von Neumann studied several quite different styles of computation—some of which do not have bottleneck problems! Nevertheless, one particular style of computation readily lent itself to electronic implementation and as a result rapidly became commercially viable. This design is now usually called von Neumann, and anything else non-von Neumann. The von Neumann design suffers from bottlenecks.

The von Neumann bottleneck is an information flow bottleneck *within* the architecture of computer systems. Figure 4.1 shows the general idea. There is lots of information in the memory (around megabytes) and this can only be transferred to the processor along a few wires, often just 8, 16 or 32. Thus either a program is slowed down transferring data to and from memory, or it has to work selectively on memory, making changes 'here and there', in which case it is difficult to design.

Typically, claims are made that recent advances in computer design and computer programming language design ameliorate the bottleneck, making programs faster and easier to write.

The von Neumann bottleneck can be viewed as an architectural, technical, conceptual or managerial issue:

▷ *Architectural*—depending on how computers are built. Computation is limited by the processor's ability to access and transfer information to and from memory. Typical solutions at the architectural level suggest having many processors, so that the task of information transfer between memory and processor can be shared out. A user interface analogue might be spreadsheets, where each cell can do some independent processing.

▷ *Technical*—about obscurities in programming languages. The standard, most widely used, programming languages gain their effectiveness to the extent that they circumvent the bandwidth limitations by such techniques as assignments to *parts* of data structures (that is, to the extent they rely on modes), a technique that is criticized for its obscurity. In Pascal, it is very easy to assign to part of a data structure like an array, for example, by 'a[i] := x'. This changes the array to something *almost* the same. After a few assignments, the contents of an array can be in considerable doubt (even when all assignments are simple, without obscurities like 'a[a[i]] := a[a[j]]'). Almost all of a conventional program is spent searching for information—calculating the value of pointers or subscripts like i, so that each assignment can be most effective in making 'just the right change' to a complex data structure.

▷ *Conceptual*—depending on how computation is thought about and controlled. Computation is limited by the expensive strategies normally chosen to implement it. The tradeoff here is that powerful languages enable programs to be written faster, but they take longer to run. For some applications, the programmer's time eclipses the computer's total run time, so sophisticated and easier to use languages (but with slower implementations) are worthwhile.

▷ *Managerial*—depending on how designers are able to manage complexity and solve problems. Von Neumann style programming, particularly the acute awareness of efficiency bottlenecks, is claimed to be mentally expensive and distracting for programmers. Programmers can become obsessed with how to avoid the bottleneck and how to design efficient programs (for example, by minimizing assignments to achieve a certain effect).

There are also clear financial tradeoffs: between the processor/memory transfer bandwidth and the cost of the hardware, and of the research and development to get it to work effectively. Gains in 'raw' bandwidth rapidly become uneconomic, and further gains in bandwidth have to be obtained by intelligent use of independent processing—itself a challenging programming task.

The von Neumann bottleneck is the subject of several major research programmes: new computer architectures and programming paradigms are heavily studied. For our present purposes, even if the conventional *spatial* von Neumann bottleneck is avoided, computers will still be affected by a *temporal* bottleneck (or depending on cost, one might be able to trade one bottle for the other). And *even* if processor bottlenecks are eliminated (quantum physics notwithstanding—see Box 5.2), electronic computers will be limited by financial considerations over how many wires can be used to convey information from one part of memory to another (from optical disks to active memory, for instance).

4.2 Example von Neumann correspondences

User interface bottlenecks can be widened by analogous technical strategies to those used for widening von Neumann bottlenecks. All the ideas in this section are quite conventional technical ideas for improving bandwidth between processor and memory. Some of them are regularly exploited in user interfaces, others are unknown and it would be exciting to try them out. The list is not exhaustive: there are probably new user interface techniques waiting to be discovered that would be more effective than some of the stranger ideas suggested here!

4.2.1 Powerful instructions

In order to make von Neumann computers as efficient as possible, designers tried to provide powerful instructions to achieve as much as possible per step. Each instruction makes the processor do something particular, maybe quite complex; to perform some task, fewer instructions are needed overall than if each instruction did a modest amount of work. This reduces the amount of information flowing through the bottleneck, yet keeps up performance. It is also relatively cheap to provide lots of instructions in the processor hardware, rather than, for instance, increasing the information that can be transferred per instruction. Whenever a computer is not fast enough, identify where it is having trouble and add some more instructions to speed up *that* problem: the result is computers with lots of complex, specific instructions. It becomes harder to decide which combinations of instructions should be used if precisely the right instruction is not available for whatever you want to program.

4.2.2 Reduced instruction sets

Recently, there has been a reaction to the problems of obtaining optimal performance from complex computers. RISCs (reduced instruction set computers) represent an alternative approach. RISCs are supposed to be simple enough to be fast (no microcode), made cheaply and be easy to exploit, particularly by compilers. Also the designers can (and do) take far more care over implementing the dozen or so instructions needed in a RISC than they can over implementing hundreds of instructions needed on a conventional computer. Roughly, the assumption is that doing a few things exceedingly well is better than doing lots of things with mediocrity. Another reason why RISCs are easier to exploit is that their design is more easily described by manageable amounts of formalism.

Even though simplified programming languages are being developed, we have yet to see 'reduced instruction set interfaces' (RISIs?), where the user interface design has been deliberately constrained so that the user can exploit the power of the system much more easily and flexibly.[2] The problem with many user interfaces, like conventional complex instruction computers, is that everything the user wants to do suffers from the overheads of providing very general features with the result that they may be slow and difficult to learn and use effectively.

RISCs are effective because complexity has been shifted from the instructions to compiling—and into the complexity of the processor circuits. Where, then, does the complexity go in a RISI? Does it go into the user's head? Perhaps it is better if the complexity simply disappears altogether, as it does in the programming language occam, itself designed to run on a RISC.

4.2.3   Very long instruction words

Another interesting approach to computer architecture is to use VLIW (very long instruction word) processors. A standard von Neumann computer executes one instruction at a time, even when consecutive instructions could in principle be executed simultaneously. In contrast, a VLIW computer has multiple instructions that can instruct the computer to perform several tasks simultaneously. If you can think of n independent things to do at once (and you have n processors and instructions n times wider than usual), then you can go up to n times faster.

An important aspect of a VLIW machine is that if there are not n independent things to do at any one moment, it is still worth doing n things otherwise some of the processing power would be idle. To use a VLIW processor effectively requires an optimizing compiler to plan work for each of the n processing elements to do which is likely to be useful, even though some of it might have to be discarded depending on events.

The corresponding form of user interface would literally permit n users to collaborate on a single task. As in a VLIW machine, some users may be asked to do work that in fact will not be needed, but at the moment

---

[2] Direct manipulation systems are not necessarily nor systematically RISI—though ideally they should be.

they are asked to do it, it is possible that the results will be required. Alternatively, instead of providing a user interface for many users, it can of course be organized so that a single user simulates them. This form of interface would provide a single user with the ability to interact with n different steps of the dialogue at any one time, rather than one step at a time: instead of having the machine waste his time, now the user can decide which things to do and within limits, what order to do them in. The nearest equivalent interface to date is **form-filling**, a style illustrated in Figure 4.3.

4.2.4 Caches

If information has been transferred once (and has not changed in the meantime), do not transfer it again. We might assume that the user can remember (cache-in-the-head), or there can be explicit mechanisms for recovering information previously displayed. For example, windowing terminals might be and often are arranged so that every information flow uses a new window as a cache. If the user wants some information again, it is already displayed in some window. (This idea exploits the ease of spatial organization: it is not so clear that users would remember cache names rather than places.) In the opposite direction, **defaulting** is the system caching what the user submitted earlier. Programming by example (which is discussed in Chapter 15) can be thought of as 'time traveller's caching': anticipate what the user will do in the future as a program, so that the user does not have to tell the computer.

4.2.5 Lazy evaluation

Lazy evaluation will be covered in detail below, in Section 4.3; in brief, don't transfer or work on data unless it is needed.

4.2.6 Compression

An obvious way to transfer less data is to compress the information, to transfer no more than necessary. Typically, this results in the use of abbreviations, single letter command names, and so on. The problem with compression is that the user (and the computer) have to be assumed to be able to decompress the data, that is, they need a model.

4.2.7 Predictive compression

Predictive compression is a particular compression technique. In predictive compression, the model is not used to expand the compressed data that *has been* sent, but is used to predict what the next item will be. Thus, instead of transmitting raw data, it is only necessary to correct the prediction. If the prediction is good, this will be quicker than explicit transmission. Defaulting is a very simple example; the computer predicts (by trivial analysis) that the user is likely to submit the same data again. If this is a correct prediction, the user merely acknowledges the prediction; however, if the prediction is incorrect, the user can change it.

4.2.8   Multiplexing

If it is not possible to transfer enough information because of the bottleneck, transfer some now and some later. Multiplexing is extremely effective if some of the user's (or processor's) activities are waiting for something to happen: the user (or processor) can get on with another activity in the meantime.

Humans have two hands, but user interfaces typically provide only one-handed input devices. A keyboard can be used by one hand; few computers have more than one mouse. Multiplexing suggests simulating extra devices, for example, when the user presses the shift key, the mouse takes on the left-handed functions—this will reduce interference between two sets of interface functions. One hand draws, the other hand positions the image: multiplexing means that the drawing implement does not have to be 'put down' when the user wants to move the image.

4.2.9   Time dependence

Since information is transferred at a particular time, and this time will be different for each interaction, then it may be possible to exploit the time to contribute to the information itself. For instance, in a von Neumann machine the three assignment statements, t:=a; a:=b; b:=t; mean different things depending on what order they are passed to the processor. Time dependence (or **serialization**) is reliance on modes, which will be discussed at length in Chapter 11.

We highlighted concurrency—freedom from time dependency, being able to do 'things at once'—in Chapter 1 as one of the important benefits of using computers. Window systems certainly allow the user to escape from serialization at a gross level (because he can choose which window to interact with), but interaction *within* each window can often be made more flexible, as indeed the brief examples in Chapter 1 suggested. Chapter 15 will give more systematic principles.

4.2.10 Non-ground variables

In von Neumann programming languages, it is an error to access a variable that has not got a value. In order to avoid this error, programs are often over-cautious and supply the values for too many variables: some of their values may never be needed. The idea of a non-ground variable is to permit a program to refer to a variable that as yet does not have a completely defined value. The value can be filled out later, but for the moment we can talk about it. For example, a user may ask a system for all the personal information it has about him. The system might reply that his age is 32, but his mortgage details are M and left non-ground. That means he will have to ask again to find out about his mortgage. The effect is that the user has not been swamped with mortgage details, equally the computer has not had to waste time discovering what this information is.

If the system is **equal opportunity** (an idea to be developed in Chapter 15), the user will be able to supply the name M, representing his mortgage details, to another program. If *that* program needs to know his mortgage details, it can get them by finding out what M is (**instantiating** it). Thus the user has been able to use some information—his mortgage details—without it ever crossing the user interface; and if he had chosen not to use the information, then the computer perhaps would never have even worked it out (so it would not have crossed the von Neumann or other internal bottlenecks either).

4.2.11 More or wider channels

Changing the hardware is an obvious, but potentially expensive, technique! If there are 8 wires between memory and processor, why not 16 or 32? Why not as many as there are bits in memory? It is surprising how content we are to live with user interfaces with very limited interfaces: keyboard, screen and maybe a mouse. And it is even more surprising when you consider that you do not get any qualitative changes if you pay more for the computer—a bigger screen, perhaps, but no new information channels for widening the bottleneck.

4.2.12 Multiple threads of control

Imperative programming languages virtually force the programmer into providing a user interface where the user can only do one thing at a time. Writing programs in Pascal that permit interleaved tasks, or multiple input devices (for example, for a system using two mice) is almost impossible. Programming languages designed for exploiting parallelism or multi-processor machines more readily support multiple tasking, and

Box 4.1   Teleconferencing: sharing information.

Users involved in a conference typically share the same screen, or, rather, have the same picture shown on their own separate screens. For example, two users may each have a word processor using half the screen; the other half of the screen shows the other user's text. Since the users can work simultaneously, the effect is as if they are sharing a *single* piece of paper, having one column each, though in fact they may be separated by a considerable distance. In general, if there are n users, the screen can be divided into n regions or windows.

The problem with such systems is that they tend to drop the social conventions for handling interruptions, so it is quite difficult to synchronize users' comments. Equally, users find it difficult to make a contribution to the conference when someone is typing—it is hard to type and read something else at the same time. Because pauses may arise owing to machine delays or users having trouble spelling or typing, users develop conventions such as writing **over** when they have finished and want someone else to respond. Even this does not solve the problem that when one person stops typing, several other users may all want to start at once.

Similar problems arise when programs are run in parallel and attempt to share memory or other resources, such as screen displays. Computers use semaphores, critical regions, capabilities and other mechanisms to organize the use of shared data. The use of the shared resource can also be scheduled using different strategies. A user might, for example, indicate how urgently he wants to contribute at the next **over** (say, by moving the mouse up or down) or even if he wants to interrupt; the interactive system allows a contribution or interruption when some combination of urgency and fairness suggests it is acceptable. The technical problems of such ideas have been solved; the social consequences have not! But the range of technical ideas suggests that there may be good technical solutions already available that would work well for teleconferencing, and may even work better than direct person-to-person contact—certainly for individuals with certain sorts of communication handicap.

permit the user to pursue several tasks concurrently. It is interesting to note (again!) that providing *simple* user interface features, such as multiple mice, is all too often a *serious* programming problem in conventional environments.

4.2.13   Handshaking

If the communication channel is unreliable, bandwidth is effectively reduced because of wasted information transmitted after undetected errors. Information that is transmitted after an error occurs, but before the error is detected and corrected, is often wasted. Instead, information can be exchanged by handshaking: send some data, wait for an acknowledgement that it appears error-free,[3] then send the next data. The handshaking protocol is often implemented in computers by using one extra wire, rather than using the primary information-carrying part of the bus (and therefore slowing normal information transfer). Errors in user interfaces occur, for instance, when the computer transmits information too fast for the user to take it in. A simple handshaking protocol can be used: the computer displays a screenful of data, then waits for the user to acknowledge, then transmits the next screenful. A good user interface would also provide a command to redisplay the current screenful, in case it got garbled.

4.2.14 Watchdogs

A watchdog is an approach to make computer systems safer. The idea is that a separate process (or a separate computer), called the watchdog, watches over the actual work. When it detects something awry, it intervenes, and, for instance, turns down the fuel supply. Typically, the main processor is required to perform 'I am awake' tasks (such as resetting a timer) every so often to keep the watchdog happy. Thus, if the main processor gets tangled and held up trying to sort out an emergency problem, the watchdog notices and can bring the situation under control by direct intervention. There are two ways in which watchdogs may be used in user interfaces, depending on whether the watchdog is a human or a computer. Both forms of watchdog look out for anomalies in interaction that indicate that either computer or human user is stuck or has forgotten to perform some task. Computer watchdogs are better and more cautious than humans at remembering to save data at regular intervals just in case the computer crashes!

(It is only by taking a minor liberty that watchdogs are included in this list of techniques—though normal plus watchdog processes together have a higher bandwidth to monitor the system than the basic system alone, in principle no extra bandwidth is made available, but the additional information is more easily obtained and acted upon by the watchdog, whether human or computer.)

4.2.15 Oracles

Oracles correctly guess what they are supposed to say, thus saving a lot of time obtaining information that a more cautious reasoner would want. This saves the bottleneck for other information. In computing, oracles are

---

[3] Information being transmitted is generally coded so that errors are easier to detect. For instance, an extra parity bit can be used so that the number of set bits transmitted is even. An error in one bit (or, three bits, five bits ...) can then be detected (but not identified). Handshaking would then ask for a retransmission.

usually a technical device to make reasoning about certain sorts of programs somewhat easier. In user interfaces, oracles would have immense benefit, so it is worth considering how to simulate them—even a partial simulation would have interesting benefits!

The simplest sort of oracle in user interfaces is a **default**. If the user does nothing, the system 'guesses' that he is likely to do the same thing again, or want something done in a standard way. This is rather conventional. A more interesting use of oracles would be in the case where lots of users are working together on a common problem. The oracle could tell each of them something different—hopefully at least one user will be given the right answer, and he will solve the problem first. *That* user will think the 'oracle' very effective.

4.3   Lazy and eager interaction

An important optimization in the use of the limited bandwidth user interface is to choose between **lazy** and **eager** information processing.

The adversarial form of Twenty Questions, where the computer does not bother to work out what it is thinking of until the last possible moment is a sort of lazy evaluation. But there are clearer examples. Suppose I want to know the meaning of a word. First, I buy a dictionary—or start running a computer program simulating a dictionary. I *do not* read the dictionary from cover to cover; I simply look up the word of interest. Even if I had a perfect memory it would be silly to read the dictionary from the beginning so that I would never need to refer to it again: it would take up too much time—and besides, I do not have a perfect memory, I would fall asleep. Using terms from computer science, the strategy for referring to a dictionary is **lazy**. The converse strategy, being **eager**, is, in this case, inappropriate.

Now, almost all computer systems are implemented using eager techniques. Eager techniques are generally much simpler: it is easier to read a dictionary once, from start to finish, and keep it handy than to have to understand how it is organized so that individual words can be looked up efficiently. Computers tend to ask the user for all conceivably relevant information before proceeding to the next step of an interaction, even though some of the information might not be needed until later. Conventional programming languages, such as Pascal, tend to encourage this style of design. A Pascal program is **imperative**: each part of a Pascal program tells the computer to do something, then do the next thing. The next thing can never be done at another time *even* if it does not rely on information generated by the first thing. For instance, consider the simple Pascal code in Figure 4.2.

This program first asks its user how old he is (let's gloss over the problems of the user typing `thirty` or something other than a decimal

```
write('What is your age?'); readln(age);
write('How many children have you?'); readln(children);
if children > 0 then
begin write('Tell me the age of ');
        if children > 1 then write('each child')
        else write('your child');
        for i := 1 to children do readln(childage[i]);
end;
```

Figure 4.2   A simple interactive Pascal program.

number really meaning his age). *Then* it asks for a number of children. *Then* it asks for the age of each child. Of course, the information obtained— your age, number of children and their ages—could have been asked for in a different order. But the system requires the information in this order only because it was written down in Pascal in that order. Even though the value of the variable **age** is never used in this fragment of the program, Pascal eagerly requires a specific value (for example, 30) before proceeding on to the next step.

There are other reasons for preferring flexible sequencing of steps during an interactive session. For instance, the user may not be able to recall how old he is, but perhaps thinking of his children's ages would help bring his own age to mind. Support for the idea of lazy use is not just dependent on the obvious limitations of time and memory I used to motivate the introductory dictionary example above.

The eagerness of Pascal-like languages is a serious problem. And it cannot be avoided by writing better Pascal programs: in general there are just too many combinations of possibilities to take account of. Instead a different programming or interaction paradigm must be used (which could be tediously simulated by writing a virtual machine in Pascal). One common approach is to interact with the user by distributing the interaction over space rather than time. The Pascal code above asks each question at certain points in *time*. Instead, we could ask the user the questions at certain points in *space*. Space has the rather nice property that we can visit places in any order. There are many ways we could distribute the same questions over space (and some new ideas might suggest themselves), but as a starting point consider Figure 4.3.

```
What is your age:  [____]
How many children have you:  [____]
Age of children:  [____] [◇____] [____] [____]
```

Figure 4.3   Form-filling style display.

We can imagine that this is some sort of screen display. The [____]
are 'slots' for the user to type numbers in. The user is about to type at the
slot marked with the ⋄. But the *spatial* layout means that the user can move
the ⋄ around the screen, perhaps up two lines to fill in the answer to the first
question, perhaps up one line to fill in the answer to the second question. It
is now obvious that the computer can easily fill in the second line from the
information the user provides in the third line. (Chapter 15 will promote
this observation into a quite general design principle.) Of course, we have
traded off flexibility against the extra complexity of learning the commands
to move the ⋄ around. The ⋄ itself is a new concept that was not necessary
in the original design. But we may hope to amortize the spatially related
learning effort because the same techniques can be used for almost every
aspect of interaction. There are also new implementation problems, such
as effective error detection and telling the user clearly which pieces of data
are in conflict.

We must note that there is a more serious tradeoff, and one that often
seems to be ignored. By distributing the interaction over space, we have in
fact made it less reactive. Unless the system still responds to each entry by
the user *as it is entered*, the potential user interface bandwidth will not be
fully exploited. Of course, there are usually technically motivated reasons
for ignoring this tradeoff: it is more efficient to implement form-filling style
dialogues if they can be made so simple (for example, by batching error
detection) to run inside a terminal without recourse to some expensive
computing facility.

Most BASIC systems require the user to submit a complete program,
entering it line by line, and only then can they run it. The BASIC system
has eagerly accepted the program *before* it is prepared to run any of it.
An alternative is to accept the program lazily, but try and run it as soon
as possible (Brown, 1982). As soon as the user submits the first line of his
program, the computer runs it—then it requests the next line of the program
from the user. Of course, if the program enters a loop, it is likely that all
the lines of program needed in the loop have already been entered: so the
loop can execute immediately. The user may submit a `goto` (or a program
line that conditionally branches): in this case, the computer requests the
destination line, unless it has got it already. The effect of this style of
interaction means that the user can never submit a line of program that is
not executed. Every line of program that the user submits is *immediately*
run and tested.

4.3.1   Laziness is general

We have only given a few examples of lazy evaluation, but we shall now
show that laziness is a quite general approach to running programs. A
concrete—though quite arbitrary—example will help. Suppose our task is

to submit 'all' the prime numbers to the computer. The solution to this problem is obviously infinite in extent: we had better be careful about the order that we use to write down the primes. For simplicity, we will plan to submit a sequence something like $2, 3, 5, 7, 11, 13$ and so on. So long as we are satisfied with our choice of order, we must assure ourselves that we can always generate more primes as the computer needs them.

The best way to generate all the primes is to use the Sieve method invented by Eratosthenes around 200 BC. His approach was, first, to write down all the natural numbers greater than 1 (2, 3, 4, 5, ...). Then write down the first number (2, a prime) and cross out all its multiples. So we cross out 4, 6, 8, 10, and so on. When he has finished *that* he repeats the process: writing down the smallest number that has not already been written down, nor yet crossed off. He has not crossed off 3, so he writes it down, and then crosses off all its multiples, 6, 9, 12, ...

It is clear that *if we had enough time* the list of numbers and the list of primes would look like Figure 4.4 after a few iterations.

Work space: 2 3 4̶ 5 6̶ 7 8̶ 9̶ 1̶0̶ 11 1̶2̶ 13 1̶4̶ 1̶5̶ 1̶6̶ 17 1̶8̶ 19 2̶0̶ 2̶1̶ 2̶2̶ 23 ...
Primes: 2 3   5   7   11   13   17   19   23 ...

Figure 4.4 The Sieve of Eratosthenes.

Of course we do not *really* cross off *all* the multiples of each prime as they are found. Instead we cross off *just enough* to ensure that we can both find the next uncrossed number in a finite time and that that number is indeed a prime. With a conventional eager approach, we would first determine that we really do not want all the primes but that we would be satisfied with, say, all primes up to some limit L. In either case we have made our auxiliary problems finite (at least, insofar as we have examined them): and we are thereby allowed the liberty of solving subproblems *completely* as and when we come to them.

Each approach, lazy and eager, has its disadvantage. The eager approach comes unstuck if our estimates like L are too restrictive. In that case, we now have to re-solve the *entire* problem with a more generous limit. This is very costly, in fact, for the present problem of generating primes we just about have to start from scratch (apart from writing down the primes we have already found) for we still have to cross out all the non-primes in our new, bigger, workspace. In 'real life', when we are generally interested in more sophisticated interaction than talking about primes, this situation corresponds to having to restart a dialogue—often from scratch, sometimes even having to reconfigure the system.

The lazy approach does not suffer from this sudden catastrophe, instead it just gets slower and slower. In fact, the first primes it finds faster than an eager method, and then gets progressively slower and slower. The reason the lazy method gets slower is that at each step we find we have more and more things to do that we postponed earlier (secretly hoping we might never have to do them).

As humans, we find the worst disadvantage of the lazy communication approach is keeping track of accumulating numbers of postponed steps, and of shifting our attention between the various subdialogues, none of which we need to finish at once. People like a sense of closure and the lazy method denies them this sense of accomplishment. Few people are prepared to be *so* lazy that they get no immediate satisfaction!

Finally notice that the best solutions for this artificial example involve giving the computer a program to compute the primes for itself. There are two ways this might be done. The user might submit a prime-generating program, written in Pascal, for instance. This may be thought to make outlandish demands on the user, but in this case, any user who wants all those primes can probably program! The program submitted by the user will be shorter than a long list of primes, so this solution justifies the comments made earlier about transferring information effectively by abstractions (programs) and, incidentally, it is a *far* lazier method than the one described at length above. Another possibility, which is outlandish because of the demands on both user and computer, is to program by example. The user submits the first 'few' primes, and eventually the computer induces the idea and writes the program itself. See Section 15.2.3 for a brief discussion of this **programming by example**.

4.3.2 Lazy interactive programming

The last section showed that lazy programming was a general technique. I now want to show that it is possible to program interactive systems lazily. Although there are lazy programming languages available, little attention has been paid to lazy interactive systems. But rather than use a lazy language, we will start our discussion by using conventional Pascal.

The Pascal program of Figure 4.2 above can be rewritten so that after the first two questions the rest of its work is undertaken by a procedure, finishoff say. Figure 4.5 is a possible way to do this.

We assume ask is a procedure that prints its argument, as a question to the user. It reads whatever number the user submits and returns it to the program. Note that ask can handle the problems we mentioned earlier of the user possibly not submitting an arabic numeral in answer. If we assume finishoff has two parameters called age and children, then calling the procedure finishoff initializes these variables and Figures 4.2 and 4.5 correspond. (The Principle of Correspondence (Section 10.9.2) states that the sort of changes going from Figure 4.2 to Figure 4.5 can be made to any Pascal program. The discussion of this section is quite general.)

```
procedure finishoff(age, children: integer);
begin if children > 0 then
      begin write('Tell me the age of ');
            if children > 1 then write('each child')
            else write('your child');
            for i := 1 to children do readln(childage[i]);
      end
end;
...
finishoff(ask('What is your age?'),
          ask('How many children have you?'))
```

Figure 4.5   Simple interaction approaching the functional style.

The correspondence is not exact, however, for the original version used the imperative feature of assignment. The user was necessarily asked his age before being asked how many children he had. In its new form, we encounter a feature of Pascal: the order in which procedure arguments are evaluated is not defined. We do not need to assume that **ask** works on a typewriter (a sequential interaction device)—it might use one window for each question for example—but its typewriter output will certainly be in one order or the other order. The new program will produce one of either of the following outputs:

What is your age?	How many children have you?
How many children have you?	What is your age?

We do not know which until the program is run. But we do know that which order will be chosen makes absolutely no difference to the Pascal program (in fact it has no easy way of telling which order is actually chosen). We can imagine that the order in which the questions are asked makes some difference to the user. If it makes no difference to the program but does to the user, why not let the user control the order? Pascal itself does not allow the programmer to use this style of programming to give the user any choice (the only person who can exploit the freedom is the language implementor), but clearly a language could be devised so that the user can make these decisions to do with the order of answering questions when the order has no effect on the behaviour of the program.

In fact the order of asking questions is not the only freedom that can be permitted. We have so far assumed that the language, being Pascal, is eager: meaning that the arguments (**ask** in this case) are evaluated *before* the procedure (**finishoff**) is called. In general it is possible to delay evaluating arguments until their values are actually needed—to delay asking the questions until their answers are needed.

It is quite possible that the program is not interested in the age of someone unless he is a parent. There might be a conditional if **age > 60**

then ask-about-social-security ... inside the existing conditional
if children > 0 then ... If this is the only way that the user's age
is used in the program, then some answers (namely 0 for the number of
children) mean that the user should never need to answer the question
about his age. Or again, the system might ask if the user is married and
what the spouse's name is. Here the second question would not be necessary
if the user is unmarried. In general eager programs quite often ask for data
that they do not need (or do not need all of).

In our example, with the program in either form, the age of the user
is always asked before the program knows whether the user is a parent
and therefore whether it was necessary to ask if he was over 60. In a lazy
programming system this need not be the case. In a lazy language *exactly*
the second form of program (Figure 4.5) would not ask the question unless it
was necessary. A lazy language does not evaluate arguments to a procedure
before the procedure is called, because at that point one does not know
whether the argument values are going to be needed.

The system being lazy does not bother to evaluate anything unless
it has to. In fact, if you look carefully at Figure 4.5, a lazy system would
simply not have asked the user for his age. The system merely keeps track
of the argument, so that if its value turns out to be needed then it can force
its evaluation to get it. The point is (which we will return to in Section 4.4),
the programmer does not have to do anything special to get lazy evaluation
when he is using a lazy language.

Getting lazy interactive systems to work well is clearly an interesting
problem (we have not discussed how the user might control the evaluation
order, particularly when there are perhaps too many permutations to make
sense of): but we have shown that it is feasible in principle and would
generally have benefits for the user.

4.3.3 Serial and parallel programming

In programming research there is now a growing trend away from
'procedural languages' (such as Pascal, Ada, Smalltalk) to 'non-procedural
languages' (such as Prolog, Miranda). This trend grows partly out of the
recognition that algorithms can often be defined without any reliance on a
specific order of evaluation. In a procedural language, for example, to find
the maximum element of an array the code, shown in Figure 4.6, might be
used.

It is not immediately clear why this particular order is necessary;
it would have been as reasonable to write 'for i := N downto 1 do' or
any other order. It is legitimate to examine elements of the array more
than once. If a procedural language is chosen, programmers have to
commit themselves to one or another of the possible representations of the
algorithm. To make their particular commitment they may waste program

```
maxval := a[1];
for i := 2 to N do
    if a[i] > maxval then maxval := a[i]
```

Figure 4.6   One way to find the maximum.

development time, especially if they begin to wonder which is more efficient on the particular computer they expect to run the program on. In such a simple case, like this one, each programmer will readily draw on his set of programming idioms (perhaps using a primitive of the programming language and perhaps the question of wasted design time hardly arises). In a more complex example it would take longer to discover whether the appropriate primitives or library routines were available, and if not it would take longer to devise the code. So why not use a programming notation that does not express sequencing? Obviously this is an idealization, the programmers now have to learn a different set of programming idioms to program effectively: but we can be almost certain that (for a wide class of algorithms) they will be able to program faster and more reliably.

If we had pursued this example in real life, it would have been intended that some computer be run, and eventually find the maximum element of some array. Whether Pascal, Prolog or another language is used, the computer will necessarily evaluate the algorithm using a particular procedure: with increasing i or decreasing i or with several values of i in parallel or perhaps some combination of these procedures. The point is that *the programmer need not have been committed to the particular procedure eventually chosen*, in this case to find the maximum.

Similarly in user interfaces, the designer need not have predetermined a particular way for the user to work through his task. Yes, the user will usually be doing more exciting things than working out maximum values, but the principle is the same. Proper programming gives the user freedom to implement his tasks in the way he finds most efficient, rather than in the way the designer assumes is most efficient (or, worse, the way that is easiest to program). Functional programming (a style of programming where order is not specified) promises to introduce new ways of interacting with computers: its advocates say it is easier to program functionally, and if so, designers *may* tend to design interactive systems where the user is not forced into unnecessarily ordered sequences. There is a difference between functional programs and their user interfaces. Functional programs conventionally have difficulty with input/output, but there is no reason why users should not interact as if in a functional language. The interface would certainly be modeless, having all the nice properties of functional programs, such as referential transparency.

On the other hand, the great advantage of a strictly serial algorithm is that there will be simple arguments to show that every element is examined (that is, correctly) no more than once (that is, efficiently). Where the user interface is safety-critical there will be similar advantages if the designer knows precisely how it will be used. By constraining the user to certain paths through the interaction, the designer can take control of various factors, such as interference in STM if the user should take on too many unfinished subtasks.

4.4   What is a paradigm?

Programming languages are different, and offer programmers different advantages. Pascal and Prolog, for instance, are good at very different sorts of job. Although any Turing Complete programming notation is formally equivalent to any other (up to choices of input/output representations, and representational completeness is readily achieved thanks to standardized character sets and similar conventions), some are more concise than others. The programming language makes certain assumptions, and the programmer need not express some things explicitly. Such differences are put down to **paradigms**. Our discussion of paradigms is important for it is analogous to user interface styles.

Certain styles of interactive systems are better for certain sorts of tasks, because of what the user does *not* need to say or see. Likewise, a paradigm is distinguished by what the programmer 'gets for free', what he does not have to state explicitly in his program. For instance, a LISP programmer gets garbage collection for free, giving him a simulation of infinite memory; he does not have to organize his program so that garbage collection works, as he would have to in Pascal. But in Pascal, you get recursion for free, whereas in FORTRAN you would have to work it out explicitly. In this sense, programming paradigms are analogous to the scientific paradigms of Thomas Kuhn. For Kuhn, normal, everyday science operates in paradigms; that is, in frameworks of unquestioned assumptions and mostly unstatable assumptions (Kuhn, 1970). The ruling paradigms govern the way that scientists think, perform experiments and interpret the results.

Let us now try to define **programming paradigm**. Since the features that are not explicitly included in a program but are used by that program (such as reliance on recursion, polymorphism, closures, garbage collection) depend on what the program needs to do, it may help to have a 'base-line' program. Then any feature not explicit in the base-line program can be said to be part of the programming paradigm in which that program is written. An obvious base-line program is the metainterpreter for the programming language. This is the smallest program that can do all that the programming language itself can do; it corresponds very roughly with the idea of a self-demonstrating interactive system. It might appear to make little difference to the discussion if we choose as the base-line program one that could implement any Turing equivalent machine. However, it strengthens the paradigm criterion if we require representational equivalence as well, and thus the metainterpreter for the *same* language is naturally suggested. The paradigm is then the set of recursively invariant properties up to identity.

Another way to put this is that paradigms provide **transparent** features. When a feature is not paradigmatic, you have to program it yourself—which means that you can *see* its implementation, it is hardly transparent! Likewise in user interfaces, most if not all of the implementation should be transparent to the user: the user should be able to get useful features to help his task for free, as part of the interaction paradigm.

By this definition of paradigm, the syntactical notation of Pascal is not in Pascal's programming paradigm, but it is in LISP's. A LISP interpreter written in LISP does not specify whether the language garbage collects, has tail-recursion removal, what precision arithmetic works at, and it does not even have to specify how to parse itself! Such features are part of the paradigm. But a Pascal interpreter written in Pascal would contain a considerable amount of code devoted to parsing. It is very interesting to see how programming language designs have been clearly divided between those that treat syntax as part of the paradigm and those that don't. Of course, this definition of a paradigm is dangerous: the metainterpreter does *not* define the paradigm, it merely uses it. At least, on this definition, we can now understand why people argue about paradigms.

The next two paragraphs discuss Turing Machines, a topic which will be properly introduced in Section 5.1.

It is well known that a Turing Machine can run a universal program (call it $\mathcal{U}$) that can read a description of a Turing Machine and simulate it. This is no more complex an idea than if you have a computer you can write a program to simulate a Turing Machine: and if computers are 'just' Turing Machines, then it is not surprising that one can be made to simulate another. So it is possible to devise a program for $\mathcal{U}$ in any suitable programming language, such as Pascal, Prolog or BASIC—the only difficult part may be deciding on how to represent the input/output and, indeed, the user interface in general.

Now any program run by the universal program inherits certain properties of the Turing Machine on which *it* is running. For instance, if the universal machine's tape is not really infinite, then the simulated machine certainly cannot have an infinite tape. If the universal machine's tape is in reality infinite, then it can provide infinite memory resources to simulate an infinite tape in the simulated machine. We would say that the infiniteness (or finiteness) of memory tape is part of the paradigm of a real (or simulated) Turing Machine.

Consider a Pascal compiler: it translates, amongst other things, string denotations, symbols a programmer uses to represent strings of

Box 4.2   Metacircularity.

Metacircularity is familiar to LISP programmers: LISP systems may very easily be defined by a LISP program. A Pascal compiler may be written in Pascal. Any system to process a language L, itself written in the same language L is **metacircular**. We say *meta*circular rather than merely circular because 'meta' means transcending or going beyond.

Technically there is nothing very difficult about creating a metacircular system. It first has to be **bootstrapped**: the system to process the language L is written in some other convenient language, possibly machine code. When that works, it can be translated by hand into L. Now we have a system in L designed to process the language L. That, then, is a metacircular system. Most, but not all, metacircular systems are Turing Complete, see Section 5.3.

Metacircular systems are a rather pleasing and elegant way of defining systems. For a language designer, writing his own compiler in the same language provides an ideal opportunity to exercise the language for a non-trivial application, namely the compiler itself. For a language user, the metacircular definition can be understood using only one language—had the language in question been defined in some other way, the user would have to know that other language as well (though it might be a natural language, like English, but then it would suffer from imprecision).

Clearly if the users do not understand the language properly, they won't understand the metacircular definition, and in turn will not be able to use the definition to work out what the language does. This is a devastating problem. Metacircular 'definition' turns out to be just that, circular.

Take a simple case. Suppose the user thinks LISP programs always print ? when they ask the user for data. Since the metacircular LISP system is just another LISP program, then the user must think that it will always print ? when *it* wants data. Now what does a LISP program do when it wants data? To find out you have to look at the metacircular system: it will ask for data on behalf of the system it is running, which means that *it* prints the ? mark. On the other hand, suppose the user thinks that LISP programs print nothing when they ask the user for data. By the same line of reasoning, it would appear that programs indeed print nothing. The point is that a metacircular system defines nothing: it does what it does. We encounter exactly the same problem when we look up the pronunciation of a word in a dictionary: most dictionaries are metacircular, and provide guides to pronunciation by example. If you have an accent, then you pronounce all the examples with the same accent, and really the guide does not give you the 'correct' pronunciation.

The features that a metacircular system does not need to define, for instance whether it does or does not print a ?, are precisely those features that come for free in the language L. Thus what is undefined by metacircularity is exactly the paradigmatic features of the language L.

(See also Section 14.7, which metacircularly refers you back here.)

characters. For instance, the Pascal programmer can write `'computer'' s move'` and expect the Pascal compiler to translate this into a sequence of character codes that the computer can print as the symbols, c, o, m, p, u, t, e, r, ', s, ␣, m, o, v, e. If the compiler is written in Pascal, we might imagine that the fragment of the compiler that translates the characters in the string to their codes looks something like: `if character = 'a' then write('a') else` ... Notice that this is correct but that the compiler nowhere need express the *actual* code for the character a, because the compiler that compiles *it* already knows the actual code required! Of course, somebody once had to bootstrap the compiler, and that would have involved ensuring that the character codes were correct. But once built into a compiler, the actual codes need never be mentioned again.

We can see how things can be left unsaid if we consider extending a Pascal compiler so that the symbol @ in a string is output as a newline. First we have to modify the existing compiler. The first code we add, to recognize @, might be something like: `if character = '@' then writeln else` ... the details are not too important. Now once we have put that into the compiler, an @ in a string gets translated to a newline, as we wanted. But *now* we can rewrite the compiler itself: if an @ gets translated to a newline, then the code for translating @ could be changed to `if character = '@' then write('@') else`... The explicit `writeln` to do the newline has disappeared! In fact we obtain the rather remarkable and useful property that the compiler is *more* portable than it would be if the conversion had been explicit. Attentive readers will notice that I have pushed the problem of decoding character codes into the assembler. The example could easily be reworked to use explicit codes (for example, `write(10)` instead of `writeln`) but this makes things even more complex when you wonder how the 10 gets translated *back* to a newline when it is printed.

It is possible to take this idea one step further—it is even possible for a malicious person to introduce bugs into a compiler and for all explicit mention of those bugs to disappear for good (Thompson, 1987). If a malicious person can do it deliberately, anyone can do it accidentally. It is not so far fetched to point out the similarities with the problem of hidden knowledge in humans: it is possible to know something, and know that you know, but be unable to express that knowledge verbally. We look at this problem in the next section; also Chapter 18, the epilogue, returns to the seriousness of bugs.

4.4.1 Declarative and imperative paradigms

The two most important paradigms are declarative and imperative. In a **declarative paradigm** the program expresses *what* is to be achieved by running the program; whereas an **imperative paradigm** program expresses *what* to do or *how* something is to be achieved. Note that almost all programming languages mix a bit of each paradigm. Assignment (for example, the :=) is the main imperative feature of Pascal: each assignment tells the computer what to do next. On the other hand, when passing arguments to a procedure you only say that you want the values passed, and we have already seen that there are several ways in which the computer might choose to do this.

Most programmers are more familiar with the imperative paradigm, and indeed most user interfaces are imperative. Interaction is broken down into steps, and at each step the user tells the system what to do and how to do it. In a good imperative system, then, the system's job is to *obey instructions*.

In contrast a user specifies goals and targets to a declarative system: the system itself works out how to achieve these goals. In a good declarative system, then, the system's job is to *solve problems*.

We will see in Chapter 5 that 'adequate' programming languages can do anything, so it is no surprise that a declarative programming language can be used imperatively and vice versa. The definition of paradigm merely says that in a declarative paradigm, problem solving is natural and easy; in an imperative paradigm, obeying instructions is easy. Of course a capable programmer can devise instructions which, if obeyed, have the effect of solving problems: but this is something that does not come easily from within the imperative paradigm.

Declarative paradigm languages attack the von Neumann bottleneck because the computer is free to solve the problems in whatever way it thinks most appropriate. It can use any strategies *it* likes to circumvent bottlenecks, so long as in the end it solves the problem. In contrast the user of an imperative program has to control the computer and tell it how to run efficiently despite the bottleneck. Thus the von Neumann bottleneck is visible, or at least an issue, in imperative programming.

Section 11.6.1 gives an example of a conventional interactive imperative calculator (a standard four-function handheld calculator), and subsequently Chapter 16 develops a functionally equivalent but declarative calculator. We shall argue that the declarative calculator is far easier to use, for precisely the reason that the user does not need to know how to do arithmetic! In an imperative calculator, the user has to convert the problem into such steps that the calculator can obey, and very often this requires the user to convert the problem into a suitable step-by-step form; in a declarative calculator this is the calculator's problem.

4.4.2 Procedural embedding

Users are likely to underestimate the implementation costs of modifications involving variation of input/output roles. For example, if a system validates data provided by the user (for example, that Tuesday 29 October 1985 is a valid date) it will be curious to users that the relevant information which *necessarily* exists in the computer cannot be used in other ways (for example, to find the day of the week on 25 December 1985). The problem is that the knowledge is 'procedurally embedded' and is not accessible except by executing a fixed procedure in a fixed way. Incidentally, people are not immune to a similar problem; the more skilled their performance becomes often the harder it is to conceptualize it: human memory is a classic example. However, we retain a remarkable flexibility even for the least conscious actions.

The more a programmer uses procedural embedding of knowledge the more he will rely on abstractions to manage the complexity of the embedded knowledge. To the user of such a system the abstractions (for example, the commands) available to him will appear limited and contrived. If a programming paradigm is found which permits the programmer to model artefacts available to the user, the user interface will inevitably be cleaner (see below). Ideally, it should exhibit the particular traits or style of the underlying model sufficiently well for the model to be of constructive use (when suitably expressed) for the user. One disadvantage of Prolog, a logic language, is that its implementation world of lists and clauses is usually completely concealed at the user interface level. In contrast, in object-oriented systems it is usual for objects to be both visible and manipulable by the user. The implementation of these objects encapsulates information about their visual form, and so the temptation for the programmer to embed knowledge in a fixed procedural form is minimized. (Thus, a spreadsheet can be implemented very easily on an object-oriented machine. The cells with which the user interacts map onto objects in the implementation.)

People are apt to embed knowledge too. For example, the fact that you can say 'Greek' out loud must mean that there is a procedural program somewhere that converts the intention of uttering 'Greek' into various physiological actions. The meaning of a program depends on the architecture it runs on: so even if some aspects of speech are dictated by anatomy, we are still correct in asserting that there is a program, even if it is not all encoded explicitly. But I do not know what my tongue does without actually saying the word (and I still do not have an accurate idea).

In general, people embed knowledge because life would be tedious if every program we ran was explicit: as we acquire skills, the skills become unconscious (without conscious control, that is, **automated**), and we can change our attention from the performance of the skill itself (for example, mouth control) to the goals achievable through use of the skill (for example, saying what we mean).

If people routinely embed knowledge, shouldn't computers do likewise? I think the difference is that people embed certain sorts of procedural knowledge, and there is great similarity between different people. Most people expect that the knowledge inaccessible to their own consciousness is also inaccessible to others—normal social interactions therefore exclude this mutually inaccessible information, or treat it as an exercise in psychoanalysis. The issue is that both computers and humans have procedurally embedded knowledge for roughly the same reasons, but computers embed knowledge in a psychologically surprising way!

4.5 Reflexive interaction paradigms

Paradigms are what programming languages provide for free, those features that do not have to be asked for explicitly. When a programmer chooses a 'good language' he can express the issues he is interested in and leave as much as possible up to the system. This results in a concise program, and one that is more likely to be correct. On the other hand, if a poor paradigm is chosen the programmer has to explicitly solve many little problems that are circumstantial to his main programming problem. His attention becomes divided, and the structure of the intended program becomes compromised. For example, if you program in Pascal, which has fixed size arrays, you will tend to impose arbitrary limits on the size of arrays. To do otherwise asks for complex programming.

Or again, trying to write a lazy program in Pascal is very difficult, if not nearly impractical; Pascal is the opposite, eager. A Pascal programmer does not ask for things to be done eagerly, it just happens that way: eagerness, then, is part of Pascal's paradigm. Non-eagerness has to be achieved by explicit programming, and it is not very easy to do that entirely correctly.

An interactive system defines a language for its user. It follows that it implements a paradigm for its user. (In Chapter 5 we will introduce the term **virtual machine** for this, but we do not need precise terminology now.) The serious matter is that the programmer's paradigm, say Pascal, is certainly not the user's paradigm.

In Pascal, parsers are tedious—they are not paradigmatic. If you want a parser in a Pascal program, you have to write it all yourself, and this leads interactive systems to have simple command parsers, often based on single character command names. The user, then, has a trivial language, all ps and qs, in contrast to the programmer's which is all begins and ends! The programmer can often—but not always—do sums anywhere a number is needed (for example, write(3+4) and write(7) have the same effect); at best the user can do restricted sorts of sums in certain places. These are just two illustrations of the radical difference between the user interface paradigm and the programming paradigm. Had we used a different programming language, such as LISP, then parsing is part of the paradigm so is no problem. Thus a LISP system typically has a LISP-like (lots of brackets) user interface language because this takes no programming.

Any language paradigms that carry over into the user interface will tend to improve the user interface. Quite simply such **reflexive interaction paradigms** encourage the programmer to think at the same level as the user. In Smalltalk, the programming language provides objects in its paradigm, and the user interface provides windows and menus in its paradigm. But every window and menu is an object. So when the programmer improves the program *from the programmer's point of view* he tends to improve the user interface *from the user's point of view*. At least that is the idea: obviously a lot depends on the relation between windows and objects—in Smalltalk it is not symmetric. It may be an important reason for the success of object-oriented systems, that they have reflexive models.

What would happen if expert systems encouraged the user to follow rule-based behaviour? What would happen if a spreadsheet used a matrix-based language, like Apl? What would happen if lazy functional systems encouraged the user to be lazy and functional (Section 4.3)? Or, conversely, how would a computer system be designed to reflect the user's task paradigm? Such questions open up a whole area of new and significant ideas; we already know that treating the user as a Pascal-style automaton causes severe problems—human brains are far more complex than one would wish to express in a Pascal-type paradigm!

4.6   Conclusions

The von Neumann correspondence is a correspondence between the processor–memory bottleneck and the user interface bottleneck. It follows that computer systems design may have ideas to suggest to user interface design, *mutatis mutandis*.

The von Neumann correspondence covers concepts from technical to conceptual; this should not surprise us, since programmers, in their efforts to interact with computers, first noticed the von Neumann bottleneck and its consequences. Programmers are now very active in developing novel concepts and questioning 'self-evident' truth (for example, the necessity of explicit sequence): it is time to evaluate and adopt some of these ideas for user interface design, and it is time for user interface researchers to put some of the programmers' claims to empirical scrutiny. Is it really the case that, say, functional programming is really 'easier' than conventional imperative Pascal-type programming? If it is, or is in certain ways, then the relevant ideas can be carried over into user interface design generally for more widespread appreciation. As it is, functional and other non-von Neumann programming styles seem to be restricted to little communities of experts.

For every technique used to improve von Neumann computers, there are analogous user interface strategies. Window systems and multi-user systems are analogues to multiple processors. Defaults are just a user interface analogue of caching. Declarative programming ideas suggest 'equal opportunity' (Chapter 15). Some analogues are fairly obvious, others are quite subtle (such as constructive use of non-determinism), yet others are specialized or perhaps inappropriate for human use—we may advocate a purely technical correspondence, but we must carefully justify technical solutions that involve human participants. It is clear that pursuing the von Neumann correspondence is likely to lead to innovation in user interface design—and as an important bonus, it might raise programmers' appreciation for user interface issues and user interface design: user interface design is certainly no easier than the design of the most advanced computer architectures or programming notations.

The von Neumann correspondence is between the user/computer and the processor/memory; we might 'escalate' it to be an analogy between the strategies user and processor adopt to interact with their environment. We would then come to the correspondence between human personality types and computational evaluation strategies, as will be discussed in Section 8.5.

Chapter 5

To the computer

The danger of the past was that men became slaves. The danger of the future is that men may become robots.

Erich Fromm

It is sometimes said that computers have a general IQ comparable to the common earthworm. But nobody would happily spend a day conversing with an earthworm. Even a professional studying worms would not devote an entire working day to prodding and playing with them. How is it that many, many people spend days on end conversing with computers? Some people even become **hackers**, thoroughly addicted to programming computers: they may even suffer withdrawal symptoms if they are separated from a computer for too long. The problem—if you've ever thought of it as a problem—is, why is it possible to interact with computers? Why do people want to interact with computers?

In some sense, computers must be closer to humans than to worms, if we can judge by the scope for meaningful interaction with them! The apparently profound question how we can interact with computers, is readily answered if (in the limit) computers can be so human-like that users cannot distinguish people from computers. Obviously, computers *look* artificial, so it should be very easy to tell one from the other. Is distinguishing people from computers a serious issue? If you were not allowed to look, there is a deeper sense in which computers could imitate people: by imitating their thought processes. So, how would you tell computer thought from human thought?

We will examine the approach that Alan Turing took to this problem shortly, but first we start with some background material.

5.1   Turing Machines

Turing was interested in the mathematics of computers. In 1937 he described a hypothetical machine that could work with pencil and paper to perform any symbolic calculation. It became known as the **Turing Machine** and was arguably his most significant contribution: he had found a precise way to define what mathematical formality was. With it, Turing was able to state exactly what was possible and what was not possible using formal rules, such as a computer would use.

Turing wanted to make his machine as simple as possible. Starting from the idea of a mathematician using pencil, paper and perhaps a rubber eraser—which are enough to perform any sort of mathematics—he went on to make some radical simplifications. First, it would not make much difference if the machine could only use a single line on the paper, provided it was long enough. So a Turing Machine uses a single tape, rather than lots of sheets of paper, and (as another simplification) there is no limit on the length of tape. The only operations that Turing allowed the machine were to write or change[1] a symbol on the tape, read the symbol on the tape (just under the pencil), move the pencil either left or right, or stop when it had finished. There were a few more rules that led to further simplifications: for instance, the machine is only allowed a fixed set of symbols from which to choose (for example, the alphabet and digits) and a fixed set of rules to decide what to do at any stage. Turing argued that his machine could do anything that a mathematician could do *despite being so simple*, though of course the representation of the final result might not be so polished, written as it would be on a long thin tape with a limited set of symbols. His argument was persuasive.

Next, Turing demonstrated that his machine could do the sorts of things mathematicians do: for instance, it could easily be programmed by defining the rules so that it could do arithmetic.

The Turing Machine is just about as simple as we can get in devising a computing machine. All the evidence suggests that anything much simpler would not have the power that we associate with computers. Nevertheless it is fairly obvious that the Turing Machine would be very difficult to use. A blow-by-blow account of how a Turing Machine adds 3 to 4 would take a couple of pages, and not much less even if we represent the numbers as simply as possible in unary as ○○○ and ○○○○ to make things easier. I shall not bore you with it. This is a nice demonstration that simplicity of design does not mean simplicity of use.

---

[1] The Turing Machine can be modified without loss of power so that it only writes on its tape and never modifies nor erases symbols, however the argument for its effectiveness becomes slightly more involved.

5.2 The Church–Turing Thesis

The **Church–Turing Thesis** states that all notions of 'computing' are equivalent (if details like speed, time and material limitations are ignored). The evidence for the Church–Turing Thesis is that all the varied attempts at defining computing turn out to be equivalent to what Turing Machines can do. If we accept that the Church–Turing Thesis applies to the human mind (or brain) doing computation (thinking), then we can adopt results from computing to say precise things about the capability of the human information processor. We can gloss over the specifically human traits, such as fatigue, inattention, motivation (though it is not obvious that computers could easily simulate these qualities) in the discussion. We are aiming at making precise statements about human (and computer) limitations which must be considered in user interface design.

Experts on the abacus, after some years of practice, can imagine the abacus and perform arithmetic faster in their head than most people can even enter the numbers into a calculator. But it is clear that the mind does not work quite like a conventional computer or even like an abacus. For instance, most of us would be unlikely to find such trivial computing devices as calculators so useful if we had mental access to something roughly like them.

Of course, there *may* be novel ways of computing that nobody has investigated as yet that are more powerful than Turing Machines. Indeed, it is possible that people have certain extra-computational mechanisms (such as insight, creativity and intuition), but it would be reasonable to assume that a user interface which *required* insightfulness would be exhausting.[2] But 'insight' (however much we may value it) is not a constructive notion: how would one improve a user interface design to exploit better the user's insight? Like many computer scientists, you may think that insight and creativity are no more beyond mechanization than thinking: 'extra-computational' mechanisms have certainly not been conclusively shown to exist. If arguments about free will suggest that humans do have special abilities, we could argue that this is no more than non-determinism—that is, making random choices. Again, if a user interface *relied* on the user making random choices it would only appeal to gamblers; for everyone else it would be more stressful. So, whichever way, for our purposes of designing user interfaces, we can conservatively assume that users are no more powerful than Turing Machines. If humans are more powerful, it would seem that there is no sane way to exploit their supercomputational powers by mere computers.

---

[2] The brain is evidently highly parallel and stochastic, but Turing Machines are sequential and deterministic—they do one thing at a time. Although it is still an open question whether sufficiently parallel stochastic machines are more powerful in a formal sense than Turing Machines, we can still argue that relying on such parallelism would be tiring for the user.

What of the differences between human and computer memory and memory processes? The Church–Turing Thesis may fail to apply to people not so much because of their limited memory capacity and imperfect recall, but because people find it *difficult* to forget. Computers 'forget' things completely and totally with ease; whereas human memory has **persistence**. For example, a person is very aware how a display image changes, so too much change in a short period of time can be disturbing (Section 11.7.5).

5.3   Turing Completeness and virtual machines

If we can prove that some notation, or some machine, has sufficient power to emulate a Turing Machine, then that notation (or machine) is said to be **Turing Complete**. It means in effect that it can do at least what a Turing Machine can do. It can compute every computable function. We sometimes use the term 'Turing Completeness' rather sloppily, in the sense that a *real* machine might be Turing Complete *if only* it had unlimited memory.

Programming languages, such as BASIC, Pascal and Prolog are examples of Turing Complete notations. It is easy to prove that these notations are Turing Complete, simply by writing (a finite) Turing Machine simulation program in them. In turn, we could test the simulated Turing Machine by instructing *it* to compute prime numbers or whatever else it is that takes our interest. We might even provide a user interface to control and monitor the simulation (though Turing envisaged the Turing Machine running in batch, one input, at most one output).

There is a hierarchy of computing notations: the Prime Number Machine description as data for our simulation program; the simulated Turing Machine itself; a Pascal system (or whatever) used to implement the Turing Machine; and beneath that, machine code; perhaps microcode; digital gates; electronic components. Each layer is built in terms of the one below. Now, it would be possible to buy some electronic components and wire them up in such a way that prime numbers are emitted, but this would be a very complex job: it would be a batch job (in the sense of Chapter 4) and after all the effort of developing it, all it could do would be to compute primes. Not a very economical investment of your time— especially as it would have taken so long to build that you would have had plenty of opportunity to think of some other things for it to do instead!

It is in fact much easier to organize the electronic components first to make gates, then when *they* work, organize them into larger units, shift registers ... ultimately a computer processor. When the processor works, it can be programmed; then we can run Pascal; then write a Turing Machine program; and so on. This may seem like a drawn out process, but at each stage we can completely ignore the machine one level deeper (at least, if it works correctly). The language used at each level concisely expresses the sort of computations handled at that level—even if that seems tautologous, it means that the level of the language is appropriate for the level of problem. We also gain in being able to make more flexible use of each level: if we no longer want to compute primes we do not need to rewire the computer—that would be working at too low a level.

The proviso, 'if it works correctly' is interesting, for when machines fail—owing to bugs in their design or for other reasons—the failures are very difficult to interpret at other levels. Thus users find bugs in interactive systems very difficult, for their consequences make very little sense at the level of the user interface.

The hierarchy techniques are so common that there is some useful terminology to talk about them:

▷ **Abstraction**: Each layer in the hierarchy of machines represents a set of abstractions over the layer below. Thus a gate represents an abstraction of its electronic components. An abstraction is rather like a 'black box', we may know what it does, but we are not greatly interested in how it works. There are good and bad abstractions: a bad one would 'leak' and to make full use of it we would have to know something about how it was made. For instance, we might find that an *and* gate only works correctly for low frequencies: at high frequencies it ceases to operate properly—the abstraction no longer works, and no longer helps us understand what the gate is doing. Conversely a good abstraction is reliable; but all abstractions hide information and will break down under the 'right' circumstances (see Box 2.1).

▷ **Representation (instantiation)**: A representation is the converse of an abstraction: a representation is the implementation or workings of an abstraction. So the Pascal program was a representation of the Turing Machine.

▷ **Virtual machine**: Each layer, made up from a coherent set of abstractions, forms a virtual machine. Virtual machines are complete barriers to the underlying representation: in Pascal we do not need to worry about currents and voltages even though these concepts are crucial representations inside electronic computers. (When at least two layers of virtual machines are the same, they are metacircular; see Box 4.2.)

▷ **Interface**: Sometimes we are concerned with doing work in terms of the virtual machine; sometimes we want to get the underlying machine to do something at its own level. In this case, the virtual machine acts as an interface between the present and the underlying level.

We can use this same terminology profitably when discussing computer systems when the interface is between man and machine. The computer becomes easier to use to the extent that the interface presents a useful virtual machine to the user. Sometimes the user interface will provide no abstraction mechanisms—the virtual machine cannot run new programs for the user—this will mean that the user cannot extend the given virtual machine to provide his own customized machine for his own purposes.

The screen and keyboard do not give the user access to a computer as such, they give him access to a virtual machine. Sometimes the virtual machine will be highly specific: it might be a word processor and provide abstractions for 'word craft'. Sometimes the virtual machine will be very flexible, perhaps giving the user access to an operating system, and permitting the user to enter programs. Indeed, most programmable systems permit the user (now called a programmer) to change levels of representation to suit his needs. Being able to shift levels of representation obviously requires the successful programmer to keep track of lots of representational detail in his head. Providing the 'right' virtual machine in the first place can obviously save a lot of effort for users later.

5.4   There are many things no computer can do

There are problems that a Turing Machine *cannot* solve at all—in fact, infinitely more than it *can* solve. Does this mean that Turing had not quite been able to formalize what mathematicians really do, or is there a similar limit to what mathematicians can do with pencil and paper? Nobody really knows, but the fact that all other attempts to find out end up making arguments equivalent to Turing's suggests that Turing had found a fundamental limitation on mathematicians' abilities—and hence on human abilities in general.

One particular task that a Turing Machine cannot solve is the **Halting Problem**: in general it is not possible to determine whether a program will halt. This is a fundamental limitation on computers. On reflection, it should not be so surprising that there are such limitations. Although the Halting Problem looks arcane, *if* it could be solved, all manner of intractable problems could be solved as well, provided only that a program could be written down that *might* solve them. Of course there are lots of programs that are so simple that we can tell if they will stop; the Halting Problem is that we cannot devise a general analyser that will work for *any* program. In fact almost all programs are too complex to decide whether they stop, let alone whether they do more interesting things than merely stop—like, whether they are easy to use!

A problem is said to be **non-computable** or **undecidable** if, like the Halting Problem, it is impossible to devise rules for a Turing Machine (or Pascal program) to execute in order to solve it. Conversely, a computable problem is one for which rules might be devised. Note that

---

Box 5.1   Turing Machines and direct manipulation.

Turing Machines can do anything (anything computable). And, yes, they work in a rather physical way, by moving a tape containing objects (symbols) in various slots. A limited number of operations are only performed at one point, involving changing the current symbol, perhaps moving it to or from a 'reservoir'. Such operations sound remarkably amenable to direct manipulation. Indeed, direct manipulation is clearly a valid style of user interface for a Turing Machine simulation.

Thus direct manipulation can be used to implement *any* user interface, if the user interface is implementable at all.

From thinking about this computational equivalence, we make two important observations:

▷ Turing Machines are not easy to operate—in fact, they are an obvious candidate for automation! Likewise, many direct manipulation systems would be better if they allowed sequences of operations to be automated, so that they could be carried out faster by machine than in tedious, simple-minded steps.

▷ Turing Machines are not the best of machines to program. They lack abstraction (being unable to define procedures), they lack encapsulation (being unable to protect and hide information). Programmers therefore use more sophisticated machines, such as Pascal or Prolog for real programming. Likewise, many user interfaces will be better off *not* being run by direct manipulation: other styles of interaction should be sought.

It is a profound and worrying thought that Turing Machines are very simple computing engines yet they are not easy to use! *Making interactive systems designs simpler does not necessarily make them easier to use.*

Box 6.1 argues the opposite view. See also Section 19.3.2 for a practical exercise.

---

because a problem is non-computable does not stop a machine embarking on its computation, it simply guarantees that it may never finish. An important assumption behind the theory is that Turing Machines do not make mistakes: if, like humans, they did, no problem could be considered 'non-computable' for there would always be the chance of making a mistake and stopping, perhaps even with the correct answer by chance.

Computability can be brought to user interfaces too. We might imagine a sophisticated user interface that may be programmed in a general way. The user could express tasks which are not only impractical to execute by computer but which are theoretically impossible to solve at all. These problems regularly surface as bugs, often as the clichéd 'stack overflow'.

Consider a librarian who asks his computer to make a catalogue of books and other holdings not in any catalogues. It is surely a very reasonable thing to do, to keep track of such books that might otherwise be lost. But if the librarian is not careful and the computer not sophisticated, such a straightforward request might lead to chaos: as soon as a book is put in the catalogue, it fails the simple criterion for being in the catalogue. This is a form of Bertrand Russell's Barber Paradox.

5.4.1   Is usability decidable?

Some user interfaces are possible to use, others are difficult or impossible to use. For any particular system, we can ask, 'do the rules which the user follows in order to use it form a computable program?' If not, then the system is impossible or at least *rather* difficult to use.

Usability, that is determining whether a user interface is usable or 'user friendly', is undecidable. We need only devise a Turing Complete user interface such as a typical command language, or a word processor with user extensibility, and ask whether the user can terminate a session. We already know that the Halting Problem is undecidable in general, so clearly we cannot tell whether the combined user–computer system will halt, whether the user will ever terminate a session. And as a final touch, we arrange for some nasty and definitely unfriendly thing to happen if the system is *not* stopped: this is easy to do (for example, the data the user has created will not be saved unless the program exits). We cannot tell if the user can stop the computer, and we know that if he cannot, the system must be unfriendly. Thus, 'user friendliness' is non-computable. If, as it appears, usability decisions cannot be automated in principle, the consequence is that the responsibility for good design ultimately rests on the professionalism of the system designers.

Even for computers, computability is not always the relevant criterion. On the one hand, some functions (such as the Halting Problem) are not in general computable, but they may be computable in certain useful cases. On the other hand, some functions (such as the Ackermann function) may be computable, but are not practical except in trivial cases. More relevant, then, than computability is **complexity**—how hard something is to compute. The Ackermann function, for instance, has a very rapidly increasing complexity that puts it beyond reasonable rather than theoretical computational powers. Complexity depends not just on the task being performed, but also on its chosen representation. Just as with humans, how a computer represents its results can have a profound effect on the complexity. Thus $\pi = 3.141\,592\ldots$ is non-computable, for it happens to be transcendental. However, it *can* be computed to any precision you like, in particular, precisions sufficient for all practical purposes—though non-computable, its complexity is simple. But change the representation of π to an analytic form and it *can* be computed, precisely: $4\int_0^1 1/(1+x^2)\,\mathrm{d}x$, for example, is *exactly* π and sometimes this may be a far more useful form than a numeric value. Our observations about computability, complexity and

Box 5.2   Quantum computers.

Does the Church–Turing Thesis, and the implied limitations of computation apply to humans and all thinking beings? There is no ready answer. But, in fact, the theoretical limitations are far too generous: so far as real computers and people are concerned, the Halting Problem and other non-computable problems are rather liberal. *Real* computers are more severely limited than Turing Machines. For instance, there is no limit on the amount of tape the Turing Machine is allowed to use (or equivalently, how small it could write on the tape it had) even though the real world is finite (and the money we have available to buy computer tape even more limited than that). Issues such as the speed of information transfer, physically limited by the speed of light, and miniaturization (which might help offset the speed limit by reducing the distances information has to travel) are limited by real physics. Both limitations stop us making arbitrarily powerful computers.

Rather than dismiss such physical limitations as irrelevant to computability *theory*, recall that almost all the advances in theoretical physics this century stem from accepting realistic limits, such as the speed of light limiting all modes of information transfer. As we currently understand physical laws, it would take an infinitely large amount of information processing (or mathematical reasoning) to determine what will happen next in a given region of space, however small. Yet, physical objects seem quite able to use the laws of nature to decide what to do next. The planets manage to solve intractable problems in celestial mechanics without any trouble! We certainly have a lot to learn about physical laws and about information processing.

It is indeed ironic that the electronic components of a computer are 'solving' complex simultaneous equations (about current flows in wires and so on) almost at the speed of light, and these equations must be Turing Complete—how else are computers Turing Complete? Yet computers run so much slower than the speed of light.

David Deutsch (1985) has suggested that the Church–Turing Thesis is on shaky ground. The thesis is tantamount to a tautology—anything that can naturally be considered as computing can be done by a Turing Machine—and if not a tautology the thesis is certainly very vague. Deutsch suggests a physically based version, which he calls the **Church– Turing Principle**,

> Every finite physical system can be perfectly simulated by a universal model computing machine operating by finite means.

Interestingly, the Church–Turing Principle *fails* for classical physics. There is only a countably infinite number of ways of preparing Turing Machine tapes, yet classical physical systems are continuous systems, with non-denumerable states. Thus a Turing Machine cannot simulate a classical physical system.

representation are reminiscent of usability, which, too, is crucially dependent on representation.

5.5   The Turing Test

So ideal computers, unlimited by natural resources and modern physics, are limited to 'computable functions', if that doesn't sound too much like a tautology. Even with such liberal assumptions, it is easy to show that there are infinitely many more non-computable functions and things that computers *might* do than things they can actually do. Are people so limited? Perhaps it would be nice to think of people as being in some way more intelligent than mere computers. What is it then, if anything, that distinguishes human thought from computer thought? What is human intelligence?

Turing worried about this problem and in 1950, fourteen years after he introduced his machine, he wrote one of the most provocative and most discussed papers on human–computer interaction (Turing, 1950).[3] He thought of a neat side-step to avoid defining what human intelligence might be—an 'imitation game' where computers pretend to be people. His game has nowadays come to be known as the **Turing Test**. The Turing Test is one of the most recent of man's attempts to find ways to distinguish himself from mere imitations: Galileo Galilei suggested tickling statues with feathers to see if they were human; René Descartes suggested holding a conversation—which of course a machine would fail because, in those days, they lacked the ability to converse. We shall now describe Turing's approach.

Turing starts with the question, 'Can machines think?' To answer this we would first have to spend some time developing definitions, and generally get involved in problems that philosophers have bent their minds over for millennia. What is the relation between thinking and consciousness? It is not obvious that a thinking computer would be conscious and have feelings, emotions, and so on. Rather than get entrenched, Turing proposed an operational approach: can computers do something we would normally call thinking? The gist of his idea is that if we cannot distinguish between a man and a computer when doing a singularly human activity, then we may as well admit that the computer can think.

The game is played with three people: a man, a woman and an interrogator who may be of either sex. The interrogator stays in a room apart from the other two but can communicate with them by using a computer terminal (though Turing, writing in 1950, suggested typewritten messages could be exchanged). The object of the game is for the interrogator to find out which of the other two is the man and which the woman.

---

[3] It is interesting to note that in the time when he wrote, the word 'computer' meant a person, not a machine.

Box 5.3   Quibbles about the Turing Test.

We might define **machine** so liberally that humans are machines by definition. Then, obviously, machines can think. Or we might define **think** so carefully that there is some doubt that humans can think, or conversely that thinking by definition is so pedestrian that machines can do it easily.

Turing's approach is reductive. In general reductionism means reducing problems to their 'bare essentials'. This in itself is appropriate, and almost always facilitates a precise formulation which will clarify matters and ease finding solutions. But the issue is whether too much gets abstracted away. Suppose, instead of asking 'can machines think?' we wanted to know whether machines could fly. Following the pattern set by the Turing Test, we choose a low bandwidth interface and employ an interrogator to see if he can tell the difference between a bird and a machine. I suspect that if we could arrange things so that the interrogator could not tell the difference, then neither would he be able to tell the difference between a brick hurled through the air and a bird. We do not say that bricks can fly (but of course they can if someone throws one); likewise, the sense in which machines can think (if they passed the Turing Test) might hardly qualify.

Many people are worried that the conclusion of this sort of discussion would be a claim that people are no more than machines—imperfect ones at that! Ridiculous! You don't feel like a machine, do you? To which Marvin Minsky—an expert in artificial intelligence—replies, 'If you are not a machine what makes you an authority on what it feels like to be a machine?' My own opinion is that it does not really matter whether we call ourselves machines or not; we are in any case subject to the same physical laws as machines, and that has never been an obstacle for our human nature. No, the problem is that computers may *treat* people as no more than machines, in the crudest sense. People have freedom of choice; but the computers they use may deny them this basic freedom.

The interrogator can ask either person—not knowing who's who—questions such as, 'Please tell me the length of your hair?' Suppose this question is addressed to the man, then it would be his task to try and convince the interrogator that he is the woman. The arrangement is shown schematically in Figure 5.1.

The woman will do her best to convince the interrogator that she is indeed the woman; but simply saying 'I am the woman—don't listen to him' will be of no avail because the man could easily make similar remarks just to confuse the interrogator.

Having grasped the basic idea, now suppose that one of the two people is replaced by a computer, as in Figure 5.2. Will the interrogator decide as easily when one player is a computer and one a person, as when each was a person? If, on this test, the interrogator cannot tell computer

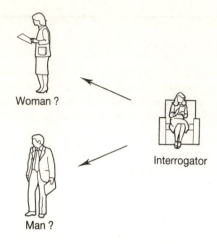

Figure 5.1   The Man–Woman Turing Imitation Test.

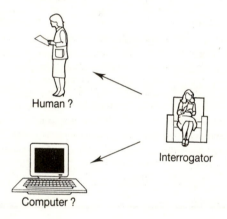

Figure 5.2   The Human–Computer Turing Imitation Test.

from human any better than man from woman, then Turing claims that the computer can think. It would be more in keeping with logic to say, more pedantically, that if the interrogator can tell the difference then the computer has failed the test. If the interrogator cannot tell the difference, we do not know: for instance another interrogator may be able to find a difference missed by the first. So, the Turing Test can *reject* computer imitations of man, but strictly not *accept* them.

A sort of Turing Test was set up by Dr Kenneth Colby, a psychiatrist, and was played by psychiatrists (presumably expert interrogators for a personality game), a computer program called **Parry**, and a weak human player—a hospitalized paranoid patient. The results of the game as it turned out can be interpreted variously, depending on your prejudices: psychiatrists may not be very percipient; paranoid personalities might be very machine-like anyway; or, just maybe, the computer was a rather felicitous simulation of a paranoid. However, a methodological difference between Colby's Test and the original Turing Test was that the psychiatrists were not told that one of the 'people' they were interrogating was a computer.

There is some danger in the Turing Test that the interrogator might not be intellectually up to making a penetrating decision. It has been suggested that the test could be modified so that the interrogator's role is played by computer, trying to tell man and woman or even man and computer apart.

It is interesting that the Turing Test hinges on the limited bandwidth of the user interface established between the participants. The participants are supposed to exchange typewritten messages. Handwriting might expose their nature; or, worse, with a visual (high bandwidth) channel it would be fairly obvious which was a machine, science fiction notwithstanding. *Clearly*, if we extend the visual bandwidth to include X-rays the test might even be trivial for a computerized interrogator! At any rate, the higher the bandwidth, the easier the Turing Test becomes. Also, as a general observation: *the higher the user interface bandwidth the easier a system is to use* (contrast, *test*)—though it may not be so much fun.

Box 1.1 suggested that you devise a program to behave like a user would do to use a display editor. (Desktop publishing, with various fonts and graphical illustrations, would be harder still.) The argument of Box 1.1 was that the difficulty of devising the program indicated that user interfaces were more complex than they seemed; now we see that asking the unidentified computer–or–user to operate a display editor, or some other 'easy to use' system, might be a good way to start our interrogation and quickly expose the computer!

5.6 Schrödinger's Cat

Erwin Schrödinger introduced his famous cat in 1935, which has more recently led to an interesting variation on the Turing Test. Schrödinger imagined a cat placed in a sealed box, with arrangements for its execution at a random time if a radioactive particle is detected by a Geiger counter. We agree to open the box after a certain time interval and see if the cat is still alive. The problem that Schrödinger wanted to raise was that quantum physicists treated particles in a way that could be scaled up to cats, and thereby made to look absurd if you don't *really* believe quantum mechanics. Electrons, for instance, can be in several superposed states and you cannot tell until you look, when the states collapse down to the particular state that happens to be observed. Electrons have never been seen, so it is possible to convince yourself that they behave strangely; but what Schrödinger did was to scale the problem up. Isn't it absurd that a cat can be in superposed states, in this case both dead and alive until someone opens the box when the states collapse to either the state of living or the state of death?

Does a person have to open the box to collapse the states? Eugene Wigner asked what would happen if you put a human volunteer—referred to as **Wigner's Friend**—inside the box. Surely there would be no need to open the box for *him* to know whether he was alive or dead? After more thought, you might well ask what is so special about humans. Why does a human observer have to be the agent that collapses the states? Can't a cat know whether it is dead or alive for itself? And if a cat can tell, what about a lower life form than a cat, a microbe, say ... and so the argument continues ... down to asking why a subatomic particle couldn't collapse the states for itself and if it could what has happened to quantum mechanics? And lastly, what about a computer instead of the cat?

If the interrogator, a role normally played by a human in the Turing Test, was instead a computer as suggested by our quick discussion of Schrödinger's Cat, we could ask ourselves an interesting question. This computer would be limited, like any computer, by the normal limitations of computability that we have already seen exhibited by the Halting Problem. What difference would it make? For instance, is making the distinction between the other two players computable?

Rather than answer this question directly, consider the more mundane problem of a person interacting with a computer. From previous chapters, we have seen that the information at the interface is insufficient for it to work, there has to be some additional modelling. Now suppose that we replace the human user with a computerized user. Straight away we have formalized what the 'user model' is: it would have to be a program.

Now this raises the crucial question: is the user-program computable? In other words, is the user interface sufficiently easy to use that even a computer could use it? If you like this idea, it can be refined: can the user-program run fast enough (what of complexity measures?); what happens if we employ a computational architecture more faithful to the human mind than a Turing Machine (for example, one that accounts for interference)?

5.6.1   Deception

Perhaps our most valuable heritage from Galileo is not his man/statue 'Turing Test' (Section 5.5) but the scientific method. He lived at a time when most people were interested in philosophical argument; instead, he insisted on observation, analysis and experiment.

The important point is that ideas should not be criticized in a rhetorical way, but criticized with respect to actual evidence. So let's move on about 30 years from Turing to the time when his speculations could start to be put to the test.

Between 1964 and 1966, Joseph Weizenbaum developed a program called **Eliza**, named after the Eliza of Pygmalion. Eliza could be taught to converse increasingly well. Eliza read what its user typed at a keyboard, and then tried to match that input with a script of patterns; and for each pattern there was some sort of appropriate reply. Eliza could run from scripts about almost any subject, though because of the limitations in what might be called Eliza's understanding one had to be quite careful what it was taught to talk about—lest it rapidly appear superficial. Weizenbaum gave it a script characteristic of a non-directive psychotherapy counsellor: so Eliza would parody the sort of counsellor that says things like, 'Do tell me more' rather than attempting an explicit analysis of the patient's problems. To make Eliza more convincing, templates in the script were added so that some sort of interesting dialogue would be triggered if the patient mentioned family, dreams, and so on. There are many tricks in counselling, not least a certain degree of pedantry; for instance, if you say that *everybody* dislikes you, your rather broad generalization is probably concealing a specific individual. It is easy to add templates in Eliza's script, '... everybody ...' or '... never ...' and so on, with replies that ask the user to be more specific. And finally, when Eliza recognized nothing of what was said to it, it looked over recent conversation for any text that matched 'my ...', and would then say, 'tell me more about your ...'

Here is a brief example of Eliza in action (adapted from Weizenbaum, 1976):

Men are all alike.
In what way.
They're always bugging us about something or other.
Can you think of a specific example.
Well, my boyfriend made me come here.
Your boyfriend made you come here.
He says I'm depressed much of the time.
I am sorry to hear you are depressed.
It's true. I am unhappy.
Do you think coming here will help you not to be unhappy.
I need some help, that much seems certain.
What would it mean to you if you got some help.
Perhaps I could learn more about my mother.
Tell me more about your family.
...
What else comes to mind when you think of your father.
Bullies.
Does that have anything to do with the fact that your boyfriend made you come here.
... and so on.

Note, in the last line, how Eliza dredges up something that the user said earlier when it can't match 'bullies' against any template in its script—it simply substitutes 'your' for 'my' and puts the clause in the fixed template 'Does that have anything to do with the fact that ...' In this case it comes up with something that looks quite insightful! To help conceal the purely mechanical nature of the replies, Eliza cycles through a list of templates for each response. For instance, if the user again types *Bullies*, Eliza might reply `Please go on`, using a template with no slots for any of the user's text. Next time the user types an unrecognized phrase, a different template could be selected for variety. But Eliza's repertoire is limited, and if the user sticks at unrecognizable replies, Eliza will eventually give itself away as a parrot. Interestingly, this deceptive scheme relies for its effectiveness on the user of Eliza not being repetitive and mechanical!

Weizenbaum published details of his program and tried it out on many people. In his book (*op. cit.*) he noted three interesting things:

▷ Professional counsellors (psychiatrists, actually) were very impressed. They imagined that with a little development the technique could become a fruitful approach to real counselling. Indeed the experimental system, **MICKIE**, developed by Chris Evans and used for screening patients before an appointment with a doctor, suggested that many people were more at ease and more honest explaining problems to a computer than to a human. In many cases this could be put down to the users believing that the computer time was free and unlimited, whereas they would feel pressurized by their perception of the doctor's limited time. (We shall discuss MICKIE shortly.)

▷ Weizenbaum was startled at how quickly and how deeply people became involved in conversing with Eliza. He relates that his secretary, who certainly knew all about the development of Eliza and that it was merely a computer program, asked him to leave the room so that she could have a private conversation with it. It is surprising that quite brief exposure to Eliza can lead people to impute remarkable human powers to it. More contemporary experience with computer games, especially role-playing adventure games, might suggest that Weizenbaum had underestimated the power of anthropomorphism on individuals.

▷ Lastly, Weizenbaum was surprised that many people thought Eliza was an example of a general solution to the problem of computers understanding people and conversing in plain language.

Turning these observations on their head: if users reacted so favourably to Eliza, finding it a definite help, then surely human counsellors might be more effective if they listened as non-judgementally as Eliza. It is often the case that users are best helped when they have been supported in the process of solving their problem, rather than having their problem solved. In the first case, the user has been helped towards learning a general strategy; in the second case, he may have learnt nothing but a particular solution and dependence on his counsellor.

Taking these observations over into user interface design: users may be best helped *in the long run* by systems that support users doing things of their own choosing, whereas many systems provide quick solutions to prepared problems that may not have been exactly those of the users.

Chris Evans developed the automated medical examiner, MICKIE, in 1971 (Bevan *et al.*, 1981). Unlike Eliza which interacted in natural language, template–matching the user's English, MICKIE used a very low bandwidth question/answer style dialogue. The user had a specially modified terminal with only three buttons on it: to answer yes, no, or don't know.[4] Here is a typical sample:

> First of all, I'd like to know if you are male?
> *Yes*
> I also need some idea of how old you are. Are you under 16?
> *No*
> Are you over 65 then?
> *No*
> I'm sorry you are not feeling good. Next I'd like to know how well you sleep. Do you sleep well?
> *No*
> Do you often have difficulty getting to sleep?
> ... *and so on.*

MICKIE was rather effective. Such a conversation yields accurate information about the patient. It can be programmed to ask pertinent questions about symptoms of illness, and can provide a standardized summary for doctors at the end of a session. This summary can be used by the doctor to prepare himself before a personal interview with the patient. The interesting thing is that many patients preferred MICKIE to an interview with a doctor: in particular they had less feeling that they were wasting the doctor's precious time, and some patients were prepared to be more candid with a dehumanized system than with a doctor. One patient was reported as saying, 'Well! I've been coming to this hospital for years and this is the first time anybody has really taken an interest in me'. Such are the advantages of a narrow bandwidth user interface for medical therapy, but notice how the narrow bandwidth of MICKIE facilitates the user forming

---

[4] By our notational convention, Yes does not necessarily mean that the user typed Yes; there could easily be a key marked yes, or the user might speak the word aloud.

Box 5.4   An accidental Turing Test.

The Vice President of Bolt, Beranek and Newman walked up to a terminal and found a note, 'Type all messages into this teletype, and end them with a period'. He probably thought this was a computer link to Daniel Bobrow, who often worked from home on a computer terminal. The Vice President started typing, but in fact was talking to a version of Eliza (Bobrow, 1968).

Do you think that I can use the computer this morning? [sic]
Why do you ask?
I might be able to make some additional telcomp sales.
Why aren't you sure?
My prospective customers have never seen a demonstration of the system.
Does this mean very much to you?
Of course it does.
You seem very positive about that.
This is ridiculous.
What do you mean this is ridiculous?
Is there any reason I can't use the computer now?
Tell me more about your prospective customers.
Please dial me up on 491-1850

The Vice President rang Bobrow, waking him from a deep sleep, and asked him why he was being so snotty. Bobrow replied, 'What do you mean why am I being snotty to you?'

Did Eliza pass Turing's Test? Of course not, for the Vice President was not playing the role of interrogator. He had projected Bobrow on to it, and the few questions, eliciting content-free answers were hardly enough to disabuse him. For more examples see Hofstadter (1986).

---

what would otherwise be an inappropriate model of the computer system. But was it MICKIE or the doctor who passed the Turing Test?

It is interesting to note that, although a narrow bandwidth is often a severe hindrance to effective communication with computers, it is sometimes useful between people. A narrow bandwidth is egalitarian. For example, if users communicate by electronic mail then there is not the spare bandwidth available for either party to disclose what race, sex, age, or other 'handicaps' the other person might have—unless the users *choose* to disclose them.

Eliza-like behaviour has an interesting application in supporting users with speech defects. Eliza can be used as output, not from a computer, but from a user (in a sort of Wizard of Oz arrangement, to be described below in Section 5.7). Social interaction is an important part of maintaining a human conversation. People with full speech do not often speak coherently—natural conversation is full of grunts, filler phrases ('you know') and signals for the participants to maintain their presence. When Eliza is connected to a speech synthesizer a user can take an active social part in conversation at normal speed, with Eliza generating and speaking filler phrases. Semantically richer utterances would, however, still have to be constructed slowly. **Chat** is one such system, and allows the user to control the level of politeness, selecting different scripts of phrases and sounds with different levels of agreement, anger, and so on (Alm *et al.*, 1987).

5.6.2 Randomness

One of the successful elements of Eliza is its apparent randomness (although *we* know that Eliza is strictly determinate, it appears random for a short dialogue that is not long enough to expose repetition in Eliza's responses). The important point is that apparent random behaviour is difficult to ascribe to a machine. If you have a narrow bandwidth interface, it is not possible to ask the system questions to distinguish between a complex model and a random model that simply gives the superficial appearance of complexity.

5.7 The Wizard of Oz

Colby's experiments with Parry the Paranoid allowed psychiatrists to converse with a program or a human. Since the psychiatrists were not told that there might be a computer involved, they could type anything at it and would expect it to reply as a human. They would make typing mistakes and naturally expect the 'person' at the other end to ignore them. But of course few computers would be able to discard erroneous and only erroneous input so easily! So Colby employed an assistant whose job was to convert the questions the psychiatrists typed into a form suitable for entering into the computer. Without the assistant it was likely that the psychiatrist would soon type something that would upset the program and make it crash, or otherwise get it to give its true identity away. Using a human intermediary like this as an assistant is the **Wizard of Oz** technique.

A hidden operator, the **Wizard of Oz**, can intercept all commands to a partially implemented system and apply some suitable interpretation if the commands have not yet been implemented (Figure 5.3). The Wizard might merely monitor the user's interaction and only intervene when things need changing, say in converting error messages into something more or less relevant to the user. Or if you want to experiment with speech input and interpretation of facial expressions, then the Wizard can hear and watch the user through a video link. The Wizard then submits commands to

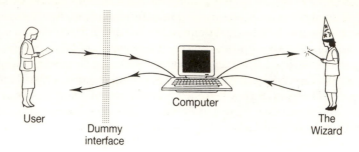

Figure 5.3 Where the Wizard lives.

a conventional sort of user interface, and this interaction generates the interface that the user interacts with and thinks is real.

Notice that for prototyping there is no need for the user interface to be programmed. A paper simulation can be used to great effect: the Wizard can still convert the user's requests to valid interactions with the 'computer'—here the Wizard will be in full view of the user, and acting rather like an amanuensis. Users can always be asked to use their imagination to use the system.

Such applications use the wizard to extend the computer's capabilities. Conversely, a wizard can be used to extend the capabilities of the users. The users may be novices with an interface, but they can interact through a wizard who is skilled with the idiosyncrasies of an existing computer system. A wizard was used in the design of an electronic mail system so that *uninstructed* novice users could develop their own dialogue conventions (Good *et al.*, 1984). Users' commands which had not been implemented, or which were in error, alerted a human wizard who rephrased the commands for the system. There was an order of magnitude improvement in the percentage of commands recognized by the system as they improved the design, guided by session logs and ideas from the wizard: the original computer system could recognize 7% of the novices' commands submitted to it, the final version could recognize 76%. Although in the situation it seems the greatest benefits came from accepting synonyms, the results are still spectacular.

Such good results may not have been expected if there had been substantial documentation or training available, or if the system had been sufficiently rich to start with. But then, you are unlikely to have detailed documentation at such an early stage in the design process: the Wizard of Oz technique permits a very early, even flaky, implementation to be tried out. And if you had implemented 'enough' user interface features so that users could not think of any more, then you would probably have wasted your time on a number of gratuitous features. Better to get the users, with the help of a Wizard, to develop a system known to be incomplete. Under the right circumstances, then, users are quite capable of contributing to the design process, even though they may not be 'good designers'.

An interesting variation of the Wizard of Oz idea is for the wizard to be an *ordinary* user. If an interactive system is used by a number of users, often some of those users will take it upon themselves to be **local experts**. Other users can ask these experts for help—and the local experts will be very effective, for they understand the user's problems from the same perspective. The difference between a local expert and a wizard is merely that they are on different sides of the user interface. Perhaps it would be useful if interactive systems provided the features necessary to support an 'over-the-shoulder' wizard, or features so that a local expert can intervene between the user and the computer application, as if playing the real Wizard of Oz.

5.8   Representation

The Church–Turing Thesis, which has been the unseen central theme in the last few sections contains the hedge, *if details like speed and material limitations are ignored*. Let us now explore some of these representational issues. The first is the choice of symbols: names for the pencil marks the Turing Machine is allowed to make.

5.8.1   Berry's Paradox with names

Names enable us to tell one identifier from another. Identifiers denote values; in general these values may be memory locations in the computer which themselves contain what we normally think of as the values of the identifiers, and these will be numbers and other programming values. However when we are using, rather than 'simply' programming, a computer much more sophisticated things get names; we have to provide names for files of text, for data, for programs, for users themselves, and for entire systems. **Berry's Paradox** is related to the Halting Problem of Section 5.4; it shows that in general we cannot know what a name denotes. Of course the turn of phrase, 'in general' is crucial—most of the time we *do* know what names denote unless we have forgotten.

The English name of 1 is 'one', the name of 1 051 is 'one thousand and fifty one': in general, the larger a number the longer its name. So consider the following number name, 'the smallest number necessarily at least nine words'. More carefully, suppose that this names a certain number, n. Now n can certainly be named in English, and by definition must take at least nine words, and of all those numbers nameable in at least nine words, it must be the least. This clearly describes a particular number, and you can

---

Box 5.5   Interacting with extraterrestrials.

Suppose that some aliens think we are sufficiently interesting to investigate. We may not be; it is merely projection to suppose that other forms of intelligence would be as curious about us as we would be about them. Suppose, further, that we conveniently establish radio contact with their UFO. These are rash assumptions, but they dispense with worrying about the extremely limited batch communication forced on us either by throwing unmanned spacecraft like Pioneer-10 out of the solar system, or by telecommunication to a distant planet—the time for a round trip radio transmission would preclude normal dialogue. If the aliens were interested, they would embark on a sort of Twenty Questions: to establish what we are. Very rough estimates of how complex we are suggests that the aliens would have to discover about 10^{16} bits to know exactly what we are made of—they would have to play at least Fifty-Four Questions, assuming that the questions they asked were 'sensible' and we were able to answer them adequately, despite trying to get answers to our own questions at the same time!

There are some nasty twists to 'sensible' questioning. What would happen if we forgot to establish whether the aliens were matter or anti-matter? How would we teach them left from right?

The Turing Test is relevant, for we are also faced with the problem: does the UFO carry computers or sentient, living beings? We also need to introduce a variant of the test: if the UFO were running a computer program—what sort of thing wrote the program? Could we tell if it had been programmed by humans and that the whole thing was a hoax?

We might indeed use the Turing Test to try and discover whether a putative UFO was a hoax: how much human knowledge seems to be built-in? Conversely, and bringing us back down to earth, we might use the variant test to see if a computer system we normally use was written by a human or an alien. For many programs that I use, I'm not so sure I can tell.

---

see it is almost certainly one hundred and one thousand, one hundred and one. That describes 101 101.[5]

101 101, then, is 'the smallest number necessarily at least nine words'—but this phrase is itself only eight words, so 101 101 has an English name less than nine words! It must be some other number that is being named. But if it is not 101 101, it would have to be 101 102 which can also be named in nine words, but if so, then the name 'the smallest number necessarily at least nine words' describes 101 102 more concisely in just eight words. And so on and so forth. The putative name *cannot* name any number at all.

---

[5] If you can think of a smaller number, then pencil it into the argument in the next paragraph, and the argument will still be correct. The actual value itself is not critical.

So far this seems a long way from interactive systems design! Berry's Paradox shows that the problem of interpreting a name as a particular number is non-computable. Obviously *some* names are easily interpreted as numbers (for example, 'twenty three'), but Berry has shown us a 'name' that we cannot interpret: as soon as we think we have grasped its meaning, it must mean some other number. Programs are a special case of names: programs are simply the names of whatever they do (or numbers they output). And Berry's Paradox agrees with the Halting Problem—in general we do not know what programs will do. Thus *there can never be a program that can understand natural language*, at least not if we allow natural language to include talking about numbers (as we were a moment ago).

You may well object that realistic use of natural language discusses issues of far more significance than mere numbers; but, surely, if something is undecidable for numbers, it will be even harder for those more interesting things. (If you accept the Church–Turing Thesis, then *anything* can be converted to a number by Gödelization.)

The real paradox in Berry's Paradox is *if* we accept the impossibility of computable procedures for interpreting names of numbers (and by extension, procedures for interpreting natural language) then how do *we* understand natural language? If we are too attached to the Church–Turing Thesis or if we ignore the tricky philosophical problems, the answer seems to lie in the fact that humans are lazy evaluators (in the sense of Section 4.3) and of limited rationality. We do not really entertain contradictions, think about names of unmentionable numbers and so on, because we never *really* bother to explore the full implications of our beliefs.

5.8.2   The Chinese Room

The Chinese Room was an experiment proposed by John Searle (1952). He uses the experiment as an argument against the view that machines will be able to become proficient in natural language, which would assume, for instance, an understanding of human emotions.

In the experiment, Searle imagines that he has been locked into a room and he has been given some Chinese writing. Searle does not know Chinese, and the ideograms will appear to him to be meaningless symbols. He is then given some rules of composition, in English, and some more in Chinese writing. If you wish, you may view the rules as a program for interacting in Chinese.

The details, as Searle elaborates them, are interesting—for instance, he assumes that the rules of Chinese he has been given do not tell him what Chinese *means*, but only how to interact—but after a while we may assume that he (locked in the room) appears to become proficient in Chinese. If a native Chinese speaker posts a Chinese letter into Searle's room, and shortly after, out pops a Chinese answer, would the Chinese person attribute understanding to Searle?

The purpose of Searle's argument is to show that if *he* does not think he understands Chinese, then a computer surely cannot. But we need only imagine that the Chinese interrogator asks the 'room', written down in Chinese, whether it understands Chinese. By assumption, it can only answer that it does, whatever Searle thinks inside!

After Berry's Paradox, we know that one flaw in Searle's argument is the assumption that he could have been given the *a priori* rules for handling Chinese. Of course, native speakers do not need to be taught their language from rule books, they learn it quasi-inductively ('quasi', because human speakers already share a considerable amount of experience and implicit brain structure and other physical attributes).

It is interesting that Searle's Chinese Room is an experiment about written, rather than oral, language. The fact that many people are illiterate, but fewer people are unable to speak suggests that written communication is harder than oral communication. On this basis, a plausible case can be made out that speech communication with computers will improve ease of use (even outside those tasks or environments for which speech is essential) over interfaces that are limited to purely written (gesture or typed) modes. It is not immediately clear that the best way to use speech is to use natural language, even though (of course!) natural language is so far the primary way humans communicate between themselves. Most interactions with computers are more complex than spontaneous speech can handle: the written medium has advantages that a user can work out and revise what he is submitting before it is actually submitted. Speech does not so easily lend itself to making dynamic tradeoffs between atomic and symbolic communication. As usual we cannot make a general statement about usability independent of the user, task and environment (see Section 7.8).

5.8.3   The Chapanis experiments

Alphonse Chapanis is interested in interactive human communication (Chapanis, 1981). He chose an experimental procedure that has interesting similarities with the Turing Test: he arranged for two people in separate rooms to communicate using a restricted medium (one time he used a computer terminal connection). The idea was for the two people to cooperate on some task, such as wiring up an electronic circuit, and he would study how they communicated.

Chapanis's experiments were not only innovative but very fruitful. Significantly, he found that people worked most effectively when they could use speech to communicate. The fact that people can talk faster than they can write or type is not in itself very surprising, but interestingly, being able

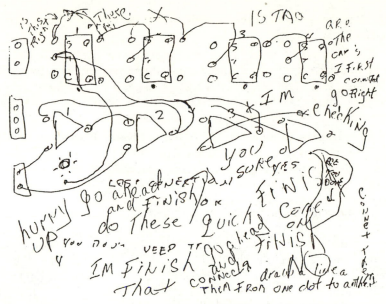

Figure 5.4   Chaotic results from the Chapanis experiments.

to see each other did not make a significant difference to their performance—at least for the sort of tasks Chapanis tried out—although the people did talk more.

What struck me most about Chapanis's experiments was the extreme chaos evident in the transcripts recorded during the experiments. During the experiments, what was said no doubt made sense to the participants, but after the event the language used seems extremely unruly, following few grammatical rules. It is interesting to conjecture what sort of program (or Eliza-style script) could handle such unruliness given that it would have to have been anticipated *before* a human–computer conversation even began.

Sometimes it is suggested that graphical interaction is vastly superior to textual interaction with computers. There is some justification for this, though it is somewhat biased because drawing tasks are much more interesting to most people than textual (or mathematical!) tasks. But Chapanis found that in human to human communication the graphical forms of interaction seemed even more unruly than textual forms (see Figure 5.4): it will surely be even harder to design satisfactory graphical user interfaces than textual ones. Probably the reason for this is that most people have a well-developed sense of composition in everything but art (for example, we know spelling rules for English). A successful graphics system will probably have to seem constraining to those of us who do not recognize the rules.

Nevertheless pictures are more fun. For instance, if you want to teach programming skills, a language like Pascal is quite a bad choice of first programming language. The sort of programs that can be written in

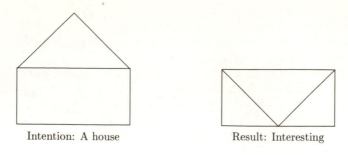

Intention: A house   Result: Interesting

Figure 5.5   LOGO pictures.

Pascal at an elementary level involve numbers. A typical first programming assignment might be to read a few numbers and print their total (or some other exciting statistic). Suppose that the user has made a mistake. The program prints 27 when it should have printed 28. You have to be *very* interested in numbers to find 27 interesting, especially when it ought to be 28. Most students, lacking this sophistication, will simply get bored and find programming a drudge.

Suppose, instead, a language like LOGO is chosen for the elementary programming assignments (Papert, 1980). LOGO is very good for writing programs to draw pictures, and a typical first exercise might be to draw a 'house'—we might intend to draw something like the house in Figure 5.5. If the user makes a mistake in this program, he might get a result like the other picture in the figure, or something even more surprising. It takes far less sophistication to find this 'failure' quite interesting—and the student will likely be spurred on to understand the bug and get excited with the possibilities opened up to him through programming.

5.9 Conclusions

We started this chapter with the question: how do you tell man from computer? We still don't know the answer, but the investigation led to insights into the nature of communication between man and computer. If man and computer are different, we ought to ask the next question: how is it that man can interact with computers at all? Computers have an IQ comparable to worms, and not many people interact with worms in any meaningful way. User interfaces are, in comparison with natural systems encountered in everyday life, very simple; and it is certainly nonsense to define 'rational' behaviour visible at the interface purely in computational terms. Ease of use certainly cannot be established by testing the computer in isolation.

It is often said that man is above all a tool maker, which indeed he is, and that the computer is a significant development over all other tools. The argument continues, that we are entering the age of the 'information society' and that the computer will be *the* tool. But what really distinguishes man from all other animals is *not* tool making—after all, birds can do that—but that he communicates *to people who aren't there*—future generations, for instance. Any animal could have discovered fire, but it would have been forgotten; only Prometheus told everyone about it. (It is interesting that when apes are taught a language so that they can communicate explicitly with their keepers, they do not bother to teach their offspring any of it.)

Above all, then, computers are tools for communication. Computers are tools for supporting person-to-person communication (you use a computer each time you use a telephone); they are tools for a person to communicate with himself (keeping a diary or a brain-storming ideas network); and they are the instruments through which their designers communicate to their users. Hitherto all normal communication tools were **passive** and made no extension to the content of a message; the computer is radically different and poses new problems for the designers of interactive systems.

Chapter 6

Easy to use?

One way of improving efficiency is by restricting the power of
the language.   *Tony Hoare*

Although making things easy to use is, self-evidently, a good idea and has
caught on as a popular slogan, the idea is simple-minded. In reality 'ease
of use' is a complex and interesting tradeoff. Furthermore it is very easy
to confuse ease of use with ease of learning, for *surely* a difficult system to
use will be hard to learn? But easily learnt systems may have to be used
in contorted ways once the user has progressed beyond basic learning to
serious use. It is an over-simplification to suppose that a system is first
learnt, then used: in reality the user grows in skill over a period of time
while using the system.

Suppose that 'ease of use' *was* a precise concept: then we ought to be
able to apply it with complete assurance to many systems much simpler than
computers—but can you say whether a paint brush, gouge, clarinet or chess
board is easy to use or not? If we knew how to make anything interesting
easy to use, we would be making easy to use educational systems, easy to
use political systems and generally saving the world. Some applications,
clearly, are never going to be easy—though they may be made a lot easier
than most computers presently make them appear.

The work done by computers could, in principle, be done by people—
this is just a corollary of the Church–Turing Thesis. Computers are on the
whole very much faster, tireless and follow instructions to the last letter. A
computer is a formal system: it does not make use of intuitive argument.
The gist of this chapter is that people have been using formal systems for

millennia and we may learn from that experience. We may draw parallels between the 'ease of use' of formal systems over the course of history with the 'ease of use' of interactive computer systems. In fact, I shall draw a correspondence between the historical development of mathematics and the development of users' conceptual models of interactive computer systems. Many mathematical concepts took centuries to resolve but computer users are often expected to handle comparable issues much more rapidly. I shall argue that if a computer system is sufficiently powerful to be 'easy to use' this implies it is also sufficiently complex to confuse its users. Or, if it is made easy to use, it becomes increasingly trivial, and may ultimately be easy to use only to do nothing worth doing. With a pessimistic outlook, a useful system might never be really easy to use!

Designing interactive systems is not just a matter of making them easy to use: it is a matter of balancing ease against other factors, such as power and security. You don't want an easy to use bank account if it means it is easy to use for *anybody*! Most people are prepared to sacrifice a little in the ease of use of their bank accounts because it mostly ensures that other people cannot impersonate them successfully. Another example is making an aeroplane easy to use, for the pilot to fly. If it is too easy to use, the pilot may fall asleep. It may be better to make the system 'harder to use' from moment to moment, to help ensure successful interaction in the long term, for safety or other reasons.

So, note the following: systems are not 'easy to use' or 'difficult to use'. Systems may be found easier or harder by different people under different circumstances. We cannot simply say that a menu system is easier to use than a command-based system, though it often is the case that we can modify an existing system to make it easier than it was. The question to ask, is not is this system easy to use, but is it easy enough to use, and if not (as is too often the case), can we find ways to make it easier?

6.1   The formal system analogy

Throughout history, people have encountered various problems when using formal systems. Even as late as the seventeenth century, well-educated mathematicians still had problems with the concept of negative numbers. Thus Blaise Pascal, after whom the programming language Pascal is named, thought that subtracting a larger number from a smaller was nonsense. Around 1659 he wrote in his *Pensées* that he could not understand why no one accepted that four taken from zero left zero! This may seem astounding: he constructed one of the first mechanical calculators; he made fundamental contributions to mathematics and science; and yet he had difficulties with negative numbers. One of Pascal's close friends, Antoine Arnauld, posed the following problem: the ratio $-1 : 1$ equals the ratio $1 : -1$, but how can the ratio of a smaller number to a larger equal the ratio of a larger to a smaller? Today, even with a somewhat better understanding, not many scientists would be able to repeat the contributions made by Pascal.

If a man of Pascal's mathematical stature had problems with negative numbers, then present-day users of computers will have really serious problems with the far more sophisticated concepts that readily arise during an interactive session. Today we expect users to handle deep ontological problems, not at their leisure over days or years, but in real time and under pressure. Of course, just as many of Pascal's contemporaries coped with the arithmetic of negative numbers (for example, for money lending) without reflecting on deeper issues, users of interactive computer systems *may* remain happy. But such users will be forced to open Pandora's Box when they are faced with non-routine tasks, bugs and other problems.

6.2   Comprehension versus efficiency

That users readily make bizarre models of what a system is and can do is, I think, nowhere better illustrated than in the history of arithmetic. Until the seventeenth century, representations and notations for arithmetic were so opaque and difficult to use that numbers were shrouded in mysticism (for example, arithmomancy). The relatively recent development of formal notations means that arithmetic can now be taught routinely in school; the subject may be well understood, but the human brain, the learning child—the user—is still the subject of controversy.

Our Arabic number system uses **positional notation**; the two ones in 113 have different meanings (the first 1 means one hundred, the other means ten). The sophistication of the notation is evident from the fact that of the many civilizations that developed arithmetic only the Babylonians conceived the positional notation.

Positional notation facilitates arithmetic but makes comprehension harder. One of the most fundamental tradeoffs to be made in an interactive system design is between the system's comprehensibility and its efficiency. We can make a system increasingly easy to use if we are prepared to sacrifice how efficient it is to use for doing certain things.

A quite compelling case can be made by considering ordinary arithmetic. Doing sums is a task with which we are all familiar, and you can easily imagine how a computer or calculator can help. If, further, we want to make addition really easy to understand, then we can represent numbers as collections. For instance, five can be represented by a collection of five stones. To add a row of five stones (○ ○ ○ ○ ○) to three stones (○ ○ ○) we simply push the groups together, and hey presto, we have a row of eight stones (○ ○ ○ ○ ○ ○ ○○). It is hard to think of

Box 6.1   Complexity versus clarity.

Systems go wrong, maybe because the user makes a mistake, so for a system to be easy to use it should be able to explain its problems. This is not entirely true—hammers don't have to explain why they miss nails, but the hammer's *user* knows (or in principle knows) why the hammer missed. Thus, more correctly, either the user or the computer should be able to generate appropriate diagnostics to understand errors, and hence recover from them, or to learn to avoid the erroneous situations in the future. In brief, the diagnostics must be computable from the error conditions. But by the time an error has been detected, the information surrounding its cause has usually been discarded or was never available in the first place, so a full diagnostic is not possible. This is why systems say 'stack overflow', instead of 'your function factorial has not been defined for negative numbers'. Perhaps in this case the issue is not one of computability alone but also of complexity: a program to make useful diagnostics would be exceedingly complex, and even then many errors would still be beyond its analysis. There are in any case many questions the user would ideally like answering (such as, does this program contain a virus?) which can never be answered. So why bother?

The practical design tradeoff is this: do you make a complex, powerful interactive system, for which most questions diagnostics try to answer are undecidable, or do you make a simple system, for which clear diagnostics can usually be given? The important principle for designing interactive systems is this: *making a system simpler may make it better*. But see Box 5.1 for the opposite view!

an easier approach to addition.[1] On the other hand, the method is not very efficient: it gets completely out of hand (literally) if you want to add much bigger numbers together. How would you add a million to sixty-three thousand and twenty-one stones? Well, maybe adding them is not the problem, but knowing what the answer was would be! Instead larger numbers are more effectively added by using a different notation, namely positional notation.[2] We can still use stones if they are arranged on an abacus, but it is convenient to write $1\,000\,000 + 603\,021 = 1\,603\,021$ using the Arabic symbols 1, 2, 3, rather than stones. Whichever way, we now have to use a much more complex procedure, and one that originally took

[1] Adding 3 to 5 may look easy, but profound assumptions are being made. Thus, each stone is counted only once (otherwise we could infer 7 plus 7 equalled 8), and we assume the stones are conserved (we get neither more nor less of them by sliding them around)—and, er, conservation is a property established by counting.

[2] The simple stone notation is linear in the size of the numbers; the Arabic notation is logarithmic. Also, because ten symbols are used, rather than a single sort of stone, the logarithm base further favours decimal Arabic notation over binary. Larger bases still (16, 60) start to use too many symbols; the cost of rote learning to add goes up by the square of the number of symbols.

us a long time to learn at school. Most people never really understand long addition with the intricacies of carries, let alone long multiplication and division. Put another way, we can understand the difficulty of the methods if we recall that the invention of the positional notation by the Babylonians was a major intellectual breakthrough, and it took civilization another few thousand years to come up with the decimal notation, then the cipher, and more recently a systematic way to handle fractional and negative values.

The problem of learning addition is not just the problem of manipulating digits on paper, it is partly to do with transcribing numbers (for example, stones) into the correct Arabic representation to start with. A number is just a quantity: for instance, the number five, might be represented in various ways; as five oranges, as ○○○○○, as the squiggle 5 on paper, or by the word cinq (the name for the pattern ':·:'). The Arabic notation (whether as digits or as transcribed into English) we now use is so good for everyday operations with numbers, it is easy to forget the difference between *numbers* and *numerals*: it seems as if 5 (a numeral) really *is* the number five. When students first start writing programs it is a conceptually difficult exercise for them to write a program to read a number and print its value (digit by digit, without using any built-in procedures for reading and writing numbers). The difficulty comes as a surprise because we so rarely need to make the distinction in everyday life between the symbols for representing numbers and the numbers themselves.

We almost take adding, numbers and numerals for granted, but it takes a good few years of intensive school training for the methods to sink in; and we must remember that there are many drop outs who are inoculated from mathematics for the rest of their lives. Surely we cannot expect training for user interfaces to be any easier—and we don't catch most users at an impressionable age!

6.2.1 Representation

The Church–Turing Thesis contains the phrase, 'if details like speed ... are ignored'. More precisely, the Church–Turing Thesis states that computational procedures are equivalent up to representation—how they are represented. For instance, symbols drawn by hand on paper can be used to represent everything an electronic computer might do. The Church–Turing Thesis says the computer can do neither more nor less intellectually, though it may look better or worse than when done by hand. That is why the Turing Test had to physically separate the interrogator from the computer and the other person—to standardize everyone's representations so that they could not be used as a give-away.

Programmers will be familiar with the idea of first writing a program (for example, to do payroll calculations) and then developing the details of the payroll representation. How the program presents its results is a quite separate matter from calculating those results. Indeed, programs can often be greatly simplified if we are able to find a clean separation between the 'work' (semantics) and the representation of their interfaces to the world (syntax).

Representation is crucial for people. Consider the following game: suppose you write the numbers one to nine on nine cards, and spread them out on a table, numbered side uppermost. You then play a game, taking cards in turn. You win by acquiring any three cards that add up to fifteen. It does not seem like a very easy game. However if the game is represented differently, like this,

6	7	2
1	5	9
8	3	4

and you are convinced that noughts-and-crosses (tick-tack-toe) is an alternative representation for the same game, then it is really easy to play! If you recall the strategy for playing noughts-and-crosses, you can now win at the numbered card game. If you play first, take five; if you play second either take five or, if you can't, take an even numbered card. Simple, isn't it, when the representation is changed!

We met the Johnson-Laird and Wason (1977) experiment with letter/digit cards at the beginning of Chapter 3. The lessons learnt from the results were that the problem was difficult, but most interactive systems would be *much* harder, and that mathematics gave the designer leverage in grappling with design problems. However, as we shall now see, mathematics is not the only representation that can simplify a problem. The same experiment can be repeated using more concrete symbols than letters and digits. Suppose, as before, there is a pack of cards, and four are laid out on a table (Figure 6.1). This time you are told that we are thinking about a trip to Manchester. The cards now have town names on one side, and modes of travel (car, train) printed on the other side; that is, a card shows the mode of travel to its destination. Four cards placed on the table show 'Manchester', 'Sheffield', 'Train' and 'Car'. Which cards should you turn over to check the truth of the statement, 'Each time I go to Manchester I travel by train'?

If you are also told that only train and car travel is involved, the rule is broadly equivalent to the original ('each card with a vowel on it has an even number on the other side'). In experiments, 80% of people tested realized that they should turn over the cards with 'Manchester' and 'car' on them—in contrast to only 10% who knew in the letter/digit formulation for the equivalent problem. You may recall that for the actual letter/digit quiz described in Chapter 3 *you* were not told that cards have letters on one side and digits on the other, but the subjects in the original experiment

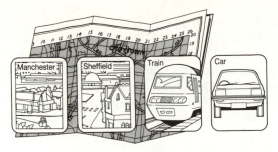

Figure 6.1 Another problem with four cards.

would have been. If you are British and hence know about Sheffield and Manchester and are old enough to have used trains, you are even more likely to succeed. This is much better performance than with the original abstract problem.

Other similar tests have been performed, confirming the idea that people's reasoning improves the more familiar they are with the concrete representation used—even if they are logicians, who ought to be able to reason abstractly. The evidence from bilingualism, too, is that people's skill in one language will not transfer to another: it is likely that skill with the travel test does not generalize to skill with a weather test (for example, using a rule like 'A yellow sky means bad weather'—which fishermen will know well).

People vary considerably in their abstract/concrete thinking abilities. People may not only prefer a certain style of dialogue but also be much more efficient using it. Do you find digital clocks easier than analogue clocks? I personally find clocks with hands much easier. I can explain why: I find an analogue face easier to remember after a quick glance; I can then interpret the time while performing other tasks. A digital watch must be read, which takes me longer and demands greater concentration. Perhaps through lack of practice, I find times like 17:44 harder to interpret than the position of hands I call 'a minute to quarter to six'. But some people may like the precision of digits. They may prefer digital *generally* for all sorts of reasons, ranging from experience, their job requirements, their difficulty in interpolating hand positions and possible confusion with short and long hands. Some manufacturers hedge their bets and provide both forms in one watch. People are skilled in different ways; not everyone likes or is able to reason in visual images.

Can you visualize a clock face showing the time 4:40? Can you rotate both hands simultaneously so that the hour hand moves on to point at 6? Where are the hands if you view the clock from behind? Can you visualize the clock with red hands and a green background? Such questions can be answered by good visualizers.

Consider the best representation to choose for describing an electrical circuit—it will almost certainly be pictorial. On the other hand, the user might find it easier to describe the circuit to the system by a command language ('`connect C3 to R1`'), and leave details of the picture (such as getting lines parallel) to the system. Similarly, if the system is to output instructions to the user, for instance wiring instructions, it could be very important to provide those instructions sequentially rather than 'all at once' in a single picture.

Mathematics is commonly thought to be a non-pictorial language. Yet the 'picture' $\frac{1+\sqrt{5}}{2}$ is unambiguous, but the English equivalent: 'one plus root five over two', which could also mean $1 + \sqrt{5/2}$ or $1 + \sqrt{5}/2$, is hopeless.

A common mistake in assessing interactive system designs is to assume that graphics is best. Many things done by graphical user interfaces are indeed done best by graphics, and they are perhaps done with such facility that it is natural to assume that graphics is the best general way to interact with computers. This is certainly not the case. In particular, graphical systems are very poor at representing the history of a task (a picture shows the last paint applied to it, not the choices and sketches that have since been concealed). This history would disrupt the picture, but would be essential in applications where an 'audit trail' was necessary. Another problem with pictorial user interfaces is that pictures may well mean a thousand words, but they need not mean the *same* thousand words to different users (or, more to the point, users and designers). The strange university mortar-board picture is a case in point: the symbol ♠ was actually supposed to represent paint pouring from a pot, which in turn was supposed to represent the notion of filling regions of a drawing with paint. Drawn as a small icon, at the low resolution on a computer screen it could easily be misinterpreted.

I have only covered a few examples of differing representations and some of the issues that arise. For further ideas, see Section 5.8.3 and Tufte (1983).

6.2.2   Concrete grammar

If you have programmed in Pascal you will have discovered that the semicolon seems to be a continual source of trouble. If a command is followed by '`else`' it must not terminate with '`;`', but everywhere else semicolons seem to be either required or optional. The relevant rule is not very obvious.

If a piece of program like the following code is edited by inserting an `else` after line 2, then you get `...x := 1; else...` which is not correct Pascal.

```
1          if something then
2              x := 1;
3              y := 1;
```

It is the sort of error that is hard to spot when you are more concerned with higher level issues like what the program means, as you generally are when programming! Some programming languages (FORTRAN, BCPL, BASIC) have a quite different approach to semicolons, so, in a sense, there is no need for the Pascal problem.

The problem is that the programmer thinks that the relevant syntax for the else is '⟨*statement*⟩ else ⟨*statement*⟩'—which it is. Unfortunately, the programmer can easily get an incorrect view of what a statement is. Almost everywhere '⟨*statement*⟩' and '⟨*statement*⟩;' are equivalent. Statements appear to need semicolons after them. In fact, the rule in Pascal is that semicolons come between statements, not after them. And, since else is not a statement, there should not be a semicolon before it.

Now the interesting problem is this: having identified a design issue, can we say *exactly* what the problem is? Could we be specific enough—*by understanding the principles involved*—to avoid similar problems in future?

What appears to be a simple issue is not only hard to pin down, but seems quite unrelated to the computer science perspective (the grammar of the programming language in this case). I suggest you examine a Pascal grammar closely (which you can find at the back of almost any book on Pascal programming): you will find the treatment of semicolons in statements is straightforward. In contrast, a language like C, which appears to use semicolons more sensibly (as statement terminators) has a more complex grammar!

The problem arises at least partly through the *use* of Pascal, and is not entirely attributable to the specification of the language. Obviously, mistakes with semicolons and any other syntactic slips *can* be avoided by using a syntax-directed editor: an extremely constrained style of use, perhaps. The semicolon difficulty should be seen in perspective too. There are many other sources of syntactic slips, such as unconventional operator associativities.

This was a batch, non-interactive example. But a user has still had to construct the program, and will have to wait for the results of running it. The task will be much longer and take more time than to submit a mouse click or a command line to a conventional interactive system. But if a system takes more time to give feedback, shouldn't the design be even more careful?

6.3   A case study

We will continue the historical analogy in the style of an extended metaphor. We will draw more parallels between the history of formal notations and how easy they were to use—how people learnt to cope with the conceptual problems—and the same issues as they arise using computers today.

The following case study transfers the development of some well-known themes in geometric thought, covering approximately 2 500 years from around 500 BC, into a few sessions with a geometric computer program. I hope you find the parable amusing (and appreciate its more serious side which will be taken up in the following sections); in any case we shall have occasion to return once or twice more to the same mathematical themes in later chapters.

The story revolves around an interactive geometry system; and given the earlier remarks about the Turing Test, it is amusing to recall Socrates' dialogue with Meno's slave. Socrates' skilful questioning managed to 'show' that the slave had an innate knowledge of geometry. No doubt a latter-day Socrates could do the same with a computer, only he might call it programming. Suspend disbelief, and suppose we have such a system ...

6.3.1   Sam and his program

Sam (not his real name) recently acquired the GEO package to help him teach his maths class. Specifically, GEO was a geometric package which was sold to him on the basis that it could prove simple geometric theorems like that of Pythagoras. The manuals which came with GEO were very long and difficult to read. It surprised Sam that the manuals were rather difficult even for him to read and used a lot of technical terms he was not at all familiar with.

He loaded the program and immediately up came a concise disclaimer of liability—probably because GEO came from the 'pure maths' stable. Then after a long pause a rather dense menu of names appeared. It seemed the program could do a great deal; perhaps this was why the manual was so long. Each name in the menu was the name of a geometric shape: triangle, square, segment, lunule ... *Lunule?*

Sam pressed the `icon` button and, next to each name, there appeared a little picture representing the geometric shape. The icon next to lunule was a crescent moon. Using a method that has now become popular, Sam selected the lunule by pointing at it, then the operation he wished to perform on it. Sam could ask GEO to perform almost any of the available geometric constructions on (or with?) a lunule. He chose 'quadrature', whatever that was, which had a little square as icon.

The system went quiet for a time. Sam wondered if it had gone wrong, but shortly a clatter from the disk drives convinced him that it was still working. The system slowly output a geometric construction, in the usual way: `Given a square ABCD, circle centre C radius CD...` There were several long pauses before GEO completed the construction;

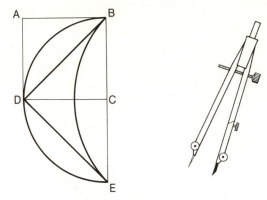

Figure 6.2   Sketch of a proof by GEO.

fortunately we need not go into the full details here. Suffice it to say the system finally displayed a picture something like Figure 6.2. The lunule has area equal to the square.

Sam did not understand what had happened, so he started reading the manual. Eventually, in Volume VI, Part 31, he came across the details. After some hard contemplation Sam understood GEO's reasoning: without doubt, GEO was very sophisticated. Sam was encouraged: he would be able to explore some interesting geometry with his class if GEO lived up to its initial promise.

It had taken Sam so long to get this far, that GEO thought he must have got stuck, so it 'helpfully' reverted to the original list of options.

'If GEO can do quadrature for various lunules', thought Sam, 'Well, circles can't be that much harder for it'. Sam was now more inspired, and—again, we needn't go into the details here—he was finally able to get GEO to construct a circle of area equal to a given square. What's this? GEO had crashed. Sam had asked GEO to do the impossible, or at any rate something that was not implemented properly. (π is transcendental, so squaring the circle is not possible using Euclid's methods of construction.)

Sam rang up the software house. Yes, they did know this was a problem with Release 1·43, but they were working on it and for a purely notional sum they would be prepared to send him the latest updates.

When the new package arrived it had a shorter manual but came on several more disks—strange that a bigger program could be described more briefly! This time Sam could enter short, stylized programs rather than going through a series of menu selections. He would try the circle quadrature again. The manual explained that it could do the problem—but it appeared Sam would have to type π. Unfortunately he didn't have the Greek-keyboard-option, so Sam had to think of another way. He played around for a few days, getting used to the new version of GEO.

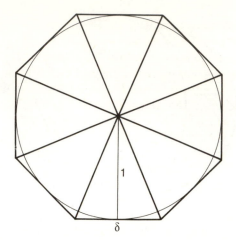

Figure 6.3   Tricky triangles.

Finally, he had a flash of inspiration one night in the bath: the circumference of a circle is 2π and its area is πr^2, so he could ask GEO to show that the ratio of circumference to area is 2 : r. GEO doesn't handle variables like r for some reason which the manual didn't explain very clearly. (In historical terms, we have to wait for François Viète.) But if he made the radius 1, he could ask GEO to show that the area was one-half of the circumference.

To cut a long story short, GEO simply said, **yes**. How did GEO know, Sam wondered? Why should Sam trust GEO—of course, in this case Sam actually knew the answer was right, but why should he trust GEO for more complex problems? A quick phone call established that GEO had a 'trace' mode and this should convince Sam whether the answer **yes** was correct. Would this trace mode be useful for his teaching?

Sam set the problem up again, though at first he found the trace output was distracting. Finally Sam could see the line of reasoning GEO took. It constructed a triangle of base δ and altitude 1, the radius of the circle. This triangle has area $\delta/2$. Rather like slicing a cake, the circle may be divided up by a number of such circumscribed triangles; eight are shown in Figure 6.3. Now GEO claimed that the total length of all the triangle bases adds up to c, the circumference, so there are c/δ triangles. Thus the total area of triangles is $(\delta/2) \times (c/\delta)$. This readily simplifies to $c/2$, half the circumference, and the answer is **yes**.

OK. But wait a minute; when the triangle bases lie exactly on the circle's circumference, δ must be zero. If δ is zero, the equation $(\delta/2) \times (c/\delta)$ doesn't make sense: 0/0 has no defined value. On the other hand, if the equation is to make sense, δ must not be zero—in which case the area of triangles will be greater than the area of the circle, as it clearly is in Figure

6.3. Whichever way we look at it, GEO's reasoning is faulty but the answer it got seems correct.

Perhaps, in some way, it would have been better if Sam had never probed too deeply into the inner workings of GEO. He used to think it was an amazing piece of software, now he knows he cannot use it in his class. It is poor pedagogy to present students with results that are inexplicable to them: if Sam used GEO he would want his students to be able to learn something they could use for themselves.

We might imagine that Sam tried returning GEO to the software house. Of course they'd say that he had broken the seal on the package (how else are you supposed to try a program?) and therefore he had legally accepted and could not return it.[3] He did not get his money back. He was a wiser man. Or maybe, like most of us, he resigned himself to working with a program he neither fully understood nor fully trusted.

6.3.2   The morals

Sam wanted to use GEO for his teaching. Some things GEO could do were very impressive, and this gave Sam confidence that he might be able to teach advanced geometrical concepts with the program. It turned out, first, that the original GEO had a bug which caused it to crash. The revised GEO didn't have this bug, but (when Sam followed exactly what it was doing) it was obviously using an unsound method of reasoning for teaching classical geometry. This was worrying; so worrying, in fact, that Sam felt he could not trust it.

Of course, the use of infinitesimals like δ is a classic point of debate— popularized by Zeno. Infinitesimals may be valid or not, but they have nothing to do with the geometric concepts that Sam wanted his class to learn. Sam wanted a geometric virtual machine; instead the 'trace mode' revealed some sort of arithmetical representation, and indeed understanding the arithmetic required a more sophisticated depth of understanding than that assumed by the GEO user interface itself.

The fourfold moral seems clear:

▷ Computer systems encourage their users to expect too much of them. Specifically, their interface notation permits users to express insoluble, non-computable or merely unimplemented tasks.

▷ The computer is disturbing: it may either crash or produce absurd results which lead the user to distrust everything it does.

▷ The inner workings of programs are normally quite obscure even to the people who wrote them, but it worries the user greatly when implementation details protrude—in Sam's case, the infinitesimals are not part of the geometric problem. They make no sense to him.

---

[3] Manufacturers are worried about illicit program copying. More about this in the Epilogue.

▷ Much of the clarity and generality of a program depends on carefully thought out notations and explanations. It took Sam considerable insight to get around the lack of variables.

There are two more abstract morals that should also be drawn out, and these are discussed in the next two sections.

6.3.3   The historical moral

The reasoning that we supposed GEO to have worked through, when finding the area of a circle, would have been familiar to Archimedes. It was a calculation which Archimedes might easily have done, although to give him the credit he is due, Archimedes would have circumscribed *and* inscribed triangles in order to have lower and upper bounds on the ratio. GEO was less formal, and only circumscribed.

Such methods were developed into the calculus by Newton and his contemporaries many centuries later. Nevertheless, infinitesimals still posed ontological problems. Bishop Berkeley roundly attacked their basis: they were zero and yet not zero. Yet infinitesimals do solve real problems, though it is best not to delve too deeply into how they work (witness Zeno's hard-wearing paradoxes)! Only in the 1960s—some centuries later—were infinitesimals placed on a solid footing.

On the one hand, we have mathematicians raving over ontological problems *over centuries*. Archimedes himself had reservations; indeed, both he and Newton felt it necessary to recast their results in respectable—that is, in those days in purely geometric—terms. On the other hand, we see *exactly* analogous ontological problems arising in the use of interactive systems, but users are expected to handle these problems in real time and probably under pressure from their boss.

6.3.4   The generalized moral

Not all programs are like GEO you may say: Sam was using a sophisticated AI program to demonstrate elementary geometry—what has this to do with real problems like process control, desk-top publishing, or accounting? For the 'generalized moral' of the story I argue that the sort of geometric proof activity of GEO is powerful enough to represent *any* sort of interaction with computers. Sam's story, then, is a model of *all* interaction. Generally, computer systems operate on internal objects (stacks, bytes, sectors, buffers, processes) which correspond to the internal objects used by GEO (symbolic infinitesimals) in the story. Life for the user is straightforward until these curious objects intrude into the user interface. I shall look more closely at this general user interface problem next by drawing on some technical ideas to handle infinitesimals.

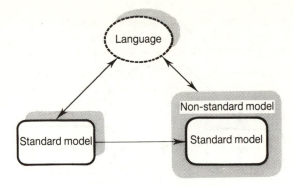

Figure 6.4   Non-standard models.

6.4   Non-standard analysis

Sam was worried by $(\delta/2) \times (c/\delta)$. Either its value was wrong if δ was not zero, or the equation was undefined: $0/0$ if δ was zero. The problem is that we wish δ to be less than any positive real number and yet not equal to zero. No such number exists in the standard model of real numbers. (The non-existence of infinitesimals in the standard real model is called the **Archimedean Property** of the real numbers.)

Abraham Robinson (1966) showed that we can construct a non-standard mathematical model of real numbers which accords infinitesimals a proper place. In the non-standard model, infinitesimals obey the usual algebraic rules for numbers and we can cancel them without problem. In our case, we would solve $(\delta/2) \times (c/\delta)$ in the non-standard model, readily obtaining $c/2$ without any cheating or tricky 'in the limit' arguments. But $c/2$ *is* a standard real number, which makes perfect sense in the standard model of reals, so it is the answer we want.

We may view this diagrammatically as in Figure 6.4.

The language is the language of algebra, which includes sentences such as our familiar '$(\delta/2) \times (c/\delta)$'. Such sentences have two models of interest to us: standard and non-standard. Note the arrow indicating the embedded standard model in the non-standard model: all interpretations permitted by the standard model are permitted by the non-standard model. However, the non-standard model permits more powerful proof techniques because (in this case) it is enriched with non-Archimedean reals.

We have seen that for non-standard analysis to work in a useful way it is important that the standard model is embedded in the non-standard model. If it is not, it would be possible to prove theorems in the non-standard model that have no validity in the standard model. In user interface terms, we might view the 'standard model' as the user's conceptual

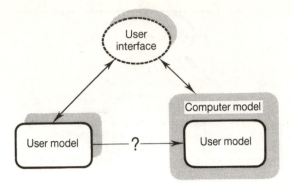

Figure 6.5   Non-standard models in user interfaces.

model, the 'language' as the language of the user interface and the 'non-standard model' as the computer's interpretation (implementation) of the dialogue. Of course, in this case the user has no guarantee that his model of the dialogue language is embedded in (or in any other sensible way related to) the computer's model (see Figure 6.5).

6.4.1   Examples of non-standard models

For a user interface flavoured example, consider the time I deleted a large program by mistake. I was using a Pascal compiler to compile a Pascal program (which I had spent a day writing) to get an object program. Let's call the Pascal program p and the object program o. What I meant to say was, '`compile p o`' but unfortunately I typed '`compile p p`'.

Now, in my standard model of compilers, this proposition ('`compile p p`') does not have a solution (or, at least, the only acceptable solution is an error message). A compiled program is object code, not more Pascal. But the compiler operated a non-standard model! The compiler found a solution all right, it deleted p.

We can view this sad state of affairs in two ways. Conventionally we might say that the compiler writer had forgotten to check that the source and object files are distinct. Having made that mistake, the next thing to do in compiling to a file is to erase its old contents. So it deletes p. The other view is that in the compiler's non-standard model the equation `compile p p` *can* be solved. A valid solution in the non-standard model is 'the as-it-were infinitesimal program p compiles into the as-it-were infinitesimal object code p'. It got that solution by cheating, in much the same way as GEO performed circle quadrature by cheating with infinitesimals. Presumably, the compiler might have complained if p was *exactly* zero, but we can only speculate.

Box 6.2   Extreme tests.

Sophisticated users often test user interfaces with extreme data, to test the boundaries of the standard/non standard models. For example, typing very long sentences, dividing by zero, making recursive nests and so on. Perhaps they are trying to find limits on the computer's model to reduce their uncertainties—they may wish to be 'optimal causal modellers'. The new calculator I describe in Chapter 16, for instance, was rapidly dismissed by one user. He first tried dividing by zero; the calculator crashed (at that stage, it was only a prototype); the user said, 'Well, I've seen calculators like *that* before'.

The designer has an internal view of computers, he knows the non-standard model; this perspective readily conceals problems the user may have. A user consults an expert system which asks the user to estimate various preferences (for example, maximize monthly profit). After many questions, the system makes no recommendation. The designer asserts that the user must have been non-committal. Suppose the user disagrees. Then the designer says, 'Ah, the weightings are non-linear, therefore your small preferences were all negligible'. So by a technical explanation (non-linear weighting) the 'bug' turns out to be caused by the way the user operated, and there is no design fault—for someone who knows the secret, or essence of the system. By the time a user understands a problem well enough to complain about it explicitly (rather than in terms of non-specific—but real—symptoms like headaches), the user is already well on the way to understanding it, and (just like the designer) not worrying about it.

Consider the problems of debugging and tracing Prolog programs. The standard model of Prolog is purely declarative. However Prolog is generally implemented in an imperative programming language, so almost inevitably the computer has a non-standard model for interpreting Prolog programs. This does not matter until the Prolog programmer writes a program which needs debugging. The programmer then encounters the non-standard model head on.

No doubt, with some loss of efficiency, it would be possible to map the non-standard model generally used for tracing and debugging Prolog into (say) unwinding rewrite rules. But instead, the implementors of Prolog trade efficient implementation for intrusions of a non-standard implementation model into the user interface from time to time.

Such tradeoffs are by no means confined to declarative languages; the conventional imperative programming language Pascal, for instance, was designed 'to teach programming as a systematic discipline based on certain fundamental concepts clearly and naturally reflected in the language' (Jensen and Wirth, 1985); yet understandable concern for efficiency *intentionally* led to many compromises which make the language harder to learn than is justified by the various gains in efficiency that are hardly crucial for teaching. (For example, can you say which of the following can be returned by functions: records, arrays, sets?)

Or consider my disk filing system which said '34 `sectors free`'. Now 'sectors' is a non-standard name for the average user, meaning nothing in their user model. It is just confusing and unnecessary. I happen to know what it means, but one day my disk system said '2F `sectors free`' and I discovered that non-standard hexadecimal numerals had been masquerading as standard decimal numbers for weeks.

Finally consider the use of a simple calculator program. First the computer displays a prompt: '?'. The problem immediately faced is that many programs, not just calculators, probably use such highly suggestive prompts, and the user may have to guess what program this is! If the program is a calculator, the user ought to be able to do sums. Let's try one: so type *3-1*↩ and the calculator prints 2. So it seems to work.

Since programs rarely do the same thing twice, let's try it again:

```
? 3-1↩
*** ERROR: BEAD UNDERFLOW
?
```

Something has clearly gone wrong—although at least we have some sort of mnemonic `BEAD` that might mean something to somebody, rather than an error number, like `E723` that means precious little even to the programmer (unless it comes up very often!); also the system has come back with a prompt, so perhaps we could have another go.

Things would make sense *if* you knew that the computer used a non-standard implementation of arithmetic: in fact it does sums by counting beads. If it throws a bead away to do the sum $3 - 1$, then it may not have enough beads left over to do the next sum. Of course, beads are a fairly reasonable way to represent numbers (witness the success of abaci), but they have some properties that are not shared by numbers! And it is only when the user encounters these representational problems that attributes of the non-standard model intrude.

Now *you* know the answer, this bead example probably seems vaguely amusing. But we should not forget that the poor user will not be amused even if we are. The corollary is that if the non-standard model was explained there would have been no problem. Figure 6.6 shows the idea of enlarging the user model by explaining the non-standard model.

Unfortunately the relation between standard and non-standard models gets rather complex if the interface languages are natural languages. Trying to make a user interface easy to use merely by being 'natural', using natural language for the interface language—especially by using speech—encourages the user to impute more powerful models (and more world knowledge) than can actually be implemented.

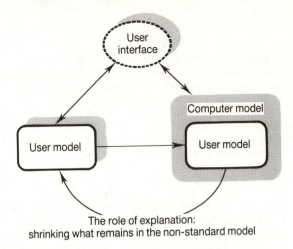

The role of explanation:
shrinking what remains in the non-standard model

Figure 6.6   Explanation explained a little.

6.5   Principles

When non-standard objects, objects in the computer model but not in the user model, emerge during a dialogue, the user interface is failing. The user interface is not 'interfacing' the user to the computer: the user is getting too raw a view of the application. Various design principles have been proposed to draw attention to this specific problem. Here are two:

▷ 'What you see is what you get' (often abbreviated WYSIWYG—see Sections 11.6.3 and 11.7.4) can be interpreted in the standard/non-standard view. If an object can be 'seen' then the user must be able to 'get' it, in other words, all visible objects must be 'standard' and therefore can be manipulated by the user. Conversely if an object can be 'got' then the user should be able to 'see' it. We will explore this issue in Chapter 11.

▷ The terms **first-class** and **second-class object** are used to express similar considerations in programming languages. A second-class object is restricted in some way, perhaps it has to appear explicitly and can never be represented (for example, by a variable); it may be possible to 'see' it but not to 'get' at it by name; perhaps it cannot be returned from a function. The **Principle of Data-type Completeness** for programming language design demands that all objects are first-class. Most user interfaces are far from being data-type complete, and compensate by providing many special-purpose features. Note that values that are first class are necessarily handled *by* the programming language paradigm, rather than built up or

---

Box 6.3   Role integrity.

Role integrity means that a system really behaves in a way consistent with its appearance, or its stated role—it presents standard models to its user and conceals its non-standard implementation models. Systems should not, as a rule, provide features that are half-implemented, giving the user the impression that the system has certain capabilities which, in fact, it cannot fulfil. Role integrity is a useful shorthand for a difficult tradeoff. It is the balance between being able to say things, and for those things to mean what you expect. It is almost always possible to say something that sounds sensible but is really gibberish. Most calculators have trouble if you ask them to compute one divided by zero. But their user interface suggests that one divided by zero is exactly the sort of problem that they can do! Yet consider a calculator designed for Roman numerals. Even if there is a division operator it would be impossible to divide by zero, for the Romans had no cipher (symbol for zero). Such a calculator would have role integrity but it would be very restricted. But would it seem restricted to the Roman users for whom it was designed?

Role integrity clearly depends on what the user expects from the superficial description of the system. It may be nothing to do with the language, but rather with the principles underlying the language.

---

implemented by virtual machines defined within it. Chapter 12 will explore the case where the user's interaction *itself* becomes first class.

6.6   Conclusions

Interactive computer systems are much harder to use than we like to think. We expect, and often require, users of interactive computer systems to handle ontological problems that are comparable to mathematical problems which defeated the best minds for millennia.

There is no such thing as simple as 'ease of use'. Although making things easy to use is, self-evidently, a good idea and has caught on as a popular slogan, the idea is simple-minded. In reality, 'ease of use' is a complex and interesting tradeoff.

In general, computer systems do not operate with the same models as their users. As a rule, the freedom of an implementer to choose appropriate non-standard objects can ensure an efficient implementation. However, what may be called lapses in the design result in these non-standard objects becoming apparent to the user. Sometimes the seasoned user may be able to ignore such pseudo-objects as 'noise'. At other times the user will be required by the system to enter into some apparently meaningless activity in order to establish some facts of relevance only in the non-standard model.

Just as the non-existence of non-standard reals is called the Archimedean Property, we suggest the term **Archimedean System** for interactive systems that have no non-standard model.   Archimedean Systems, then, are good things.   Sadly designers' and users' casual acceptance of bugs, minor and major, makes Archimedean Systems—actual or attempted—rather rare.

Chapter 7

Basic design problems

> The need for more elaborate man/machine interaction can certainly be enhanced by designing more incomprehensible systems.
>
> *Edsger Dijkstra*

It is usually obvious when an interface fails or is not a total success. Many people can easily say what is wrong with a particular interactive system from their point of view, maybe they will even be able to offer or suggest hardware or software solutions to the immediate problems posed by the poor design. Such would only be palliatives—the designer really needed preventive medicine in the first place. Industrial and other realistic timescales are too short for the designer to have several serious attempts at getting a design right—to say nothing of the effects of the training overhead on the users exposed to the prototype versions. If the designer wants to stay in business, the next system must be 'compatible': the failures of one design are then carried into the next generation of systems.

Designers need to be aware why they design badly, why design is just so difficult. In some cases, designers need to be aware that by falling into traps they are perhaps designing worse than need be. This chapter shows there are lots of possible problems that arise when designing interactive systems. Design problems have a daunting scope which we can see here.

User interface designs fail not just because of technical errors but because of failures of communication between user and designer and because of different perspectives of the role of systems. These we can view as consequences of differing models in designers' and users' heads, irreconciled because of the low information channel available between them. Some of the design issues that follow are **systemic** in that they apply to systems generally; some are specifically to do with interactive computer systems.

7.1 Divergent commitments

The user and designer have quite different commitments in their approach to the computer. The designer is concerned with the programs, hardware choice, and so on whereas the user is concerned with information manipulated by those systems. The designer is not in the least committed to the user's data, and the user is not in the least concerned with the implementation of the computer system—in the normal course of events. At worst, this is unsatisfactory; the designer should certainly make a commitment to save the user from loss or corruption of information! Another reason, quite pragmatic, for divergent commitments is that the range of possible designs is just too large for the designer to explore unless he has commitments that limit the range of designs he is willing to consider.

Designers usually delay devising the help and documentation until the *last* moment. If help was written earlier it might have necessitated revision as the system design iterated. Yet users often need the help *first*! This aspect of divergent commitments has serious consequences for prototyping and iterative design, where some users are exposed to systems which the designer intends to have a short life—and hence effort expended on documentation might be 'wasted'. The designer should always be present at user tests to say what the help would have been if it is needed. (Box 17.5 gives an interface design method (the 'think aloud' method) that turns this recommendation into a technique.)

7.2 The 'ergonomics issue'

Designers design for themselves. Designers often think of themselves as exemplary users and evaluators. In the past they will have certainly designed effective systems for themselves; the apparent success of which lends support to this opinion. We saw some reasons for this in the conclusions to Chapter 3, but we now want to define and name this pervasive phenomenon.

Programmers are often trained to produce systems which are academically evaluated on their technical merits, or on the value of the system for the academic or peer environment of highly skilled users; if a programmer is successful in these terms then he naturally expects to be as successful using the same approach when he works in industry—despite *not* 'researching' the users, the business and social setting and constraints, and so on. Thus design training and experience, which rarely extend beyond the technical aspects of design, understandably lead programmers to underestimate the communication problems in real-world design when the three roles (designer, user and system evaluators) are embodied in different groups of people. This is **cultural dominance** (and not a good thing).

In computing, the problem is exacerbated because there is no intermediary (for example, craftsman, or producer) between the designer and user to flesh out the design abstractions. Current trends away from von Neumann style programming and towards higher level languages (for example, using CASE, Computer Aided Software Engineering) encourage even more abstract specifications which are immediately executable and hence further reduce the gap between abstract formalism and user. Because there is no intermediary, programmers are forced to promote their status to that of designer, and we've seen they do not usually have the training for this. The computer scientist implements a system and by calling that process 'design' assumes that the user interface has been 'designed'. But a real designer knows he does not know how to design, and therefore he knows he *has* to take considerable care over every design he attempts.

As we have seen the ergonomic rule is that designers will be unaware of the relative level of their threshold of complexity and the differences in their and users' value systems unless they are specifically trained to appreciate the different needs of ordinary users. On the contrary, the designer is trained with various formal methods such as structured design, stepwise refinement, even mathematics ... techniques specifically to enable *him* to avoid unmanageable complexity. In addition, the designer will often use a formalized or automated design tool which enables him to abstract out the representational complexity of the user interface; this sets his threshold even higher. Top-down methods, abstract data types, separation of concerns, and so on, aim precisely to conceal representational complexity from more abstract design levels: thereby complexity is successfully hidden from the designer.

We saw in Section 3.3.3 that users act so as to maintain their environment, so too, designers impose a certain level of complexity on the things they design. Although technology allows tasks to be made easier, it is often used to introduce new complications—partly to maintain the perceived level of complexity *for the designer*. Some of the most exciting developments in computing are at the user interface: high resolution colour displays, speech, special devices for new ways of interacting, advanced software— you would think these would contribute to better usability. But we do not know how to use these advances effectively, often they seem more to introduce gratuitous complexity. This is **the paradox of technology**: technology can make things easier, yet it is used to make things more complex (Norman, 1988).

Users can be expected to be much better at the task than the designer. Word processors should be designed for typists, chemical systems for chemists, and so on. Many computer scientists are not touch typists and this leads them to over-emphasize keystroke counts or direct manipulation because typing is relatively hard for them. A good typist is likely to prefer a more verbose and more mnemonic interface than the designer, since the time to type is less significant compared with the time to learn or understand. (A professional typist will type in much larger bursts than an inexperienced typist; he may be able to type familiar words faster than a non-skilled typist can type individual characters. Non-familiar abbreviations may be slower to type than complete words—but then, on the other hand, a skilled typist might enjoy learning an extension to his existing skills.)

In general, the user interface designer is well advised to seek expert help in all representational issues—and to design the user interface so that such things are parametrizable, so that the user or installation engineers can configure the system, changing colours, command names, and so on. Section 8.6 gives general reasons—delaying commitment—why parametrization is a good thing.

7.3   The Sapir–Whorf Hypothesis

The ergonomics issue can be summed up in the **Sapir–Whorf Hypothesis** (otherwise called the **Whorfian Hypothesis**). Edward Sapir and his student Benjamin Whorf suggested that how we perceive and think about the world depends on the language available to us; or, put in a more dogmatic form, the language we have available to us controls the way we think. Interesting examples can be given by comparing, say, European and Amerindian languages; but it will suffice to say that if users are not trained in programming they cannot think the same way as designers, and even if they could, their thinking would inevitably be terribly woolly and unreliable. Or again, a FORTRAN programmer would not think recursively even if (for a programmer with wider experience) recursion were a 'natural' approach to a certain programming problem. The Sapir–Whorf Hypothesis identifies language and thought, and we know that almost all natural languages are Turing Complete, so the only real effect a language can have on thought is one of efficiency, and various emotional influences. Inappropriate design language will not only make a designer blind to certain possibilities, but make it difficult to express those blindnesses to the user.

The programming language can have a direct effect on the user interface. Some Pascal-based systems produced very poor diagnostics simply because Pascal had awkward string operations. Designers will almost certainly use computers to design and develop the user interface, so there will also arise an implicit confusion between *designer* and *user* interfaces. It is perhaps too cynical to suggest that most user interfaces start off life as debuggers for a program under development—in a sense, anything that cannot be discovered via the user interface doesn't need fixing so is there any point making the user interface different from the debugger?

7.4 Design is too easy

Designing computer systems is very easy: programming is easy, and it is very easy to get a program working. The faster a program is written the harder it is to modify and improve—and it becomes increasingly difficult to improve the more modifications are made—and the more likely the designer will stop improving the system and present it to its users. Of course, *real* programming is very difficult but this doesn't hinder most practitioners.

Design *is* too easy when details are ignored! Should this part of the program work *exactly* like that part? Should the user be able to change this data later? ... Diagonal lines are thicker than horizontal lines. The program can't open more than four files. Well, most users won't notice any of these design issues—or, at least, they won't notice till after they have bought the system!

When a program does not work in the intended way, just add a bit of code, `if problem then do something-completely-different`. So it is easy to fix obvious bugs here-and-there, without any overall view of the system's design. It is even easier to 'design' in an object-oriented environment: object-oriented programming allows existing program code to be reused and overridden very easily, in fact, without doing anything special—overriding is part of the object-oriented paradigm. Furthermore, the better the designer, the more programming techniques he will know—compiler-compilers, program generators, and so on—that will make his job easier still.

Perhaps because the designer's job can be done with 'simple' programming, the designer is tempted to dismiss anything which is not technical as trivial: generally the designer is more interested in what a system does than in how it does it and, because of the ergonomics issue (Section 7.2), supposes that the same will be true for the unfortunate user.

7.5 Solutioneering or 'instrumental primacy'

The designer has to have an eye on machine efficiency, utilization of resources, cost-effectiveness, speed, mathematical tractability and program correctness. Technical training encourages this emphasis, and it is but a short step to pursuing these instrumental goals as an end in themselves. This will often result in solutions to gratuitous problems, so-called **solutioneering**—another manifestation of cultural dominance. They may be very impressive solutions in their own, technical, frame of reference, but they will contribute more to the designer's job satisfaction than the user's. Thus we see a move away from designing quality user interfaces to defining metrics over user interfaces, and then improving the interface purely with respect to those metrics.

Box 7.1 Words for talking about bugs.

Arabs have many words for camel; Eskimos have many words for snow; Aborigines have many words for hole; we have many words for vehicle (car, lorry, bus, sedan ...). A language has lots of words for concepts that its speakers are interested in. Eskimos live in a land of snow, and they need to talk precisely about it.

Bugs cripple programs. And how many words do we have for bugs? Just one. Everything else is circumlocution or computer-centric; that is, *nobody is interested in bugs* and their effect on users. If some of the worst programs around were improved, had their bugs fixed, whole professions and career structures would be destroyed! Of course, it would have been better if the bugs and low standards of programming had never been accepted in the first place. But because there are no words, it is difficult to talk about the problems, let alone get excited about them.

Brian Reffin Smith has suggested some more words for bug. A 'smug' is a bug you don't worry about; a 'hug' is a deadly embrace; a 'mug' is a silly bug; a 'thug' is a bug that is destructive. A 'plug' perhaps should be a bug deliberately installed to help sell a system. Even with these words, and more like them, we still need to change the way bugs are talked about. 'Programs *have* bugs', we like to say. But we ought to say that programmers *make* bugs; bugs don't come out of nowhere, they are caught from sloppy programmers.

It is very worrying that the computer industry is so complacent about bugs. It is terrifying that the prevailing social climate is not just complacent but *encourages* bugs. It is something of an intellectual challenge to design a decent bug. And it is quite acceptable to do so. Both the law and social pressure are very weak in this area: crime is often fun, but usually there are various pressures to behave sociably. Not so in computing.

We do have some words for special sorts of deliberate 'bug'. These are *virus, Trojan Horse, worm, bomb* (Witten, 1987). Unlike the bugs we have been talking about, these things are deliberately, intentionally introduced by clever, malicious programmers. Some of them are very destructive, and destructive in ways outside the jurisdiction of the law. By giving you a virus I can destroy your company records, possibly your company as well. And not be held responsible, and not even *feel* responsible. It was an intellectual challenge to get the virus to work, and besides it is your fault that it destroyed your data, I mean, don't you backup every day?

Instrumental primacy can often be seen in the way many fifth generation projects are presented: 'get the system engineering right (enough logical inferences per second, say) and the user interface effort will be trivialized'. Of course, this may be the case, but it would be more realistic to make the consequential 'ease of use' explicitly hypothetical.

Instrumental primacy encourages the designer to ignore informal principles (especially those concerned with appearance or representation) unless they can be transformed into technical statements. One of the reasons for this book is to show (shortly!) that some principles can be expressed precisely: the designer can make some important design decisions *as technical decisions*.

It is perhaps easier to recognize the same traits appearing in areas in which we have less personal investment: when I try to draw a cartoon face, perhaps trying to emulate a newspaper cartoonist, I fail miserably. One reason I fail is that I am tempted by the obvious solution, to add detail, resolution, because I know how to add detail, and adding detail is a lot easier than getting the whole style into proportion. Exactly the same happens in user interfaces where the display designer wants more bits-per-inch. For many graphics applications one can get adequate realism without high resolution, but resolution and corresponding processing power is the most direct way of enhancing realism.

7.6 Bottom-up design and the fallacy of composition

User interfaces can easily grow by adding unrelated features; no method is used to specify coherent sets of user interface techniques (top-down selection), so user interfaces grow bottom-up. We've seen that bugs can be fixed locally; display design follows after higher resolution. Features are added because they are locally powerful, and no orthogonal[1] 'neat' design theme ever emerges, or if one does, the user cannot rely on it being uniformly applicable. Indeed, design conflicts and limitations in the initial design can often be camouflaged by adding new features. Bottom-up design is much easier than rethinking the entire structure of the system.

If it takes a user 30 years to understand his job in order to do it well, it is unlikely that the designer (or his intermediaries) can understand the requirements of the system in a few days. Instead, the designer will identify specific features that can be woven into the system, each feature supporting part of the user's task. Again, there is a tendency for designs to grow bottom-up, by accruing features.

Design tradeoffs are often driven by low-level details of the computational model of the implementation. Thus undo is unlikely to be very powerful in a system implemented in an imperative language. Programming languages like Pascal require the programmer to fix the size of most data structures before a program is compiled; this means that features of the user interface will come in predetermined sizes, perhaps powers of two or some other machine-oriented quantities. And even when the programmer has a more flexible language at his disposal, it is still easier to plan a program for fixed data sizes. But if there is a good reason to suppose the user

---

[1] Orthogonal: meaning that the components are independent; roughly, self-contained.

may ever require something up to the fixed size n (n files open at once; n characters in his name; n cells in his spreadsheet), he is likely to need $n + 1$ occasionally. So the system should have supported $n + 1$. Now we have an argument for $n + 1$, so by the same reasoning the interface should have supported $n + 2$. By induction, then, there should be *no* limit. So there is a good design principle: put features in in units of 0 (that is, not at all), 1 or ∞ (that is, without any limitation).

All too often the user has no warning *before* attempting a task that a machine restriction may be invoked, that he cannot do or type any more than n things. Far better to have provided programmable features, and no intrinsic limitations (apart from computability). (This is an example of Parkinson's Law: things multiply to fill all available space.)

Alternatively, features are provided simply because they can be implemented as opposed to being well considered and integrated into the rest of the system—for example, a text editor may provide some ingenious and abstruse scheme to handle long lines wider than screen or paper. In all cases the user interface could be improved by having the courage to generalize the implementation of a restricted interface, and never the other way around.

> Raisins may be the best part of a cake; but a bag of raisins is
> not better than a cake.   *Ludwig Wittgenstein*

The fallacy of composition is that properties of the parts are not necessarily the properties of the whole. Thus good, even excellent, interactive systems may have bad parts; systems with good parts may be bad overall. The fallacy can be expressed as a logical formula, the **Barcan Formula**: $\forall x \; \Box f(x) \Rightarrow \Box \forall x \; f(x)$—if for all x, it is necessary that $f(x)$ then it is necessary that for all x, $f(x)$ is true. The $\Box$ (sometimes written L) means 'it is necessary that'. This formula is true for some models, *not* for others. The formula expresses the main problem of bottom-up design: properties composed at the 'bottom' may not be the properties visible at the 'top'.

Suppose we are contemplating the design of an interactive system: it is obviously necessary to include useful commands. Suppose the $\forall$ quantifier ranges over all those useful commands that we could include in the system, and we define $f(x)$ to be true if we will include the command x in the system. Obviously, since we are only ranging over useful commands, it is true that $\forall x \; \Box f(x)$: that is, for *each* useful command, it is necessary to include it. But, this does not mean that we consider it necessary to include *all* useful commands, $\Box \forall x \; f(x)$: this would result in a system with an overwhelming number of commands—creeping featurism. The Barcan formula is not true when there are side-effects; in this case, each true $f(x)$—each command included—affects how we evaluate $f(x')$ for some as yet to be included command, for we may only want to include the useful command x' if we do not include the useful command x, and vice versa.

The fallacy of composition has applications in many other areas, for instance, a jury made up from indecisive jurors might be decisive, but made up from decisive jurors it might pass an indecisive verdict.

7.7 Design is fun; work is not

The designer is in a unique, exciting position to develop and repeatedly redefine the system at will. The users will have to put up with whatever completed system results, and they will never have such a creative, inventive control over it as the designer had. This point is rather well made by the **Adventure Analogy** (Carroll, 1982). Adventure is a computer game where users get 'lost' and caught up by unexpected events and, indeed, it is very exciting to play. But this exciting scenario parodies what happens when using a work system for work: users get lost and quite inexplicable things seem to happen. Users get very frustrated, let alone excited!

Gregory Bateson abstrusely defines **play** as composed of actions which do not denote what would be denoted by those actions which the actions themselves denote. In other words, things happen in games, but they do not *really* happen, except in the players' imaginations. Thus a vivid flashing screen in an arcade game may denote a personal disaster, possibly even the death of the spacecraft pilot, but it does not denote what would be denoted by an actual disaster, namely, the player *really* dying. If Bateson's definition is as succinct and reasonable as it can be, think how difficult it must be for a user to disentangle the different referents of denotation!

Constrained by his job role, the user may not be able to make the subtle distinction. System responses will be interpreted as signs which *do* denote what the real-life actions they denote denote. In other words, the user takes things more seriously than the designer—things the designer may treat as 'fun' may be a matter of employment for the user. Such confusion is illustrated by the user who wonders if he has irrevocably broken a system which has 'crashed' or 'aborted', but the words hardly denote *really* crashing or *really* aborting for the designer. An emotive expletive like 'aborted' is an unfortunate choice of word for a pregnant user.

Recognizing that users may prefer fun to improved work conditions, many serious systems are now provided with games and gimmicks. There is a serious side to this: the temporary relief afforded by *suitable* games may revitalize the user. Programming is probably the best game and we can no doubt expect enjoyable but totally unreliable user-programmed systems in the near future—certainly, various people have argued that games playing and designing games programs is a good (and not just superficially motivating) introduction to programming.

7.8   'Feature ticking'

Confusion between functionality and speed- or ease-of-use leads to evaluators requiring systems to provide certain features, which are then ticked off a 'feature check list': things such as menus, mice, colour, speech, direct manipulation. If a system does not provide menus, say, it cannot be user-friendly! Designers provide systems with $n + 1$ features often for no better reason than because rivals provide systems with n features. User interface features cannot be evaluated independently of the entire context and purpose of interaction. If a user is colour blind, colour coding is a disadvantage; if a task involves working in a group, then speech or sounds directed at a single user may be inappropriate; if the environment is such that the user needs his hands for other purposes, then speech is a good idea.

Generally a system becomes easier to use *for a designer* as more capability is added. Contrariwise, a system becomes harder *for a user* the more that needs to be learnt—and the more that can be done accidentally. Interactive systems often have an excess of technical options; users are not necessarily computer experts nor wish to become so by using a system which apparently expects them to be.

One of the more interesting consequences of this confusion is that designers grossly underestimate the potential of special-purpose peripherals. A good bitmap display, a general-purpose peripheral, can do almost anything, having high graphical functionality, but it may be hard to use precisely because the user does not know what it can do, or how it will do it.

7.9   You can't see programs

Once a system is running, it can be sold and used, without anyone ever realizing the underlying mess—or elegance! Commercial software houses often have clauses in their licensing emphasizing that they are not liable for any undesirable features of their program: even they do not know what it can do (see Chapter 18).

Imagine that you have just designed a system, and you invite someone to try it out. They give it a quick try and then try to do something you had never intended the system to do. Or perhaps you have been the user in such a situation: you wanted to do something that you thought could be done, but the system provided no support for your task? The situations are rather like someone jumping into a jeep and trying to drive it like a racing car. *Obviously* jeeps excel racing cars off the road, but if you want to accelerate to high speeds you are better in a turbo-charged racer. But few people would get in a jeep with expectations so awry: jeeps and racers look rather different (though both of them might be equally bad from a human factors point of view).

Programs, unlike cars, cannot be seen; there is no visible 'style' for a program—you have to run it to find out what it is like. Even then, you do not really know what it is like, as this following example makes clear:

Like many other university departments ours puts on a show for the public every so often. The problem is, how do you show people what computing is *really* like? For if you demonstrate a system that can be understood (or is easy to use), you are open to the criticism that a ten-year-old could have done it better, or that similar programs can be bought at the little micro-computer store down town. Why, then, do you need a computing science department? This might be called the **building bricks problem**. Playing with building bricks does not give someone much idea about real, full-scale, building. The complexity of computer programs cannot be seen as easily as the complexity of real buildings, and this results either in people thinking they know more than they do (the public show problem) or in knowing less than they want (the normal user interface problem).

The 'you can't see programs' problem is the so-called **frame problem**: a problem of knowledge representation. How do you represent the 'right' information for each purpose? Consider, say, climbing into a car. First of all, perhaps you will check that the car is not completely full of people (but you want it to be full of air); then you might check that the car is manual or automatic, but you don't check whether the seats face forwards or backwards. Clearly there are a vast number of checks you *might* make to convince yourself that this thing is indeed a drivable car, but you do not make more than a rather small number of checks.

The frame problem is about making changes to knowledge efficiently, given that there is an enormous amount of knowledge (for example, about cars) out there. Because there is a von Neumann bottleneck, it is not practical for a computer to examine much of its knowledge to perform 'trivial' tasks; similarly, because there is a user interface bottleneck, it is not practical for a user to know much about the system he is using.

'You can't see programs' suggests that the impenetrability of computer systems is a disadvantage. Well, one man's loss is another's gain: designers *may* exploit the hiddenness of programs to make systems appear better than they are. This trick escalates to a problem, the 'out of sight, out of mind' problem, when the designer, too, is caught up in the deception, and loses sight of the complexity of the system. The result may be more error prone in use.

7.10 Ergonomics is experimentally based

Technology continues to outstrip any experimental basis. This is not entirely true, but sound experiments are rare and are usually highly specific in their terms of reference. As designers are usually not experimental scientists, it

---

Box 7.2   A simple-looking interface.

A fax (a facsimile machine, telecopier) is a cross between a photocopier and a telephone. A user can ring up another fax, and copy text or pictures from one place to another. To sell such systems, it is an advantage if they appear to be simple and, by implication, easy to use. They certainly need a keyboard adequate to perform the telephoning function: normally ten digits plus two special characters (hash and star). Maybe we can assume that our users are more sophisticated, and might expect telephone-type features like last number redial—this will add one or two more buttons.

A common problem with a fax is that the receiving machine is busy. The user transmitting therefore wants to delay the copy until the receiving machine is ready. So fax machines, since they have a computer inside anyway, are provided with all sorts of features, like delayed dialling, polling, page counting and error correction. *If* there were buttons for each feature the system would look complex; if there were a QWERTY keyboard (which could obviously be used to construct any command) the system might look like the user had to learn a language. Instead, the manufacturer might decide to stay with the modestly enhanced telephone style keyboard. This *looks* easy to the purchaser. But to access the more advanced features will require learning some very obscure conventions: for instance, how to use the ten digits to enter the alphabetic names of stored numbers.

---

is therefore very easy for them to over-generalize naïvely from experimental results (and their own personal experience). Designers are often not in a position to distinguish between mere anecdote and respectable experiment.

It is quite proper that ergonomics is experimental. Suppose we have a group of users here who are operating at 50% of some objective level of performance possible with the system they are using. The reason for their low performance is that some commands are never used and that certain sequences of commands are used in a particularly inefficient manner. So the system is redesigned (the *system* redesign might include new training). The experimental ergonomist would now say that *this* new system needs further experiments: the effect of the redesign might be counterfinal (see below, Section 7.12)—for instance, the users may have chosen to operate below some theoretical level of efficiency for other reasons, and the new efficiencies expected of them might, for instance, so pressurize them that job turnover increases. Increased job turnover in turn means higher organizational costs in training; thus the increased efficiency at the interface is traded for higher training costs.

The last point has apparently defined ergonomics in such a way as to exclude the possibility of it providing useful contributions! I am reminded that the early 1950s efforts at formula translation (parsing) were categorized as artificial intelligence until they were better understood. Almost by definition, AI cannot be a useful branch of computer science, since anything that is useful is immediately appropriated by the rest of computer science. So it may be with ergonomics: any result that is sufficiently constructive for interactive systems design purposes is—by definition—computer science.

7.11 Schismogenesis

Schismogenesis is the sort of interaction between two parties where one reacts to the other in such a way that each further provokes the other. Imagine a restrictive sort of dialogue where the user might easily fall into a role of feeling helpless (the system is out of control), so requiring the system to control the dialogue further. Now the user feels even more at a loss. Imagine a database system which structures its help in the form of a database: asking for help could mean that the user needs help even to operate the help system—and he might quickly lose sight of his original goals. Text editors often present help text via the editor, often using the same interface.

To avoid schismogenesis, the user needs additional information, training or documentation, and most likely collaboration with the designer—that is, cooperative design. The user requires **metainformation** about a dialogue to understand its as-it-were intentions and the best way to respond to its quirks.

The **Prisoners' Dilemma**, a non-zero sum game, is the classic example where there is no obvious rational strategy for either player (call them the designer and user) *unless* there is some common agreement made outside the terms of the 'game' itself.[2] Computer systems are *par excellence* systems that play by 'the rules', and they almost certainly do not provide the user enough information about themselves for the user to 'play' rationally, or at least to the user's best advantage. The bandwidth of the user interface is barely enough for the dialogue itself, let alone for allowing the user to form a goal-oriented model of the system—even if such a purposive model could be deduced from the facts available at the interface.

The Prisoners' Dilemma becomes interesting when it is played with the same prisoners several times. This is the so-called **Iterated Prisoners' Dilemma**. This naturally arises in commerce and other social transactions. Each 'prisoner', or manufacturer, can then use his knowledge of how the others behaved earlier to help choose the current best policy. The game

[2] **Prisoners' Dilemma**: Imagine two prisoners arrested on suspicion of the same crime. They are separately confined in isolation, and are told that making statements will help their case. Since a crime was committed, let us suppose that each prisoner would like to make a statement exonerating himself but implicating the other. If they *both* make such a statement at least one of them must be lying, and both would be tried; if only one makes the statement, he might be set free because his evidence convicts the other; but if neither makes a statement, each misses out on the possibility of being released immediately (see Axelrod, 1984).

Box 7.3   Organizational deception.

People working in organizations are generally responsible to more senior personnel. Since time is limited and workers generally want to create a good impression with their management, there is a problem that the managers confuse the successful end results, which they are told about, with the work actually undertaken to achieve those results.

For example, much of an emergency call telephonist's time handling emergency calls is spent calming the caller, who may be in quite a panic. But, from the management perspective, the operator is merely producing factual information about fires, burglaries, and so on. There are many other examples, almost all where the workers gain their job satisfaction at least in part from smoothing out irregularities in applying official procedures to everyday circumstances.

Now, management is in a position to specify the requirements of computer systems introduced into the organization. Managers are likely to try to computerize what they think is done, rather than what is actually done. Once their idea of what goes on is embedded into a computer, the workers are then forced into particular ways of operating which may greatly reduce their efficiency and job satisfaction.

In the telephone operator example, the management decided that word processors would help the telephonists. In the original scheme *after* each call, during which the telephonist would take shorthand notes, the telephonist would type up the factual details from her notes and then send them to the relevant service departments. The management assumed that the telephonists' product could be made more efficiently by imposing a computer system that facilitated typing *during* a call, this would speed up production of one of the few tangible parts of the telephonists' work that management actually saw.

The result was that telephonists (after a short experiment) returned to working in their old ways, taking shorthand notes and then typing them up. The reason being that one of the 'helpful' things the computer did was to time-stamp the message, supposedly saving the telephonist doing it. As originally designed, the time-stamp was made when the telephonist *started* typing—and if the caller took half an hour to explain the circumstances (being in a panic they may need some help to describe the address the fire engine must go to!), it might well look as if the telephonist was a very slow typist!

---

becomes interesting because the 'prisoners' may try to cooperate to get the best results for both of them now, or one may choose to punish the other for being exploitative at an earlier stage of play. Each prisoner may try to infer the other's strategy for cooperation or exploitation, trying to act to his own *long-term* advantage—at the same time trying to convey the best impression to encourage the other to cooperate in the future. Fortunately most interactive systems do not get so introspective—but adaptive systems, that try to adapt to their users (for example, becoming verbose after a series of errors) may have surprises in store for their users.

The generalization of the Prisoners' Dilemma to any number of 'prisoners' is the **Free Rider's Paradox**—from an individual point of view, the best thing seems to be a 'free rider', but from the higher, socially aware position, knowing the long-term effects of free riding suggests more circumspect behaviour. The individual point of view corresponds to the prisoner in the Prisoners' Dilemma cheating his accomplice, to his own advantage but to all other prisoners' disadvantage. A free riding user is a problem whenever there are shared resources. For example on a timesharing system, everything a user does slows the system down a bit for everyone. A free rider would therefore conclude that the best results are obtained when he does as much as he possibly can, even though, alternatively, his doing less would generally mean that *in total* everyone got more done. We will meet the free rider paradox again in the Epilogue (Chapter 18): it is one reason why manufacturers do not make very good interactive software.

7.12 Counterfinality

Even when we have perfect information and are able to make perfect decisions, we may still make mistakes: the consequences of our decisions may have unfortunate, unwanted, or so-called **counterfinal** effects.

Three examples are mentioned below.

▷ First, OS/360 is often thought to be a horrendous operating system; it is certainly extremely complex. Now, suppose that the designers of OS/360 had been able to pay more attention to human factors issues, and had in fact been able to produce an easy to use system. That would have meant that the whole profession of helpers and consultants that has grown up around OS/360 would never have happened. The very grottiness of OS/360 has been sufficient to base whole career structures on! The fact that OS/360's complexity ensures that some people know lots about it, and others are helpless perhaps made it all the more successful.

▷ For the second example, consider an operating system that is far simpler, UNIX. UNIX was initially designed as a portable operating system. It rapidly moved onto the PDP-11, and then became widely popular and spread to many systems. But its very portability has led to a terrific diversity in implementations and versions. UNIX, because of its very portability, is no longer portable, in the sense that you'll be lucky if a program written on one UNIX system will run on another. The same story could be told about Pascal or Scheme (an originally simple dialect of LISP).

▷ Last, consider MS-DOS. In the 1980s, everyone accedes that MS-DOS has an out-of-date user interface. So when a new computer is advertised, you would expect the manufacturer to claim that not only does the hardware represent a great advance, but the software has been improved also. But what happens is that the adverts are careful to claim that the hardware, improved beyond recognition, nevertheless remains entirely compatible with MS-DOS, warts and all. In other words, because MS-DOS is difficult to use, and therefore users can be assumed to have learned to cope with its idiosyncrasies, it is better to keep its idiosyncrasies than improve on it. If MS-DOS is improved on, users will have to learn something else, and they probably suspect that the 'improvement' will, in the end, be just as difficult to learn. The counterfinal effect is that the aspects of a system that make it difficult to use become the very aspects that make people retain it!

7.13 Conclusions

Almost all of the design problems we have met arise from poor communication: low bandwidth between the designer and user. This results in assumptions filling in the missing information. Worse, they may be *unconscious and unstated* assumptions that, if ever noticed, are too easily rationalized. There is little hard knowledge around to help designers and so designers tend to design for themselves. It is the *basis* of ergonomics that the designer cannot rely on his intuition—yet he needs intuition to innovate and produce a distinctive product.

It is interesting that the goals of design are very similar to the goals of interaction, a point first raised in Section 2.1. Conversely, many of the techniques for interaction (for example, undo, natural language) might be profitably used—with the same caution—in the design process. Would it not be nice if the user could use a clear natural language dialogue to establish the requirements of the design, and when it goes wrong, use undo? Or would direct manipulation be better?

Chapter 8

Attitudes to design

The meaning of things lies not in the things themselves but in
our attitude towards them.   *Antoine de Saint-Exupéry*

Design is difficult, so designers tend to take a stance as they cope with the
complexity of the design process. This chapter explores attitudes to design
and some of the consequences for the user interface.

8.1 Levels of intellectual sophistication

If you ask a 'knowledgeable' person which text editor (spreadsheet,
operating system, computerized teaching package, programming language,
and so on) he thinks is the best one, he will be able to come up with a
limitless list of irrefutable reasons why his chosen system is best, and how
it excels any editor you might personally prefer. And vice versa: if you
ask someone which his least liked system is and why. It becomes clear,
on reflection, that designing a user interface is an optimization problem,
and unless there is agreement on the terms of optimization, that is, what
things are important, no constructive discussion can follow. When problems
arise in the use of interactive systems, it is probably because user and
designer have different perspectives and different objective functions. The
strongest opinions are often expressed by people who fail to distinguish
clearly between user and designer roles. These were the issues of Chapter 7.

What is *right*; what design is *right*? Our approach to doing design
is often not very sophisticated; we are too naïve, over-simplify, and expect
right and wrong answers immediately.

Box 8.1   There are no standards.

There are no standards by which the designer can judge his success, or use
it to help him improve designs; far less are there standards for training
or assessing designers. Sometimes this will mean that designers become
over-confident: they *know* what is right. Yet centuries of design practice
have only led to two forms of training: apprenticeship and vicarious
apprenticeship by reading biographies and case studies. If there was more
certain knowledge it would be written down ...

Following Willema Perry (1970), students' attitudes to knowledge are
said to develop through **levels of intellectual sophistication**. Following
Perry's choice of names for these levels, 'Position 0' is the least sophisticated
level of intellectual sophistication ranging through levels of increasing
sophistication to 'Position 9' of greatest sophistication. We will use the
labels to discuss the increasing intellectual sophistication of a designer of
interactive systems.

Although Perry charitably starts at Position 1, for our purposes it
is useful to start at Position 0 where there is no intellectual sophistication.
Here designers just forge ahead and build a system. There are no user
interface issues as such; no problems or tradeoffs arise about what the
user interface should be like, it simply emerges as a consequence of the
programming, probably as an extension of the debugging. The designer
does not pause to wonder whether the system could be easier to use, for it
has the right features to sell; it does what is needed (for example, by having
enough functions), but *how* it does it for the user is not a design issue.

Next, at Position 1 we are aware of such issues and start to seek
their answers. Position 1 is characterized by seeing the world in clear-cut
terms: 'we-right' versus 'others-wrong'. Answers are yes/no. For a person
at this particular level in a particular subject, there are right answers to
all problems. Authorities, such as teachers or authors of research papers,
know the right answers. The problem for the discerning designer is to find
the right courses, books or research reports where he supposes he can find
the right answers for his design problems. The designer perceives that the
main blockage to his progress is his lack of definite knowledge: the more
techniques (metaphors, paradigms, user-models, algorithms) he knows the
better equipped he will be to design better interactive systems.

This first level of sophistication can be most damaging when designers
work in teams—either concurrently or independently but on a single system
over a period of time. One designer may easily be convinced that his
ideas are *right*, and who wouldn't be after expending so much effort
(cognitive dissonance)? It seems better to provide his 'super' facilities
than compatibility with the rest. It is often impractical to rewrite existing

software (and rewriting would also mean retraining users), so as time goes on, systems become more and more fragmented precisely because of a euphemistic 'policy of continuous improvement'. This sort of creeping featurism knows no bounds on modern computer systems; at least early computers did not have enough memory to support all of the features the designer would have liked to pack in—modern computers are too easy to program!

By Position 2, the designer is becoming more sophisticated: he realizes that authorities disagree on some things. However the designer thinks at least one of the authorities must be right.

By Position 3, the designer accepts differences between authorities and accepts the uncertainty as legitimate but temporary. At this point the designer starts following up and reading the references in research reports. It appears that the right answers have not yet been found.

By Position 4, either the designer realizes that uncertainty is legitimate, but confined to those areas where people have a right to their own opinions; or the designer realizes that reasoning is relativistic. The designer only accepts that reasoning is relativistic because that is what the authorities say!

By Position 5, the designer sees all knowledge and values, including authorities', as contextual and relativistic. He still accepts the right–wrong view of design as being appropriate in some areas.

By Position 6, the designer sees that he must orientate himself through some form of considered commitment, for which he alone is responsible. The designer has realized that there is a difference between technique ('manner of execution', *Oxford English Dictionary*) and design ('purpose, intention', *Oxford English Dictionary*).

It is perhaps easy to read through these levels of intellectual sophistication and decide on your 'considered commitment' in order to reach Position 7 rapidly. Position 7 is attained when the designer has made his initial commitment. Obviously one should be committed to expert user-friendly menu-based systems with icons and mice, maybe bitmapped colour displays with knowledge-based user interface management systems. It is then only a short step to proclaim the universal merit of this commitment; perhaps expert systems are *the right* answer to the muddle of interactive systems design. That is a fall back to a Position 1 level of intellectual sophistication! The sort of commitment the designer should be making by Position 7 is a personal commitment, which will affect his whole approach to design and will bring into prominence certain design issues which he now considers especially worthy of attention.

Perry's final Positions 8 and 9 are related more specifically to personal growth. Computing, specifically human–computer interaction as a discipline, is not neutral. It is extraordinary that the two disciplines which are combined in interactive systems design, computing and ergonomics, both stem largely from military initiatives and requirements for more effective hardware and more effective exploitation of human behaviour and performance. The designer is, perhaps most so in the user interface field, implicitly an agent for social change and he should intentionally guide the transition to a humane, paperless, networked, ... worldwide society. For this, he needs a personal commitment. By Perry's Position 8 the designer is experiencing the consequences of his commitment and is exploring the responsibilities this position carries.

By Position 9, the designer has gained a self-identity through his commitment and, furthermore, has realized that his own commitment is dynamic and, indeed, expresses his lifestyle.

You may wish to compare the changing view of knowledge over the range of levels of intellectual sophistication with the contrasting epistemologies ranging over reductionism to phenomenology discussed in Section 2.3 and Box 2.1.

8.2   Theories X and Y

Early computer systems were expensive and centralized: an organization might have one computer shared between several users—often the users would be in the organization's data processing department, and in any case would have carefully circumscribed job descriptions. It would never do to squander the investment in the computer by failing to control its users and uses. Programs designed to run in such environments generally emphasize that the system (the computer or the organization) is in control.

Increasingly, computers cost less; desktop machines compete in apparent power with mainframes; and so there is less centralized control over the work of users. Indeed, many computer users are discretionary— they perhaps bought home micros on their own volition, to do with as they please. Programs designed to run on home computers emphasize that the user is in control.

D. McGregor (1960) proposed a simple binary classification of views of human nature, which he termed **Theory X** and **Theory Y**. His starting point was that behind every management decision there underlies a 'theory' of human personality. Thus these theories are not to be taken as theories in a scientific sense: X and Y are names for the generally unexpressed models in people's heads (generally the manager's) about what is best for other people (generally his employees). (They are theories in Popper's World 3— see Chapter 9 for more discussion.) The ideas are interesting from our perspective because designers (and their clients) carry similar notions about what is best for users.

8.2.1 Theory X

The basic assumption of the Theory X view is that people dislike work and avoid it if they possibly can; therefore most people must be coerced, controlled, directed—even threatened—to get them to work and to put effort into organizational objectives. McGregor points out that rewards have a short-lived effect and that punishment can be used as a far more reliable incentive. Finally, the adherent to Theory X assumes that people *like* to be directed, want to avoid responsibility, and above all want security. This is projected cognitive dissonance.

There is circumstantial evidence that people do behave like this, and that Theory X is a reasonable working view. Of course, it is in part a self-fulfilling theory: if you treat people like this, they are likely to lose motivation and must therefore be coerced.

Man can be viewed as an animal of needs; first of all, we need the necessities of life: air, water and food. If these needs are not met, we become hungry and finding sustenance becomes of major importance. But when those physiological needs are properly satisfied, we are conscious of higher needs. Each in turn can become sated, and we become motivated by still higher goals, such as self-respect, creativity, development and in general **self-actualization**. The Theory X approach to work simply keeps workers at a lower level than they need be, for this makes needs at that level explicit and more easily controlled. Once sated, a worker would only be influenced by punishment if rewards at higher levels were not available.

8.2.2 Theory Y

There is no question that the Theory X approach, exemplified by monotonous paced work on production lines, has brought benefit to us all. But could things have been done better? Theory Y is an alternative and recognizes people as humans, rather than mere animals of need.

The assumptions of Theory Y contrast with Theory X. Under Theory Y, the expenditure of physical and mental energy in work is seen as natural as play or rest—thus the average person does not dislike work. Work may be a source of satisfaction; external controls (such as threat of punishment or offer of reward) are not the only means for directing effort— man can exercise self-control and self-direction in the service of objectives to which he is committed; people seek and accept responsibility; the average person has greater capacity for imagination, creativity and problem solving than he is normally permitted to utilize. The intellectual, physical and social capacities of the average human are only partly fulfilled in modern life.

McGregor makes an interesting point about integration: both the organization's and the individual's needs must be recognized and a sincere effort made to meet them. If not, both suffer.

Box 8.2   The 'human factor' euphemism.

To be successful a computer system must benefit at least somebody, so **human factors** are *necessarily* involved in the design and assessment of systems. Nevertheless, hardware and software designers may be ignorant even of elementary human factors; worse, they may be ignorant even of this ignorance—and so on recursively! People often compensate for ignorance by using intuition. And in the case of designers, their training and personal attitudes may magnify the unfortunate consequences.

The user is perceived all too often as a source of trouble; many of his troubles, if noted by anyone at all, are classified as irrelevant to the functional specification of the interface. The consequences are dismissed as the user's personal responsibility. This point of view is summarized by the succinct phrase, 'You asked for it, you've got it' (shades of Bellerophon).

A well-known system provides two two-letter commands, one edits a file and the other deletes it. The commands differ only in their first letters, which are adjacent on the standard QWERTY keyboard. If the designer can argue that there is nothing wrong with the user interface from a technical point of view, any faults must surely lie with its users.

Human Factors is often, incorrectly, supposed to be concerned about making systems for people. It isn't. Human Factors is about enabling people to make more effective systems for people; enabling designers to make more effective systems for users. Seen like this, Human Factors is obviously 'done' by the designer. The usual understanding encourages the strange view that Human Factors somehow magically changes systems on its own—that is, Human Factors is always someone else's job.

8.3   Condescension in 'ease of use'

Making computers easier to use is certainly a rational design policy if the designer subscribes to some form of Theory Y. If, however, the situation for which an interactive system is being supplied conforms to the views of Theory X (for example, a typical production line), it is not clear how conventional views of ease of use will improve the users' lives. There is the danger that 'improving' part of the users' lives (that is, the part they spend working with computers) will have a negative effect on other parts (see counterfinality, Section 7.12). For instance, if a new computer system really is easier to use, shouldn't users' productivity increase, or their error rate drop, and would this mean that management perhaps exerts pressure to maintain that higher performance? What happens if users, for their own reasons, want to maintain the *status quo*?

Figure 8.1   A typical under-determined dialogue.

8.4   Dialogue determination

What sort of systems correspond to McGregor's alternate theories of management? If the designer adheres to Theory X, he will tend to build **over-determining** systems; if he adheres to Theory Y, he will tend to build **well-determining** and possibly **under-determining** systems (Thimbleby, 1980).

8.4.1   Under-determination

An under-determined dialogue is mystifying. The user knows what he ultimately wants to do but not how to express his subtasks for the computer. He does not know what the computer is requesting nor at what level it is functioning. The computer is failing to help or guide the user. He does not know what to do next and is effectively disabled. Figure 8.1 shows an under-determining screen.

Though Figure 8.1 is manifestly under-determining for a command-based interface, in a direct manipulation interface, however, the user is not under-determined. Rather, he cannot do anything because there is nothing to manipulate! A direct manipulation interface, then, cannot stoop to the extremes of under-determination possible in some other interface styles.

In short the computer is unnecessarily or inappropriately secretive. The basis of the dialogue is insufficiently defined for the user to operate adequately.

8.4.2   Over-determination

When the dialogue is over-determined the user is unnaturally constrained into expressing more subtasks in an unrelated sequence in terms of *his* model of the intended dialogue. He may not be allowed to do tasks his way with his sequencing and his structuring—or even at all. For example, the user has just entered a date, the computer says it is wrong, and asks for another date. The user is trapped, unable to get help or other information from the system until he has successfully entered a date the computer is satisfied with.

Over-determination *can* be exploited to help the user avoid termination errors, but more likely the user will be forced into apparently *unrelated* activities (and it is likely that the dialogue will then become under-determined). Thus he is forced to reformulate his task and thereby lose sight of his primary goals. The result is that the user is strained, which will reduce his ability to orient himself to the computer-defined schemata—engendering more and more deterioration in the dialogue. Clearly it is difficult to operate using an over-determined dialogue, perhaps it is less clear that it can give rise to personal feelings of lack of freedom.

In short, the computer is unnecessarily or inappropriately authoritarian. More definition (rigidity) than is necessary is imposed on the user.

8.4.3   Well-determined design

When I say that the **system** is secretive or authoritarian I am not implying that the computer is the scapegoat for the design decisions made by designers. Both $\frac{\text{over}}{\text{under}}$ determination are ways to conceal the responsibility of the decisions behind the machine interface, and this manipulation does in fact deskill the user.

Humans have considerable conversational skills and part of the problem of having a dialogue with machines is that they do not have the same skills. Indeed, the way the computer works often tends to invalidate the person's skills. Determination is a concept borrowed from interpersonal psychology: it is closely related to the sociotechnical systems principle of **minimum task specification** which states that for optimal work satisfaction, no more than the minimum necessary should be specified for each individual worker.

Dialogue determination helps distinguish between information (an objective measure) and informativeness (a subjective measure). It is easy to provide the user with information that is not informative, and paradoxically, providing more information may make it less informative. Consider trying to tell the user the value of π. The system could display, 3·141 592 653 589 793 238 462 643 383 279 502 884, and perhaps a bit more. *Now*, did you read all of it? Can you remember the 18th digit? Given the time you wanted to spend reading it, it might have been as informative to present the value as 3, *and* you would have had more time to digest other information. So presenting *less* information may make the user interface *more* informative. The difference between informativeness and information is called **clutter**.

There is a correspondence between dialogue determination and Marshall McLuhan's classification of media into **hot** and **cool**. With a hot medium for carrying messages the meaning is delivered in the message itself; whereas in a cool medium the meaning is furnished more by the person receiving the message. The hotter a medium the more it denies the receiver (that is, the user, if the medium is a human–computer interface) choice and participation in its interpretation. There is clearly some connection between these 'thermal' distinctions and the earlier distinctions between imperative and declarative paradigms (Section 4.4.1): an imperative system tends to come across as a hot medium; a declarative system tends to come across as cool. McLuhan used his terminology to help explain insights into, for instance, the contrast between the effect of television and oil painting. A hot medium tends to be over-determining and a cool one under-determining.

A computer is powerful enough to exhibit any behaviour, so the user has less confidence that it will exhibit any *particular* behaviour. The **human window** is the range of implementation which is neither too shallow (devoid of explanation, under-determined) nor too deep (incomprehensible, over-determined). Broadly speaking, the implementation method shifts the human window: shallowness is often due to excessive use of data (the system, at best, appears to be rote), and depth to excessive use of computation (the system's algorithms have to be understood). It is interesting to note that two of the earliest computer systems envisaged were at opposite poles of the human window. Vannevar Bush's (1945) vision, **Memex**, was shallow, being all user interface. The Memex was a large multiple-medium database system, but it behaved little better than an electronic encyclopedia: it did not compute in a visible sense. But Turing's Machine (of eight years earlier) was deep, all semantics and no user interface whatsoever. We looked at it in Chapter 5.

8.4.4 Extremes may be good

An example of a *useful* over-determining system is one that attempts to reduce the consequences of user (or machine) errors. It asks questions it knows the answer to or could have deduced from previous responses; perhaps it requires the user to perform his tasks in a certain order to reduce the probability of termination errors. Also, over-determination is useful if there is some reason not to trust the user, or not to trust his stated identity— requesting passwords over-determines users but is frequently a good check against fraud.

An under-determining system will effectively stop system-naïve users doing much that is useful. Conversely, if the input to a system is through using a menu (Section 15.2.7), an untrained person would be able to construct valid commands quite easily without knowing what he was doing—this is less likely when the system gives no clues about how it works. Indeed, the more obscure the interface, in whatever ways, the harder unauthorized users will find it too. Many users will enjoy the challenge of under-determining systems, although this depends to a great extent on the availability of reasonable documentation and social determinants.

The quality and effectiveness of the dialogue is personal: what is good or liked by a skilled user is unlikely to be appropriate for a computer-naïve user and vice versa. We want to

▷ **Avoid under-determining dialogues**: for instance, by providing help where necessary, by reducing the number of options open to the user—perhaps by requiring his responses to the system in a particular fixed order.

▷ **Avoid over-determining dialogues**: for instance, by abbreviating help (or ultimately not showing it at all), by permitting the user to undertake many interleaved activities in any order in a way to suit himself (compare VLIW systems, Section 4.2.3).

▷ **Maintain well-determined dialogues**: a well-determining system must, in general, provide ways to support alternative styles of interaction—or, at least, get the user's tasks done so efficiently that interaction with the computer is not significant compared with the rest of the user's responsibilities.

Or, if none of these, wait, hoping. The user will always adapt to the given system.

What is under-determining today may become over-determining later. The same dialogue may be under-determined for one user and over-determined for another user, or even the same user at another time: an ideal computer system should adapt itself (or should have been adapted in the design stages) to the specific needs of the users, even on a day-to-day basis.

8.5   Personality types

Theories X and Y are different stances about personality and human motivation. People themselves, not just their views, vary considerably! It is particularly important to realize that there are personality differences between designer and user and to anticipate the consequences of these on whether the system under- or over-determines the user.

It is obvious that the job roles of users can be very different. Some users may be managers, who only want help in making decisions, but are not interested in computers; some users may be keyboard operators who have no choice but to use computers; some users may be specialists in some areas and choose to use computers to further their goals (for example, for geological analysis); and some users may be computer experts designing for any class of user, including themselves. Each class of user has different needs with respect to computer interaction. Some may suffer from loss of motivation and interest from over-familiarity; whereas some may only use a system casually, and suffer from not being able to recall the intricacies of the system, and so on. People differ not only by externally imposed constraints, such as we have just discussed, but also by their internal approach. It is arguable that internal (mental) personality differences between designer and user *exceed* externally imposed role differences: in any case, it is certain that personality differences are the more subtle, and deserve more careful consideration. Equivalently we could argue that external differences, say between different sorts of job, are partly chosen by the person's disposition to certain styles of environment complementary to their personality. The designer may prefer certain aspects of a system certain ways, not because of some absolute judgement or knowledge about the user's job, but because of traits in his personality. When these traits differ significantly from the user's own, the user interface may not be used so effectively. Clearly the designer should have some way of talking about these issues.

Carl Jung identified four dimensions by which to assess people's personalities. We will use the terminology from the **Myers–Briggs Type Indicator**, a system developed from Jung's and routinely used for personality assessment, for instance for job counselling (Myers and Myers, 1980). There are, of course, many dimensions we could use to evaluate users (for example, How do they take risks? What is their hand–eye coordination? How old are they? Have they a technical training?) but the present dimensions have the advantage that they are significant and, as we will show, there are analogies with computational strategies. Interactive programs, too, can be classified using analogous dimensions— though convention and propriety would lead us to use somewhat different terminology. There are four dimensions, as follows.

▷ **Judging/Perceiving**: A judging type makes decisions as soon as possible; a perceiving type of person would consider it a waste of time deciding what to do when the situation may still change. Put another way, a judging person looks for **goals** in life; a perceiving person is interested in the **processes**. In a tradeoff between means and ends, a perceiving personality will emphasize the means, a judging personality the ends ('the ends justify the means'). A judging type of person is generally interested in goals: in making and having goals; whereas a perceiving type of person would be more interested in the process, and might never make the decisions necessary to recognize attainment of his own 'goals'. Computationally: judging corresponds to eager evaluation; perceiving corresponds to lazy evaluation.

If, of two people, one person is a judging type and the other a perceiving type, then the judging one will tend to over-determine the perceiving one in all his instructions. Conversely, when the perceiving type takes the initiative, he will tend to under-determine the judging type. This is often a source of friction in relationships; in user interface design, it can result in user interfaces that trap their users in a style of dialogue that they find most frustrating, and hence which they use inefficiently.

▷ **Sensing/Intuiting**: Sensing personalities tend to rely on external stimuli to make decisions (for example, by measurements or questions); intuiting personalities make decisions with less reference to external events. Computationally: sensing corresponds to interactive processing; intuiting corresponds to batch processing. An intuitive type of person may be annoyed if nothing is left to the imagination when using a system, whereas a sensing sort of person may be annoyed if everything is not explicitly stated. (Sensing types tend to over-determine intuiting types.)

▷ **Thinking/Feeling**: A thinking person has explicit reasons for doing things, whereas a feeling person has hunches. Thinking people tend to rely on verbal thought processes. Put another way, the thinking user wants to understand a system before using it; a feeling user would happily use a system in order to 'get the feel of it'—to understand it. Computationally: thinking corresponds to algorithmic strategies; feeling corresponds to heuristic strategies, also to the sort of computation performed by neural networks. (Thinking types tend to over-determine feeling types.)

Rationalization is the conversion of feeling into thinking (serialization, if we consider intuition to be parallel processing). Rationalization is necessary because without it there would be no way to justify intuition to other people.

Of a design, a predominantly sensing type of user would like it to be workable, a thinker would like it to be systematic, a feeling type would like it to be humanly agreeable, and intuitive types would like scope for development in the design. A perceptive type would want a system that can be enjoyed; a judgemental type would want a system from which results can be obtained.

People are oriented in outlook by these types, but their source of information may come from within or without. They may be more concerned with their mental worlds or they may be more concerned with the world at large. This brings us to the introvert–extrovert dimension:

▷ **Extrovert/Introvert**: Extrovert personalities get their 'energy' (what motivates them) from outside; introverts get their energy from themselves. Curiously, an introvert may have a strong outgoing personality, since he perhaps has more to say and is less dependent on others' approval of his actions than an extrovert. Computationally: extroversion is being input/output bound; introversion is being compute bound. (Extroverted types tend to over-determine introverted types.)

Note that the terms have technical meanings that differ from normal usage. Thus, in colloquial use, an introvert is shy; but by technical use an introvert merely directs his attention inwards by preference. Whether he becomes withdrawn in demanding social situations is another question: an introvert might be quite able as an outgoing person, but likely he would not try to be one. The colloquial usage of the terms is superficial, it is about how people seem; the technical usage is deep, it is about how people implement their behaviour.

It is interesting to locate the 'implementation' of these personality traits in the anatomy of mind. Thus, the sensing function is located in the lower brain stem; the feeling function in the limbic system. Conscious thinking occurs in the left hemisphere (in most people, particularly right-handed people) and intuition probably occurs in the right hemisphere.

People are generally assessed along the dimensions by using questionnaires. Many hundreds of questions are asked to identify trends, since certain concrete situations that the questions are about may push people into atypical responses. A question trying to identify a thinking/feeling trend might ask, given some situation, whether the person considers fairness is preferable to mercy. The power of the personality type idea is that by asking specific questions a questionnaire can identify habitual traits (judging, perceiving, and so on) that generalize to other situations such as interacting with computers.

Naturally people's personality types tend to guide them towards their profession: they may choose a vocation that best fits their personalities. Thus a designer should be especially aware that his personality type is almost certainly different from the personality types of the users of the systems he designs. For example, a designer is likely to be an intuitive thinker, but a bank employee is likely to be a sensing thinker, and a nurse is likely to be a feeling senser. Or, rather, a person with developed traits in feeling and sensing will have a disposition to work in an area like nursing, rather than work in computer system design. This means that, as a rule, managers (the people who control the choice of systems bought for users), designers and users will each have fundamentally different views of what constitutes a good system. This underlines the seriousness of the ergonomics issue (Section 7.2).

Most interactive systems are written in imperative languages and a thinking/judging style of design follows naturally. *Thinking* because of the planning to ensure the algorithms used in the implementation are correct; *judging* because all choices in the dialogue are fixed and must be evaluated in the same order as the program expects them (that is, eagerly). This tends to result in inflexible interaction: dialogues have to proceed in fixed paths with predetermined order. A language such as Pascal, particularly with its awkward input/output conventions, further encourages introvert design. This type of design appeals to certain users, and is appropriate for certain classes of application (for example, secure or routine).

8.6   Delaying commitment

Designers often forget that design is a series of open choices; too often a design just grows, with no particular reason for each feature, except that its design was decided yesterday. The result, of course, is a system with no coherence, and no chance of getting any. The alternative is to spend more time thinking—scientifically or mathematically, approaches we will examine later in this book—or to employ heuristics that increase freedom and facilitate change. Design freedom is the topic we explore now.

Delaying design commitments is a fundamental approach to computer science and problem solving in general. Programming, as an extreme example, is a means to delay committing hardware to a particular purpose; distributed computing further delays commitment about the location of the hardware. Programmable user interfaces (sometimes called **customizable** or **extensible**) are a means by which the designer can delay some of the final design, the final commitments, to the user. Delaying commitment to a choice of order results in lazy evaluation, a topic we covered in Section 4.3.

Delaying design commitments to the point where they can be properly analysed and justified is essential. At that point, commitment trade-offs should be made explicit and carefully reasoned through.

In many disciplines the difference between amateurs and professionals seems to be that professionals delay their commitments as long as possible. Experts also know how to conceal errors (that is, to delay widespread knowledge of their errors as long as possible)—their skill is as much in repairing errors as knowing the right procedures to avoid them. But amateurs generally try to get things completely right first time (and often fail, trying to solve too many problems at once). Perhaps in their anxiety to avoid error they make early commitments (precommitments)—and often the wrong ones. The experts' postponing firm decisions as long as possible and waiting to discover constraints before filling in details of plans are in fact standard heuristic strategies for coping with interacting goals in problem solving. Often relaxing problem constraints, that is, delaying commitments, leads to new insights.

Two of the personality types, perceiving and judging, correspond to delaying and precommitment strategies. Thus certain people have a tendency to favour delaying commitment as a general strategy for facing life's problems; other people have a tendency to make early commitments; and, of course, balanced people may approach each situation in a way appropriate for them in that situation, neither strategy habitually prevailing. It seems however that most people facing *new* problems have a tendency to make early commitments, to evaluate eagerly, to prejudge. Early commitment is a natural strategy for it tends to reduce both the number and complexity of remaining problems.

Notice that hackers typically choose to know as much as possible about computer systems: eagerly consuming every available piece of information, whether or not they will eventually use it. To make their consuming interest feasible, they have to be committed to a particular sort of computer or operating system—one can only learn a lot about a few things. The term 'hacker' is often used pejoratively, and perhaps few would want to be associated with the extreme, addictive forms hacking sometimes takes. But I should point out that almost all computer scientists when faced with a new system to design, first of all commit themselves to a certain piece of hardware (and often the fastest and most recent). Of course there are generally very practical reasons for doing so: except that early commitment may blind them to more creative designs.

Whatever one's personality or disposition towards persistent judging, deliberately delaying design commitments, even when there is no computer-based method to support it, is a useful design heuristic. Specifically in user interface design, delaying commitments promotes the role of the user in the design process; for, the earlier commitments are made, the less impact the user can have on them. There are, of course, times when you do not want to delay as such (perhaps because of the generality it may impose on the user), but here delaying commitments is a useful design heuristic: it may help suggest alternative approaches to the system design. (Commitment will be picked up again in Section 17.2.1.)

8.7   Iterative design

Which came first, the chicken or the egg? Which comes first, the user's requirements or the system?

Although we want to separate design and use, to do one then the other, and in that order (for that makes both tasks much easier), it is possible that the introduction of a system may so change users' attitudes that maybe the system is not required nor even wanted. The system may have given users new ideas, which is quite possible due to changes in job prospects. More often, the working system will help suggest—or enforce—new ways of working that are better for the user. But adopting such methods would revise the original design tradeoffs.

Generally designers and users do not really know what they want. What users ask for is probably not what they want either. When they get

---

Box 8.3   The next-system trap.

The present system is admittedly bug ridden and inadequate, but the next system will cure the problems. No self-respecting designer will cure problems without being tempted to introduce a few new features which he had always wanted to include but did not understand how to fit in. The result is that the next system is not better but merely different with different problems.

---

an interactive system, it may do what they said they wanted but it may not do it in the way they assumed it would and, now they can see it working, it is not working in the way that they would really have liked. Users tend to assume that a small change to the way a computer does something is easy once the computer can do it, as indeed it often is for humans.

Most user interfaces are implemented in imperative programming languages, so making changes to their interface requires the designer to devise new instructions for the computer to obey. This much is obvious! But over a period of time, *ad hoc* alterations make the program increasingly obscure, and many 'improvements' accidentally introduce other problems— either by simple programming slips or by fundamental problems with the unanticipated interaction of new features, data structures or whatever, with old features (that themselves have probably been changed once or twice). To help the designer manage program development, various normative programming methods are employed. Although there are many, **structured programming** is perhaps the commonest, and also one of the vaguest. Nevertheless structured programming, however it is enforced, is designed to protect systems against unintentional change. It does this largely by introducing redundancy in the structure of a program: for example, Pascal requires the use of a variable to correspond with its declaration. You cannot change the way a variable is used without also changing its declaration, and doing that will help identify other uses of the variable that you have failed to change in the same way. That is one of the simplest techniques.

But if structure programming can protect against unintentional changes, it is equally good at protecting against intentional changes once the system has been tried out! Apparently simple changes have to be effected in many places in the program. After a few iterations the original program structure has disintegrated and user and designer are no longer on speaking terms! Increasingly the fractured structure becomes subverted and the original 'mere design' omissions or errors shift to serious technical implementation errors. Often they are left like that, as bugs that 'are not worth fixing'.

> A feature which is omitted can always be added later, when its design and its implications are well understood. A feature which is included before it is fully understood can never be removed later.

> Earlier attention paid to quite minor requests of our customers might have paid as great dividends of goodwill as the success of our most ambitious plans.   *Tony Hoare*

An initial system may not be acceptable.   Acknowledging this and *deliberately* setting out to repeat a design in the light of feedback from users and other insights gained from real use of a system is called **iterative design**. A system design is tried out on a suitable set of users. The users are watched, quizzed, their ideas solicited and generally scrutinized. Did users persistently make a certain sort of mistake? Was there a common misunderstanding? Did they frequently suggest certain improvements that could be made?   Such information helps the designer improve the next version of the system.   Since this round of improvements may still not lead to a design that is acceptable, or because some of the suggested improvements appear to conflict and cannot all be achieved, the design–use–evaluate process is iterated.

Clearly iterative design is well motivated, and so far as the designers are concerned with users things are likely to improve. Nevertheless, there are several pitfalls:

▷ Iterative design can be unimaginative. Although it may converge to a design far better than the starting design, it may converge to a system differing only in details from the initial design—and these differences may be no more than palliatives, worse they may be no more than unrelated features superficially satisfying user suggestions but together contributing to complexity. A different initial design may well have converged to a far better design. This is a problem of local optimization (satisficing). Iterative design puts design in the hands of users and so is bottom-up (Section 7.6).

▷ Iterative design can be abused. It is cheaper and far easier to get users to detect bugs. They may even suggest nice fixes!

▷ Iterative design may ignore its local impact. Iterative design is more reliable the more users are involved with the evaluation, and the longer they use it: comments and other data will be more useful the closer the evaluation corresponds with realistic use. Each iteration may use different groups of users to avoid bias; some iterations may be controlled, so using several groups of users each employed using variants of the system. The better the iterative design, the greater the number of people affected and the greater the burden on each

---

Box 8.4   Make the user fit the system!

The conventional approved approach to design is to make the system fit
the user. To do this, the needs of the user (or the targeted user group)
must be carefully identified and the system must be evaluated to assess
its impact on the users and their performance and behaviour.

Alternatively, we could approach design by making the user fit the
system.

To do this, we simply design the best system we can and then
advertise it. Those users who want it will acquire the system, and
doubtless be suitably pleased with it. We call such design **non-
deterministic**, particularly after the way in which oracular non-
determinism is used in programming. In programming, oracles make the
right choices (in effect, the programmer is only interested in the oracles
that make the right choice; some may fail but will not be heard about)—in
non-deterministic design, the design has been made 'right' by the selective
choices of the users.

For non-deterministic design to work, two things are required. First,
that there is enough variety on the marketplace for users to have choice;
secondly that the claims made by manufacturers are clear and valid. It is
unfortunate that licensing requirements often make it impossible for users
to test interactive systems for themselves. This bad practice is criticized
in Chapters 9 and 18, but otherwise the ideas expressed in this book are
particularly aimed at creative design and making useful, accurate claims
about interactive systems.

---

user. Of course, if millions of systems are to be sold there will be an
acceptable tradeoff (from the designer's point of view).

▷   Iterative design may be slow. A design *may* be overtaken by changes
in computing technology or even by your competitors producing
a better system first. It might be worth committing to the
present design now. You can then improve its general presentation
(for example, organizing documentation and training courses) and
perhaps beat competitors to a marketable product.

▷   Iterative design makes subtle assumptions about the political control
the designer has over the class of user. Suppose you want to design
a system for streamlining call-outs for a motoring organization. You
already have enough difficulty getting servicemen to come when your
car is broken down. So, what sort of additional problems will you
have getting them to use an incomplete, buggy system (which they
probably cannot use on the move)? Most professionals have a hard
enough time doing their own job *without* helping you do yours.

▷   Commercial interests may be compromised by iterative design. A
company developing a novel interactive system may not want to give

competitors any chance of discovering details. Obviously field testing cannot be used.

▷ Iterative design happens on a *big* scale. Each iteration may take several years and occupy the life of one company per system! Commercial pressures force a product on to the market well before iteration has established useful things. Once a product is on the market there is strong pressure for future versions *made by that company* to remain compatible, improved only by adding more features! It is interesting to note how visible iterative design appears to go on, not within companies, but by forming new companies just in order to be able to break away from corporate images built up around user interface styles that have become entrenched.

Is iterative design a *process*, an end in itself, or is it a means to the *goal* of a more usable system? Perceiving or judging? What is 'best' must be seen in the light of the interacting personality types of the designers, users and evaluators. Some designers, by inclination of their personality type, would like to get a system design 'right first time', but in fact it might need iteration; other designers may habitually opt for iteration, when in fact the original is good enough.

The motto of iterative design should be 'post factum nullum consilium'—advice comes too late when a thing is done. Exploit iterative design, but do it on things that are not 'done' and practically entrenched (then it's not too late for advice). Iterative design can be effectively coupled with the Wizard of Oz technique (Section 5.7) so that modifications can be cheaply made—and without major reimplementation effort.

8.8 Conclusions

What is the best answer to, 'How do you design an interactive system?'

We have seen that the answer depends on the designer's attitudes. If the designer is at Position 1 on Perry's scale, then showing him some guidelines may be the best answer. What is the designer's view of the users and their job role? Is it X or Y? Do the user and task call for over- or under-determining interfaces? How do the designer's personality traits relate to those of the users? Should the designer deliberately work against his own natural—and often unnoticed—inclination to forge a certain style of interface?

Realistically, design is complex, and it is more, not less, complex when we admit that the designer's attitudes are crucial to it. Systems are not going to be optimal first time, there will be noticeable mistakes because the designer will now know more than he did earlier in the design process before anything was working. Hence iterative design is a sensible approach: that is, design knowing that designs must be improved. Yet the designer has to be at least Position 5 to skirt the problems we raised in Section 8.7: there are no right answers, and paradoxically none can be given until the designer has started answering the question for himself by *doing* the design.

To learn anything from iterative design, so that improvements can be adopted for the next round, requires the designer to have a scientific attitude. Each iteration is an experiment, and like experiments, the designs are not 'wrong' as such but opportunities to test and hone theories about the design. Thus we are now led naturally into Chapter 9, about the relation of science to user interface design.

Chapter 9

Science

Only science can hope to keep technology in some sort of
moral order.   *Edgar Friedenberg*

With Figure 2.1 in Chapter 2 we started to explore user interface issues (see
Figure 9.1).

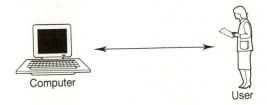

Computer

User

Figure 9.1   Computer–user interaction (again).

Our present concern will be what the laws underlying interaction may
be, where they come from, how users acquire them, and how users may
make effective use of these laws to interact. These problems are analogous
to epistemological problems in science: we need only substitute *world* for
computer as in Figure 9.2.

The 'user' acquires rules about the world, and for exactly the
same reason—to understand and to control: ultimately to understand and
interact with the world. Science is arguably the most successful human
enterprise underpinning this purpose. This chapter explores: the user as

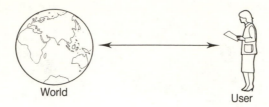

Figure 9.2   The analogous world–user interaction.

a scientist; the designer as a scientist; design as science; and the field of research in user interfaces as science. We shall prepare the way by a discussion of the philosophy of science. Science posits fundamental natural laws, which it aims to discover supposedly following the 'scientific method' for technology to exploit.

This chapter is a mild attack on the popular stance of doing little experiments with interactive computer systems. We can do as many 'experiments' as we like on complex systems, evaluating systems with vast numbers of people, doing sophisticated statistical tests, and so on, all to no avail unless we know what we are doing, and how the results of the experiments can bear on future work. I have often designed interactive systems and come to a point where I would like to make a decision between, say, two design ideas. I search the literature for **theories** that I can apply in my case (because I cannot really do any experiments until I have actually made the decision!); instead I find reports of experiments— sometimes related to my particular problem—but without some underlying theories, how can I know how safely I can generalize those results to apply in my design, with my users, in my language? As usual, the safest approach in 'design' may simply to be to copy what we *think* are the successful ideas we have already seen in use, or which have already been evaluated in the same context as the planned system: but we still need to ask what we should do, and what approach we should take when trying to design a new system.

9.1   Science, design and use

The world was made by and follows natural laws; the 'user' interacts with the world (see Figure 9.3).

What we think of as natural laws are but our attempts at describing what we perceive as regularity in God-given nature; that the so-called natural laws have a certain form is a result of our limited view of the world, not because the world is necessarily as we imagine it. To make things more complicated, the laws may change as well, though so far as we can tell such changes are negligible: or, at least, we like to find laws that are

Figure 9.3   The user interacts with a world governed by laws.

constant! Figure 9.4 is therefore a more accurate diagram than Figure 9.3. It also makes quite clear the direct analogy with the user interface diagram of Figure 9.5, glossing over a few philosophical problems and differences in commitment between designer and nature (see Section 7.1).

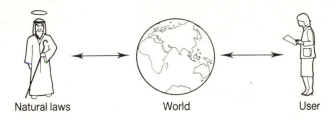

Figure 9.4   Laws affect and are affected by the user.

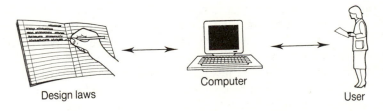

Figure 9.5   An analogy with human–computer interaction.

When we design we are making laws about the future use of a system. These laws must be based on observations and expectations of what the users of the system will get up to. This is an analogous problem to that faced by science: science tries to explain natural phenomena by laws. The problem of design is to determine what laws would be best to embed in an interactive system: if 'science' is an attempt to understand the real world, design is a 'synthetic science' that attempts to build a world (the system) that can be understood. This analogy is the motivation for the investigation pursued in the present chapter. By better understanding science, we can

▷ **Help the user**: The user is a 'scientist' trying to understand and exploit the computer system. Some of his activities will be experiments, to find out what the system does.

▷ **Help the designer**: In two ways: first, the designer faces enormous problems in design—scientific method will help manage this complexity (and help it be performed and reported in such a way that it helps other designers); secondly, the designer strives to build a particular system with desirable properties, or 'natural laws', for the user to understand and exploit. Can the system be designed so that experiments produce valuable knowledge for the user without risk?

▷ **Gain insight into user interface design as a research programme**: Standing above individual use and design is the subject that studies the common features and draws generalizations. This, too, can be a scientific endeavour.

9.2   What is science?

In the previous chapters we have seen user interface design touching on diverse topics and science must have seemed far away, particularly since the main characteristics of scientific disciplines are coherence, interrelatedness and the ability to make accurate predictions.

Nevertheless making predictions is philosophically tricky. If the premises of some argument (for instance, that something will or should behave in a certain way under *some* circumstances) are about certain things, and if the conclusions are about other things (for instance, that something will or should continue to behave in this way under *all* circumstances), then the argument must logically be invalid. We need only substitute *design* for *science* to see that the same problem arises in design. Indeed, we know that when people start using a system their ideas about what they really want to do will probably change—so even the premises (that is, design requirements) change.

Designing interactive computer systems is certainly a very complex task. But science has been developed as a systematic method for handling the complexity in the natural world—so we may ask to what extent is it relevant to user interface design? We shall see that there is some science in user interface design and it would be better if there was more of it. However the very method of science is to home into issues and this may make the designer lose sight of the broader context. So science is necessary, but it is not sufficient; what is done could be done better by adopting scientific methods and attitudes (which we shall explore in this chapter), but the rationalistic tradition of science deliberately and quite rightly excludes subjective opinions. And, of course, at least half of the user interface is concerned with the subjective experience and well-being of the user.

To make matters more complex, there is a lot of bogus science. It is possible to amass vast quantities of facts, even devise plausible explanations without really testing ideas (consider psychoanalysis). The cargo-cult South Sea Islanders, having seen real aircraft land, made their own airstrips, lit guiding fires along the sides and had men wear wooden earphones with bamboo aerials ... all in precise imitation of how they had seen it really done. Yet the aircraft did not land! Similarly, a lot in design goes under the name of science, yet no science is done.

9.3   Popper's Three Worlds

What is science about? What is design about? The common view is that there are just two sorts of knowledge: subjective and objective. Science is objective, and feelings are subjective and must at all costs be excluded from proper science, although they might be studied by science. Karl Popper argues that it is more productive and clearer to think of *three* worlds, as follows (Gaines, 1988; Popper and Eccles, 1977).

▷ The *objective world*: reality, things. World 1 includes computers, and in particular, systems running on computers.

▷ The *subjective world*: of experience, sensations, memories. World 2 of course includes the feelings of computer users.

▷ The *world of objective knowledge*: the meanings of thoughts. World 3 includes formal knowledge, mathematics, the theories of science and the thoughts underlying artistic expression.

Thus Popper retains the common distinction between subjectivity and objectivity, but argues that there is a third position, independent of the other two, neither subjective nor objective. This World 3 contains the meanings and concepts of all human, and perhaps non-human, intellectual efforts.

To demonstrate the independence of World 3, Popper suggests two contrasting thought experiments. First, suppose all tools, machinery and computers are destroyed. But with our knowledge, we could (albeit with much effort) rebuild our present standard of civilization. Secondly, suppose that along with the tools and machinery, that books and all representations of knowledge were also destroyed. In this pessimistic case, mankind would only return to the present standard of civilization by the same sort of difficulties, over the same sort of time (assuming that mankind still wanted to get there after such a disaster). Thus, Popper argues, we can see the importance of World 3 and of its influence on the other two worlds.

There are many equivalent ways of expressing the roles of these worlds. In World 1, of objective physical objects, things are true to the extent that they *correspond* with reality. In World 2, of subjective experience, things are true to the extent that they *perform* well (or feel right). In World 3, of statements as such, things are true to the extent that they are *consistent* within themselves. As an approximation, we can take World 3 as the world of mathematical statements: mathematics is 'right' to the extent that it is self-consistent—there is no need for mathematics to correspond with reality (World 1), nor with our feelings (World 2): it need only be coherent (but see Section 14.7).

Another view is based on distinctions. There are *necessary* distinctions, as arise in the physical world, of World 1; they are necessary because we have no choice about them. There are *independent* distinctions, as arise in World 3 of imagination, and there are *distinction makers* in World 2. Thus, computer systems are in World 1—imposed on their users who are in World 2. Both the designer's and the user's models, different or not, are in World 3. Some people specialize their interests: a person mostly interested in World 1 is an instrumentalist; a person mostly interested in World 2 is a humanist (though the word has various associations); a person mostly interested in World 3 is a theoretician.

We are now in a position to define science: it is a combination of Worlds 1 and 3, using statements as such to express the behaviour of real objects. The goal of science is to find self-consistent descriptions of reality. Computer science, then, is also a combination of Worlds 1 and 3, using statements as such to *define* the behaviour of real objects, namely computers. Science methodically excludes World 2—subjective experience.

Figure 9.6 makes it clearer how the three worlds overlap. Some systems may be in several worlds at once; some systems may be viewed strictly within one world, but a recursive analysis would find other world views. For instance, a certain configuration of neuron activity in our brain is certainly properly in World 1, though it may arise as a result of a process of abstract reasoning (World 3), which in turn is a subjectively experienced activity (World 2).

Work within the field of human–computer interaction tends to fall within one, rarely more, of Popper's three worlds. Some people concentrate on building interactive systems (a World 1 approach); some people concentrate on the effect on their users of using systems (a World 2 approach); and some few people are interested in formal statements about the specification of interactive systems (World 3). The Popperian worlds cannot be used to make a value judgement on the relative merits of these stances, but they can be used to support argument of their mutual interrelatedness.

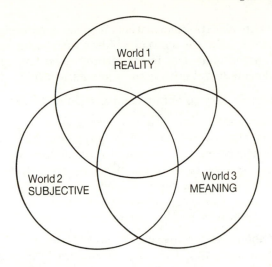

Figure 9.6   Overlapping Worlds.

9.4   What is good science?

For our present purposes it will (just about) suffice to present a conventional view of science, but also acknowledging that in actual fact few people *really* do science in this way at all. Quite probably very few people need to be good scientists—just as very few people need to be good interactive systems designers: half-a-dozen is enough to provide ideas on which the rest of us can work.

There is no such thing as the 'scientific method': for if there were a method, as Peter Medawar liked to point out, scientists could be reprimanded for not using it. If there were a precise foundation for scientific method we could in principle program a Turing Machine, which could then discover everything that we know, and thereby pass the Turing Test. The so-called scientific method is not a method as such but merely guides scientists in **justifying** or **falsifying** what they already suspect. People often do this without exactly following scientific methods: there is always the lingering debate whether what they did could have been done scientifically or is beyond science. The scientific method is itself beyond science, as are the underlying assumptions that there are natural laws to be discovered. For example, suppose we hypothesize that there are natural laws. This hypothesis is not falsifiable; for if we somehow managed to falsify it, we would be forced to conclude that there were *no* natural laws, itself a natural law.

Paradoxically the most important feature of science is that it is prepared for, indeed encourages, its own criticism, testing, refutation and eventual replacement. This is what distinguishes it from other disciplines, such as art, where all extra information and endeavour is often extension—in science we want to criticize and replace ideas with better and more powerful ideas. Good, acceptable ideas in science are called **theories**. Popper puts down the following list of criteria for a good scientific idea:

(i)   It should be easy to obtain confirmation and support for the idea.

(ii)   Confirmations of an idea only count if they are **risky**: if the contrary observation would have invalidated the whole idea. There are obviously an infinite number of supportive experiments and observations we could make if we so wished, simply by staying within the bounds of our experience upon which the idea has already been based. But these observations should not count as scientific confirmation because they are too contrived.

(iii) Every good idea forbids certain things to happen. The more an idea forbids, the better. Certainly, if an idea forbids nothing, then no observation can falsify it!

(iv)   An idea that is not falsifiable by any conceivable event is non-scientific. Irrefutability is not a scientific virtue, as some people think, but a vice.

(v)   Every genuine test of an idea is an attempt to falsify it—not to corroborate it. There are degrees of testability, some ideas are easier to test than others.

(vi)   Supportive observations should not count except when they are the result of genuine tests of the idea. Thus, support for an idea comes from as-it-were failed attempts to discredit it.

(vii) Some genuinely testable ideas, when found to be incorrect can still be accepted if they are modified in some way. For instance, some *ad hoc* assumptions may be added, or some exclusions may be specifically added to the domain of the idea. Such modification is always possible, but it rescues the idea from refutation at the price of reducing its scientific status.

There are three points Popper doesn't mention: a theory must be computable—it must, at least in principle, be possible to express it precisely enough for a Turing Machine to run (better still, it should not just be computable, but have a manageable complexity). Secondly, a scientific theory should fail *systematically*. Only if a theory fails systematically will experiment be a valid procedure to discover more about the world in terms of the theory. And thirdly, a good theory must be *communicable*. That is, a theory must not have too much information in it; in particular, it should have less information content that its confirming instances (otherwise, a theory could simply list rather than 'explain' all its confirmations).

Given the analogy between science and design, the principles of good science suggest what good design should be. How would a designer try to

---

Box 9.1 A debate on the science in HCI.

Allen Newell and Stuart Card gave an address at the 1985 ACM CHI Conference which was subsequently written up (Newell and Card, 1985). They were concerned that the 'hard sciences', such as computer science, would drive out the 'soft sciences' of human concerns. They proposed the sort of psychology presented in their book (see Chapter 19) as paradigmatic of a hard science that could be applied to user interface design. But their article provoked a response from John Carroll and Robert Campbell (1986) who claimed that Newell and Card may well have some particular ideas that could be developed, but their broad thesis— to do 'hard' science—did no more than impose additional burdens on scientists. Carroll and Campbell argued that the major issues centred on understanding the real problems and on providing better tools for people to use. Newell and Card's thesis was a scientific programme; those practitioners who might be squeezed out by 'hard' science had more pressing things to do than compete in hardness. Newell and Card (1986) replied; they defended their position, suggesting that Carroll and Campbell had missed their main point and, besides, argued against a view Newell and Card did not subscribe to either.

---

corroborate his design? When observations with users demonstrate some inadequacies of the design (as they surely will), should the designer make *ad hoc* modifications, or replace the design with a completely different one, one that took these new observations into account from scratch?

Clearly a sensible approach will depend on the context, for instance if the users have already spent a long time getting to know the system before they find it is inadequate, then perhaps minor changes would be better than complete replacement. Short-term ease of use against long-term ease of use and productivity? But this is the same dilemma as in science: do we replace a scientific theory as soon as it seems incorrect, at the same time discarding the theory-specific expertise that has already been built up? Or do we replace it with a new theory that may lead us eventually into new insights that could never have been afforded by the old theory? Compromise is the general approach; patch up what can be patched up for now, and leave the more radical paradigm shifts for another time and place.

Another promising analogy arises if we concentrate on the *user* as scientist rather than the designer: the user has hypotheses about how the system works. Are these good or bad hypotheses—how should the user learn to distinguish reliable methods of using a system from unreliable methods? How can the 'experiments' reveal information that will help users to pursue their task better?

9.4.1   Closure under consequence

In mathematics a **theory** is a set of facts and everything that can be deduced from them. Any consequence of the theory is part of the theory: the theory is closed under consequence. Let us give two examples of theories that may not be closed under consequence.

Consider a boring theory about apples. Expressed as simply as possible, the theory is based on two facts: one apple is a piece of fruit, and secondly if I have some fruit and add an apple, I still have fruit in my hands. From these facts we can discover a consequence that two apples together are fruit (one apple is, by the explicit theory, and to that (by the other fact) I may add one apple and still have fruit). Similarly, from this consequence and the second fact, I can infer that three apples are fruit ... and so on, discovering one more consequence as we add one more apple. But for all I know about apples, if I have a billion, adding one more might initiate some strange reaction (the police might intervene), or a few might suddenly get squashed, or a nuclear reaction might start in the core. It might just be that the theory breaks down if I try to make one billion and one consequences from it. But because we are scientists rather than lawyers, *we refuse to accept a theory that has limited liabilities.*

Now suppose we have a theory about an interactive system. Most likely this theory might have been sold to the users, or other customers, as some sort of description of the system and its behaviour. You can imagine the users using it, and one day discovering a bug. Is this like a scientist with a theory that predicts something that does not happen? Does the designer say, 'Well, if you will do that, then what do you expect?' If the designer acted scientifically he'd say, 'Have a replacement system, and upgrade'— have a new theory, in other words.

9.4.2   Repeatability

There are three reasons for repeating scientific work. *One*, due to World 1: perhaps the world has changed. *Two*, due to World 2: perhaps the people first doing the experiment made different assumptions or otherwise affected the results. *Three*, repeating experiments making small systematic changes (for example, changing the scientist!) will help uncover any hidden assumptions built into the experiment but not the theory: it is possible that by coincidence the theory explains the result of the experiment because of some factors it failed to take into account.

If a scientist wants to continue other people's work, he needs to be certain that he can do what they were doing already. Typically a scientist will want to do a new experiment that has never been done before. Suppose he does the experiment and finds out something surprising. He must then decide whether this is because he did not perform his experiment in quite the correct way, or because he has found out something really new. He should have repeated some similar experiments whose results were already known: if he could obtain the same results (or explain why they were different), then he would be more certain that his method was not at fault.

The situation in user interface 'science' is quite interesting. We find three sorts of experiment frequently reported:

▷ Some experiments examine very simple hypotheses (like a user can find entries in a menu faster if it is sorted alphabetically). In Popper's terms, these hypotheses are not very risky. None the less, it is worth adding the results and data to our lists of design guidelines: until—if ever—there are ways to unify the results.

▷ Some experiments use many users as experimental subjects, often with idiosyncratic traits. Some users who do not perform adequately may be eliminated. The experimental users are often college students or colleagues.

▷ Some experiments explore the potential of complex systems running on proprietary hardware. Such experiments are almost impossible to repeat simply because of the cost of the equipment required to run the experiment—especially when compared with the expected significance of the results of the experiment. Frequently, the software is commercially licensed, and obtaining it in order to repeat an experiment (even if we had the appropriate hardware) would mean paying some huge fee. Very often experiments will mean modifying programs, perhaps to add timing information or to make records, or simply so that the investigator knows exactly what is going on in the user interface. Programs are surprisingly difficult to transfer from one sort of computer to another (even when it is legal), and it is more than likely that few scientists would bother. Besides, if they could port the software to a totally new machine, to check that the experimental results are invariant over the two sorts of machine, they have immediately got themselves a commercial software product they could sell to owners of the different type of machine! *Selling software is a better paid job than understanding it.*

It is interesting that commercial pressures (for example, imposing software licensing fees) hampers repeating scientific investigations. Some recent computer hardware has been intentionally designed so that it is difficult to replicate (to **clone**). User interfaces sometimes have gratuitous features—with almost the status of trademarks—to make them harder to replicate without seriously infringing the otherwise difficult to apply copyright laws. From a commercial perspective, if you are going to design something successful, you may as well ensure that no one else can plagiarize the ideas; but from the scientific perspective, this insularism can only be criticized. In particular, you may never know exactly what factors contribute to the putative success.

Science cannot flourish against personal or commercial interests. There is hardly any commercial advantage in distributing software in source form so that experimenters can know exactly what they are doing! They might modify it and sell it, and what would that do for business? On the other hand, recent developments in freely available software (so-called **shareware**, software available for small distribution fees) may mean that shareware-based experiments can be readily repeated. Apart from a few altruistic shareware suppliers, most software suppliers have discovered that they can make more money selling documentation than software (a floppy disk is cheaper than a paper book). Theories (documentation, in this case) are more valuable than systems.

Many 'experiments' are actually observations to establish a tradeoff between alternatives. When alternative features of a system are evaluated, it is easy to slip into the cargo-cult and call what you are doing an experiment: but what is the hypothesis? Surely the hypothesis is that one system will be better (presumably in some well-defined sense) than the other—but that is hardly an interesting hypothesis, let alone a risky one in Popper's sense. Really, what is being done is that several observations are being made and those observations are not intended to test any hypothesis, instead (and at best) they are to find parameters for a design. Thus various forms of menu design may be evaluated: are users faster or do they make fewer errors per second with different hierarchical structures (for example, shallow with a high fan-out; or deep with a narrow fan-out)? A *real* experiment would have some theory (say, based on information theoretic notions or some cognitive architecture of the mind) about what sort of user performance to expect— and this theory could be refined by the results of the experiment. *Real* experiments may well lead on to insights that enable designers to build systems that excel either of the two 'experimental' systems.

A more constructive view of evaluation is that the alternative system designs are analogous to competing theories. An experiment is performed which falsifies one theory with respect to the other (though we must accept a statistical falsification, because the differences between the two designs are likely to be marginal in comparison with the differences between experimental subjects). But the temptation to confuse evaluation with science probably results in many researchers not looking for really interesting hypotheses to test experimentally. For instance, it is widely claimed that display screens should not contain too much clutter (and there is much anecdotal evidence to support this hypothesis, which is clearly true in the limit). But I have not yet seen any experimental studies: who has built an experimental system that could *not* be used (the riskiness in the hypothesis here is that it would almost certainly be usable)? It is so incredibly difficult just building a system, it is not surprising that most experiments are intended to corroborate the design quality, not bring it into question! According to Popper, the fate of all ideas is to be tested, and all hypotheses will be found wanting in due time. The scientist is relieved thereby from thinking of falsification as failure. The user interface designer is also relieved: not everyone should even want to use his system, but the designer would certainly be unscientific if he failed to have that flexible attitude to perform just those experiments that might expose weaknesses in his system.

Notice that falsification, like all aspects of science, is interpreted with respect to a prevailing **paradigm**. Aristotle falsified the idea that the earth rotated by jumping up and down. He landed where he jumped from—so he concluded the earth could not have moved in the meantime. All Aristotle did was falsify 'the earth rotates' in *his* paradigm. His paradigm did not account for, nor express, concepts such as inertia. Without inertia, Aristotle necessarily found fault in the idea that the earth rotates. So there is always a subtle hedge around any scientific statement: something like, 'it works where it works'—Heisenberg's applicability argument. For instance, it is an accepted law of nature that the laws of nature themselves are symmetric under translation: that they are invariant everywhere in the universe. Thus we expect the law of gravity to be the same on Mercury as it is on Earth. But the symmetry only works under special circumstances that are impossible to state in advance (because there are an infinite number of conditions and influences, and we cannot think of nor characterize them all in advance): I can do an experiment on my laboratory bench that will not work if I translate it only two metres to the North where it would be partly inside a wall: my experimental write-up should mention the wall ... and all sorts of other 'silly' things. This brings us to **controlled experiments**.

9.4.3 Controlled experiments

The original meaning of an experiment was more like an *experience* to be had rather than a systematic attempt at discovery. A badly done experiment is no more than a one-off experience.

▷ Experience is unassailable. If I report my experiences with interactive systems honestly (and you accept that I am not deranged), then you are obliged to accept what I say as true. It is my experience that things are thus, you were not around at the time in any case, and so on.

▷ Experience is not general. *Your* experience may not be the same as *my* experience with interactive systems. Asseveration is the final authority in disputes. Incidentally, a requirement of sound statistical sampling (that is, for experiments from which generalizations of calculable reliability can be made) is to take *random* samples (for example, when taking the temperature, not to choose only those days warm enough to go outside): and my personal experience is far from random!

▷ There may be hidden variables (for example, inertia in Aristotle's experiment mentioned above) that the original experimenters did not know about (or, horrors!, knew about but did not tell about).

Experience, as opposed to experiment, is **uncontrolled**. The fact that I have a different experience from you (or vice versa) discounts our experiences as experiments. Instead, an experiment—especially in behavioural sciences—should be designed with a **control**. The controlled experiment has been called *the* method of discovery (by Alfred North Whitehead).

Suppose we wish to see if a menu-based dialogue would improve (for example, in terms of user preference, or in performance, or error rate or some other metric) the existing command-based approach. We cannot simply change from one to the other, since the change itself may affect users (the Hawthorne Effect, Section 3.3.5), and we might have to make incidental changes to the system that turn out to be the real cause of the improvement. In a controlled experiment, exactly the same system (bar the feature we are interested in, menus in this case) is tested on as near as possible the same conditions and users. If the experimental system (with menus) shows improvements, these improvements must be compared with performance from the control (that is, unchanged) system, *not* the system before menus were provided. We might justifiably worry that the screen layout required by menus might contribute to the user's performance; there should also be a control system that has the menu system's screen layout, but retains the command-based interface of the original. And for each factor there should be a control; to say nothing about controlling for the confounding effects of variability between the users! Some users will come from different backgrounds, some might be colour blind, there may be ethnic differences, some may have career ambitions that motivate them harder. How do you distinguish between differences between users and differences between systems? How do you design user-controlled experiments without over-stepping the moral mark? The usual answer is to perform a statistically designed experiment so that the experimenter can attach statistically sound degrees of certainty to any experimental results obtained.

Controlled experiments are scientific attempts to make empirical results more objective and more easily repeated so that they can be checked; but the 'objective' results themselves are interpreted within a paradigm. Ultimately, all science is subjective to a greater or lesser extent. The purpose of the controlled experiment is to make results objective *relative* to an accepted paradigm. We again ascend Perry's ladder of intellectual sophistication: so-called objectivity is just appearances when the current paradigm is not made explicit (Section 8.1).

9.4.4 Anti-essentialism

Computer scientists can easily explain the behaviour of a computer system by appealing to its **essence**: since it was programmed this way, it is bound to have this sort of behaviour. Typically, a user finds—and is upset by— some limitation in a program, but almost any programmer can say, 'I bet the buffers are 512 bytes or ... ' Rather like Aristotle appealed to the innate nature of stones to explain why they fell back to the earth when dropped: because they 'wanted' to get back to the centre of the universe. So good science is against essentialism.

Francis Bacon wanted to escape from superstition; he wanted to avoid explanation appealing to essences. To do this he proposed the opposite: to go out into the world and observe nature. How do you find out about things? You observe rather than philosophize.

9.5 Scientific method—scientific values

In summary, the scientific method is first to separate out ideas, to tease out ideas that can be examined and criticized independently (sometimes called **divide and conquer**). Some wag said that science is the art of drawing sufficient conclusions from insufficient premises. But these conclusions must be subjected to rigorous testing by experimental methods. The testing itself is admitted to be fallible, and should be repeated by other scientists working elsewhere.

Less widely discussed is that the scientific method only works when it is executed by reliable scientists. Sadly there are many examples of fraudulent science. Very often a scientist cannot be bothered to do the hard work of an actual experiment. He makes up the data, then other people do not bother to repeat his so-called experiments ... a lie gets perpetuated, and gradually the weight of supporting literature makes a reinvestigation very difficult, and apparently quite unnecessary. More frequently, through no direct fault of anyone involved, the original experiments may just be imperfect and produce data that is in some as-yet unnoticed way unsatisfactory. Later research may take the data uncritically. Eventually the weight of circular evidence becomes convincing. (Is this what all paradigms are?)

Along with the espoused scientific method (Section 9.4), there are some scientific values, that aim to direct scientists to doing good work. It is perhaps strange that these values are hardly discussed in the literature, nor on courses in schools—like all morals we think it is perhaps easier to acquire them rather than to teach them.

9.5.1 Argue rather than convert

I believe that the most typical scientific value is that a scientist would be more satisfied *arguing* some case with you, rather than trying to *convert* you to his point of view. A scientist has reasons for doing and believing things, and he ought to be able to communicate the reasons explicitly, rather than using his authority or personal experiences—which you would have to accept as a matter of faith—as a point of departure. The rest of science is simply making the reasons for argument universally recognizable, and for structuring the reasons so that all parties have common methodological ground for assessing the merits of various arguments.

So: reason rather than asseverate (asseveration is persuasion by fervour). However much a scientist is convinced of his hypothesis, however daunting the scientist's reputation, however right he may have been proved in the past, none of this should in itself overtake reasonable assessment of the ideas.

By now, we do not need to spell out the parallels with issues in user interface design, if we accept the scientific stance. We ought to be able to convince ourselves or others *by argument* that a particular system design is better or worse than another; and, for instance, that the system design may have come out of a large respectable company or research laboratory is no proper part of the argument. It may, of course, be a proper part of a wider argument, perhaps that this company can provide unequalled after-sales support ... but would a *good* system need such after-sales support?

9.5.2 Prefer error to confusion

Francis Bacon was keen on the idea that if we are confused we can learn nothing; if, however, we are wrong, we can at least find out and take steps to correct our mistaken views. In fact, the propriety of Bacon's idea is demonstrated by the *opposite* approach that is taken in much sales practice. Advertisements often seek to confuse their readers, or to present 'facts' so vaguely that they cannot be refuted (for example, by drawing graphs that demonstrate astounding performance trends, but omit to mention their scales and origins). Sadly, the legal standards of advertising encourage confusion rather than error (because you can get sued for libel)—but that is only because some people may be taken in by an advertiser's asseveration. That is why 'prefer error to confusion' takes second place after 'argue rather than convert' in the order of our sections.

9.5.3 Prefer simplicity

William of Occam (or Ockham) the 'invincible doctor' of the fourteenth century gave us his famous razor, **Occam's Razor**: that for the purposes of explanation things not known to exist should not, unless it is absolutely necessary, be postulated as existing. His razor is often more briefly expressed as, 'do not multiply entities beyond the necessary'. Ernst Mach applied the razor to the whole of science: the purpose of which, he said, is to organize experience in as economical a way as possible. If it were not for the scientific razor, there would be a danger that we would simply rephrase empirical data without trying to explain it. The razor means the explanation should be shorter and simpler, it should have 'power' to be of worth.

Occam's Razor is based on the notion that reality properly understood is simple, or that simple explanations can be used most effectively by our minds. There are some sorts of reality that are not shaved by the razor: generally those of an ecological nature, in the widest sense, where there are many interacting factors. For instance, many sociological issues not only depend on individual user preferences but on changing preferences as situations change. The **Hawthorne Effect** and other homeostatic phenomena certainly conspire against Occam's Razor. Designs often have to be enlarged to handle more features than were originally intended.

Einstein's well known dictum, 'Everything should be made as simple as possible, but no simpler' is often quoted in this context. Glegg (1969) points out that when a system appears to be too complex this is probably because *part* of it is too simple. (In other words, local optimization may not lead to global optimization.) We could merge Einstein and Glegg:

▷ *Make the entire human–computer system, user's tasks, manual, user interface, software implementation, hardware, as simple as possible, but no simpler.*

Simple must include 'simple to describe'. Complex documentation means the system must be even more complex! We'll spend Chapter 17 pursuing these ideas.

9.5.4 Challengeability and radical honesty

A scientist must be honest in reporting the results of his experiments, that is, in explaining what he has done. He must not write what he would have liked to have happened, but what really happened. He must admit as many of his circumstances, assumptions and methods as necessary so that he can be challenged on well-defined ground.

The only way to have a risky hypothesis is not to be sure what will happen when the hypothesis is tested. If you are sure, you are prejudiced. And your preconceptions will no doubt colour both the experiment and the way in which you tell others about it. It is a very sad fact that computer science seems to have more than its fair share of imaginary experiments reported as real experiments. It is so difficult to get a program working just so, that it is very tempting to write up experiments with programs as they should have gone, rather than how they really went. Often the program doesn't work well enough to do an honest experiment.

When experiments are performed that involve people the confounding effects of prejudice are worsened. Not only may the experimenter report the experiment untruthfully, not only may the experimenter be blind to certain facts, but the other people involved in the experiment may be affected by the experimenter's expectations and hopes of a 'good result'. Thus good experimental design will use techniques such as automating the recording of data, using a **double-blind procedure**, that is, not being present (and having no influence) when the experiment is performed, and so on.

Double-blind procedures involve an intermediary helper who performs the experiment. Great care is taken so that the intermediary does not know what outcome for the experiment is expected. The helper therefore cannot influence the other people involved in the experiment to get 'better' results. Typically a double-blind procedure will be used to compare two or more sorts of interactive system. Naturally the experimenter will hope that one system will be better than the others. Somehow, the people must know what to do for the experiment; but if the experimenter tells them, he might give away his aspirations accidentally. So the intermediate helper is used to instruct the people in the experiment. Neither the helper nor the subjects know what is expected: hence the double blindness. Double-blind experiments are routinely used in medicine: for example, some patients are given either a medicine or a placebo. Clearly the experimenter hopes the medicine will work better than nothing (the placebo), but the experiment *must* be arranged so that there is absolutely no chance that the patients know what sort of pills they are taking. It may happen that if they *think* they have the medicine, they get better anyway.

A conflict between objective science and radical honesty?

Scientists tend to report their work using the passive voice, and they generally distance themselves from their writing. This gives an impression of objectivity; possibly even that things might have happened without the personal intervention of the scientist. Many of us must have used the passive to disguise our dishonesty; compare, 'The window broke' with 'I broke the window'! It is more honest to write in the first person in the active voice. Material expressed like this is also easier to understand.

The difficulty of radical honesty in computing

Computer systems are complex and they rarely work quite as their designers would wish. It is therefore very tempting to publish articles about programs that conceal these unwanted flaws, simplify accidental complexity, and, overall, describe the system as it should have been in an ideal world, rather than the actual system. Here are two quotes taken from two recent scientific articles,

> ... to simplify exposition and more clearly highlight the modelling issues, what is described here is neither the same as implemented, nor precisely what we intend to implement.

> Because our prototype is so fragile, we regretfully cannot make it available to other investigators.

They were actually good papers—and the better for the admissions! I think it would be pernicious, and not very constructive, to give examples where there is not even a disclaimer. Sadly there are many examples in the literature.

Perhaps the authors of such articles gain in some ways—greater acclamation, easier style of writing—but the losers are the rest of us, who do not know exactly what happened; we cannot even learn from the mistakes, to take steps to avoid them ourselves. We cannot distinguish what happened from wish fulfilment.

If that is a statement from academic life, the commercial world has its problems too. Instead of academic papers, manufacturers publish adverts. An advert may make claims about a product (and we know this is probably what the managers want the product to be, rather than what it really is—perhaps because of time pressure in its production, or other reasons). So you buy some software. It comes inside a plastic envelope with a big warning on it, 'This software cannot be returned if the seal is broken'. Now the user has to believe the manufacturer's claims (though the legal small print probably disclaims everything) or the user has to return the package unopened. In fairness it must be said that this irritating marketing policy is no more than a reaction against those dishonest users who freely pirate (copy) software for their own benefit.

9.6 What is good design?

If the natural sciences are concerned with understanding nature—the given world in which we live, then, as I argued above (Section 9.1), design is a synthetic science that attempts to understand synthetic worlds in which users will live, at work or at home. After such a long discussion of science (some of it illustrated with parallels with user interface design), it would be tedious to go over the same ground again, just to make the point that user interfaces could be better designed if their designers did more science in the scientific spirit. However, it will serve to highlight a few important points.

▷ *A design should be task-specific*: In other words, it should not only be designed for a certain purpose, but it also should be clear what that purpose is to its users. Just as a theory should be domain specific, it would be good if users could know what they are getting with a system.

▷ *A design should have predictable performance*: Personal computer users often have to commit their own money on buying software that they are not quite certain will do the job, but opening the software seal is taken (by the software company, that is) as a legal act accepting the software. It is a fact, brought about by the complexity of computers, that it just may not be possible to know what you are getting without using it (see Section 7.9).

▷ *Design should be iterative*: Iterative design is the term used for the approach to design where the first design is admittedly a prototype, and is used as a starting point for acquiring data and users' comments to improve the design. Iterative design is no more than presenting designs as hypotheses, accepting that the hypotheses need testing, and perhaps revision in the light of the tests applied (see Section 8.7).

▷ *Design has more control than evaluation*: At the design stage, the designer can do practically anything; but once a system is built, it—and only it—can be evaluated. Thus we cannot rely on iterative design to converge to a good system: the initial design must be almost good enough. Put in other words: evaluation (and iterative design) are **local optimization** strategies; design itself is a **global optimization** strategy.

▷ *A design should be simple*: Apart from the Occam Razor arguments (Section 9.5.3), a system should be simple enough for a user to be able to perform useful experiments. If a system is complex, and every action the user submits has some side-effect, then the results of any experiment the user undertakes can only be interpreted in the light of the possibly unknown side-effects.

▷ In summary, a good designer attends to detail in a detailed way.

We can ask, 'Is there a science *of* user interface design?' If so, we could imagine such a science taking one of two forms. It might be a general theory, rather like thermodynamics (that is, perpetual motion machines are rubbish). Alternatively, it might be a specific theory, a probably sophisticated version of what we already know (but better presented). The latter sort of theory would most likely enable designers to proceed even faster on to totally new techniques that are *not* covered by the theory. What sort of output do we want from the science—are we interested in explanations (so we understand), or in predictions (so that there is early guidance for designers), or in performance (so that we can make correct claims for interactive systems under use)?

Should a theory of human–computer interaction be able to explain the most fundamental problem: how on earth do man and computer interact? Indeed, if there is a non-trivial answer, would we recognize it? How should a science of design be interpreted? Would there be a bag of rules and theories that could be fed to an expert system—a turbo-charged Turing Machine? Or would the importance of a scientific theory lie in its method rather than in its assumptions and application?

9.7   Is 'computing science' science?

Most cynics think that the only interesting things in computing science[1] are the *other* subjects of which computing is composed. For instance, electronics, physics, psychology, mathematics. Typically computing science is seen as 'just' programming, which almost anyone can do; anything substantial in computing must be because of its roots in other disciplines. Sadly, this view also pervades human–computer interaction: many people seem to think that the computer is no more than a tool for implementing interactive systems. By now this book should already have made clear, at least so far as human–computer interaction is concerned, that there is more to computing science than programming. Anyway, computing scientists could retaliate by claiming that psychology is 'just' computing science applied to human computers; that sociology is 'just' distributed computing, and so on!

The natural sciences set out to discover properties of the world. In a sense computing 'science' cannot make discoveries, since it is not clear that there are 'things out there' waiting to be discovered. Of course, we may find out things we did not already know or know for sure, but it is not as if these things were already there waiting to be discovered. Contrast Alexander Fleming's discovery of the penicillin fungus which was (presumably!) already there, waiting for someone to discover. (But we are getting on to philosophical ground about Platonism, *a priori* knowledge ...)

Programming is science in the practical sense that programmers operate at the limits of their abilities and knowledge, testing hypotheses, 'it will work', 'it will work faster'. If you think these are trivial hypotheses, there is no doubting how risky they are! The systems that are devised are experiments often on a massive scale, which push the designers' grasp of theory and technique to limits. Perhaps the most amusing illustration of this

---

[1] This section makes a pedantic distinction between *computer* science and *computing* science. Computer science is held by some to be the study, specifically, of conventional computers; whereas, computing science is the study of computing, performed on any conceivable computing device, 'computer' or not.

Box 9.2   The perfect program syndrome.

The perfect program syndrome is the notion that a program is perfect if it can do anything: if the designer can show that his system is Turing Complete then it can *obviously* meet any effective functional requirement. (The commonest method used is to include a macro processor.) This often enables the designer to slide the responsibility of design on to the user; in effect the designer can say, 'Although my system may not be the easiest thing to use at first, you can customize it any way you like'.

Which of these cynical reasons best explains the popularity of customizable user interfaces: because designers are so bad at their job of designing; or because every designer (as a user) wants to do design and will feel let down if a system does not permit *him* to reconfigure it?

The *perfect* program, like non-science, never fails. But a system which is *designed* to fail is much better. For some applications, a modest, but anticipated, crash once a week is a small price to pay for 20% better performance (that is, human–machine performance) all round. Even a perfect machine will wear out, and if it was not designed to wear out, when it finally does, probably irreparable disaster will ensue. On the other hand, if a machine *is* designed to wear out, the designer will have built in facilities for servicing it; a long life can be ensured by scheduled, and cheap, servicing. Similarly, if we design programs assuming them to be imperfect they may well be much easier to use: for instance, if a user interface is not perfect, then how do you expect a user to know how to use it without help? How do you expect the user to avoid making mistakes? How do you expect the user not to embark on one line of interaction and then find another should have been done first? If one is designed to be imperfect, these problems would have to be faced and solved.

is part of the history of programming languages themselves, that is, even the very notation which many designers employ in the design process. When the major programming languages FORTRAN, Algol 60, Algol 68, PL/1, Ada, Prolog were introduced nobody could implement them effectively because they were just too complex for the programmers to implement and for the machinery to run well. Even for the successful language 'experiments' (for example, Algol 60), effective theory generally lagged by over seven years. Even today, aversion to recursive programming techniques can be traced back to the bad name recursion got under the early hard-pressed Algol 60 implementations.

Few programmers compensate for their ignorance and inability to understand even modest-sized programs by building in safety mechanisms— whether internal to the program or also available to the user. In fact, quite the contrary. Many interactive programs crash or get stuck in endless loops, losing the user's work. But with only slightly more thought, the user's work could have been made easily recoverable (for example, if the system had kept a record of what the user was doing). Some computers have a 'programmer's button' that invokes a debugger: this is a simple enough idea—but to help the *programmer* not the *user*!

The designer may adopt an attitude to programming which assumes the program cannot go wrong. His program does not check that preconditions are met, nor take steps to 'recover from the errors which can never happen'. Even if a programmer takes a more mature, egoless, approach to programming, it is still in his cultural background to disown programming faults; programmers do not talk about design errors so much as 'bugs', and bugs that almost have a life of their own—they 'creep in', as if the programmers were not entirely responsible for them in the first place. The normal attitude to finding bugs is to test programs—but to test programs half expecting them to work. A more scientific way to test a program is to test it with monstrous data trying your hardest to get it to fail. That is how a scientist would treat a hypothesis—after being as satisfied as possible with the underlying mathematics—and a program is no more than a hypothesis. The user deserves no less!

9.8 How does science in use fail?

Science has developed into a powerful tool, yet scientists (and designers) have human limitations, and there is a gulf between the idealized values of good science and its actual practice. One of the most elementary misunderstandings is that science somehow proceeds from observations to hypotheses. This misunderstanding results in bias in reporting scientific work: it becomes biased to observation and, indeed, observations carried out on the most recent machinery. Instead, *real* science would be performing observations in order to test and refine hypotheses, with the bias on testing and refining to develop understanding. As it is, the literature is crammed with trivial observations. Much work in user interface design has led many people to reject conventional scientific methods.

9.8.1 We expect too much of formal methods

Computer science is gradually becoming a more mathematical discipline: there is a growing emphasis on mathematical specification, proving properties of programs, formal derivation of programs, and so on. Formal methods suggest innovative approaches to design, and help us avoid the impossible. And in the middle ground, where we are most of the time, a formal inclination is merely beneficial—if we, as some, were to imagine that formal methods were essential, then we would have an enormous and daunting task ahead. The argument for formal methods is simple: systems are far too complex to understand (or check, or evaluate) when they are finished; instead, we must have formal theories about them first. This is much faster, when it can be done. Consider a *very* simple system that purports to add one to any number the user submits to it. How would you check such a system? You would have to sit there forever, submitting each number in turn. You never know, one day it might get an answer wrong! Of course if you could see the program you could formally check that the program really did add one to any number in principle.

It is worth being reminded that formal methods rely on models, and bring with them all of the same problems (see Section 2.3 and Box 2.1). For instance we may convince ourselves that the program adds one to any number *if* we believe that the computer system the program is running on (that is, the model) is correct. Of course, the computer's adding unit will also have to be checked, not by experiment, but by formal methods, ... and so on, until we come to artefacts (for example, how individual electrons and holes migrate) whose modelling relies on our choice of world view.

Overall we probably expect too much of formal methods, especially their basis. For instance, mankind spent at least 3 000 years before worrying about the formal basis of the number system, and most of us still do not worry about it. Examining formal models is supposed to facilitate clear thinking, and of course it does subject to blindness. It does not necessarily *improve* our thinking: Newton's mathematical skills, impressive as they were, hardly helped him think clearly about prophecy. Not confusing clarity with quality: impeccable formal methods should never be used as an excuse for a bad design.

Science is advanced by making abstractions—statements in World 3 about the facts of World 1. Clearly for the statements in World 3 to have any advantage, they must be more compact, they *must* have excluded some 'irrelevant' information. Because the scientist has selected certain problems as worthy of investigation, he must have ignored all the other issues that were not salient. Thus the computer system designer may get interested in some algorithm or some detail of hardware—this may be the crucial problem of the moment. Everything depends on its solution, but at the same time he must have ignored all the other potential issues, for instance the social ones. The scientist and the designer are **blind** (see Box 2.1), because they can only do one thing at a time. We may be expecting too much of science, scientific methods and formal methods if we expect them to help solve all of the problems of good user interface design. If they are efficient at solving some problems, then necessarily they must be bad at solving other problems, for which the methods, too, are blind.

Formal methods tend to be sterile, to abstract away from things of real significance to people. An example from art would show this most clearly. What sort of formal statement can be made about a painting? That it has a certain area, or that so many metres of wood are needed for its frame. For certain sorts of picture we might, if clever enough, be able to say something trivial about perspective or lighting. But to say something about composition, to say something about the impact on its beholders is way beyond formal methods. In computing systems there is the same problem: ease of use is not easily characterized, let alone by 'scientific methods'. But we can easily avoid buying a canvas too small for the planned painting.

9.8.2 Pseudo-formality

If formality is a good idea, *appearing* to be formal is a danger. Let us illustrate the problem by talking about numbers—in many cases, the first step towards precision.

It is almost always possible to attach numbers to ideas, and thereby gain credibility. Galileo, for instance, wanted to quantify how falling bodies moved. This led him to review the facts and initiate the overthrow of Aristotelean physics. Numbers clearly facilitate more exact reasoning. Unfortunately the converse is not true; even when numbers are quoted to high precision, the reasoning may not be precise.

Many numeric measures have no useful properties that enable them to be used in a formal way. For example, by counting how many questions I get right in a certain sort of test, I can determine my IQ. Psychologists have been studying intelligence for quite a while, so we may suppose that there are many opportunities for formality. For instance, we might want to know what the effective IQ of two people, each with an IQ of 100 would be. Is IQ conserved like some physical properties (for example, electric charge)? Ultimately, there is nothing that can be done with a number like an IQ, other than use it to categorize things as being better or worse endowed with respect to the way it is measured—which is enough for some purposes.

Using numbers does not necessarily make you more precise, despite the close association of numbers with precise arguments. Likewise, using formal languages does not itself hoist an argument to formal respectability. A lot of so-called formality in computer system design has really been no more than programming in a language that *some* people can use formally. What in the 1960s was programmed in FORTRAN, is now programmed in a formal definition language. It is not necessarily being used in a more formal way, in the sense that the programmer has rigorous proofs or a complete and consistent model of what he is defining. It may only be formal in the rather weak sense that it is abstract and concise, and therefore errors are easier to spot (for example, inconsistencies might fall on the same page of the program).

9.8.3 Realism and non-monotonicity

Science in use may fail because we try to make theories too realistic. We live in an imperfect world, with imperfect information about what is going on: therefore science must assume approximate data; make approximate predictions and rely on approximate explanations. This is not enough for our inclinations are to do better: theories can be idealized ('assuming no friction or other loss of energy' or 'assuming a spherical cow'), that is, realism can be avoided; or they can be made realistic, that is, extra hypotheses can be added to increase their accuracy, and indeed the whole structure of the theory may be such that it can be indefinitely refined. Newton's theories of gravitation and motion fall into the first category: they are idealizations. In contrast, Ptolemy's theory of planetary motion, with its epicycles, can be indefinitely extended to make it as realistic as desired. Indeed Ptolemaic astronomy fitted the facts *better* than the Newtonian theory because it could be made as accurate as observation permitted and had benefited from a few centuries of observation-based improvement. Furthermore Ptolemaic theory is more easily used to make accurate predictions! But we reject Ptolemy's theory in favour of Newton's because making Ptolemaic theory more accurate gives us no insight into cosmology. Making Newton's more accurate helped predict hitherto unobserved planets.

The Popperian view is that Newton's approach is more easily falsified, whereas Ptolemy's is all too easily modified. But here lies a more subtle point: Newton's theory gives more information the better the data it is used with; Ptolemy's just gives 'more of the same'.[2] This is an important information-preserving property of a good theory: a theory like Newton's is **monotonic**.

One major problem with facing criticism of a user interface design is that it is possible to respond to each criticism in a piecemeal fashion, making small unrelated *ad hoc* improvements. One can add 'realism' (appropriateness, ease of use, and so on) by adding features, and possibly thereby losing sight of an altogether better design. It would be impossible to find fault with such a system—especially if the designers are willingly involved with the policy of continuous development—for any defect can be remedied by a new feature.

Suppose the user is provided with an explanation of the behaviour of the user interface: he is given a theory, and can use this theory with respect to the user interface just as a scientist can use a theory to plan experiments and make predictions. Will the explanation the user has be monotonic: will it give the user more information about how to use the system the more the user knows about the system? It would be better if it did.

---

[2] Note that Ptolemy's theory *only* describes simple astronomical events, whereas Newton's not only describes the details of planetary motion but describes tides, weather, ballistics, the results of gravitational experiments in the laboratory. Since experiments can be devised with the intention of falsifying Newton, and (within limits) Newton survives tests in so many domains, it is normal—and natural—to claim Newton's theory *explains* rather than merely describes.

Box 9.3   The theories of synthetic science.

If design is synthetic science (see Section 9.1), then anything designed represents the theories of that science. In other words, when a designer presents a user with an interactive system, he is in effect saying, 'here is a theory': an implicit theory that the system can be used, in turn relying on possibly implicit, possibly explicit, theories about how interactive systems are used. In particular it is a theory about how *this* particular system can be used. John Carroll (1989) has taken this view, arguing that designed artefacts can serve the traditional role of theories in applied science. The advantage is that designed artefacts—interactive systems—codify current knowledge by example and hence guide future efforts. Actual systems do this in a form that is possibly more appropriate than science.

Further interactive systems necessarily contain assumptions about their usability and about their suitability for certain tasks. Carroll argues that such assumptions are falsifiable. This is true but only if the assumptions are espoused: you cannot falsify something that is merely assumed unless it becomes clearly stated. The theoretical statements, then, may *follow* design rather than precede it, which would have been the ideal of design *qua* synthetic science.

It is interesting to note that the artefacts-as-theories view is a World 2 view (that is, performance knowledge), a contrast to the earlier definition of science as *excluding* World 2! We can however place the artefacts-as-theories view, retrospective theorizing, as an essential part of normal design activity. We shall do this in Section 17.5.

9.9   Conclusions

This chapter explored the parallels that can be drawn between science and design (as synthetic science) and between science as use (the user as a 'personal scientist'). Figure 9.7 shows the analogy by diagrammatically combining Figures 9.4 and 9.5 in such a way as to suggest a comparison with the Turing Test described in Chapter 5.

The analogy is productive, but emphasizes fundamental differences in approach:

▷ In science, 'good ideas' are tested by experiments with 'risky ideas' (ones that, if workable, should criticize the good ideas).

▷ In real-life design, it is too late to experiment.

The dilemma is exactly that between the judging and perceiving types of personality (Section 8.5): a judging person tends towards reasoned judgements (sound theories), whereas the perceptive person tends towards empirical data (experimental evaluation). The process of iterative design, which experimentation implies, is a perceptive-type undertaking; whereas the 'get it right first time' is a theoretical, judging approach. Our examination of the role of science in user interface design has reminded

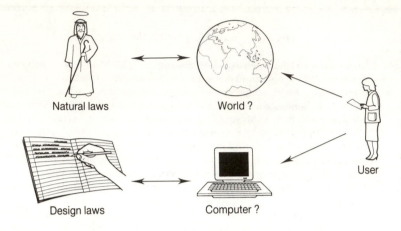

Figure 9.7   The Turing Test analogy.

us that designers need to be balanced between the judging and perceiving extremes of personality—perhaps most easily achieved in design teams with a spread of personality types. Theory is no use without experiment, for then how do you know what a theory implies in the world? Experiment is no use without theory, for then how do you interpret the experimental results? Design is no use without evaluation (for the effectiveness of a design depends on how it is used, not on how it is meant to be used), and evaluation is no use without knowing the design, for *what* is being evaluated?

Is there science in user interface design? The answer is 'Yes, and there should be more of it, done better'. Even so, science makes us blind to many crucial issues; this is an unavoidable fact of life, and we have to take account of it if our hopeful systems are not to fail when used. Designers need a personal commitment to their systems' users, particularly because science is normally dogmatic—once an experiment is done and some idea 'becomes science' there is a tendency for it to gain an authority it may not really warrant—particularly when imposed on new users. Thus there is a need for iterative design, involving the user, of bringing democratic processes back into design.

Chapter 10

Principles
for principles

The Golden Rule is that there are no Golden Rules.

George Bernard Shaw

Ignore this principle.   *Anon*

User engineering principles are rules of thumb that are available to guide designers. There is a great range of them, from vague precepts to detailed and precise rules. If they are specific there has to be rather a lot of them, or if vague no one is quite sure when they really worth applying. It is clear, for instance, that a guideline to help make a coin-in-the-slot arcade game exciting and worth playing will be quite a different sort of guideline from one appropriate for helping to design the user interface for a military command, control and communication (C^3) system—despite their obvious similarities. However, there is a nagging feeling that there ought to be some sort of consensus: after all, all these systems are being used by people who undoubtedly have the same sorts of needs whatever they are doing.

Many principles have been derived from small experiments, and it is somewhat dubious to promote exploratory hypotheses to principles for widespread use, except as a way to suggest possible design approaches. Would an experiment be strongly enough controlled for its results to generalize to the sort of system that one might want to design a year later, on different equipment, in a different country? Guidelines should not be over-generalized by inexperienced designers—and yet the whole point of guidelines is to extend the design arena so that inexperienced designers can do a better job!

Box 10.1   Keyboards for terminals.

One typical design principle is that function keys should be grouped logically. For example, keyboards often sport a cursor pad of four or five adjacent keys for moving the terminal cursor. I once used a terminal that had a logical group of three keys: called SETUP, SAVE, and RESET. This logical group controlled all terminal features, such as background colour and character set. The SETUP key let me examine the current settings and change them; SAVE stored the current settings so that they would be retained when the terminal was switched off; and RESET restored the previously SAVEd settings. Terminal features could also be controlled by the host computer, and occasionally the host would leave the terminal in a bad state (for instance, using an unreadable character set). I would then need to hit SETUP, then RESET, to restore the previously saved settings. The key carefully and 'logically' positioned between these two keys, and therefore very easy to hit by accident, was the one called SAVE and hitting that would ensure that the terminal stored the *incorrect* terminal features. If I hit that key under these circumstances I should have to spend about five minutes restoring the terminal features I really wanted one by one.

Today *thousands* of guidelines are available (Smith and Mosier, 1984). They attempt to cover every eventuality. Following such guidelines closely gives a design a coherence that the guideline researchers have tried hard to achieve. The purpose of the guidelines is to help designers make well-informed choices, to avoid mistakes (which others have already noted) or to design using techniques or in certain ways which others have already found particularly effective. However, it is still very hard for the designer to anticipate the consequences of following the advice until something is working. By the time something is working and in use, it is probably too late to improve it at the sort of level that most guidelines operate.

Designers are often sceptical of guidelines because they seem either trivial or difficult to implement. For instance, a guideline about the colour of warning messages is trivial: whatever the guideline is, the designer could ignore it, because the colour can always be changed after the system is finished. Adopting guidelines that are not so trivial will mean revising part of the design: and the designer may be reluctant to do this.

There are also **attitudinal guidelines** whose purpose is more to raise consciousness than to provide specific direction: they identify issues for which there may be no general answers. For example, 'find out exactly what the interactive system is supposed to do before designing it'. Or, 'know the user': find out how the user expects to use the system, and how skilled he is and how well he will be able to use it.

Another standard guideline is 'present informative feedback'. But of course you don't design a secure system to offer informative feedback when the user fails to enter the correct password. `You got that wrong.  Why not try this password? sdfgweu90.`

Input and output should be **compatible**. For instance, if a pointing device is moved up then a cursor on the screen tracking it should move up. More complex things can be compatible, but compatibility is exposed as an arbitrary property: things can be compatible *when* interpreted in a particular model—and who provides the model? For instance, if the pointing device is a mouse, then moving it *away* should move the cursor *up*. And compatibility is not always a good idea: it makes verification much harder for the user. For instance, suppose we want the user to submit the date. The user might submit the date as *year/month/day*, in the international format. A compatible system would display it in the same way. But if the user submits 87/9/10, does he mean the tenth day of September or the ninth of October? There are even more problems for dates in the first thirty-one years of the next century! To avoid circularity, the system should display the date **incompatibly**, perhaps as 10 `September` 1987, if that is what it means.

There are principles about using pointing devices. For instance, **Fitt's Law** states that the time to move your hand depends logarithmically on the ratio of the target size to the distance you have to move to hit the target. Thus items that are a long way away should be bigger if the user is not to spend extra time. Such a performance law can suggest to the designer that pop-up menu entries can be made smaller than pull-down menus with no loss of time, ignoring any effect on readability. But Fitt's Law will not help to decide between a pointing device like a mouse and using keys to select entries from a menu. Experiments suggest that a mouse is faster for unanticipated selections. For instance, if I tell you to choose the green item, you would find the mouse useful; but if *you* wanted to select a particular item and you know where it is (say, three down), you might well find cursor keys faster and more accurate. Any general principle—say, use a mouse—interacts too strongly with user skill, task dimensions (how often the user performs this task; how open-ended the task is), task requirements (for example, the user must interview a client, and cannot pay full attention to a screen; or often holds a telephone handset, and cannot use a mouse well in his other hand), hardware (for example, screen resolution, response times), psychosocial issues (such as the consequences of user performance, especially of error), and so on. Quite often these considerations may be in mutual conflict. Really, a user engineering principle, so simply stated, can only be used as a *hint* for the designer. If using a mouse is generally a good thing, then certainly consider how to exploit it to the full: nevertheless there may be far better ways of designing the user interface that do not use a mouse.

As the examples above show, the use of guidelines is certainly dependent on the application. They are also user dependent. As the user develops from non-user to user; or from non-programmer to programmer;

from casual to regular; from inexperienced to experienced; from naïve to expert; from employed to employer; from work to home; from school child to pensioner; ... the sorts of guidelines for 'good' systems will also change. The most useful attitudinal guideline is to know *the* user, and to let him know you know.

On the positive side, guidelines are now used routinely as a contractual part of design: the user has a book and requires the designer to adopt certain standards. This ensures greater consistency between various systems, even if their design is contracted out to various companies.

Really vague guidelines are generally phrased as slogans or pithy statements, such as 'avoid modes' or 'make it easy to use'. Designers have a vested interest in keeping as many guidelines as possible vague! The vaguer a principle, the more convincingly a designer can adhere to it.

To show the danger of vagueness, consider the classic **Sorites Paradox**. We need only take a simple example to exhibit the form of paradoxical argument clearly, though we can make it as sophisticated as we wish, and substitute more subtle or contentious interface features than plain 'commands':

(i)   An interactive system with *no* commands is clearly not easy to use.

(ii)   Adding a command to a difficult to use system does not make the system easy to use. (Adding a help command will not in itself make a system easy to *use*, though it may make it easier to *learn*.)

Treating (i) as a base case, and (ii) as an inductive hypothesis, we have demonstrated that *no* number of commands makes a system easy to use. One resolution of this paradox is that 'easy to use' is not predicated on the number of commands, although we tried to make it look as if it was by the way we expressed (i) and (ii); the paradox arises, then, because we abstracted away from (lost) some *necessary* vagueness in the relation between ease of use and commands. Thus a core concept of ease of use is that it is vague, and not amenable to the sort of precise argument that the Sorites Paradox presents itself as. An alternative view to resolve the paradox is that vagueness is a deficiency exposed by the paradox. Therefore vague concepts such as 'usability' are imprecise, possibly invalid and certainly of little use in design.

10.1   The Principle of Least Astonishment

If the designer makes claims for the behaviour of a system, what assurance has the user that the claims made for it are applicable throughout the system? It is highly probable that at boundary conditions (for example, the ubiquitous stack overflow) a system would cease to conform to espoused principles. If the list of exceptions to a principle is much longer than the explanation of it or, worse, if the manual (or other training/reference material) sets up unrealistic expectations, then there is little to be gained in suggesting principles to users in the first place. For example, Dan Swinehart's **Principle of Least Astonishment**—design a system, or its features, to surprise the user as little as possible—might be so poorly implemented in such a way that it only applies in the least astonishing ways; it is, of course, in the 'astonishing' boundary situations into which users invariably get themselves that they will most rely on general rules. One of the worst things that can happen to a user learning a new system, by making a slip, is to be thrown into an aspect of the system he is not yet expected to know. Clearly, there are significant advantages in expressing general principles of system behaviour or use in a form accessible to users.

The Principle of Least Astonishment highlights the issue of subjectivity: for whom is astonishment minimized? Hopefully the designer can distinguish between his own astonishment and the deeper astonishment felt by users faced with, for them, already unmanageable complexity.

Note that the hoped-for generality of principles across the interface may conflict with providing certain features. Certainly there may have to be careful balancing of performance against uniformity; perhaps not *everything* can be undone! An office system which seriously claims to be WYSIWYG will not support certain functions conventionally associated with word processing, other than as exceptions to the rule: the designer has to weigh up carefully the conceptual leverage of consistency against the apparent power of arbitrary functionality. Conversely, it is also possible that strict adherence to a principle may be too difficult to achieve, and limitations rather than 'features' in the implementation will compromise the idealizations.

10.2 A new orientation

Descartes wrote in his *Œuvres*, 'Each problem that I solved became a rule which served afterwards to solve other problems'; he was in the privileged position of both making and using his rules; the more normal case is the designer makes the rules, and the user employs them—*if he knows them*—to help him solve other problems. Thus the designer should not only have laws about his design, but also he should tell the users. It will often be better if designer and user are able to cooperate beforehand!

At present the best designed interactive systems are built partly by inspiration, possibly guided by formal considerations, but in a large part by *ad hoc* accretion. Many such accretions are details for handling special cases and are usually afterthoughts to the main thrust of design. They may even be accreted over years rather that during the initial development and, as often as not, are as much the fault of the designer as the fickleness of the user. Despite adherence to user-engineering principles, it is unlikely that a coherent system will result. Of course, the result is a disaster for introducing new users to a system, especially systems intended for casual or non-expert use.

Ernest Rutherford, the physicist, said that a scientist does not know what he is doing unless he can explain his work to the laboratory cleaner. We might ask, does a designer know what he is doing unless he can explain the system design to a user?

The point is we need guidelines that are accessible to *both* designer and user. We will draw on the science analogy to suggest a methodology and attitude to go along with these guidelines. **Generative user-engineering principles** are risky assertions about interactive system behaviour that have equivalent colloquial forms: thus they are intended to help bridge the conceptual gulf between designer and user (Thimbleby, 1984). In a rigorous form, the generative user-engineering principles provide constructive consistency, and guide the designer in his development of the system specification. In colloquial, or everyday, form they can help clarify design requirements for participative design, help explicate documentation and give the user 'pegs' on which to hang his growing understanding of a system.

For brevity 'generative user-engineering principle' is abbreviated to **guep**. Before examining gueps in detail, it is worth intimating the power that might be expected from such dual principles:

▷ *For the designer*: Without reasoning, the designer may be unable to resolve conflicting principles at the right level. For instance, it is suspicious when designers adopt high resolution displays, colour, mice, voice, undo, and so on just in order to solve design conflicts. It seems, rather, that such technical solutions are more likely to be palliatives, perhaps no more than concealing conflicting design principles.

▷ *For the user*: It is obvious that the user needs some model of a system in order to use it in a meaningful way. Whatever form this model takes, it is very likely to be more effective if some of it has a grounding in laws suggested by the designer and which are known to be felicitous descriptions of the system behaviour.

We may wonder whether people normally use laws or learn to use a system largely by rote memorization. Obviously it depends. We can give examples like learning natural language. Children make mistakes (for example, saying 'goed' for 'went', using a rule that present+'ed' = past) based on over-generalization of laws they have inferred for themselves. So, if English had more regular laws it might be easier to use; on the other hand, the actual choice of the word 'go' for movement can only be learnt by rote (to say nothing of forms like 'go about', 'go down', 'go for').

Would telling users gueps help them, or are they better inducing rules for themselves? Certainly, if users are to be told gueps, then there is the issue of explaining them in a way that can be clearly understood. This may be problematic if attempted before the user has any experience of the system! And yet, if explained after experience with the system, then the gueps are not being explained early enough! I suggest, that *if* the gueps can in principle be expressed in an intelligible way *then* this suggests that the user might also be able to induce them more effectively. Certainly, if there was no easy way to explain a design rule, it is highly unlikely that the user could work it out for himself, explicitly or unconsciously. *Howsoever* the dual form of a guep is used (for example, in training), its mere existence will often make a system easier to use and learn. We might also add that the effort expended by the designer in finding good explanations will in itself be beneficial, particularly as the design is modified to bring it into line with clearer explanations.

10.3   A rhetorical design process

Much has been written, and even more said, about the design process; using terms like structured design, top-down refinement, design cycles, and so on. For the present purposes it would be awesome to contemplate the role of gueps within a respectable design paradigm. Instead I shall consider, as a purely rhetorical device, a totally naïve approach to design. It's naïve, and by no means idealized.

After deciding, or being told, what sort of thing to do, the typical design process proceeds with generating design ideas. These may be discussed with potential users, or they may be picked out of the air. Some thought will be expended polishing the ideas and determining the essential features so that at some stage a fairly formal specification will emerge. This might be a *real* formal specification in mathematics, or it might be a rigorous specification written in some program development notation; parts of it might be written in some convenient programming language (perhaps a fourth or fifth generation language). Next this specification is transformed into an implementation. The transformation itself may be a formal process, partly automated, or it may be treated as a programming exercise. Sometimes the design ideas are so 'obvious' that all these stages may be collapsed, and they may even occur in a single programmer's head.

Ultimately, anyway, we get a runnable computer system: the implementation. This will be presented to users and to documenters, though not necessarily in that order.

What I have summarily called 'documenters' are meant to be all of the people who present the information about the system to the users: they will not only write documentation, but they may devise training courses, advertise the product, run telephone help lines, and so on. For the sake of brevity, let's assume that what they do can be called **documenting**.

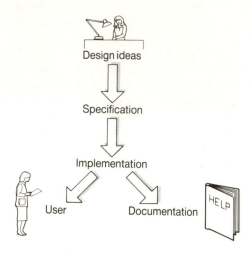

Figure 10.1   Simple design.

There are two things to note about Figure 10.1, which illustrates the process. First, it represents an ideal: in reality, lots of things go awry, and there are lots of little iterations so things can be improved. These fragments of reality would mess up the nice diagram. Secondly, and more important from our point of view, the documentation stage has to come *after* implementation, for until this stage it is not clear exactly what the system is like and how it can be documented—of course, some of the documentation may have occurred earlier, just like we might cheat and write some program code earlier than the formal specification. The reason that this is an important point is that the documenters are in an only slightly better position than the users for whom they are writing. If the documenters misunderstand the system, they will perpetrate *worse* misunderstandings for the users. *Worse*, because the users will feel that the documentation they read is authoritative.

It is interesting to consider where Human Factors and ideas of usability impinge on this design scheme: *they are not mentioned*, except implicitly in the initial design stage, in the design of the documentation, and in any iterative design based on actual use (rather than merely fixing bugs). We might obtain some Human Factors insight *out* of our design process: the system might be evaluated for its ease of use, and this, in turn, might lead to insights or results for use later. There are certainly no Human Factors to do with the formal specification step; the initial step is most isolated from the overall goals of the design process! Indeed, the usual qualities admired in a formal specification: tractability, elegance, simplicity, abstraction ... if pursued with the sort of zeal we know that a conscientious

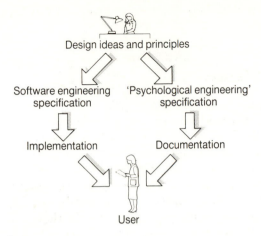

Design ideas and principles

Software engineering
specification

'Psychological engineering'
specification

Implementation

Documentation

User

Figure 10.2 Designing with principles.

designer would apply, would draw things further from the most mundane consideration of usability—the same problem faced by our unusable Turing Machine of Chapter 5.

If we call this idealized design sequence **software engineering**, then the guep idea suggests it should be developed in parallel with as-it-were **psychological engineering**. A guep is a concept that is expressible both formally, hence software engineering—and colloquially, hence psychological engineering. Both routes are illustrated in Figure 10.2, software engineering on the left and psychological engineering on the right.

Of course, psychological engineering might be quite formal too. 'Colloquial', which I really intend to mean human-oriented, might be taken to mean colloquial for the psychologists. It might, for instance, mean expressing something as production rules for an expert system simulating the mind. Nevertheless, at some stage, I hope the formalism can be converted back into colloquial-for-the-user language.

The software engineering route down the left of the diagram produces computer programs as its end result. The route down the right, what we might call **psychological engineering**, produces *user* programs— otherwise known as documentation, training material, golden rules, and so forth.

The diagram emphasizes that user interface design is about the design of the complete human–computer *system*, and if this involves writing programs for the computer then, symmetrically, it also involves writing 'programs' for the user. Note that computer programs define what is implemented at the user interface, and what sort of dialogue with the user can ensue; likewise, the documentation and so on, can be viewed as a program which the user interprets. Symmetrically, the user's program (plus the user's world knowledge) dictates what can and will happen in dialogues with the computer.

10.3.1   Bugs in design

Design will surely go wrong; there will be errors in defining what the system is to do, there will be errors in transforming the requirements to a documented, working system. There will be bugs of various sorts in the computer program, and there will be various bugs in the user program. The user program, the manual or training, and so on, may be poorly written and easily misunderstood in places. The analogy of computer and user program runs deep! The user program may be susceptible not just to bugs of an accidental nature but to outright lies, after all there will be commercial pressures to sell the computer program by the claims made for it in the user program.

Normally the user program will be accepted when it is expressed clearly, adhering to certain documentation standards, and correctly describes the computer program. Yet the guep duality suggests that the computer and user programs have equal claim to priority. Why not modify the computer program so that it is correctly described by the documentation?

▷ *An interactive system can be improved by improving its documentation, and then fixing the computer program so that it is correctly and fully described by the improved documentation.*

10.3.2   Interface bugs

Interactive systems have bugs, bugs both in the computer programs and in the user's description of them in their manuals and other documentation.

A system may fail outright to perform some reasonable operation; the computer may crash. This is the conventional sort of programming bug, and its cure is usually sought in better programming practice, software engineering methods, formal methods, and so on.

Less drastically, a program may perform some operation badly, perhaps with detrimental side-effects. Here the cure is more subtle, for the problem usually lies in the designer's poor understanding of what the user wants to do. The solution, then, is better Human Factors practice in eliciting what users want to do.

The system may simply not implement some operations. Rather than crash or have deleterious effects, the computer simply forbids certain things. It was not programmed to work that way. The cure here lies in both Human Factors and in software engineering. The requirements should have been more complete, or if they were, the requirements should have been transformed into operational bits of program.

There are also **structural bugs**: the system may allow the user to do X and Y and even XY, but not YX. The response to the complaining user is, 'you don't do it that way, use the Z command instead'. The easy way to solve bugs of all sorts is to add features, like Z, so that in principle the user can always do what he wants. This adds gratuitous complexity, especially if Z cannot be explained in terms of X and Y, whose functions it is supposed to combine. More often than not it would be better to redesign the system so that these extra features were not necessary.

Just as in programming language design, the best way to get a more powerful language is to provide the right primitives and flexible mechanisms for combining them, for instance into procedures. A language with idiosyncratic mechanisms may do 90% of what it is intended to do, but the extra 10% is unavailable. It is easier, too, to design and implement simple programs than complicated ones with *ad hoc* accretions. The exciting thing is that computing science has a lot of structural knowledge, and as a rule this can be exploited in user interface design. Using computing science notions to design user interfaces will make them both more powerful and easier to use. This book's aim is to motivate this approach.

User interfaces have to be understood by their users. This principle does not apply to 'mystery games' where the intention is for the game-player to find out how to use the interface! But we might assume that, even for this extreme case, if everything was a mystery the user would be reduced to the position of a newborn baby. At least the user—in every case—has the right to understand something, for there to be some recognizable constancy. If interfaces are to be understood, then they have to be explained. The user may read a manual that had to be written. There may be on-line help of some sort; interactive prompts or the design of icons, or whatever, help the user understand the interface.

Accepting this elementary premise; we now present the design principle,

▷ *Make explanations brief.*

It should be taken for granted that the explanations should be complete and truthful (see Box 10.5: equivalently, you can concentrate on making the system simpler rather on making the explanation more comprehensive). To 'unpack' this design principle, let's consider a typical piece of explanation: 'Filenames can have a maximum of eight characters, optionally followed by a period and a three-character extension'. If you recognize this filename format, you will realize that the reasons for these rules are steeped in history and accident. Neglecting history and 'compatibility', would it not be far more pleasant to explain to the user that, say, filenames could be any length? Maybe (for ease of implementation) we might still want a restriction—but why not have a footnote that explains that, well actually, only 256 characters are permitted. Of course, had the original designer, who first imposed this filename format thought about the amount of paper and reading time that would be wasted explaining and understanding it, he may have made a different decision. An argument *not* to have a separate profession of technical authors!

This simple principle highlights a central issue in good interface design: what should take priority? If the ease of implementation or the speed of the computer is to take priority, then filenames should be as short as possible and have lots of arcane conventions (so that they may be efficiently processed). Conversely, if ease of use is to take priority, ideally there should be no artificial restrictions. But no restrictions whatsoever would be extremely tedious to implement, if indeed it was feasible. And, in particular, we cannot see 'ease of use' in complete isolation: what if the user actually wants backwards compatibility? What should the user interface designer do when he is developing a wonderful user interface manager for an existing system—over whose idiosyncratic conventions he has no control at all?

The best way to polish a user interface and indeed the application behind it, is to develop the explanation for it concurrently. Adhere to the 'minimize explanation ' guideline (Occam again) ruthlessly. Of course, you should explain bugs and curious features (radical honesty again) in sufficient detail. And (hopefully) you will find that it is often easier to fix bugs and other restrictions rather than explain them! Sometimes it may be preferable to leave a problematic feature out than explain exactly what it does. Emphasizing the connections with science once more: the purpose of explanation is to provide the user with a basis for *correct* inductive laws about the user interface: the rest, ultimately, must be left to the user's powers of induction.

Explanation is easy to undervalue. This may be because those people who are best positioned to explain the design—namely the designers themselves—rarely feel the need for a good explanation: they know it already. And the under-evaluation is propagated again and again: very few program development environments (compilers, debuggers, editors, and so on) provide any support for explanation beyond simple text editing (and perhaps text formatting). For serious projects it will be worth while to develop simple tools which permit designers to explain and design at the same time. One way to do this is **literate programming** (see Section 17.4.1).

The interesting thing about explanations is that their success is purely psychological. A formal explanation, that perhaps goes back to first principles, can easily lose someone in the sheer quantity of detail and of the combinatorial explosion of mutually dependent and interacting assumptions.

Consider finding that a spreadsheet balances a column of numbers. Why does it do that? How could I get it to do that with my numbers?

Perhaps it uses some algorithm; perhaps it has to be in a certain mode and certain keys pressed. But why does the algorithm work? Why does it have to be in that mode? And so on. Inevitably we come to a point where the explanation is going to be so long that we lose sight of the original thing that was supposed to be explained. Nor would it be acceptable to abbreviate an explanation by leaving the reasoning to the user: simply stating axioms does not explain theorems.

Thus the most pertinent property of an explanation, beyond its empirical acceptance, veracity and completeness which are in any case its *sine qua non*, is its brevity. If a designer cannot explain a system (at a given level of abstraction) both coherently and briefly, one is justified in thinking that the designer does not fully understand the system. If the designer cannot produce a concise explanation, whatever hope is there for the user to formulate *his* understanding? Thus,

▷ *An essential part of designing user interfaces is to explain them.*

This is such an important point that we will re-present it later (Section 17.4) as an integral part of creative design. For the moment, we may be inspired by Mendeleev who discovered the periodic table by writing an elementary chemistry book, that is by explaining a complex phenomenon as clearly as possible: we'll come back to Mendeleev also in Chapter 17.

10.4 JOSS

The idea of gueps is by no means new, and I can trace it back to one of the earliest interactive programming systems, the Johnniac Open-Shop System, JOSS, in regular use by 1964. The designers of JOSS used the term **rubric** (for the brief summary—usually in red—that precedes an Act of Parliament) for their principles. JOSS was an innovative interactive computer system, a sort of BASIC calculator. C. L. Baker wrote a short note on the principles that designers of JOSS-like systems should keep in mind. Bearing in mind the date of the note, March 1967, it ought to be a minor classic (Baker, 1967).

JOSS was a complete self-contained system, the hardware and software of the system were isolated from the user: JOSS was intended to be machine independent. Indeed the technical ability to isolate JOSS was *also* isolated from the user: the user always dealt with JOSS and there was no 'operating system' to contend with; it was also unusual in those days to have a system that needed no operator and for the user to need no special hardware knowledge. It was intended that no experts be required to help users: JOSS's behaviour could be described in simple English without having to describe how it was implemented. Wherever possible the general case applied, there were simple rules with no exceptions. There were well-defined boundaries of applicability for the rules, and it was claimed that

---

Box 10.2   Using JOSS rubrics.

Consider the following real examples and decide which JOSS rubrics they violate. Invent additional rubrics to tackle other problems, actual or potential. Are any of your new rubrics domain independent—can you usefully apply them to other systems?

Saving information on a floppy disk requires either that the disk is formatted or that the user does not mind replacing existing information on the disk with new information.

Often saving data to a disk is part of a larger operation, such as backing up a hard disk. It is important not to have to restart that long operation if there is some problem or doubt about the just-inserted floppy disk. But some backup programs cannot format a floppy disk! That means that the backup has to be abandoned, and the format program run specially. Another problem is that the backup might ask you if you really want to lose information on the disk—but how are you to tell what will be lost unless it provides facilities to find out? Or does it provide facilities to rename files you want to keep?

Most backup systems have a facility to save files that have changed since the previous backup. The problem is that that is *all* they save— anything else already backed up, but not changed, is ignored. And furthermore, if you put in a blank disk (so that nothing can be lost) the backup program assumes nothing has been backed up, so it backs up everything, not just the changed files! There is a facility to add files to the backup disk, but that is an option (what if you forget it?), probably because it *adds* changed files (so you need lots of backup disks to keep track of all the versions, even if you only want the most recent backed up), rather than *replacing* out-of-date files on the backup.

---

these could be discovered without extensive probing—so the boundaries presumably conformed to simple rules. With JOSS, then, the user could be a successful 'interface scientist'.

JOSS was a modeless system ('single active agent' in Baker's terminology) in the sense that the user always communicates with the same set of commands, and commands are always interpreted in the same way.

Just these points would make JOSS an exceptional interactive system today—and JOSS ran in 4K words shared between up to eight users! It used valves (vacuum tubes). JOSS was also designed iteratively, starting out on a pool of cooperative users. Here are more:

▷   JOSS execution steps are always completed. There are never partially executed commands: either all commands run to completion or they cause no side-effects. Thus the type command could be interrupted— so it would not run to completion—but doing so would cause no state change. In particular, JOSS produced a complete record of a session with it, and this may be used to reconstruct any situation in the dialogue; if JOSS had had modes, this would not have been possible.

▷ Errors detected by JOSS do not lead to catastrophic results: that is, they are reported as potential errors, and are reported before trouble happens. The user can repair the error, and JOSS continues as if *only* the repair had been made. Thus a command causing an error report has no other effect, and the user can correct the command without also having to correct some possibly unwanted consequences of running the erroneous command.

▷ JOSS never perceives its own internal state differently than it presents it to the user. JOSS was a WYSIWYG system (see Chapter 11 next). An example Baker gives is if JOSS reports that a variable x is undefined, the response to the user's command *type* x would never be that x had a value.

▷ Control of the typewriter (JOSS used an electric typewriter for the user interface) was proprietary: either the user was in control or the system was in control. Some effort was expended to ensure that the user was quite clear which state the system was in: visual, audible and tactile signals were employed. There was a light (red or green), a beep and the keyboard would be physically locked when JOSS was in control. Apart from error messages and a few other occasions, JOSS did not need to announce completion of a task: the switch from red to green was in all cases unambiguous. The typewriter technology enabled input and output to be printed in different colours: green was used for input but, surprisingly, black for output. Black light bulbs don't work, and I suppose they could not obtain a green/red ribbon for the typewriter.

▷ JOSS insisted on 'letter-perfect' input and output: it never tried to anticipate or second-guess the user: there were no defaults or abbreviations.

In all there were 28 rubrics; I have omitted some rather specialized ones, such as those specifying JOSS's numerical properties. But the last one is most telling: 'The JOSS language cannot, in general, be extended simply, because each of the above factors must be taken into consideration'. It would be an advantage to be able to 'take factors into consideration' precisely: hence the need for a formalization of principles.

10.5 Collaboration

Ideally, user interfaces should be designed by collaboration between representative users, psychologist (ergonomist; cognitive scientist . . .), task expert (if different from the user; perhaps the user's manager) and computer scientist. The terms are general; indeed, for some applications the roles might be devolved into one person. However, each view has limitations which restrict communication and often curtail the emergence of an overall design approach. The idea of gueps is to give the participants of the design process something of a common currency. With a guep the user might have well defined (and clearly expressed) expectations, the computer scientist might be able to express them as theorems over the specification, and the psychologist might be able to evaluate a working (or prototype) system against them.

However we define the term 'user model' (of the system), we know that with or without guidance, users will construct their own models. And without guidance these models will be over-complex, difficult to generalize, with no assurance of validity and magical. By magical I simply mean unscientific: a user may one day find that the system works when he taps the space bar between commands; the next day he discovers it works even better if the CAPS LOCK button is depressed *and* he taps the space bar. It may be that neither action has any effect; perhaps once in desperation the user typed extra spaces and that seemed to help (but what *really* helped was something else; perhaps the user could think more clearly if he typed rhythmically). In any case, superstitions tend to grow: and when things go wrong (as they will) users will likely add more superstitions, rather than stripping away the ones they already have. It is easier to add to the complexity of a model to help it cope with special situations than to start all over again. Note that superstitions, just like epicycles, may work extremely well.

Nevertheless, a system is natural if it is in some way compatible with the user model. If so, then as a general principle of user interface design,

> ▷ *The designer is obliged to ensure the user constructs and can use an appropriate model of the system.*

How can he do this? 'He' (surely, more than one person is needed—see Section 1.2!) can copy existing conventions (the user's not the designer's!); he can train local experts to be a resource; he can build in system guidance; he can demonstrate systems (perhaps even get the system to run demos with animation); he can emphasize inconsistencies; he can write documentation (and, no doubt, go on courses to write clearly). And so on. Any one of which is a major undertaking, and probably worth a research degree! It is too much to take in as well as all the other problems when designing a new system! Instead, I suggest that the user needs a brief, catchy, memorable and accurate maxim (or 'golden rule') as a foundation on which to build the user model *and* the designer must be able to use the same maxim (plus appropriate reasoning) to constrain the system design.

Hence, we could try viewing the user model as a guep of sorts: the design principle, 'use the user's model' now becomes the easier, 'use the right guep'! It is interesting to list the differences:

▷ The user model is rarely verbalized. Careful introspection or experiments are needed to elaborate it. A guep, in contrast, starts off as an explicit statement. There is considerable discussion on the best interpretation of the user model: for instance, whether it should be normative (*tell* the user how to model the system; or perhaps *tell* the designer how to build it). At least with gueps we have a new term, and once abbreviated the name is not ambiguous English!

▷ A user model is generally as simple as possible, just good enough for the present purposes. This means that when a user first encounters a system, his model will be just adequate for what he has seen of the system so far. It may be hopelessly inadequate for features yet to be experienced. Gueps are initially and always sufficient.

▷ The user model often changes as the user develops and acquires more knowledge about the system. Gueps are fixed.

▷ If user models are supposed to be realistic in some sense, they should certainly conform to psychological requirements. Instead, gueps can have a much weaker psychological status: even if they are misguided with respect to research, if they help the user understand a system, then they are successful. A bad system would be even worse if it was not explained adequately! Thus, in a sense, gueps can be made compatible with real design guidelines after the fact: we might even imagine arbitrary gueps being employed in a design—simply because anything that imposes some sort of consistency will help.

10.6 Domain independence

What use is a principle that applies only to a narrowly defined category of systems? Such a principle cannot be used to guide the design of new systems outside this category, valuable though it may be within it. Similarly, it cannot contribute much to the general education of users of interactive computer systems, but can only inform their use of one particular kind of system. If a principle is not **domain independent**, general throughout many systems, its development effort cannot be amortized over several different systems. On the other hand, it might be evaluated more rigorously.

The 'What You See Is What You Get' (WYSIWYG) principle is conventionally viewed as appropriate to the office information processing domain. Thus WYSIWYG is taken to mean that what text the user can 'see' on a display screen (and can manipulate) is also what he can later 'get' printed on a piece of paper. However, WYSIWYG can also be used in other domains and is probably a useful principle for any system where the user has available functions for manipulating state information (for example, editing) and for viewing the information (for example, printing). It is an interesting principle because it is unlikely that the user will want to manipulate the entire state as a single object (perhaps his screen is not large enough anyway) but he will want to view the entire state. We shall have a lot to say about WYSIWYG later (see Sections 11.7.4 and 15.4.1).

Many user-engineering principles are as-it-were compiled hindsight. When somebody writes up a successful system (for a research report, or to advertise it in a magazine), he wants to put down its success to certain distinctive design ideas. Of course, the design may exhibit distinctive ideas *in most places*, but had the principles been applied from the start, then the system might be uniformly distinctive. It is quite possible that non-uniform application of principles (which is inevitable if you don't know what principles you are using until after the event is written up!) does more harm than admittedly *ad hoc* design.

Although we shall try and make gueps realistic, there is a possibility that purely mathematical gueps exist, which of course would be domain independent. For instance, we can readily imagine that there are essential properties of interactive systems that are not apparent to their users, in much the same way that gravity is an essential part of our lives on this planet, but most of us get along perfectly well without being aware of it as such.

10.7   The hypotheses behind gueps

Gueps are still a relatively new idea: there is time yet for them to fizzle out, develop into a distinctive methodology, or be sublimed into the general approach to interactive systems design. Already, writing this chapter five years after the initial ideas, it seems so obvious to me that you can't *just* formalize a design, and you can't *just* explain it to users: you have to do both, and with gueps you at least have a common factor from which to start.

With a little experience using gueps, it has been found that:

▷   They are hard to think of.

▷   'Good' ones are restrictive and often mutually incompatible.

You only need a few gueps and it becomes apparent that no sensible system can be designed satisfying all of them all of the time (see Chapter 13). If a guep was not restrictive, it would not tell the user very much about the system: and if each guep tells the user a useful amount about the system, only a few gueps will cramp the designer, leaving hardly enough elbow room to get anything working at all!

That gueps appear to be so restrictive can be taken two ways. Either they are *too* restrictive, and a more relaxed approach to user interface design is called for, or else their restrictiveness can be equated with the fundamental nature of user interface design (Newton only had three laws of motion). Under the latter view, gueps are probably an essential part of the user interface design toolkit.

With these disadvantages, what are the possible benefits?

The idea of gueps is based on hypotheses, and it is well to make them explicit. First, there is a practical hypothesis: gueps exist and are useful tools in the design process. Second, there is a strong hypothesis (that I expect to be disproved) that gueps are unfailingly successful, even when arbitrarily chosen. Third, there is a weaker hypothesis, that gueps can be selected for effectiveness if the design problem is defined: that is, in principle there could exist a corpus of gueps from which designers and users could select according to explicit criteria already established by experiment. Fourth, it may not be possible to evaluate gueps before their use in a specific system, but once embedded in a proper context they facilitate evaluation. Finally, gueps may have negligible effect on usability but none the less are useful in specification, or even for orienting the designers somewhat more towards the users.

Clearly we are still at a stage where more research is needed! There are many user-engineering principles, and they cry out to be formalized. What does WYSIWYG *really* mean? How would you know if a system really was WYSIWYG? Can the idea WYSIWYG be tested independently of a particular system? Could we find criteria to help designers decide whether it was an appropriate principle for a new system they were considering? And, lastly, an interesting spin-off from attempting to be more formal and rigorous: we may also discover *new* user-engineering principles by converting formalisms back into colloquial form—we shall see examples of this creativity in later chapters.

10.7.1   Against gueps: why the hypotheses are risky

The hypotheses above seem very reasonable (to me); but, in keeping with the Popperian stance, we should think gueps are good hypotheses only if they have good reason to fail. If they are risky hypotheses and they survive, then they have a useful role in user interface design. This section suggests two simple and direct arguments *against* gueps. And note that by criticizing gueps, I am not trying to make a perverse appeal to scientific values to make them appear better than they are! I am trying to improve their scientific standing: if they are rubbish, the sooner they should be forgotten.

First, real life is essentially unpredictable, and yet to a greater or lesser extent we do survive, and it might be argued that chance and variety give us much of our satisfaction. Predictable computer systems might be easy to use, but they won't be satisfying.

Secondly, a guep is only so much information and it cannot constrain the design of the user interface enough to worry about. If we imagine a small computer system having 10^7 bits, a guep factors maybe 100, maybe a lot less. That still leaves 10^5 bits unknown! It is no counter-argument to insist that a guep has structure, for equally so do most of the 10^7 bits inside the computer—they might be program, for instance, with a compactly encoded structure.

Counter-arguments

First, concerning predictability. I accept this point, but I would argue that complete unpredictability (for example, the system might disintegrate) is chaotic and probably not a workable concept, though *constrained* unpredictability is already a useful design idea—for *games*—and it is such constraint that a guep should express. But anyway we don't always want to play games: people at work are enforced by social constraints to perform certain tasks. The user's satisfaction under such circumstances is likely to be related to predictable closure rather than uncertain novelty! Another point is that unpredictability in the real world is distributed between all our senses—for example, you may be able to smell a meal, but the colour is as yet unpredictable—but in most computer user interfaces very few sensory modalities are involved. The users rely very heavily on visual input and tactile output (that is, from themselves) there is no redundancy to smooth over unpredictability, nor is there much redundancy within the modalities that are used. Keyboards cannot express the nuances of handwriting, facial expression nor speech; the output from a computer is terribly bland, and unpredictability is generally disastrous.

As for the second argument, if we fixed *all* the bits by a guep we would have essentially given the user the system specification (and we would have to find a way of expressing it more intelligibly than by computer program). But giving the user so much information would introduce user interface problems of its own. So there is a tradeoff: give the user a little information so that he can better understand and use the actual system, but not so much information that understanding *that* information becomes a major issue in itself. In order to make a good tradeoff, the designer will decide what information is interesting and best suits the purposes of the anticipated users: and I think that interest and utility are beyond information theoretic arguments of this sort.

Underlying guepery is the notion that user interfaces should be *consistent*, specifically with respect to a set of engineering principles. In fact this is no more than a convenient assumption: if things are consistent then we can use formal methods more easily. However humans live in an inconsistent and unpredictable world and it is not immediately clear that they would best interact with consistent machines. We could argue, rightly I think, from Chapters 3 and 6 that inconsistency at the interface would encourage the user to attribute more to a system than it was capable of. On the other hand the formal consistency of a system may be so sophisticated

---

Box 10.3   A lesson about consistency.

Teacher, '... and every system should be mnemonic ...'
Interruption, 'When you type **A** mine aborts'
Teacher continues, '... and consistent ...'
Interruption, 'In fact, when you type anything my system aborts.'

---

that only the designer recognizes it. It is easy to imagine systems being built that although strictly consistent, appeared inconsistent to their normal users. Indeed almost all systems fall in this category: for unless there is a hardware fault, computer systems operate to fixed and determinate laws. In principle they are consistent ... though the structure may not be apparent. Obviously consistency is a word that we should not use unqualified. Far better, I think, is the term **predictable**, which simply means that a system seems consistent to its user. And a technical term is **compatible**, meaning consistent with some inbuilt habit of the user, perhaps formed through long experience with other systems.

10.7.2 Two types of guep

Gueps come in two flavours: they may *restrict* or *liberate* the user. In the terminology of Chapter 8, they may over-determine or under-determine the user; they may reflect a Theory X or Theory Y attitude of Section 8.2. In other words, a guep may tell a user what he *has* to do in order to achieve certain goals; or, alternatively, the guep may inform the user that he can achieve his goals in a variety of ways, or take advantage of certain reliable hints from the system (for example, about which mode it is in).

An example of a restrictive principle would be one that relates to security. For instance, to modify a database, the user must supply a password at a certain point in the dialogue. We might imagine that in a very secure system the password is never explicitly requested—the guep would tell the user how to recognize those points when he must supply the password. Conversely, a liberating principle might tell the user that, whatever he does, the system never loses information. We can ensure this by equal opportunity (Chapter 15) or by providing undo (Chapter 12).

Now the interesting thing about the restrict/liberate view of principles is that the user and designer may not agree on what restricts or liberates! A simple example will illustrate the problem. Suppose a guep is expounded that the system will operate correctly in whatever order users submit commands. The designer intends this to be a great liberty and, no doubt, would have gone to great lengths to ensure that the rule really worked (for example, having a functional programming system underlying

---

Box 10.4   The purpose of scientific theory.

The purpose of a theory in science is not to explain facts, it is to explain them concisely and therefore to help the scientist reason economically about the facts. But all facts can be explained by alternative theories. So a further criterion must be levelled at a good theory: a good theory *improves the facts*. The standard and easily appreciated example concerns the theory of planetary motion; at one stage the theory was based on epicycles, and almost any data (right or wrong) could be accommodated. Then Kepler proposed a theory based on ellipses; this step could almost be considered an improvement on the empirical data! Then Newton proposed a theory of gravitational interaction: Kepler's Laws both serve to corroborate Newton's Laws and, by doing so, expose themselves as approximations. Later still, Newton's Laws explained the anomalies in the orbits of the known planets; yet there were still anomalies, and later still the mathematicians Adams and Leverrier were able to calculate the position of the unseen planet Neptune. Thus the good theory explained the known facts and led to the discovery of new facts: the good theory actually improves the evidence.

---

the user interface). This lack of structure clearly under-determines the user: but, as Colin Runciman discovered, some users may interpret such a rule as a restriction.

Users with rudimentary programming experience found the 'any order' guep a liberation: they could do things in any order, and not worry about getting it 'just right'. But experience-hardened users and programmers were suspicious—they could imagine how complex the system must be to ensure the property—and they interpreted the guep as a restriction: they thought commands would commute (work in another order) *only if they were correct*! Thus, programmers over-determined themselves, for they had to think very hard to find a way of expressing what they wanted which they also believed would commute!

10.7.3   The role of principles in design

So far I have presented principles as being golden rules appositely chosen for the user and his tasks. Good principles will help the user understand an interactive system, understand how his tasks can be broken down into steps appropriate for the structure of the system, and, as a side-effect, give him extra confidence: users will achieve their goals more readily and more confidently. But there is another perspective on principles: *principles help designers*. And, quite possibly, principles will help designers *more* than users—but thereby helping users indirectly.

The purpose of principles in design is to explain the design (this is the 'conventional' role) and to improve the design. Imagine that a designer is developing a system; he is probably juggling with both abstract design principles and concrete design ideas. If he hits on a good principle, it may only describe *part* of the proposed system, or it may describe *more* than he has yet considered. In either case, the designer can adhere to the principle and improve the system. The designer is in a rather privileged position in comparison to the scientist: the designer can 'change the world' so that a good theory works!

Gueps may also be of direct use to the implementor once a design has been fixed. If a guep is telling the user something useful about the behaviour of an interactive system, then it can equally be viewed as a hint to the implementor to implement the relevant groups of features in a uniform way. Conversely, being able to implement superficially disparate parts of the user interface by the same primitives might suggest an incipient guep. We can develop this line of thought to an interesting conclusion by noticing that many systems (including all Turing Complete systems) can be implemented by metacircular methods. Thus precisely the properties available to the implementor, which he can take advantage of in writing the metacircular system, will also be available to the user. For instance if a guep assures the user that he need not worry about storage management (that is, there is a garbage collector), then the implementor has a hint that his implementation may be clearer if garbage collection is abstracted away. Using the terminology of Chapter 4, the metacircular gueps would be called **reflective paradigms**, of which one is object-oriented programming.

10.8 Metagueps

Sometimes gueps are too rigid, and the ones we have just been looking at have a tendency in this direction. Systems that always satisfy gueps might be very constrained: there are always reasons for the exceptions. Thus to allow a design to cater for exceptions, there should be metagueps:

(1) *If a guep does not or cannot hold, the system says so*: This metaguep (which always holds!) allows other gueps to be relaxed, but the user is always warned or made aware when the laws are being suspended. For instance, the JOSS-like guep that errors have no consequences (Section 10.4) could be waived for some errors if the system told the user what the consequences of each error were.

Perhaps this first metaguep is too strong: it would either be difficult to implement thoroughly, or it would constrain the design overly, and it would probably be a nuisance for the user if every breach of gueps was reported. An alternative would be to require that the user is always able to tell if any guep applies:

(2)   *The user can in principle determine whether a guep applies*: Thus, the system does not have to tell the user something he may not be interested in, but, however, the information is available.

Principle 2 is rather weak for the user. There is a cost in establishing whether a guep is valid: this guep does not prohibit the nasty sort of system where determining whether a guep applied would change modes (and hence the applicable gueps). You might know where you had been, but you could never be certain what principles applied now, where you are.

For a better principle, it would be important to reassure the user that any reasonable experiment to determine whether a guep applies had, or need have, no long term effect:

(3)   *The user can determine whether a guep applies without changing the state (or results) of the system*: This third formulation suggests that either there is a general method for returning the system to an earlier state, or else there is a subdialogue available for experimenting with or discovering system principles. Help systems are one such dialogue, though they are rarely experimental except in some text editors.

A fourth possibility is that if the user cannot determine what the current situation is, at least he should be able to get it into a known mode with known properties:

(4)   *There is a set of fixed commands that always put the system into recognized modes where recognized gueps apply*: Metaguep 4 limits the scope of modes: there are some (particularly useful) commands whose meaning is unaffected by the current mode. This guep is consistent with the 'eyes-shut' principle: whatever the system mode, the user can force it into any particular mode by using predetermined commands (see Section 11.7.1). For example, there might be some function keys that put the system into particular modes, each function key always having the same effect. Metaguep 4 suggests the advantage of commands that get *into* modes, rather than commands that *exit* modes and get into the previous mode: whether this really is an advantage, and under what circumstances it might be so, is an idea that could and should be tested experimentally.

10.9   Closure

Closure, as a mathematical rather than psychological term, means that doing something does not take us out 'into the open' beyond the system. For a guep to be useful, the system must be closed under the guep. It will help to give a concrete example, but first based on libraries rather than interactive systems:

Box 10.5   Training wheels.

It is crucial that users have a good enough model of the user interface right from the start. If they start off with a poor user model it will only get worse. Gueps address this problem by giving the user 'golden rules' to understand the fundamental behaviour and properties of the interactive system. Alternatively, we could make the system *much* simpler, so that acquiring a good enough understanding of the system is not problematic.

We present the user with a very stripped down version of the user interface. Such systems have **training wheels** interfaces (Carroll, 1984). In a training wheels interface, advanced operations are not initially provided: the user simply cannot make mistakes with them. The user is started off on a simple and safe user interface, but the advanced user interface contains the original interface: nothing the user learned is wasted. Building a sound model of the training wheels interface is easier, and because it is sound it should readily generalize when the 'training wheels' are removed.

It can be frustrating for a library user to read a book and then find that some of the books it cites or refers to cannot be found in the same library. 'Refers to' is a relation between books, and it will help clarify what we mean by closure to look briefly at how the library design would have to change if we imposed closure on this *refers to* relation:

▷ **Simple closure**: This would mean that every book referred to by any book in the library is also in the library. Note that closure can be achieved *either* by buying in all books that are referenced, and all books they reference, and so on ... until there is no book missing, *or* by buying very selectively, so that very few books are referenced! Both strategies result in closure, but one in a big library, the other in a small library or a library of non-academic books with few references. Another possibility would be to censor references; we could then enforce closure.

▷ **Reflexive closure**: This would mean that each book refers to itself. Depending on how serious we are about the *refers to* relation, this is either pointless or essential! Of course you know what book you are reading, so there is no point in it referring to itself. On the other hand, if a book did not refer to itself somewhere (not even on its spine), how would you know what it was called?

▷ **Symmetric closure**: This would mean that if a book A refers to book B, then B would refer back to A. This relation would be very useful: if you find an interesting idea in a book, the book will tell you which other books follow up the idea (because they refer to this one, and by symmetry this one has to refer back to them). Of course, this is a feature that is fantastically useful for the research user, but practically impossible for the library to implement! Note that symmetric closure may mean changing existing books as new ones are added to the collection.

▷ **Transitive closure**: Sometimes a researcher will follow a chain of references: this book refers to that book, and that book refers to the next. If the relation was transitive, then a book would refer to all books that were referred to by any book it referred to: in other words, there would be no need to follow a chain of references through several books, for all the details would be contained in the first book. This would clearly save the researcher a lot of time running round the library, but it would make some books enormous (imagine a book that refers to an encyclopedia).

So, some sorts of closure seem pointless, some have benefits, some are costly to implement. What we see is that closure of a relation does not necessarily make a design better (in this case, a library design), but it certainly suggests new ideas. The issue with non-standard models is that they are outside the ideally closed world of the standard models.

Clearly our ideas on closure in libraries is no more than a convenient example to help convey the idea. The design consequences are in almost all cases simply infeasible, or put severe constraints on the books permitted on the shelves! But with a little imagination we can use the same ideas to help design an *interactive* library system.

A computerized bibliography need only *appear* to be closed, whether it really is or not. Here we can exploit the relatively small screen through which the user has access to the bibliography. The computer can compute the closure of the *refers to* relation faster than the user can take in the information about the referenced books via the interface. Thus, a computer system can provide the advantages of transitive and symmetric closure. Good-enough simple closure might be obtained by on-line access to a major library.

We may readily justify the liberal application of closure in the specification of user interfaces. Suppose the user discovers that some relation ρ holds between certain objects (in the library example above, ρ is *refers to*). If ρ holds in several contexts over different objects, the user may reasonably induce its more general application. The designer may anticipate this by requiring the design to be **closed under** ρ. Naturally, the designer cannot anticipate the mental models of the user, in particular the nature of some arbitrary user-induced relation such as ρ. There are many relations that the user might like, but which are incorrect with respect to a design that is intended to be useful for some given task. However, by seeking closure in the specification for a variety of operations, the designer improves the reliability of such user induction; indeed, the designer (by way of user manuals) can encourage the user by stating that certain properties are *generally and reliably* true of the system. Note that, as in the case with the lazy library bibliographic system, it is enough if the user cannot tell that the system is not 'really' closed under whatever properties are claimed for it.

In summary, then, closure is a useful design concept because: (*a*) we can often close a design under some property by a purely mechanical procedure; (*b*) a closed system can be defined both for computer and user more briefly; and (*c*) attempts at closure often lead to insights in the design process.

10.9.1   Closure in interactive systems

Very often some feature of an interactive system is available in two different contexts. The command processor (or window interface) has a means of accessing files, and many applications will have internal means for accessing files, for instance to allow the user to save work on disk. There is a relation between the two situations: *corresponds to*.

In the command processor, it may be possible to list the current set of files, select a file and perform operations on it. Within an application, it may not be possible to list the set of available files. If there is a correspondence, why not close it so that features in the two contexts correspond more closely? Then the user does not have to learn exceptions; learning one is as good as learning the other.

10.9.2   Closure in programming language design

The **Principle of Correspondence** (Tennent, 1981) is a simple (symmetric) closure principle about the way variables are declared in programming languages.[1] On the basis that there is some correspondence between definition and parameter mechanisms, it states that, in principle, definition and parameter mechanisms in programming languages should correspond completely. Let's see what this means in Pascal.

In Pascal there are two ways of introducing variable names, as ordinary `var` variables, or as parameters to procedures or functions. There is a rough correspondence between the two mechanisms: in both cases a name is associated with some memory location. The full correspondence is made clear by looking at the two program fragments in Figure 10.3. If you

---

[1] Since a definition corresponds with itself, correspondence is a reflexive relation—so we would not discover anything stunning by examining the reflexive closure! Similarly, correspondence is transitive: if A corresponds to B and B corresponds to C, then A corresponds to C. But correspondence need not be symmetric: if A corresponds to B it is possible that B has some features not in A, so B would not correspond with A. Therefore it may be interesting to find the symmetric closure of correspondence.

```
var x: integer;          procedure dummy(x: integer);
begin x := 3;            begin write(x)
        write(x);        end;
end                      begin dummy(3)
                         end
```

Figure 10.3   Corresponding fragments of Pascal.

work through them, *exactly* the same thing happens to the variable x: it is bound to new storage, has the value 3 assigned to it, and is then written out using the `write` statement. (We used the Principle of Correspondence in Section 4.3.2 to argue about the generality of freedom from evaluation orders.)

Given this correspondence, we can set up a simple relation between the semantics of definition and parameter mechanisms. But, in Pascal, the relation is not closed under symmetry: there are features in parameters that are not in definitions, and vice versa. There is a `var` parameter mechanism that has no corresponding definition mechanism; `with` has no corresponding parameter mechanisms. The correspondence could be much closer if definitions of variables permitted their simultaneous initialization; when a procedure such as `gargle(2,3,4)` is called, its three parameters are simultaneously initialized to 2, 3, and 4.

Initializing variables in Pascal is a problem for programmers: the definition of a variable comes early on in the program, then there may be pages of procedure definitions, then the main body of the program where, finally, the variable can be initialized. This is an unnecessary separation which not only makes programming harder but also makes it harder for the compiler to optimize. It is very easy to declare variables in a Pascal program and forget to initialize them. On the other hand, it is *impossible* to call a procedure without initializing its parameters. If the principle of correspondence had been adopted, then Pascal might have required—or at least permitted—that all variables be initialized. Perhaps the programmer would have to or be able to write something like, `var x := 3 integer;`

Another closure principle arises from consideration of the relation between Pascal expressions and functions. As a rule, it is possible to replace any expression with a function giving the same value. For instance, 3+4 can always be replaced by a call to a function `seven` (say), if `seven` is defined to return the value 3+4 (in Pascal, it would have a body, `begin seven := 3+4 end`).

But the converse is not true: the relation is not symmetric. Very few Pascal functions can be written out in full where they are called. If a Pascal function contains any commands (for example, an `if` statement), then it cannot be used directly in an expression. Yet other languages

(Algol 68, BCPL to name two) permit arbitrary commands to be embedded in expressions: and it is a very useful programming feature. For example, the standard Pascal problem of trying to test two conditions in the right order (for example, the generally incorrect `(i > 0) and (j/i > 0)`) is easily solved (by using `if i > 0 then j/i > 0 else false`). In Pascal you can call a function to evaluate a conditional expression, but you cannot write conditional expressions out *in situ*: here closure fails.

Such observations, of being able to do something some of the time and not always—in this case convert expressions to functions and vice versa—can be promoted into a closure principle, if we like the idea. In this case the principle is called the **Principle of Abstraction**: any meaningful unit can be replaced by an abstraction, and conversely any abstraction can be written out in full. In the present case, the 'meaningful units' are expressions and the abstractions are functions. Pascal provides just one other abstraction mechanism, for commands, which is the procedure. The principle of abstraction suggests that we might search for other meaningful units and see what good their abstractions would obtain. Unfortunately this would lead us into a digression, but to whet your appetite, note that abstraction of types (Pascal provides rather limited type expressions—called definitions) would permit **abstract data types**, or **classes**, a step towards object-oriented programming.

Macro processors are the main form of abstraction mechanism available in user interfaces. Any sequence of commands (although often with restrictions, for instance, that the sequence is not too long and does not contain ↩) can be given a name. When the user submits the name, the macro processor expands it into the original sequence. (We will examine macro processors further in Section 16.9.2.)

There is great variation in the design of macro processors, but the following three observations are generally correct:

▷ Macro processors are **accelerators**. A single command submitted by the user can be expanded by the macro processor into a long sequence (possibly involving further macros). Thus, macro processors can speed up the interface.

▷ Typically a macro processor operates on the text of the commands (or other basic actions submitted by the user). There is no prior restriction on what text can be stored as a macro body.

▷ Conversely, if there is no restriction on the text, the principle of abstraction does not apply precisely: the principle suggested that *meaningful units* (syntactically well-formed structures) could be abstracted. Most macro processors are quite independent of the syntax of the system with which they are used. This results in the most obscure problems for the user, and the loss of a number of design principles (for example, all algebraic laws (Chapter 14) and the principle of commensurate effort (Section 15.4.3) are lost).

10.10   Conclusions

Gueps, generative user-engineering principles, are special *dual* explanations, easily understood—assuming they are expressed in an appropriate form—and used by *both* designer and user. Of course, both designer and user may have to put some effort into understanding them: one in attempting to formalize the guep (and all that that entails); the other in attempting to understand how to reason with the guep for the use of the system. Gueps can be expressed in such terms that:

▷   The user *and* documenter have a sound basis on which to construct an understanding of the system behaviour, even before making any use of it.

▷   The user has a sound basis on which to generalize his knowledge reliably. The user relies less on debugging skills: he can be more confident about what has happened and how new things may be made to happen.

▷   The designer can use gueps to meet predefined expectations in the user, often with specific techniques.

▷   The user interface is designed top-down, using gueps as theories about desirable interactive behaviour.

▷   Even if the gueps are psychologically ill-founded, they are better than arbitrariness.

Having once suggested a basis for the user model, the designer is under an obligation to ensure its coherent implementation through careful system design, which should maintain the model as understood by the user. This approach will facilitate both evaluation and refinement of the original design permitting proper iterative design. If the iteration is to be worthwhile, the iterated design must have scope for improvement: that is, the gueps must be risky, in the sense of Section 9.4.

I believe that gueps, plus attention to detail (which is anyway an essential part of the formal process) provide a constructive approach to top-down design of effective, acceptable interactive systems. At the very least, even if a guep is unfortunately chosen and is ergonomically unsound, an interactive system built around it will have greater internal consistency and be more faithfully and clearly documented than the average system available today. But let's finish with a warning:

In many cases it is anticipated that adherence to a guep actually makes the effort required to design a user interface considerably greater, not least because a guep is useless, indeed counter-productive, for the user if the designer permits exceptions to it. Thus we return to the adage that successful user interface design requires attention to detail. Now at least we have a frame of reference to indicate the relevant level of detail.

Chapter 11

Modes
and WYSIWYG

No presentation without representation—a taxing issue?

The previous chapter ended in a discussion of gueps, generative user-engineering principles, suggesting that they might profitably form part of the science base in user interface design. But very little was said about the actual content of gueps. This chapter turns to the issue generally recognized as the most significant, the role of hidden information, the so-called **modes** of the interactive system. Modes form an excellent concept on which to construct gueps. The chapter on gueps and principles followed one on science; the motivation for this present chapter is simply that modes hide experimental observables—in short, they stop the user being a scientist and being able to experiment sensibly with an interactive system. Even if the user does not want to be a *real* scientist, the fact that he is inhibited in principle severely limits what can be done just in simple tasks like word processing.

Modes are necessary to provide versatility, yet this versatility must be traded against increasing confusion in the user's head. We shall see that a useful motto for the designer is the ancient legal maxim, '*De non apparentibus et de non existentibus eadem est ratio*' ('what does not appear is presumed not to exist'); and the user should be able to act *as if* this maxim were effective. Thus we have a principle for design.

Box 11.1   Modes and the Johari Window.

Joe Luft and Harry Ingham invented the **Johari Window** as a visual aid to self-disclosure (Luft, 1963). The chart is a 2 × 2 matrix, with columns for information known or not known to the person in question, and rows for information known or not known to others.

	known to self	*unknown to self*
known to others	shared information	blind-to-self
unknown to others	hidden information	unknown information

Typically, a Johari Window is used in a group of people or in pairs, each person filling in sections according to his perception of himself and of others. If a person is given feedback from others, then the top vertical division moves to the right; if the person discloses more information about himself, then the left horizontal division moves down. Each activity increases the area covered by the top left region: doing both feedback and self-disclosure increases it most.

As a project, try using the chart for visualizing the disclosure of information between user and computer in some particular application. As designer, you have privileged access to otherwise hidden information! Identify techniques that move the boundaries between the individual regions of the window.

11.1   Modes as hidden information

Modes can be defined concisely, but somewhat vaguely, as the *variable information in the computer system affecting the meaning of what the user sees and does*. A mode is the *variable* information, since we assume that the choice of system (the gross information affecting what the user can do) is fixed: modes are variations within a particular choice of task. A mode is information *in the computer system* because this focuses the concept from, say, documentation or social issues.

Crucially, by defining modes to be artefacts of the computer system design we have a chance of being precise about them: this is a prerequisite for the scientific goals we have set ourselves. A mode affects what the user *sees and does*, because we want to treat input and output symmetrically— most other analyses of mode concentrate exclusively on what we will call **input modes**.

Typically, the user finds modes difficult because much important information is *hidden*, perhaps forgotten or not noticed by the user. Modes are normally a great disadvantage to the user. Typically, a system gives the user no clue about how it got to its present state or does not tell the user enough for him to be quite certain what the current state is. It may seem strange, to be so secretive, but it is in fact extremely common. As we shall see, making design decisions about modes involves very complex design tradeoffs, and often modes are allowed to remain for the gains they obtain.

In fact modes do have advantages for the user. Hidden information, if the system and user can successfully 'get away' without that information, allows the system to be used much faster—the hidden information is not transferred across the user interface. Thus modes help the user avoid interface clutter.

The central importance of modes in the design of interactive systems rests on the following two observations:

▷ Modes are perceived similarly by both designer and user.

▷ Modes contribute directly to complexity, particularly under error conditions (that is, precisely when the user and system need extra information).

Designer and user are united in fighting a common enemy!

Thus we might well seek ways to 'shave off' the number and scope of modes in an interactive systems design. This 'mode razor' is as good as Occam's Razor in reducing unnecessary design complexity. Karl Popper has suggested a sharper variant of Occam's Razor that he proposed be called **Berkeley's Razor**, after the Bishop Berkeley we met in Chapter 6, that *all entities are ruled out except those that are perceived*. If we equate 'entities' with information, then Berkeley's Razor rules out hidden information that the user cannot perceive. If a designer used Berkeley's Razor, fewer modes would be tolerated. Berkeley's Razor will lead directly on to WYSIWYG, a topic that will be addressed at length below (see Section 11.7.4).

All well and good, except that *nobody* knows or agrees precisely what a mode is. The terminology itself is open to misunderstanding: the word 'mode' can mean information channel to a psychologist (examples would be visual, aural, tactile modes); logic programmers use 'mode' in another way, which we will explore in Chapter 15. And, as we shall see below, *even with* a rigorous definition there is still a choice of abstraction level: a system can have different modiness at different levels of abstraction—just like a calculator has on/off modes, but these are of no great interest if you are *using* the calculator, for it is surely on.

We shall see below that the ambiguity in the use and identification of modes is inevitable, but the ambiguity can be used profitably by the designer, who may be able to make subtle tradeoffs in a system design if he is able to control what modes mean in his design.

11.2 Low-mode or modeless?

Modeless systems are supposed to be good. Yet using our definitions, a **modeless** system is unachievable, because at least one mode is needed to give commands an interpretation so that they might be run by the system. Strictly, a truly modeless system would have to ensure it was never switched on! Instead it is more accurate to talk of **low-mode** systems. This may also help the designer to reduce modes, rather than give up reaching for modelessness if he is convinced that a few modes are necessary.

For the sake of consistency with conventional usage it is nevertheless useful to retain the word **modeless**. But we can use it more precisely: henceforth **modeless** will mean that the user is (or is able to be) unaware of the mode in which the system is. Thus modelessness is a perceived quality of the user interface, and is generally the result of a well-designed low-mode system.

If we mean strictly modeless, then the term **mode free** can be used. Many simple public-access systems are mode free: they are always switched on, and have one key for each operation (generally a local knowledge query).

11.3   The Principle of Non-sufficient Reason

The user generally assumes that what cannot be seen at the interface does not exist and, conversely, what he can see does exist. If the user perceives response delays, these may be interpreted as significant: and if the delays are really random, the user will form an unnecessarily complex model of the system. A more frequent concern is the existence of states or information in the computer that influence the mode, but which are not directly visible to the user.

George Pólya suggests a problem-solving heuristic which he calls the **Principle of Non-sufficient Reason**:[1] if you do not have sufficient reason to doubt things are different (when solving problems) treat them as the same. When looking for eligible ideas when problem solving, no one idea should be favoured without sufficient reason to choose it. For example, the unknown variables in an equation to be solved that play the same role in a problem may be expected to play the same role in the solution to the problem.

Or, in a window manager, for instance, if two windows look the same then they should be the same; alternatively, perhaps the window manager should ensure that each window is visibly unique, for example, by providing a distinct and visible numeric (or more sensible) identifier.

It is interesting that our concern for modes could easily have come from the following argument. People have been solving problems for millennia and, over this period, others have been searching for heuristics

---

[1] Not to be confused with Leibniz's **Principle of Sufficient Reason**: nothing occurs without sufficient reason—another principle derived from everyday experience that would be useful to maintain in interactive systems! Pólya's Principle of Non-Sufficient Reason, and many others, can be found in his books (Pólya, 1948 and 1981).

and general methods for attacking problems. One of these methods is Pólya's Principle of Non-sufficient Reason, which is likely to give insight into problems if a person follows it. Conversely, if you are in the privileged position of designing problems, why not arrange for the known heuristics to work well on them if you want people to find them easier? Of course, this is just what user interface designers could be doing, and Pólya's principle suggests that systems should not work differently (that is, be modey) unless (*a*) they have sufficient reason or (*b*) they give the user sufficient information or other reasons to tell the modes apart.

11.4 Are modes good or bad?

Modes are necessary, it seems, and in the limit unavoidable, but are modes good or bad?

Modes are good: they help simplify programs (because then simple tests are sufficient to decide what to do), and they are used frequently and naturally by people (consider the number of modes that yes may be interpreted in; the mode being represented by the preceding question). Modes can be used to protect the user from mistakes: a command (such as destroy something) might have no effect in the standard mode other than cause a warning; a separate mode must be entered before destroy is activated—and entering that mode can be made as difficult as appropriate to the sort of things that might go wrong there in careless hands. The example with the word yes shows how important the effect of modes on the user depends on how much information the user has about the system. Generally we only say yes to a recognized question; with a computer it is all too easy to say yes (or, as most computer systems want it put, just y) to inappropriate actions.

So, modes are not necessarily a bad thing (except that it is easy to ignore modes that we like as being modes). For instance, if you are using a word processor and you happen to be at the end of the text it would be nice if down was an error (you probably do not want the cursor to move into nothing, and for the screen to go blank); on the other hand, elsewhere, you *do* want down to move the cursor down. The interpretation of down is modey, albeit in a trivial sort of way.

On the other hand, modes are bad: it is all too easy to forget what the state of a system is and how it will interpret your commands: the more modes there are the more likely the system will use an inappropriate mode. Even if the user knows exactly which mode a system is in, his reaction time will increase. By **Hick's Law** (Hick, 1952), the user's decision time is proportional to the logarithm of the number of choices known to be open to him. And Hick's Law is optimistic: a choice can only take logarithmic time if the user knows the options open to him well (or knows how the options are organized, so that he may search them effectively).

11.5   Spatial versus temporal modes

The reason input modes arise is quite simple: we generally want to do more things with computers than the 100 or so keys on the keyboard directly allow given a single interpretation each. Output modes arise because we want to do more things than a small display directly allows. Palpably more information can be displayed by using a sequence of several screens (or using a single screen providing a scrolling view on to a larger 'virtual' screen), but this just brings history back in: the information in the earlier screens becomes hidden in history. There are generally fewer ways of interpreting what the system does, via output to the user, than what the user does, because the output medium (for example, eyes and screen) has a much higher bandwidth than the input medium (for example, fingers and keyboard). There results an understandable—but narrow-minded— tendency to limit 'modes' to mean input modes alone.

Information requires time and space to communicate. The more space that is used, the less time is necessary; conversely, the more time, the less space. The tradeoff is perhaps easiest to understand by imagining a keyboard. If the user is restricted to a two-key keyboard (very little space at all), typing a message—in a Morse code perhaps—would take ages. Alternatively, if there were lots of keys (taking up lots of space), some messages might even be transmitted by typing a single key—saving a great deal of time. Now, it is far easier to type a four-letter word one letter at a time than to find the right key out of the about 500 000 keys that would represent all possible four-letter words. Thus, Western typists are faster than Chinese ideograph typists. Furthermore, constructing information over a period of time gives users more opportunity to reflect and (if the system permits it!) to correct errors.[2]

There are more tradeoffs complicating the issue. For instance, the more space is used, the greater choice the user has and he will tend to be under-determined. More choices will tend to slow the user down (as his brain has to select a choice from a larger set), yet perhaps give him a greater sense of achievement or control over the system.

The argument that communication is more readily distributed over time is supported by noting that degradation can always be graceful. If you have time to wait, there can always be more time to correct errors. On the contrary, space has definite boundaries that restrict error correction, and make error-corrected communication in the presence of errors (or backtracking) impossible under some circumstances. The computer's screen may simply not be big enough for some purposes, communication relying

---

[2] Chord keyboards permit users to press more than one key at a time, and thus increase the effective space of the interface exponentially. Rather than provide millions of combinations of keys, chord keyboards are usually designed with fewer keys than conventional QWERTY keyboards—five keys on a chord keyboard can simulate 31 keys on a conventional one-at-a-time keyboard.

Box 11.2   The method of loci.

People find it very easy to structure tasks by spatial position. I cook in the kitchen, I work in the office, I drive in the car. I am very unlikely to try and steer the kitchen or put a cake mixture in the car filler. But I sometimes make errors in the same place: I have been known to put coffee in a tea pot and I have put tea leaves in a cup. The ancient **method of loci**, to aid memorization by attaching mental images to various places in one's imagination, puts this spatial ability to impressive use.

---

on space will be abruptly—not gracefully—interrupted when the limits are reached.

Unfortunately, almost everything done with a computer is done in one place, looking at a screen surprisingly indifferent to the different roles the user takes on from one task to the next. This is a recipe for confusion, exacerbated by more modes, and the less distinguishable they appear to the user. And remember that the user may be unable to pay undivided attention to the system, and might easily miss announcements of mode changes. The mode in the head and the computer mode can easily get out of synchronization.

Many recent systems have **spatial modes**. The meaning of the mouse keys depends on where the mouse is pointing. The mouse has not got rid of modes, but has simply replaced temporal modes with spatial modes—and as I argued above and in Box 11.2, users are probably less likely to make mode-related mistakes with spatial modes. Nevertheless, replacing temporal modes with spatial modes is not a simple tradeoff: for instance, the user might easily forget which region of display space currently represents their dialogue. The system might be over-complex (with respect to the user's model of it); the user might hit the mouse with his elbow; he may be distracted; he may come back to the system after a cup of tea—*he* may be having a conversation with one part of the system, but the *system* thinks it is having a conversation elsewhere. As usual, the problem is that the user interface bandwidth is not wide enough to provide additional sensory cues to indicate which mode the user is in—in real life, for instance, the kitchen is decorated and smells different from the living room … and all the other senses provide extra cues. Furthermore, in real life, the user actually moves around in space: in a user interface, this spatial motion is only metaphorical.

For convenience it is often possible to drive a system by the mouse and its two or three buttons alone. Three buttons are not enough to do much that is interesting, so **temporal modes** are generally employed for those buttons: press the left button and a menu appears (which menu would depend on where the mouse was), move the mouse and a press from the right button selects from *that* menu displayed at that moment. Because there are so few buttons and they could mean so many things, it is clear that the user cannot be expected to remember all combinations for all modes: instead such systems display menus (transient spatial modes) to make it clear which mode the system is in. Mice and other analogue pointing devices cannot be used without watching the screen (without feedback the user would get lost and not know where the cursor was), so the user generally sees which mode he is in.

An interesting characteristic of most mouse-based interfaces is that most non-standard modes, like menus, are used for short durations only, and indeed if no button on the mouse is pressed the system will revert to a standard or initial mode. It is useful to recognize such **transient modes** as an essential technique and part of the reassuring robust feel of such systems.

11.6   Illustrating modes

11.6.1   Input modes illustrated

Take an example from the early 1960s, MIT's Compatible Time Sharing System. In CTSS, a colon was used for 'backspacing' but inconsistently:[3] aaa:::bb← could mean bba, bb or bba (where the first two as have been overprinted with bs). The colon is consequently a potential source of error, to say nothing of the problems of how to delete colons themselves. There are additional problems when we wonder whether the colon was merely typed and caused characters to be deleted without itself appearing, or whether the colon was echoed (printed) as an ordinary character, the others being deleted when the entire line buffer was processed.

Coming more up to date, Figure 11.1 shows a typical four-function calculator; a simple interactive system.[4] We shall see that the limited user interface bandwidth results in the display region being used for different purposes at different times—and there is no way for the user to tell which is which, except by remembering what he has been doing. Furthermore, there is a significant amount of information that is *never* displayed, and which the user *always* has to remember. All this hidden information contributes to modes in the calculator's user interface, as we shall see in the discussion below. But what is worth pointing out now is that, even so, the calculator remains a very useful tool. Indeed, it is not clear how some of the modes of

---

[3] The code of colon happens to differ from backspace by one bit—you see how easily implementation concerns intrude into the user interface!

[4] Arithmetic and calculators form a frequent example used in this book. Calculators have the advantage of being simple enough to bring out salient features without copious description. Also, we can invoke Gödelization to argue that arithmetic is semantically rich enough to satisfy every computable example we care to think of. Of course, such a wild claim leaves aside serious issues of representation. Gödel numbers are virtually impossible for human use!

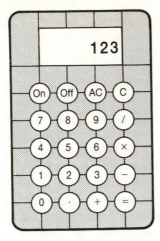

Figure 11.1   A simple four-function calculator.

the calculator could be avoided—at least, if we wanted to retain its range of features. As usual, then, design is a tradeoff, in this case, between too many features for the available interface bandwidth and suffering modes.

Our calculator has 20 buttons, although once the calculator is on, the ON button has no further use, and it could be given another meaning (for example, as a reset or 'all clear', which is what the bottom left button AC is supposed to do).

It will be useful to review quickly how to use this calculator. First, the user has to switch it on. He has to press the ON button to do this. The calculator will then remain on until the OFF button is pressed (or until its batteries run down). Fortunately, we can give the user a simple rule:

> ▷ If nothing is displayed in the display region (and you want to use the calculator!) press the ON button. You can use the calculator until you next press the OFF button.[5]

The calculator will display 0 (with a decimal point) as soon as it is switched on. It is now ready to accept commands from the user. Not every command will have an effect at this stage; for instance, if the user hits the decimal point '.', nothing will appear to happen. Of course, hitting ON will have no further effect (this may not always be true)!

If the user hits a digit, that digit is displayed. Of course, if the user hits 0, 0 is already displayed, so the 0 button doesn't seem to do anything yet. Hitting digits again has an interesting effect: the number displayed is multiplied by ten, and the digit pressed is added—this gives the appearance

---

[5] Can you see how to get rid of this rule? The calculator could be switched on all the time (or on all the time there was enough light to see it, which is easy if the calculator is powered by solar cells); or hitting any key could switch it on—and still do what it would have done had the calculator already been on.

of the number sliding in from the right. In fact, this is a general rule, and explains why hitting zero would not have had an effect at first, since $0 \times 10 + 0$ is still 0.

It is arguable that this rule is too complex. Why not arrange the calculator to work like paper? That is, as the user hits keys, the number simply grows from the right as if the user were writing it down, left to right. Certainly there might be problems with insignificant leading zeros taking up too much room: but the user might find this a quite understandable sort of limitation. Besides, most calculators anyway work incorrectly if the user hits more significant digits than the display can handle.

The decimal point changes the last rule: after the point button is pressed, subsequent digits are divided by 10, 100, 1 000 ... (depending on how many digits have been pressed since the decimal point), and then added to the display. If the decimal point is hit more than once, the calculator will multiply the display by 1, 10, 100, 1 000, depending on how many digits the user has pressed since the last time the decimal point was hit.

Of course, as the user hits digit buttons, the display gradually fills up. Eventually, the display will be completely full: and two different rules apply as to what happens next depending on whether the user has hit the decimal point. If the decimal point has not been hit: the calculator jams up, and the C button must be pressed (which also changes the display to 0). If the decimal point has been pressed, further digits hit by the user are completely ignored.

These rules seem quite intricate when they are spelt out and we have not even started to see what happens when we hit other buttons! Of course, the user gets the idea pretty quickly; the way numbers behave has been understood since childhood—emphasizing the point that interactive systems rely implicitly on an awesome amount of user knowledge, and indeed knowledge that was not learnt in a few days.

The calculator becomes more interesting both for us and the user when some arithmetic operation (+, -, ×, ÷) is pressed. Pressing any of these four buttons has no obvious effect, but the *next* digit pressed works in an apparently new way: it will start a *new* number.

What is happening is this: there are really *two* numbers relevant to the interaction, but at any given time only one of them can be displayed. There is the number the user is currently entering; and there is the number representing the running result of the current calculation. So as soon as + is pressed, the displayed number changes from being 'number being entered' to 'running calculation'. As soon as the user next hits a number, the display reverts to 'number being entered', which is of course a *new* number. There are two rules for controlling the display:

▷   Hitting a digit or the decimal point changes the display to 'current number' or if already the current number, it has the effect described earlier.

Box 11.3   Emily Runciman, age 6, is given a calculator.

Child: '... can it add any numbers?'
Adult: 'Yes.' *Adult explains method. Child taps keys.*
Child: '... it doesn't work.'
Adult: 'Did you press the equals key?'
Child: 'Oh yes.'
Adult: 'Did you use it like this?' *Explains again.*
Child: 'Yes.'
Adult: *Exasperated.* 'Well, what were you trying to do?'
Child: 'Work out nothing plus nothing.'

▷ Hitting an operator changes the display to 'running calculation'. It has no effect if the running calculation is already displayed.

Now, calculator buttons are notoriously unreliable, they make no noise and hardly move when pressed. We can safely assume that there will be many times when the user is uncertain whether he has successfully pressed a key; in general, the user will not know whether the display shows 'running calculation' or 'current number'. There are many other reasons why the user may not know, for instance, part way through some calculation he is interrupted by a telephone call and the display meaning gets lost from STM.

The calculator has two modes. Depending on which mode the calculator is in, keys mean different things. Furthermore, this particular calculator provides no way for the user to tell which mode it is in without destroying the calculation. Real calculators have even more modes, for instance if an operator is pressed twice in succession then the 'running calculation' may be copied to the 'constant'. The effect of this is that subsequent uses of +, −, ×, ÷ add, subtract, multiply and divide *by the constant*. There is probably no direct way to display the constant (one could of course try 0+= to see it, and lose the current calculation). Calculators often provide special features, exploiting key press sequences that our rules have not otherwise defined: for instance, to add proportions or perform percentage calculations.

A user may not think of such a simple calculator as having even two modes. He is more likely to shout out that 'the calculator has lost my calculation' or worse. Part of the problem is that *there is no way to find out which mode the calculator is in without otherwise affecting it.* Thus, a cautious user will always write down the running calculation, in case it gets wiped out by an accidental key press. (Chapter 13 will formally address just this sort of issue.)

Lastly, note that one of the most important modes of the calculator is whether it is on or off and, as it happens, this is readily detected. If anything at all is displayed, the calculator is on, otherwise it is off. This may seem an obvious point! But many interactive computer systems are designed in such a way that it is not possible for the user to tell whether they are working or not, whether the user is able to submit commands or not.

Is the machine on or off? You may think it a joke to worry about on/off modes: but consider the sort of computer system where both the display monitor and the keyboard (or the computer itself) have on/off switches. To switch the computer on, and know it is on, requires both switches to be on. If the last person to use the computer only switched off the monitor, the next person may have a very frustrating time—especially when the on/off switches are push-on/push-off buttons which do not indicate which state they are in!

11.6.2   Pre-emptive modes illustrated

Modes are ways of interpreting what the user does (though we shall see below that they are also ways of interpreting what the system does); there is, however, an alternative and equivalent way of looking at them. Modes determine the meanings of commands the user submits; it is therefore possible for the user to get the system into a mode where the meanings he wants are not available.

Typically, in this **pre-emptive mode**, the user can still submit the commands he would like to do, but the mode interprets them as errors or perhaps ignores them. Thus the user is pre-empted: he must provide the commands the mode deigns to interpret. A pre-emptive system is sometimes called **modal**—which it is, for it provides one mode, pre-empting the user from alternatives.

The last two paragraphs certainly describe a new aspect of modes, but no doubt it seems too abstract to follow! A simple example will show how common pre-emptive modes really are. Imagine that you are in a spreadsheet program and you wish to save some data on to a floppy disk. You put in a disk, and submit the 'save on disk' command. So far, so good. The disk clatters, but then the system announces that it cannot write to the disk because it is not formatted. Clearly, the user is supposed to format the disk before attempting to write data to it ... but the format command is not available in the spreadsheet. The user knows there *is* a format command somewhere in the system, yet the modes imposed by the spreadsheet do not provide 'format disk' as the interpretation of anything the user can do. The only solution is to exit the spreadsheet, so that the format command can be issued in *that* out-of-spreadsheet mode—which, of course, is a disaster for the user, as he loses all the data he wanted to store on the disk! To summarize: in the modes provided by the spreadsheet, the user can write data to a disk, but cannot format the disk. In the non-spreadsheet mode, the user can format a disk but naturally cannot write spreadsheet data. If the user happens to have entered the spreadsheet before formatting his disk (and he has data that needs saving), then he is in for trouble.

Since some systems avoid this particular problem (for example, by automatically formatting new disks), consider one further example. The user is working on a drawing, and has perhaps drawn a rectangle of a certain size. It turns out that this box is 6 cm long, but it should be 5 cm. The drawing program has a scaling feature, select the rectangle and type a number: the rectangle is then shrunk or enlarged by the percentage submitted. The user therefore needs to enter 5/6 as a percentage (500/6) but the system only accepts numbers. Quite likely the computer will provide a calculator that can do just this sort of sum, but while the user has the percentage question in front of him the calculator is—for some reason—inaccessible: the user, having selected the scaling operation, *has* to submit a number to scale by. In short, the scaling dialogue pre-empts the calculator dialogue. This problem, too, can be solved (by permitting expressions wherever numbers are required—so called **substitutivity**; see Section 14.3.7): the issue is that more often than not, the problem is left as a piece of restrictive, unnecessary pre-emption.

Particular problems, like the ones just illustrated, can be tackled by the designer in a piecemeal fashion. Yet each operation has many ways of failing: in the first example, the disk might be full (what file does the user want to delete?); the disk might be write-protected; the user might need some help; there may be a file of the same name on the disk already … and this is just writing to disks! The user clearly needs a command that takes him from spreadsheet mode to disk manager mode, where *any* disk management commands can be interpreted. It only takes another problem for the disk manager itself to 'mode the user in' ('Don't mode me in': phrase coined by Larry Tesler, 1981) so that some command the user now wants to submit cannot be interpreted. In general, rather than a piecemeal approach, the underlying operating system has to support concurrency (indeed, make it so easy that the programmer is encouraged to use it freely). Users may or may not need concurrency very often (depending on their work), but it is a great relief to have any mode available at any time, whether or not the designer anticipated the user requiring that mode in certain circumstances.

A special case of pre-emption is **delay**. In normal pre-emption, the user is restricted to a certain set of commands. When a system pauses, the user cannot do *anything*: he is restricted to a set of no commands. And exacerbating the problem is that being in or out of this mode may itself be hidden information. The user may submit a command thinking it will be interpreted, but it will not, at least until later—by which time other things may have changed.

For instance, consider the problem of **mousing ahead** (also, **type ahead**, typing faster than the system can process, has similar problems). The user submits a command which the system undertakes to execute—causing the delay. Next, the user moves the mouse to a menu (say) and selects an item: but the system is still working out the last command. The user has moused-ahead. Quite possibly, the command terminates normally, and the relevant menu item is selected. But it is also possible that the result of executing the command is to display something which conceals or moves the menu: then, the user has selected something else, not what he saw on the screen when he performed the selection, but what is now in the same place. There are worse problems, for instance, the user may be uncertain that he has selected the menu entry correctly (after all, the system is still working on the last command and cannot yet respond to the menu selection); so perhaps the user tries to select the menu entry again. When the system gets around to processing the menu selection, it will find two consecutive selections, which will almost certainly have some unanticipated effect. In both cases, the information the user needs to understand what the system will do when he selects (or thinks he selects) the menu item is hidden in the uncertain future.

Mouse ahead could probably be solved by providing some visual feedback on progress, for instance, changing the colour of the screen or the shape of cursor. Presumably the user is watching the screen so that he knows where he is moving the cursor? It is interesting to wonder how and under what circumstances such feedback could be automatically provided by suitably designed hardware that monitors the progress of the user's application program.

11.6.3   Output modes illustrated

System output is interpreted by the user, who will assume it is displayed in some specific mode (there are usually fewer output modes than for input since the output bandwidth is usually larger). An interesting example showing output mode problems arises when diagnostics can be confused with ordinary text. Suppose there is a 'list *file*' command, and a file listed happens to contain the text `file does not exist`. On many systems, the user will interpret this text in the wrong mode, and assume the file really does not exist! This example can easily occur if diagnostics from commands can be saved in files. When the user lists a diagnostic file he can easily assume `file` refers to the file being printed, not the file that was missing when the diagnostics were saved.

Some display editors distinguish between various types of blank text, calling them 'written', or 'required' space, being spaces that are 'really there' or submitted once upon a time by the user. Other spaces, although being visible, are not actually part of the text the user is reading. Typically the user cannot tell which is which—output modes again. It is worse when there is a screen pointing device, such as a mouse, which the user can move to anywhere on the screen, whether or not it is over a place that the editor allows editing.

Escape codes

One of the most common sources of output modes arises with poor design decisions about increasing the number of symbols available to the display. For all sorts of reasons, the designer wants to display more information than there are symbols to represent it. He may also want to distinguish between equally displayed symbols (for example, between spaces and tabs, or between written and required spaces). A word processor may want to display the codes, **attributes**, that format text (but displaying the codes would upset the format); or a terminal can only display a subset of the ASCII character set, yet some application uses 128 or even 256 characters. Such problems frequently arise in operating system design: the operating system output routines must be able to print any character, *and they should indicate the character code unambiguously.*

The standard solution is to reserve all but one of the standard printing characters (that is, letters, digits and punctuation) for the corresponding character codes. The special character will be called the **escape**, and might be '^' or some other little-used character. To print any character code outside the standard range now only requires an escape combination, for instance '^A' can denote ASCII code 1, or control+A. Since there are about 96 standard characters, a scheme like this (which almost doubles the number of symbols) can easily cater for a seven-bit character code.

Since the system may have to display '^' itself, the code '^^' is conventionally taken to mean the single symbol '^', not the escape command—but many systems are not consistent! Output modes arise because of the ambiguity in output like '^^A': does it mean '^' followed by 'A', or possibly '^' followed by control+A? If the symbol '^^' *always* meant '^', there would be no problem because the choice would be known—the display '^^A' means '^' followed by 'A'.

11.6.4 Inertial modes illustrated

Modes also arise when the internal state of the system is used to provide part of the meaning of a command. Hidden information can be used to make the user interface more efficient by exploiting information the user (or designer) supplied in the past.

When the user submits a command a second time, the system may remember how it was used the previous time. The system is able to fill in details by **defaulting** them. Of course, the information that provides the default values is normally hidden, for it only appears when the user resubmits an earlier command. In the case where the designer supplied the default, the system will typically supply what the designer thinks is the most likely fragment of missing information. (Some recent systems use a sophisticated profile of the user to choose the information.) The excerpt in square width? *1·2471* ↵

· · ·

square width 1·2471? ↵

Figure 11.2   Defaults in action.

Figure 11.2 is from a dialogue that shows how user-supplied defaults can be used.

The user is running some drawing program, where (for instance) squares of certain size may be drawn. The first time the user wants to draw a square, the system has no idea how large it should be, so it asks. The user supplies *1·2471* (in units that the system has presumably defaulted from information supplied even earlier—perhaps by the designer). Later on, the user wants to draw another square. The size information obtained last time a square was drawn can now be used by the system to save the user submitting the information again. The user need only use **passive recall** (that is, 1·2471 has only to be recognized as correct, rather than actively generated by the user); there is also a reduced danger of making typing mistakes (though there is a heightened danger of defaulting *completely* the wrong information).

Consider if the user is running an editor. First he wants to edit a file. Later he wants to delete a file: if the system defaults the filename, the user can delete the file he was editing by only one typing mistake. Also, passive recall has greater danger of the user automatically affirming the system without really thinking. Defaulting is generally *not* a good strategy if the result can be expensive (or, in the limit, irreversible).

This particular scheme for defaulting has used a 'syntax error', that is a missing number, as acceptance of the suggested default value. An alternative would be to ask the user a question, such as 'width 1·2471?', to which the user replies *y* or *n*. If the user replies *n*, then he would be asked for a specific numeric value, 'what width then?'. Another alternative is to allow the user to imply a no answer by simply submitting a number. This uses the 'syntax error' the other way around.

Some menu user interfaces require two actions of the user: first a choice, then a confirmation (for example, move the cursor over the desired element, then click or press enter). Such menus are often designed so that the last choice made by the user is inertial. Next time a menu is displayed, the default choice will be the last one the user selected. Thus, if the user immediately clicks, the last choice is selected. For this sort of menu, enter is a postfix command that requires a choice to be made first; if no choice is made, the system can default its value.

Other forms of menu where the select and submit steps are not separate cannot be inertial. Typically the user selects a menu entry by typing its number, which will be a single digit. Since it is a single digit, pressing it needs no `enter` step.

Menus are very often organized in a hierarchical fashion: selecting from one menu brings up another, and selecting from that brings up a third. Each menu may have a `go back` entry, that allows the user to go back to a previous menu and make a different choice at that point, perhaps going back again, ultimately to reach the first menu. Inertia can often be used to help the user orient himself within the menu system.

The simplest form is that each menu remembers the last choice that was made with it. Thus, when the user selects a `go back` entry, the previous menu is displayed and it shows the selection that was last made in it, which of course is the menu the user has just come from. More radical inertia might allow the user to jot down notes on each menu (or on the surrounding screen), or to change attributes like the background colour. Inertia would ensure that these features are fixed. Next time the user comes across the same menu, it will show the user's original jottings and other choices: the user will be able to distinguish this menu from others much more easily. Users will be less likely to get lost in a large anonymous menu system. (Obviously, some of the attribute coding might be supplied—defaulted—by the system, imposing conventions deemed to be helpful, for example, in typographic details.)

Inertia in user interfaces is named after the inertia of mechanics. It is instructive to compare inertial laws of motion (Newtonian mechanics) and non-inertial laws of motion (Aristotelean mechanics).

Newton's three Laws of Motion are not at all obvious. If we take the time for them to be discovered as an indicator, or the time for which Aristotle's Laws were accepted, they must be quite counter-intuitive. Aristotle thought that for continuous motion there must be a continuous force, or *cause* (hence angels pushed the planets around—some cause was necessary to explain their continued motion). Thus, Aristotle claimed that motion required a cause, and given the lifetime of this idea, it must have seemed obvious. Nevertheless, Newton claimed that motion was a state requiring no continued cause, the reason being that mass has inertia.

Newton introduced inertia: the motion of a body depends on the history of its influence by forces. For Aristotle, there was no such thing as inertia; without a cause, a body would fall back to earth or heaven. If you like, Aristotle's Laws of Motion are modeless, but Newton's are modey, but modey in a certain way: Newton's Laws are *inertial*.

The point is that 'inertia' is a form of modiness as seen by the Aristotelean user, but is a useful form of modiness as seen by the Newtonian. We shall see below that what is a mode depends very much on how the user views the system. Crucially, how the user views the system depends, in turn, on how the designer constructs and explains the system.

To summarize the analogy from mechanics: *some* forms of modiness, which we shall call **inertial**, are useful and help the user progress without

---

Box 11.4   Unmediated sound.

Long ago, when a 'big' computer had less memory and speed than a modern personal computer, it was common practice to attach a loudspeaker to the machine's program counter or to its bus. A typical arrangement would make a click each time the program counter was changed. The computer then made different sorts of noises depending on what it was doing. This is **unmediated**, since the computer does not impose an interpretation or structure on the sound generation. A computer operator (what this book calls a user) would soon get to know what various sounds meant. Probably things got too complex on timesharing computers for sound to be useful, but nevertheless computer technology seems to have lost sound, except for a single beep. Also, in the old days, the sounds came from the only computer in the room; nowadays, sound made by every computer in a typing pool can be socially unacceptable—especially if some sounds are used to announce user errors. Whatever the historical reasons, very few interactive programs make good use of the beep: consider the guep, 'commands have the following properties x, y, z except if the system beeps' (for example, consider cursor motion which fails at screen boundaries).

Mediated sound, using synthesized sounds, could be used to reduce mode errors. In one mode the system sounds like a waterfall, and in another mode the system sounds like a motorway. Choosing such mediated sounds will be very difficult.

---

effort. However, inertia is (or can be) a sophisticated concept, and perhaps goes beyond the comprehension of the user, carrying him off into places where he does not want to go—without his doing anything. Then, inertia turns to modes.

11.7   Gueps for modes

Gueps are dual statements that should be useful to designers and to users. Rather than develop each guep in both directions, which would be tedious and lose sight of the wood for the trees, this section *suggests* rather than *describes* gueps. The discussion about WYSIWYG (Section 11.7.4 below) will give the clearest indication that gueps represent design tradeoffs rather than simple decisions.

11.7.1   Gueps for input modes

Informally, an **input mode** is a way of interpreting what the user submits to the system. The user types q, say: in one mode this will be interpreted as an abbreviation for quit, in another mode it might mean a letter q (as part of a longer submission (for example, equal) that is yet to be interpreted), in another mode it may simply be an error. So far as keyboard applications are concerned, the colloquial form of a typical mode-related guep might go something like, 'The interactive system is so consistent and predictable that it may be used effectively with your eyes shut'. (Referring to the user's eyes may be too 'psychological'; an alternative 'technical' formulation is, 'The interactive system is so consistent and predictable that it may be used effectively with the display switched off'.)

This guep is perhaps rather extreme, though not unrealistic. The formulation above is tantamount to requiring the user to be able to touch type—so he really can use the system, including the keyboard, without looking! More seriously, it means that either commands always have a single interpretation or, perhaps, that exceptional circumstances are announced by making a sound. It can also be taken to mean that, if there are several modes, then the user can change between modes by fixed, mode-independent, command sequences: whatever mode the system is in (whatever the display says), the user can submit fixed sequences to get the system into desired modes—for instance, escape always exits to the top menu: this is **idempotence**, which is defined in Section 14.3.3.

The 'eyes shut' principle would be ideal not only for desk-top publishing or word processing applications, but also for systems intended for writing notes during personnel interviews; tasks when the user of the system would be unable to pay undivided attention to visual feedback from the system. We also require gueps to be expressed formally so that they can be used precisely in design.

The guep 'you can use it with your eyes shut' does not make sense for direct manipulation applications that require the user to see what he is pointing at and manipulating. This is another reason why direct manipulation is a good thing: the designer does not need to employ a *discretionary* design rule to reduce modiness.

11.7.2 Gueps for pre-emptive modes

A phrase like, 'you can do anything anywhere' is a possible colloquial form of a guep outlawing pre-emptive modes. It means that wherever the user 'is' in the system, all commands are available to him. In particular being able to 'do anything anywhere' outlaws the pre-emptive, 'Do you want X?' if the *only* response is *yes* or *no*.

There are two standard design solutions to achieve non-pre-emption. In a conventional (small screen) application, non-pre-emption must be achieved by a temporal feature: the user can enter any command at any time, provided it is prefixed by (say) '!'. Even if the system requires yes/no responses, the user would be permitted to submit any command instead,

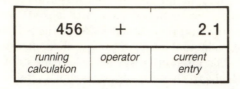

Figure 11.3 Declarative calculator display.

so long as he prefixed it by '!'—in a sense, meaning neither the command nor its result is to be taken as the user's answer to the question. In more recent systems with multiple windows *and the continuous ability to bring up any window to submit any command*, non-pre-emption can be achieved by allowing the user to move into another region of the screen. There he can either continue with an old mode, or create a new mode. There are advantages in providing both techniques—and, of course, making them available all the time and in all regions of the screen.

11.7.3 Gueps for output modes

One of the commonest forms of output mode is due to **history**, that is, to the user interface being imperative. The calculator example with which we started the chapter had two output modes, and which mode the system (calculator) was in depended on, for instance, whether = or a digit had been pressed most recently. In the calculator, the output mode depends on the recent history of interaction.

If, instead, the system was declarative, there need be no alternative output modes. In colloquial form, we might tell the user that he can do sums on what he can see *alone*. Typically, then, the calculator has to be designed to show *all* of the calculation that is relevant.

With such a radical departure from the original design, it is tempting to over-generalize and provide lots of new features that were not thought necessary in the original (for instance, providing brackets). However, if we retain the original functionality of the calculator, a display slightly larger than twice the original size is required.

Figure 11.3 shows the basic idea: the display simply shows *everything* pertinent to the calculation. The original calculator had a single display that showed the running calculation or the current number; now the new design can display both at once. The operator region of the display (which will display +, -, and so on) is used so that the user even knows what the last operator key press was. Nothing is hidden.

Every button has a well-defined effect on the calculator in terms of the information displayed *alone*. What a key does is in no way dependent on the history (except insofar as the history changes the display). In Berkeley's terms, the only relevant entities are those that can be perceived. To give one example of the improvement this declarative idea entails, notice that the = button is now redundant (it might therefore be repainted and used to take over a function that might previously have been assigned to some obscure button sequence, for example, for calculating proportions).

11.7.4 WYSIWYG: a guep for output modes

'What you see is what you get' has become a popular slogan for describing a certain style of interactive systems design. Abbreviated WYSIWYG—pronounced wizzy-wig—the phrase has become a byword for requiring that what the user can see (the output from the system) is indeed what he has got. In other words, that there is no hidden information that cannot be seen. If, for some reason, what can be seen is not what the user has, there is hidden information—and modes.

WYSIWYG is usually taken to mean something like a concept of text display in word processors where you can use interactive commands to modify the displayed text so that you can immediately see exactly what will be obtained when the text is printed.

This approach avoids the use of conventional formatting commands with obscure codes embedded in the text (for example, `.PARA` to start a paragraph, `.CENTRE` to centre a line). The exact effect of commands like `.PARA` is not known until the text is printed. They are programs, and just like any other program they have to be run to see what their effect is. In a non-WYSIWYG text editor, running the program (a process called **formatting**) is performed non-interactively. This means, in particular, that to debug a text format (for example, to get running headlines to correspond properly with section names) requires sophisticated programming skills. WYSIWYG avoids these problems, but limits the control a *sophisticated* user might wish to have over the format. The design could compromise: simple things could be WYSIWYG, advanced things could be programmable. What you get would not be exactly what you see, but the rules might be precise enough for the principle 'what you get is what you can see *plus* the details supplied by the program' to apply. The meaning of '*plus*' would need clarifying.

If you cannot see it, you haven't got it—but merely providing dynamic formatting does not, of itself, achieve getting what is seen, and (not least) word processors provide many other functions which this formulation does not consider. Nevertheless, if used with care, WYSIWYG is a principle that has the advantage that it can lead both the designer and the user to have a considerable overlap in their conceptualization of an interactive system. We ought to explore how to make the overlap as large as possible.

The features that make a WYSIWYG system easy to use are exactly the features that make it tedious for an expert to use. There can be no 'power commands' that affect data not displayed, nor commands that structure it in sophisticated ways without actually showing ('what you see'ing) the structure. Consider the following example, based on a word processor that can display text in several font styles. Suppose the text, 'abc◇**def**' is displayed, with the cursor (shown here as '◇') in the space between the abc and the bold **def**. What happens if the user types another character? Will the next character be bold or not? The problem is that the user cannot see whether the space is bold (or whether the bold font starts to the left or right of the cursor position). The user cannot see everything he has got. One design idea would be to make the font changes explicit and visible (for example, displaying either 'abc↑ **def**' or 'abc ↑**def**', as appropriate, where ↑ means 'become bold'), or simply to live with the problem, perhaps it doesn't happen often enough, and anyway, since this is a word processor, the user can recover from any errors easily enough (Section 10.8).

Interestingly WYSIWYG encourages under-determined dialogues. A non-WYSIWYG system generally separates the various stages of preparing an object (for example, separating editing and formatting a textual document), whereas WYSIWYG presents the user with the finished article all the time. The user must therefore have concurrent access both to content-editing and form-editing commands. The chances are that this will improve the user's satisfaction—for the system does not constrain him to structure how he performs his tasks; he doesn't have to first supply content *then* its form—but choosing amongst the extra alternatives will tend to slow him down. For complex activities, WYSIWYG has the same danger as programming: if all you can see is the final program text rather than its evolution, then some changes may be too difficult; this problem is particularly apparent when trying to edit very detailed pictures with a drawing (or painting) system, since the user can only change what it looks like *now*, rather than how he originally drew it. For example, it might have been better to have drawn that circle larger a few minutes ago, but now it is 'underneath' things that have been drawn since. (Undo and redo, to be discussed in the next chapter, provide one way of changing how the user actually drew a picture, but they are general techniques and not—at least in their basic form—ideal for visual tasks.)

11.7.5 Gueps for inertial modes

Inertial gueps can be divided into two classes: local and global. A local property says something about what is happening now or here; a global property says something about what is happening everywhere.

Box 11.5   The tense of WYSIWYG.

It seems to me that the usual formulation of WYSIWYG is more hype about the sort of hardware than about the style of interaction. WYSIWYG is usually expressed in the present tense *with future implications*: What you see is what you *will* get. What you see on the screen is what you will get when it is printed on paper. This encourages people to buy expensive high resolution displays, then fancy printers that can print with the freedom they have discovered without the restrictions of a character mapped display. WYSIWYG suggests hardware remedies for improving user interfaces: improve resolution (and ensure screen and hardcopy resolution are compatible). This is clearly useful, but it is interesting to see how a slight change in wording would make WYSIWYG a principle applicable to interaction *per se*.

'What you see is what you *have got*', expressed in the present perfect, is about what is happening *now*, rather than what will happen when the user presses the `print` button. We can still call the principle WYSIWYG, but take it to mean that what the user can see *is* what he has got *inside the machine*. This interpretation is roughly what I called **passivity** before anyone had thought of WYSIWYG. But it is important to think of catchy principles. 'Passivity' is neither catchy nor, crucially, of any intrinsic meaning to a user. Er, just like WYSIWYG?

Expressing WYSIWYG in the present perfect tense (or at least viewing it to be about interaction) makes it clearer how gueps represent tradeoffs rather than thresholds. In the conventional sense, any display or printer resolution above the strictly necessary is just a bonus. In the interactive sense, a certain amount of power is required, but too much is proscribed. For example, if what can be seen is what one has, then the display must preserve the structure of the underlying data. Commands that do powerful things would not be acceptable.

A comment command would be unacceptable if the body of the comment could completely cover the screen without the user being able to see it was in fact commented out: the user could see something (by being comment, it could say *anything*), but it would not represent what he had got. The user sees some Pascal '`write(1); {This prints 0!}`', which really *does* print zero—because the comment is mischievously '{*backspaces* 1}; {This prints 0!}'. What the user can see is not what he has got!

An example inertial guep of the local kind would be, 'The screen (or rather, the data displayed on the screen) moves as little as possible', or 'Everything stays as you left it'. These principles are asking for **display inertia**, so that information tends to stay still, where the user left it on the screen. If a display is non-inertial, the user might spend a lot of time rereading the screen to assure himself that nothing other than the position had changed. Special cases of display inertia are limiting the movement of the cursor (except when explicitly moved), and limiting the number of places on the screen that the user *has* to read. Some systems expect the user to enter data in one part of the screen (where the cursor happens to be), but provide instructions at the top, sometimes at the bottom, and sometimes where the cursor is. A consistent place would probably be better, and more inertial.

The problem with WYSIWYG is that 'what you see is *all* you've got' is a bit restrictive. We often want to have more than we can see. A text editor would be a bit limited if it could only edit a few dozen lines. In most systems, the user has to remember information not displayed. A display inertia guep can be wielded to guarantee that the information not displayed at any moment does not change; or, conversely, the user can only affect information that he can see. Thus, an example inertial guep of the global kind would be, 'When you go back, everything is as you left it'.

This last guep makes (or with a little adjustment could easily make) an important guarantee for the user: that he can examine all his data (for example, by scrolling the screen) and be certain that by doing so he is not changing it.

Menus provide a good illustration of inertial principles. We need to clarify some terminology: some menus provide selections in two steps. First, an entry may be **highlighted**, then **activated**. Key or numeric menus often do both steps at once. Just hitting a digit activates one of several menu entries. This entry may *then* be highlighted by the system as a side-effect, to remind the user that that was his last selection.

The user interface provides two sorts of operations: change the highlighted entry, and activate the currently highlighted entry. On a mouse-based system, merely moving the mouse changes the highlighted entry, and hitting a mouse button activates the entry. The combined action flows easily, and is generally called **selection**.

Now imagine that whenever the user submits ? a menu comes up to provide an easy way to submit any of the available commands at that point in the dialogue. The user might be drawing a rectangle, hits ? and the menu comes up displaying a variety of line styles with which to draw the rectangle. The user might select dotted lines, and then continue drawing. Later the user is drawing another rectangle, hits ? and the line style menu reappears. Now, the question is, which menu entry is going to be highlighted? Is the system inertial, in the sense that it remembers the last line style chosen was dotted? Or does it always highlight the first entry or the entry nearest the cursor? Maybe it should highlight none: the user would have to explicitly move the cursor to get a highlight—and nothing could be selected by default.

Hierarchical menus have entries that, when selected bring up further menus. Suppose the user selects a menu entry, then another, then another—which causes some command to be run. Thus the system reverts to the previous menu. What entry will be shown highlighted? If the system is inertial, it ought to show the last activated entry as highlighted, even though this may be several levels down.

Actually a moment's reflection shows that this form of inertia is 'most recently used', and other equally sensible choices might be 'most likely to be used' (see Section 16.9.4), or 'most frequently used' and so on: in these cases some sort of modelling will have to go on, and care must be taken so that the system does not out-guess the user.

11.8 Domain independence?

Domain independence was mentioned in Section 10.6 as an important characteristic for design guidelines. It would be too exhausting to take every guep and show that domain independence can be achieved. Instead I shall just examine WYSIWYG, partly because WYSIWYG is 'obviously' just a principle for word processor type applications—and there does not appear to be much domain independence there!

So in what way is WYSIWYG domain independent—or is it specialized, and only of interest in the limited domain of word processing? In short, is WYSIWYG a way of summarizing *past* designs, or can it be elaborated in a way that is useful for *future* designs in new fields beyond word processing?

WYSIWYG is touted as a style for interactive text processing systems: the text you see on the screen is the text you will get when you print it. But it could apply with equal force to a drawing system (the picture you can see is the picture you will get), or more or less straightforwardly to any system that ultimately provides output on a sheet of paper or any other two dimensional medium. Things would get slightly more complex with computer controlled machining systems that could produce three dimensional objects, but WYSIWYG would certainly give both designer and user insights.

11.8.1 SLR cameras

SLR (single lens reflex) cameras are perhaps hardly sophisticated computer systems, but they represent the commonest literal form of WYSIWYG. In an SLR camera, the user looks through the same lens system as is used to take the photograph on film. Thus the user sees exactly what image the camera will record, even if special-effect lenses are being used. This is in contrast to the cheaper viewfinder arrangement where the optics of the viewfinder are separate from the film optics. A very easy mistake to make with a cheap camera is to photograph someone, but miss out the top of his head. His head may be fully in the viewfinder, but not on the film—what you see is not what you get.

This example makes a most important point. WYSIWYG, or any other guep, may make excellent sense and even obviously make a system

easier or more reliable to use. But it is quite a different matter to work out
how to design a system so that it is WYSIWYG. The WYSIWYG principle
itself does not suggest the crafty arrangement of lenses, prisms and mirrors
needed in an SLR camera. The creative part of design is still fully in the
hands of the designer.

11.8.2   Cooker timers

Sometimes, however, a guep may almost directly suggest a means of
implementation. Take electronic cooker timers. A cooker timer provides
three basic functions: since it is a clock, it can be used to tell the time; it
can be used for timing short intervals (for example, to cook eggs); and it
can be used to switch on and off the main oven (for example, to switch the
oven on at 3 pm, and leave it on for two hours). Some cooker timers also
provide other features which we need not consider here.

With the few features mentioned, a WYSIWYG timer needs four
numeric (analogue or digital) displays. One for the time; one for the egg
timer; one for oven on time; one for oven off time. These times all represent
information that may be inside the timer, and if WYSIWYG is to hold,
there must be some way to view the information. Since it is possible that
you may want to know what time it is while cooking an egg just before
an oven-cooked supper, you might even want all information at the same
time. That means four displays and four knobs, including one to set the
clock to the correct time of day. However, most modern digital timers have
only one display; older analogue timers needed several knobs and pointers
just to enter the times—this avoids multiplexing the mechanical linkages
which is much harder than electronic multiplexing. (The mechanical input
knobs could also serve as output displays for the user, a form of **equal
opportunity**, the subject of Chapter 15.) The display will show the time
corresponding to whatever the timer is doing. If it is not doing anything
else, it will show the time of day. If it is timing eggs, it will show a decreasing
count. If something is waiting in the oven, it might show a count-down to
when the oven is to be switched on.

Suppose the user has set the oven timer for a meal to be cooked in the
evening. Now the user wants to cook an egg. Dare he? Might fiddling with
the timer so that it works as a simple egg timer disrupt the oven timings?
A single-display clock may make the user think that changing the display
(from oven count-down to egg timer) must also change the internal state,
so that it forgets the oven timing instructions. With a WYSIWYG timer,
it would certainly be clearer to the user that each display was independent.

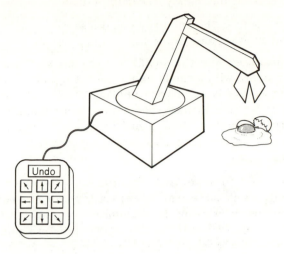

Figure 11.4   A programmable robot arm.

11.8.3   Industrial robots

I have used an industrial robot which was programmed by a handheld
keypad. It looked something like Figure 11.4. The robot had a single arm
and grab that could be moved in three planes, and the whole contraption
could be rotated about a vertical axis. The control panel had keys that
moved the arm in a specified direction for the duration that the key was
pressed. It was possible to move the arm around and pick up small objects,
swing round, and drop them in a bin—the sort of operation that would be
very useful in a simple production line. Of course, it would be even more
useful if it could be programmed to perform repetitive operations. And it
could. The control panel had another button for programming, though all
it did was to record a sequence of key presses so that they could later be
replayed.

Of course, it was very easy to make mistakes trying to control the
robot. The control panel also had an 'undo' key, to undo the effect of the
last program step (actually, a delete key). Unfortunately it undid just the
program step, and did not undo the robot arm movement. So imagine that
the user makes a slip: the arm has been programmed to go to the wrong
place. Easy, just undo the last step. Oh!—and move the arm back—and
that move gets programmed in. So when the 'corrected' program is finally
run, it doesn't do the mistakes, but it does do all the corrections! What you
can see is the arm position; what you have really got, though, is a program
(a sequence of relative moves): what you can see is not what you have got.
It is an interesting comment that the very command that was meant to
improve the user interface—the undo—has in this case probably made it
much worse than it was before.

This problem should be easy to rectify.

▷ A first idea is this: the undo key could also cause the robot arm to move, undoing the effect of the last motion.

▷ Second idea: there might (instead) be a 'merge' key that replaces the last two motions with a single smoothed-out motion. The merge key would be used as follows: move arm from A to C. Whoops, we meant B! Move arm to B. Hit merge key. Now the program is modified to contain the instruction 'move arm from A to B', and that is where the arm is. Undo is submitted before a correction; merge after a correction.

It is also interesting to note that the robot's programs would have unpredictable effects unless the arm always started from the same position: you could ensure this by resetting the machine, or by moving the arm to an extremity. But when I discovered this limitation of my program, it was too late to insert a reset at the beginning of the sequence of actions—the undo only affected the most recent commands. (I therefore put the reset at the end, ready to initialize the next run.)

11.8.4   Menu systems

Menu systems provide another application of the WYSIWYG principle. The user should be aware when there is more to the menu than the first screenful. I have used a system that suggested the user select menu entries by typing a digit; seven entries were on display, numbered 1 to 7. The designer had probably heard of the magic number 7±2. I typed 8, I think, and something funny happened. In fact, as is obvious in retrospect, the menu *really* had more than seven entries, but I was not aware of their existence. What I could see was not what I had got. Would it not have been better to have been warned, not allowed to submit 8, or at least shown what 8 meant?

11.9   The elusive mode

To obtain the very best form of domain independence we need to be mathematical. If we can correctly express properties of user interfaces in abstract terms, then we can apply those principles very widely—by changing concrete details that have been abstracted away. This is no more profound than stating properties about numbers (that is, abstractly) and being able to apply the properties to apples or oranges (that is, to different concrete representations of numbers). If we can find a mathematical way of describing modes then we should be able to apply the precise ideas to a wide range of systems.

A mode is a mathematical function[6] mapping commands (for example, the letter e, a mouse click, a command like `delete intray`, or even an entire Pascal program) to their meanings within the system.

In principle we might be able to calculate the number of modes a system has, once we have committed ourselves to a definition of modes; though in general we would certainly not be able to count them by empirical measurement without knowledge of the program. But the user may not have an accurate idea of the modes in a system: for instance, some mode information is so easily carried in the head that it hardly counts as a 'mode', some command meanings seem equivalent: the meaning of all the alphabetic keys seems 'the same', though of course each letter has a different meaning!

Some information is hard to acquire—the computer may not tell the user when it changes modes—and the user may assume it is in one mode when it is in another. If the user makes frequent mode-related errors, he is more likely to over-estimate the number of modes a system has than if the system's mode transitions naturally follow the user's task. Much of the user's perception of modes will depend on how the system structures tasks.

The idea that a modey system changes the meaning of commands is readily expressed in algebra. The commands of a non-modey system simply change the state of the system; they are functions that map the current state into the next state. We can express this formally as follows: $I[\![c]\!] \in S \to S$, which means the interpretation, I, of a command c changes the current state of the system to the next state.

The user's command is put in **emphatic brackets** (written '$[\![$' and '$]\!]$') a convention that is pedantic. Think of them as ordinary brackets, provided the commands that are being interpreted are simple; otherwise, see Box 11.6.

Consider typing the letter i to a word processor. The meaning of i is $I[\![i]\!]$, which is a member of $S \to S$, meaning that it is one of many ways of changing S, the state of the word processor to the next state. The commands e, v for instance, would change the state in other similar ways— they would have different meanings in $S \to S$. Since the notation $S \to S$ means a functional relation, then the meaning of each command is fixed (we are still considering a non-modey system).

Another example may help. The command 7 typed at a calculator changes the current state. 7 is a command that changes the display by multiplying it by 10 and adding 7: the interpretation of 7 is to modify the display: $I[\![7]\!] = s \mapsto 10s + 7$, where s is the number displayed. If

---

[6] A function can be thought of as a recipe for determining something from something else, following rules that depend *only* on the thing explicitly being considered. If the result depends on the time of day or what previous things have been looked at, then it is not functional. Thus the naming of the language construct **function** in Pascal is unfortunate, since we can easily introduce global variables that make the value of the 'function' depend on things other than its parameters. We will use the more convenient and precise notation $f: A \to B$ rather than Pascal's **function f(x: A): B;**.

Box 11.6   Emphatic brackets.

If you don't like the $[\![c]\!]$ notation, you might prefer the Pascal equivalent: `function Interpret(c: command; s: state): state`—a function that implements all commands. Note that in Pascal, we usually try to have mnemonic names like `Interpret`, whereas in mathematics we tend to have brief names like I! Programs are normally large and involve lots of names; people spend a lot of time *reading* them, so names have to try and explain themselves. In mathematics formulae are comparatively short, and the 'user' spends more time per formula, *using* it, for example, copying it down, working out its consequences or value. Thus, as a rule, names in formulae should be chosen to encourage efficient use, names in programs should be chosen to encourage efficient recall. Since some parts of programs are predominantly formulae, the rule should be applied thoughtfully.

Alternatively it might be clearer to write the Pascal using `function DoCommandX(s: state): state`, with one function `DoCommandX` per command. `DoCommandX` merely says that $I[\![X]\!]$, the interpretation of command X, is a function that takes a state `s` and produces the next state that would prevail after the user has submitted the command X. The mathematical notation would forbid the Pascal from using any global variables in the function definition—what the function I does depends only on its parameter values, even though in Pascal it would be efficient to have `state` as a collection of global variables.

---

the calculator displays 1 and the user submits 7, the display changes to 17 and nothing else changes. In general for any digit d we can write: $I[\![d]\!] = s \mapsto 10s + \text{val}(d)$, where `val` gives the value of each digit—not very difficult for decimal numbers, but necessary in case we want, say, hexadecimal numbers, where $\text{val}(\text{A}) = 10$, $\text{val}(\text{B}) = 11$.

However in a modey system, commands cause changes to the state *and* affect the meanings of subsequent commands. The interpretation of a command now depends not only on the command but on some variable mode information $m \in M$. We can write this: $I[\![c]\!]m \in S \to (S \times M)$. This could also be written equivalently as $I[\![c]\!] \in (S \times M) \to (S \times M)$.

Submitting a command c now maps the current state to a new state *and* can change the mode. A calculator may have a button that changes the mode between decimal (numbers in base 10) and hexadecimal (numbers in base 16). The mode part, m, could be 10 or 16 respectively, and the meaning of digits would be mode dependent: $I[\![d]\!]m = s \mapsto \langle ms + \text{val}(d), m \rangle$. Note that a digit does not change m, the mode component.

In a word processor a command like i has a meaning $I[\![\text{i}]\!]m$, and this meaning may affect the meaning of subsequent commands. In fact, this is what really happens—*strictly* the meaning of i depends on *where* in the text it is typed. The i key does not always mean 'insert i at the end of the text', i could be inserted anywhere. After inserting it, the next character will be inserted in the next place to the right. So the mode component must go something like: $I[\![\texttt{i}]\!]m = s \mapsto \langle s', m + 1 \rangle$, if we take m to represent the cursor position, which is increased by one. s' would be the new state, based on the old s, but including the letter i at position m.

Of course, the cursor position is hardly hidden information for the user. Almost everything the user does is located at the cursor position, so its position is generally in STM. Typically the cursor moves in response to commands in a simple fashion, so the cursor position does not often get out of step with the user's model of where it ought to be. In fact, we would rather put the cursor position inside the state S and 'pretend' that the word processor was modeless (so far as it goes).

It is possible to do this. Consider: $I'[\![c]\!] \in S' \to S'$ where $S' = S \times M$. The new S' conceals the mode M, but the result is that I' has the form that earlier was claimed to be modeless!

So mathematically we can treat a system as modey or modeless as we please. It all depends on how the system state is factored into S and M. If we want to think of the cursor position as part of the state then we can have a modeless word processor. If we do not want to consider it part of the state, we can have a modey editor. How do we decide?

11.9.1 Bottlenecks locate modes

The elusive mode problem revolves around the von Neumann bottleneck (see Chapter 4). What is data (or state, S) and what is program (or mode, M), and to what extent can mode be treated as part of the system's state? In the user interface case, we have the system state, S', and it can be factored into pure data (the original S) and a component (the M term) that represents mode information. Exactly how the state is factored is not fixed, and this is the problem.

The conundrum can be side-stepped by defining a mode as a dependence on any information, data or procedure, that is not apparent to the user. Thus, from a formal view, $I'[\![c]\!] \in S' \to S'$ is modeless, but by our revised definition, it will *not* be modeless if the component M of S' is hidden from the user. The word 'hidden' simply conceals all the usual user interface problems: how do we reveal information to the user? What are the consequences of overloading the user by revealing too much mode information? And some information that is never revealed may not change the meaning of a command so far as the user can tell!

By the mathematical definition of mode, I am side-stepping an important representational issue: for instance simply displaying the state as a binary number (or a screen bitmap) would not make it *apparent* to the user, even though formally there is enough information present to deduce everything about the system! We are reminded that the user needs an effective model of the system, and this will be used in part to interpret the state of the system: if the system displays its state by a funny number then the user's model needs to be *very sophisticated indeed*—Gödel numbers are only one step removed from trapdoor functions and decoding them is anyway an exercise in cryptanalysis. Hopefully simpler representations can be used in real systems.

Why do we want to make the mode/state or data/program distinction clear? Suppose that you are using a word processor, and hit the `delete` key. You want this key to delete the last character you typed. But clearly the change to your text depends crucially on what you have already typed. Are you deleting a line break? So do you consider *that* a mode because it affects meanings? Or are you prepared to say that the meaning of `delete` is effectively the same in all cases? *Even* at the top of the file where there is nothing there to delete?

Do we really need to make such pedantic distinctions, and if so, how should we correctly make them? They are necessary, for in the limit it would be possible to say that everything provided by the system was program and everything provided by the user was data. That way, there would be no modes whatsoever. Modes arise because some data appears to have significant meaning that is partly hidden from the user—which means that sometimes in a modey system the user's input (or system's output, for output modes) is treated like program, invested with a deeper meaning.

Here are just two ideas about making the distinction clear. You will see that each attempt to pin down the distinction depends on what the user is assumed to be doing.

▷ *Data and program can be distinguished by testing for equality*: Data are equal if and only if they are identical. Lazy evaluation systems generally permit infinite data structures, which cannot be tested for equality in finite time. The user interface analogue to this is that the data may be supplied by the user: until the user has 'finished' the data may be tested for equality with other data, but only so far as it goes. Program, on the other hand, does not have a unique representation: two different programs may mean the same function. For instance the *data* 123 and `delete` are different (they are clearly different sequences of characters), but `write(3)` and `write(1+2)` both result in 3 being printed when run as Pascal program.

In general, there are rules that can transform one program into another: in Pascal there are so-called 'constant folding' rules to transform `write(1+2)` into the equivalent `write(3)`. But since some programs may or may not halt, and in general you cannot tell which (see Section 5.4), program equivalence is in general non-computable. Thus, the **computability** of equality distinguishes program from data.

Unfortunately the equality test does not really help distinguish program and data, for it depends on the prior choice of model being used. Thus `write(3)` and `write(1+2)` are equal programs if modelled in Pascal, but unequal if modelled in Prolog. The prior choice of language model is crucial—hence the early definition of mode as specifying *variable* hidden information.

The distinction suggested based on testing for equality is interesting, but circular. We first need a way to decide what model to employ before we can establish whether information is data or program—we need to know what a system is about. Thus we try the next idea:

▷ *Program and data can be distinguished because the program part is what the system is* **about**: Thus a word processor is about word processing—and obviously works because of a word processing program inside it!

Notice that the ideas allow different interpretation by designer and user. Other ideas—like program is partial, data total—have the same weakness. Effectiveness of equality can be based on either Turing computability or cognitive computability—and computability may be 'in principle' or may be based on the commands available at the interface, and again, on commands *in principle* available, or commands *actually known* by a particular user to be available. Data might be incomparable simply because no commands are available to observe it without changing it. Secondly, designer and user can very easily disagree what a system is about and what it *should* be about.

Just as the von Neumann bottleneck forces a pragmatic distinction between data and program, the user interface bottleneck makes a pragmatic distinction that makes it is easy for the designer to think that modes are fixed by the design. But our exercise in formalizing modes has emphasized that they are actually user referenced. What a mode is depends on what the user is trying—or thinks he is trying—to do. Naturally designers hope to influence the user by apposite choice of gueps and other expository material. Bad explanation can make a 'simple' system seem extraordinarily complex; good explanation or training can make a 'complex' system seem trivial.

11.10 Conclusions

Modes are an important topic in their own right, but they help illustrate how gueps can be formulated.

The advantages of modes in their inertial and protective forms suggest a resolution of the **mode paradox**. Modes occur in everyday items, like cookers, washing machines, alarm clocks, radios, bicycles. So if there is some universal significance in the concept of modes, why don't designers capitalize on their experience of modes in everyday life? Presumably because *those* modes are often worth while. The mode paradox is perhaps the most blatant form of that little mystery why there are so many bad designs around when there are plenty of good examples to copy. (An advantage of modes, of no concern to the readers of this book, is that they often ease the implementation of user interfaces.)

The quickest way to make something incomprehensible is to conceal something from the user. It is even better if what you conceal keeps changing: whence modes. Modes arise because of the user interface communication bandwidth bottleneck. Information *not* transferred between computer and user increases modiness. Modes are perceived by the user to the extent that the omitted information would have been relevant to the tasks in hand. Modes are not necessarily bad: modes may improve the efficiency of the user interface, but at the risk of the user failing to understand the hidden information.

WYSIWYG provided an ideal example of a property of systems. It requires that there be a simple relation between information transmitted from the computer to the user and the results obtained. That is, what the user can see (information transmitted from computer to user) is what the user gets (information transmitted from computer to results).

WYSIWYG is a prototypical guep. It is easily understood by both user and designer:

▷ The user is inspired to confidence: the system has no hidden tricks; the user can manipulate what he can see, without fear of unseen side-effects.

▷ The system model can be understood and (relevant parts of it) readily memorized by the user without prior system experience.

▷ The user may generalize his knowledge. The user is confident as to what *has* happened (for instance, after an error). Quite unlike the popular terms 'user friendly', 'fluid dialogue', 'ease of use'—which impart no knowledge to the user!

▷ The designer can use the principle to meet clearly defined user expectations with specific techniques.

The exact meaning of WYSIWYG is debatable. The tense problem of WYSIWYG (Box 11.5) showed that precision of expression is essential for a right understanding of principles: or at least that we should be careful to interpret principles carefully and lay aside our automatic assumptions. This was also the concluding observation of Section 11.9.1: correct, complete explanation must be clear. *Improve the design to make it so.*

'Out of sight, out of mind'. So if something is out of sight, make sure that the user can operate the system with it 'out of mind'. Avoid modes.

Chapter 12

Undo

Irreversibility is the effect of the introduction of ignorance into
the basic laws of physics.
Max Born

I used to call this chapter *Apocatastasis*, but I have since undone it. The
word means re-establishment or returning to a previous condition, and is
too rarely used to be a sensible choice of title. We wish to avoid spurious
jargon, so the English word **undo** serves us far better, except that I can
no longer make the point that names in interactive systems must be chosen
with care. Who would take 'a' as the name of the command to undo?
Those people who most need mnemonics are those least able to understand
a system, and every concession helps.

In a batch system a user needs to plan his work well ahead and
anticipate the computer's quirks. In interactive systems the user adapts
the details of his plan as the computer responds to each step. This is
incremental interaction, and it means that a single error does not destroy
an entire session. Instead, each error can be dealt with separately, and the
user can try a different approach at the point where the error occurs. The
errors can arise from bugs in the computer system, from misunderstandings
of the user about the computer, from accidents due to the complexity of
the task the user is trying to attack, and so on: there are no simple ways
to avoid errors.

Even an interactive system may occasionally lose too much as the
result of an error. The user may reply *no* when *cancel* was intended.
Perhaps hours of work will be discarded by the computer as a result of this
one slip.

▷ The system should have asked a clearer question. The *representation* of the user interface can be improved (see Section 12.1.1).

▷ The system should be aware of the costs of its actions and ensure that what it does is information-theoretically related to the user's actions. Thus, a single mouse click (clicking on **no**) should not be enough to destroy thousands of user actions. The interface could be more *principled*. See, in particular, the principle of commensurate effort in Section 15.4.3.

▷ We can add more *features* to the user interface. These features provide for greater flexibility in recovering from error; they also—putting it cynically—camouflage problems in the user interface by making it appear more powerful and attractive. Features may encourage a user to buy the system, and once they have bought it, so what about errors?

▷ The system can provide a mechanism to undo actions (see this chapter).

In general, the user of an interactive system must be able to undo errors, so that he can resume interaction at some point just before the error was detected. In a batch system, the strategy is that the user can indeed recover from an error from a point, but a point a long time ago. Batch systems rely on a pre-stored 'batch' of information previously devised and stored (in a file) by the user; interactive systems do not rely on the user thinking ahead so far, and certainly not thinking ahead far enough to cover the entire session.

In a normal interactive session, the user is 'merely' interacting; with a session that in addition involves undo, the user can talk about the interaction itself. The advantages of undo are not merely in flexible approaches for the user to correct errors, but include:

▷ The view of the interaction can be changed from temporal (do this; then do this; then this) to spatial (perhaps a diagram of the history of the interactive session). The provision of undo and other meta commands allows the user to choose, as it were, a left or right brain style of interaction to suit himself.

▷ The difference between the designer's and user's views of interaction is reduced: both designer and user can think about the course of interaction.

▷ Properties of the interactive system are naturally expressed in terms of the history of interaction; now both user and designer have access to this history, and the formal properties will seem more relevant to the user.

▷ With a good undo available, users will be encouraged to experiment, and we gain all the advantages of science as described in Chapter 9.

Undo is not just a safety net, its provision encourages the user to take on a backtracking approach to solving his problems. The user is given confidence, and may, for instance, learn to use the system in powerful ways much faster. A good undo is not just for undoing mistakes, but enhances the way the user can interact.

▷ Although undo is usually understood to be a way of undoing user errors (or for facilitating experiments, as mentioned in the last point), note that errors can arise from a wide variety of causes. The user may want to undo the effects of *computer* error—or *design* error. One of the calculators discussed in Chapter 16, in Section 16.9.3, has undo to correct the calculator's, not the user's errors.

There are very few interactive systems where undo has been designed in from the start; until a system is in use, user error recovery is often ignored as a design concern. In consequence, undo-ish functions are tacked on to a finished product: they are then characterized by incompleteness and being difficult to use. Nevertheless, users may be very pleased to be able to recover from certain catastrophic errors if even with some difficulty.

When undo is considered from the outset of design, and ways are found to implement it speedily and reliably, this can have a profound influence on the rest of the design. For example, defaults no longer require confirmation—the system can be bold and proceed, for if a default turns out to be incorrect, the user will be able to undo the corresponding action. It is not really as simple as that however: the chosen default will be stored in STM—only if the user is attending!—and by the time an error is noticed, interference may mean that the user cannot remember the actions that caused the error.

There are two quite legitimate reasons why it may *not* be a good idea to include undo in prototype designs: first, undo minimizes the consequences of user errors, and hence the motivation to improve the design to lower the probability of those errors occurring; second, it is exceedingly difficult to implement undo thoroughly (only trivial systems can have complete undos), because of non-undoable interactions with the world at large—striking a balance between undo for errors, or better guards to protect from them is best done in the light of experience with the system. On the one hand, undo may not be considered much in the design process; on the other, it may be given too much emphasis and become treated as a palliative—all design faults contributing to the user making errors can be redeemed by undo.

There is one legitimate reason why undo should not be provided in a final design: it may be inappropriate for the task. In chess, for example, undo is more often called cheating. Although undo might be desirable in a chess training system (so the user can experiment more easily), it would still be inappropriate in an emergency medical training system, where—amongst other things—the user has got to learn not to make mistakes.

There are two philosophies pulling the would-be undo designer in opposite directions. First, undo should be sophisticated and permit the user to undo and change his interaction history in any conceivable way. This is the glamourous choice! But, alternatively, undo is recognized as a feature provided *merely* to rescue the user in distress. If the user is panicking, the undo system has to have a straightforward user interface itself, or else the user may need to undo mistaken undos. The aim now is to make undo simple and reliable in use; perhaps it will be slow but the aim is to ensure that the user may undo everything with well-placed confidence.

12.1   Introductory remarks

12.1.1   Confirmation is not enough

Sometimes the user submits a command that will have serious consequences. It may delete a considerable amount of work. So the computer asks the user to confirm that he really wants the computer to proceed.

The computer asks, 'are you sure?' and the user can probably only reply yes or no. Very often such a question is pre-emptive, requiring the user to answer the question, and forbidding the user to do anything else to check—the user is over-determined. Furthermore, the designer has made an implicit assumption that the user *may* have made a mistake, and this is a put down.

The user's response, yes or no can be combined in a menu, which at least avoids the possible problem when the user does not know that to reply yes he actually has to hit the Y↩ keys. The user would move the cursor over the desired reply, click the mouse (or whatever), thereby submitting that answer. This makes a mistake even easier than before.

Suppose a user submits the quit command to a program: does the user really want to quit, and should the data be written back to a file before the quit? If it is not saved, the user runs the risk of having wasted his time. The computer responds to the quit with 'Do you want to quit without saving?' and offers a menu of three choices: yes, no and cancel. Selecting yes clearly leaves the editor without saving the data. But what about no and cancel? Does answering no mean, 'no, I don't want to quit without saving' or does it mean 'no, I don't want to save before I quit'? Clearly, some users will select no under the circumstances the designer expected them to select cancel which means neither saving nor quitting: 'cancel my attempt at quitting'. As usual, a simple positive rephrasing would help. The question might have been put: 'Do you want to save? yes, no or do you want to continue?' Better still, it need not have been a question: after all, this is what menus are for. A menu could have presented the choices: 'save and quit', 'lose changes and quit', 'don't quit'.

Maybe the fourth option, just save changes, should be available, since the dialogue will arise at a point of closure.

If the computer (that is, the designer) was worried that perhaps the user was unaware of the significance of a request it might better respond, 'if you wish to do this, say "really do this"'. Now 'really do this' can be a command submitted in the same context as 'do this'—the user is not then trapped in a pre-emptive mode to answer fussy questions. Yet the system still protects the user from doing something really dangerous—the extra interaction at dangerous points is always a good safeguard.

Whichever approach is taken, the designer has to anticipate the circumstances where the user may want to revoke a command, and his view of the value of the user's work (and hence when confirmation is required) is no doubt different from the user's own view. If everything the user does is subject to confirmation, this is over-determining and probably too tedious; but if only a few things are confirmed, then the user is bound to make a mistake that the designer did not choose to catch in a confirmation. A more general approach is often required.

12.1.2 Very simple undo is worthwhile

Almost all textual systems provide a rudimentary form of undo. Typically, the user can submit commands to the system line by line. If the user spots a mistake on a line, he may be able to correct it. For instance, there may be a rubout key that deletes the last character typed. In general, the user might be able to do any sort of text editing of the sort that one might expect to be provided by a word processor. All corrections to the text are a form of undo, and are very useful.

Of course, this is not *real* undo, for there are generally severe limitations on what may and what may not be undone. Typically, it is not possible to edit outside of the current line: there will be some key, enter, say, that submits the current command line so that the system can execute it—and commits it beyond the reach of mere text editing.

12.1.3 Undo in text editors

All users make mistakes; merely improving the design of user interfaces will not change this fact. Indeed, text editors exist solely to enable users to correct their mistakes—although some 'mistakes' only become apparent over long periods of time as the user changes his mind about the way in which he wishes to express himself, rather than merely correcting slips. The reason text editors 'work' is that most corrections are shorter than the incorrect text: if we simplistically assume that the user makes mistakes at

---

Box 12.1   The sad story of a painting program with undo.

I have used a very expensive painting program which has an undo. Yet the manual says 'make frequent backups of your work in case of mistakes'. You wonder why the system can't make its own backups ...

One drawing I did with it took about an hour, and I was very pleased with it. I had used undo several times: for instance, when I rotated an arrow anticlockwise, I could select undo from a menu and rotate the arrow back again. Actually, undo at this level is not really necessary, since I could just as easily submit the rotate command again, and rotate the arrow back manually.

I had just painted a white arrow, and had noticed the text I was writing beside it was also white. At first I did not understand, so I selected the whole drawing and moved it so that I could see my writing a bit better in the middle of the screen. It was invisible white. So I clicked the mouse on `paint` and chose `black`. This made the writing go black, as I wanted.

It also made the *entire* drawing go black (remember, I had selected it all to move it as one piece—so the system made the 'one piece' a uniform blackness).

Guess what? *The system removed the undo command from the menu.* Here was the first mistake I had made that I could not undo myself with other commands, and the system was refusing to undo it too! I need hardly add that the manufacturer did not undo my purchase for such a *trivial* complaint!

---

a certain rate, he will make fewer mistakes correcting text than entering it in the first place.

The trouble with being able to correct mistakes in the text is that the user may make mistaken corrections: it is not always the text he is writing that needs editing, but the choice of commands that he uses. Suppose the user deletes a paragraph or sentence by mistake. Whether he has just read the paragraph or not, he is unlikely to be able to recall the text accurately— and besides it is a bother to have to type a few hundred characters to undo the effect of the one or two keystrokes that deleted the text. It would be even worse had the user deleted an entire file or destroyed the day's work in some other way. The user wants to undo his mistake.

As an example where undoing is useful, word processing applications are rather tame, since the word processor does nothing with the user's text other than store it. Text editing can correct any typing error made at any time. Quite often the user will arrange for other applications (such as programming language compilers) to interpret the text that has been typed. Once erroneous text has been interpreted, the interpretation—not just the text—also has to be corrected. The erroneous interpretation has to be undone too. How does the user correct a mistakenly executed command?

12.1.4 Changing history by keeping records

There are advantages for both user and designer if the system keeps a log of interaction. A log can be used explicitly, rather than kept as a passive record of the story of interaction that will only be *after* the interactive session (for example, to aid iterative design or to determine productivity bonuses for the users). This section gives some concrete implementation ideas.

We have already seen how the user may edit text. But text is just an interpretation for keystrokes, and editing functions are often just a different mode of command. Why not provide functions for editing editing functions? In general, why not provide functions for editing the history of the user's interaction?

We may imagine that the user interface keeps a log of every keystroke the user makes. Undo operations may be considered as text edits on this log. (If we have a graphical interface, the log may be textual or graphical, and the edits permitted on it will be of the appropriate kind.) Note that keeping a log provides the user with security: should the system crash, on rebooting it can replay the log and recover the lost work. In this case, the system must flush log buffers sufficiently frequently, otherwise the last half-hour of the user's typing may go down with the crash. The log buffers can be sensibly flushed after long pauses and when the user makes a change of context indicating closure. When a log flush is due, it may make sense not to flush the buffer completely: suppose the most recent command itself causes the system to crash—if this command is flushed, then replaying the log at a later time will simply cause the system to crash again. The purpose of keeping a log is to make the system more reliable against user and system error. Be careful to ensure that when flushing logs itself goes wrong (for example, when on to full disks, or when the network goes down) that the system winds itself up gracefully!

Commands to the user interface are partitioned in two. Conventional commands are executed as submitted but also recorded in the log. When the user submits the undo command he is able to truncate or otherwise modify the log. The system then resets itself to the last checkpoint and re-executes the log, including the modifications the user has just made. When the log is rerun, the user may choose to get the system back to the intended state as rapidly as possible. Alternatively, the user may wish to watch the system, and perhaps take over at some point before the end of the rerun. This second approach is most useful if the rerun is being used to recover from a crash or other disaster! The recovery may also be made at a much later time, and an animated rerun serves to remind the user of his previous actions.

Undo by rerun demonstrates two things: that simple undo is generally possible; and that, even though reruns may be slow, the user is given confidence. Only concern for more rapid response, or for easier or more sophisticated undo motivates the designer to consider other implementation techniques.

Note that a log can be provided not just at the level of a text editor, but can be system wide, built into the architecture of the machine. When, say, a file gets updated, a record of the change is made, preferably on another medium, like a removable disk. Why is it that when my computer crashes it takes with it everything I've been doing? If it had kept a log, I might have been able to restore what had been lost.

12.2   The user interface requirements for undo

We can now summarize the requirements for undo provided in interactive systems. Later, after building some formal models, we shall have more detailed ideas: the points here are very general.

There are two extreme classes of user: programmers (who may even be able to reverse editing sessions by mechanisms outside of the editor itself) and others who have no interest in computing skills as such. We assume that an undo command must meet the requirements of the more casual class of user, as the more experienced user will be aware of the alternative mechanisms available to him.

▷ *The undo command must be simple*: The user has already made one mistake, and undoing the effects of the undo command could get unnecessarily awkward. The undo command should obviously be easier to use than the explicit reversing of a command: to undo a deletion should certainly be no harder than retyping the deleted text.

▷ *Make unavoidable limitations sensible and apparent to the user*: Some operations cannot be undone, and some commands may stop subsequent undos (for example, transmitting mail to a remote computer). It is essential that such limitations are made clear to the user, and where possible coincide with expected closure. Note that making something apparent to the user is very different from telling him: the user may be so keen to do something that he does not attend to the warning that what he is doing is not undoable.

▷ *Some commands should have specific undos*: An undo is supposed to undo any command, but the user might prefer to invoke undo only when he has made a 'serious' error. There may be many common errors for which the user does not want to invoke the conceptual or implementational overhead of undo. For instance, if the user types x by mistake, he *could* submit undo, but surely it would be easier to have a delete-last-character command that deletes characters quickly; having specific undos helps avoid capture errors.

▷ *The undo command should be general*: It would be exceedingly frustrating to make some accidental transformation to the text and then find that the particular sequence of commands which made it could not be undone (see Box 12.1).

▷ *The scope of undo should be unrestricted*: Slips may not be noticed immediately and further commands may be issued after the slip. These commands should not affect the ability to undo. Nonetheless it is unlikely that a full 'change history' command would be desirable— the average user would not be certain that the previous commands following the undone command are still relevant. Besides, the possibilities of changing an undo later defeat the first requirement of basic simplicity.

▷ *Any undo is useful*: It may help the user in times of need. Like many generic commands (`help`, `move`, `copy`), `undo` deserves a consistent name across all parts of a system (perhaps a dedicated key on the keyboard).

12.3 The Archer, Conway, Schneider script model

The conventional view of interaction is that the user first constructs each command (possibly aided by editing features), then submits the command for execution. Each command is considered separately and processed successively. The conceptual leap into undoing is that the sequence of commands can itself become an object for the user to manipulate.

If the user submits the command c_1, then a command c_2, then a command c_3, somewhere, perhaps only in the user's head, is the notion that the history of interaction is '$\cdots c_1 c_2 c_3$'. The idea of undoing is to make this history an explicit part of the user interface. The user will be provided with various commands (of which `undo` is the most obvious) that change the history.

Typically, if the user makes a mistake in submitting, say, the third command, he can change the history by submitting `undo`. This will change the system from having the history $c_1 c_2 c_3$ to behaving *as if* its history were $c_1 c_2$. The '*as if*' is needed because the history is *really* $c_1 c_2 c_3$ `undo`. Thus we have to distinguish between the following:

▷ **History**: This is a complete record of what the user has done.

▷ **Script**: The record of interaction that the system treats as its effective history. Depending on the system, the script may be an approximation to and simpler than the true history, or it may be more sophisticated than the actual history—for instance, common episodes in the history may be abstracted.

▷ **State**: Different actions by the user (different histories) may result in the system being in the same state. Thus the histories/scripts '$c_1 c_2 c_3$ undo' and '$c_1 c_3$ undo c_2' are clearly different, but they result in the system being in the same state which can be represented by the simpler equivalent history $c_1 c_2$. Formally states are the equivalence classes of scripts; this formal definition clarifies how the script is considered part of the system state.

In Archer, Conway and Schneider's **Script Model** (Archer *et al.*, 1984), the user is viewed as constructing a script, and the system is viewed as providing a continuous interpretation of the script. The ACS model views the user interface cycling between two sorts of activity:

▷ The **edit activity**: The user is editing the script. Each edit activity is terminated by submission. In many systems, the end of the edit activity is signalled by a special command, such as `enter`.

▷ The **execute activity**: The system interprets the script. Execution terminates when control has passed back to the user, and a new edit activity commences.

In the classic batch system there is only one cycle through the two activities. The user prepares the script 'off-line' and then submits the script. The system then executes the entire script. The user has no facilities to change the script if the execution phase turns out to be undesirable in some detail: the user has to devise a new script, again off-line, and submit it in its entirety.

In an interactive system, the cycles are iterated until the user is satisfied or he runs out of patience. Ideally, anyway, we may imagine the user iterates, converging on his intended goal of a certain desirable system activity. The user receives feedback, possibly null, from the system at each iteration as the system executes the previous submission. This feedback will help guide him in making further submissions.

Typically the user will append new commands to the end of the script, and the system will execute the most recent command as each extension to the script is submitted.

When we consider undo mechanisms, the user may now make more interesting changes to the script than merely appending commands. Other parts of the script may be changed. Most likely, both the user interface (to help the user navigate and edit the script) and the application (which now has to interpret a mangled script) will have to be much more sophisticated.

Consider two successive iterations through edit and execute activities. For the first iteration, we assume the user has constructed a script S, composed of n commands $c_1, c_2, c_3, \ldots c_n$. The user submits this script, and the system will perform some activity. But there is no reason to presume that the system will interpret the entire script: indeed, in a line-based dialogue the system will not interpret the last line of user commands until an enter or similar key is typed by the user. Thus execution divides the script into two parts, E (executed script), perhaps up to the last enter command, and P the pending script, submitted by the user but not yet executed by the system. The ACS model assumes that the script is necessarily evaluated sequentially, that E and P are in order and never interleaved: $S = EP$.

Given a script $S = c_1 c_2 \cdots c_n$, execution will result in

$$\underbrace{c_1\ c_2\ \cdots\ c_{i-1}}_{\substack{\text{executed} \\ \text{commands, } E}}\quad \underbrace{c_i\ c_{i+1}\ \cdots\ c_n}_{\substack{\text{pending} \\ \text{commands, } P}}$$

Note that the commands c can be mouse clicks, words spoken by the user, complete commands or letters typed at a keyboard. In the latter case, c_{i-1} may be a distinguished command, such as enter or newline. To analyse a particular system we would first decide on a suitable level of detail at which to analyse it.

After the execute activity terminates, control returns to the user who now edits the script. For convenience, we shall write everything after the execute and edit steps with a prime, writing x before, x' after. Thus the edit activity results in a script S' of commands $c'_1 c'_2, \cdots c'_{n'}$. Unless the user has made radical changes, c'_1 will be equal to the original c_1, c'_2 will be equal to the original c_2, and so on up to the first command c'_j which is different. (Strictly we should write j', since we don't know j until after the end of the edit activity.) c_1 to c_{j-1}, then, make up a common initial sequence of unchanged commands in the scripts. Subsequent commands in the script will have been modified by the user. Call the unchanged prefix U' and the modified suffix M'.

$$\underbrace{c_1 c_2\ \cdots\ c_{j-1}}_{\substack{\text{unchanged} \\ \text{commands, } U'}}\quad \underbrace{c'_j c'_{j+1}\ \cdots\ c'_{n'}}_{\substack{\text{modified} \\ \text{commands, } M'}}$$

Recognizing the categories represented by S, E, P, S', U', and M', we may distinguish various forms of interaction and undo:

▷ Execution policy is **complete** if after all execution phases, P is empty and $E = S$.

▷ Execution policy is **partial** if P is not empty or E is not equal to S. Execution policies are classified as either complete or partial.

▷ In the **non-undoable** case, where the user cannot undo or affect already executed commands, $U' \equiv S$ and the modified suffix M' is a pure extension of S.

▷ A prefix of the script is **committed** if the user is prohibited from changing it.

▷ Script modification policy is **extending** if, at the end of every edit activity, $U' = S$. In other words, the user may only change the script by extending it—an extending policy commits the script as soon as each execution activity commences. (The ACS model uses the term **incremental**, a term which we have pre-empted; extending is more precise.)

▷ Any cycle starting in the condition where E is not a prefix of $U'M'$ starts in an **inconsistent state**. This is simply because the user has changed commands in the script that the system had previously executed.   Before the execution activity can proceed sensibly, consistency must be restored.   This process is called **recovery**. Recovery is never necessary under an incremental modification policy since executed parts of the script never get changed by the user.

12.3.1   Script modification

The user may be restricted in the ways in which he may modify the script. Most restrictively, we have extending modification.   The user may only append to the script.   Least restrictively the user may be able to edit the script in any way whatsoever—rather as if the script were a text being edited with a word processor: the user can add and remove commands from the script, or reorder and change the script in any way.

▷ A system with a recovery mechanism powerful enough to handle arbitrary script changes is **complete**.

▷ **Block-truncate** is a script modification policy where there is a distinguished command `checkpoint`.   Script modifications are restricted to undoing all commands since the last checkpoint. In other words, M' is empty and U' must end with a `checkpoint` command. Some systems will restrict the number of `checkpoints` in the script; many systems will permit a complete erasure of the script, as if the script is always preceded by a notional `checkpoint`.

File editors (such as text editors) are often provided with a 'write to named file' command.   The user may use this command to establish implicit checkpoints.   Block-truncate may then be achieved by various means, for instance aborting the current edit and renaming the 'checkpoint' file. The user may be helped enormously if the system administrates the checkpointing; the system might store change-files rather than complete files, so gaining in efficiency.

▷ **Single-truncate** is a script modification policy which only permits two sorts of modification: appending single commands and truncating single commands (deleting the last command from the script).   Truncating more than one command is not permitted—all but the last command of the script are committed by the system, and are therefore inaccessible to the user's modification.

▷ So-called **truncate*** is similar but lifts the *single*-truncate restriction. The script may be truncated indefinitely, so long as it does not go negative! Truncate* is powerful and permits the user to undo anything. Its disadvantage is that, to undo something, the user has to discard every command back to the command to be undone. It may then be difficult to recall the unnecessarily undone commands.

The next style of modification stores the undone commands in a buffer, thereby removing the memory burden on the user—and perhaps permitting their rapid resubmission, faster than the user might have submitted them incrementally.

▷ In **truncate/redo** the system makes provision for storing the truncated part of the script. This script buffer may then be used to resubmit commands to be redone. The user interface will have an `undo` and a `redo` command.

Notice that these classifications do not assume that the undo treatment of commands by the system is uniform. This is not usual in real life! Generally commands have differing degrees of 'undoability'. Some commands are easily undone: inserting letters in a word processor is undone by deleting them. Some commands have special provision made for them: for example, block delete in a word processor. But other commands, 'complex' ones like moving a paragraph and certain errors like accidentally overwriting a cut-and-paste buffer, may not be undoable.

That some commands have simple inverses (for instance, `left`/`right`) that undo themselves, that undo is difficult to implement anyway, together conspire to make most undo implementations non-uniform. As always, good user interfaces are hard work to design and implement.

A very common trick (let's call it **flip-undo**), which admittedly is better than nothing, is to provide single-truncate with an undo command which itself gets appended to the script. Therefore a subsequent undo command undoes the effect of the first. This 'trick' (treating script and history as identical) ensures that the system may safely commit all but the last command in the script. Flip-undo makes sense, since it satisfies the rule, 'all commands are undone by `undo` (including `undo` itself)'. One reason why the treatment of undo is non-uniform in most systems is that the designers have chosen flip-undo, but realizing its limitations have chosen to decouple it from 'minor' commands. Minor commands may not be undone (by the explicit undo mechanism, at any rate), thus the single-truncate scope of the flip-undo can extend to the last major command, even if it was not the most recent. And if `undo` does not apply to every command, why make it apply to itself?

12.3.2   Undo/redo animation

An undo interface may be symbolic or manipulative, with or without incremental feedback. In the symbolic case, the user specifies an undo of so-many commands, or back to a certain command (all the usual text editing commands of searching and locating are applicable). In the manipulative case, the user issues step commands that truncate the script incrementally.

Feedback for either form may be the (name of the) command about to be undone back to, or it may be the display at that time, possibly plus a region devoted to the undo subdialogue. If display feedback can be implemented efficiently, undo/redo provide animation of the user interface: the display from the system shows a speeded-up version of the session, in either direction: undo backwards or redo forwards.

Forwards animation is easy to implement and may provide useful insights both for the designer and user. Animation of a user's session may help the user to improve his performance or interaction strategies. Forward animation plus an 'interrupt' command provides a pleasant interface to undo, implemented internally by a 'return to checkpoint and rerun' method: the animation also gives the user feedback that the system is actually doing something while it is doing the redo.

12.3.3   Side-effects: The world beyond undo

Undo is fine if nothing has been changed *outside* the system. If the user launches an intercontinental missile, the scope for undoing the last command will be severely limited. Even for ordinary systems, some commands are going to have side-effects on the world at large, and these effects may not be undone merely by changing the state of the interactive system.

Having sent information to the outside world, it is not generally possible to recall it if the recipient has acted upon it; or having accepted and received information it is not generally possible to return it, if, say, the sender of the information should have sent it somewhere else.

In fact, *every* command submitted has an effect on the real world, namely the passage of time. No amount of undoing will run real time clocks backwards. A system that supports undo should therefore take care how it evaluates time-dependent commands. Perhaps time-dependent commands should be evaluated lazily, as necessary, after commits. Imagine an airline reservation system: A tourist reserves two seats, but later wants to change his reservation to one seat. Undoing the reservation may allow another tourist elsewhere to reserve the released seats quickly before our tourist can re-reserve one of them.

Note that lazy evaluation will make commands generally cheaper to undo. It would be possible to undo commands, not by running their inverses but by running the lazy interpreter backwards. Laziness often has surprising

---

Box 12.2   Virtual time and distributed undo.

Suppose that the user is working on a distributed system, a system of interconnected computers (not necessarily all in the same place). We still have the problem of side-effects in the world, but *some* of this world can be designed by us; we could arrange for remote computers to handle undo commands themselves.

Suppose the user submits a command c that is transmitted for execution on a remote machine. Then the user submits undo; clearly, that undo should be transmitted to run on the same remote machine, and (hopefully!) will take the remote machine back to its previous state, as if c had never been submitted. The user interface problems are unchanged if we decide that the transmission of commands to remote machines is transparent; however, interesting design issues arise if the user can select machines on which to execute commands. Then, the user might want to have as many scripts as there are remote machines, and to be able to redo commands originally intended for one machine on another one.

A problem of distributed systems—and for their users—is that you have to wait for all information to arrive before daring to do anything. David Jefferson (1985) made an interesting observation: if there is a system-wide undo, then instead of waiting, a system (or its users) can just go ahead and do whatever seems right at the time. If at a later time, information arrives that shows your original course of action was ill-advised, you simply issue undos (which are transmitted to remote systems as necessary—Jefferson calls these **antimessages**), and have another go *with* the new information. Apart from helping the user realize what state the system has gone back to, the whole process can be done automatically.

Jefferson saw the user as outside the system; he was concerned with virtual time as an efficient lookahead mechanism in an asynchronous environment. The problem with the user being part of the system is that he may make mistakes even when all information is present—the user may want to undo arbitrarily far back in time. If the user never makes mistakes (or is excluded altogether, or has a commit command, or simply has no mechanisms to undo the commands he submits), it is possible to determine when each system may safely checkpoint.

---

benefits: in the present case, if the interpreter runs backwards lazily itself, and the user repents of the undo at a later stage, then there would only be administrative overhead.

12.3.4   Explicit versus implicit command parameters

Undo and redo should work as the user expects for commands with explicit parameters. However, implicit parameters (for example, defaults, commands acting on the current state) are heavily used and can make redo very confusing. Suppose we undo the last command (delete current line, say; the state-dependent binding of 'current' is the implicit parameter), then type a new line somewhere else in the document, then redo the delete. Which line will be deleted?

If commands are to be redone without such ambiguity all their parameters must be bound directly to objects or values, not names (like current, more often '.').

In a graphics system similar problems arise: suppose the user picks an object and moves it 1 cm left, placing it at a position 2 cm in from the side of the screen. When this command is redone, should the system move the object 1 cm relatively, or 2 cm absolutely? Here the absolute/relative choice was an implicit parameter that was bound in the user's head, not in the system. The system cannot resolve the problem without querying the user when the command is redone, or (better) distinguishing the user's intent when the command was originally submitted. Perhaps there should be two sorts of move command for the relative/absolute cases—but then the user might conceivably intend a relative horizontal move and an absolute vertical position.[1]

Note that similar problems arise when the user's name bindings to objects in the system become outdated. Suppose a compiler informs the user that there are syntax errors on lines 447 and 523. The user binds these names (line numbers) to the concept 'must be edited' in his head. Suppose the user fiddles with line 447, perhaps adding some extra code. Now the name 523 is no longer bound to the original line *in the system*, but it still is in *the user's head*.

12.4   Undo, Skip and Redo

The undo/redo concept is not well modelled by the ACS script model. Consider a script $c_1c_2c_3$. We undo commands c_3 and c_2 (which are saved in a redo buffer). We then submit a command c_4 and redo c_2c_3. The result is a script $c_1c_4c_2c_3$. Suppose we now want to undo back to the previous *state* c_1c_2. The ACS undo model takes us successively back through the script, but not through the history. The following sequence makes this problem clear. We start from the point where the script is c_1c_2 and the user is just submitting the command c_3.

---

[1] This raises an intriguing design problem if you want a WYSIWYG interface! Without additional information being displayed the user cannot tell absolute from relative positioning; therefore the system should not make the distinction; therefore it should not provide undo ...

Script	Commands submitted
$c_1 c_2$	
	c_3
$c_1 c_2 c_3$	
	undo
$c_1 c_2$	
	undo
c_1	
	c_4
$c_1 c_4$	
	redo
$c_1 c_4 c_2$	
	redo
$c_1 c_4 c_2 c_3$	
	undo
$c_1 c_4 c_2$	
	undo
$c_1 c_4$	
	undo
c_1	

The final ACS script has not recorded the historical state $c_1 c_2$, although it happened; in fact, it occurs twice in the sequence—so the user is likely to remember it! This previous state cannot be reached by any sequence of undoing and redoing. More complex cases, as arise in real situations, are *far* more complex and the user may have no idea what is possible or worth while trying by using undo and redo. In such cases the user will probably construct command sequences explicitly, avoiding the 'advantages' of the system's support for undo.

The limitation arises because the ACS model is based on a strictly linear script, but the changes brought about by undo and redo are better modelled by a graph. Recognizing this, Vitter has introduced a new framework to handle graph-script undo (Vitter, 1984). He calls his technique **Undo, Skip and Redo**—or when abbreviated, *US&R*, which very nearly spells *USER*.

Over the period of a session, a particular command may be redone at different times, following any commands and followed by different commands. In general, the command script can be represented by a graph. Commands are represented as nodes, and actual sequences of commands submitted by the user as paths through the graph. The current state of the system is then represented by some path through the graph from the first command to the current command.

Instead of the general graph implied by this view—and the complexity of employing it in a practical user interface—Vitter employs simple precedence rules at each node and uses a directed acyclic graph (DAG) to represent the script. Each node on the DAG corresponds to a command, but not all paths are represented explicitly. The state is represented by a list of commands which may be implemented as part of the script.

Since the script records history by using a DAG it can only represent the successor command choices for each command, and not the complete history. Thus, the user has to make decisions to choose which child to take when redoing a command. The claim is that this choice is sufficient for almost all purposes, and is certainly not as complex as it would have been had a full history (and hence all possible choices) been stored in the script.

We shall run through the problematic example shown above to see how the idea works out and, indeed, solves the particular problem of redoing the elusive $c_1 c_2$.

For simplicity, we shall assume the script and state list corresponding to the initial script $c_1 c_2 c_3$ considered above has no alternatives, and therefore only nodes of order one (that is, with no choices):

> **history**: $c_1 c_2 c_3$
>   **script**: $c_1 \rightarrow c_2 \rightarrow c_3 \diamond$
>   **state**: $c_1 c_2 c_3$

The **history** line shows the complete sequence of commands submitted by the user; there is no structure in the history itself, and this would make it hard for the user to manipulate. The second line, **script**, shows the DAG that Vitter's scheme constructs; and the last, **state**, line shows the current state of the system. For clarity, the last command submitted by the user is marked by $\diamond$ in the **script** line.

Submitting undo twice, and so undoing c_3 and then c_2, results in:

> **history**: $c_1 c_2 c_3$ undo undo
>   **script**: $c_1 \diamond \rightarrow c_2 \rightarrow c_3$
>   **state**: c_1

Notice that the command undo itself is not present in the script. The script represents a simplified version of the history of what the user has done, but the state represents what the user has effectively done; in the last example the system is in a state *as if* the user submitted the command c_1 alone regardless of how he really managed to get there. At this stage the user can readily redo command c_2 (a command **redo** would simply submit the command to the right of the $\diamond$, and move the $\diamond$ right). But as before, we suppose he submits a fourth command c_4. There are then alternative successors for c_1:

> **history**: $c_1 c_2 c_3$ undo undo c_4
>   **script**: $c_1 \rightarrow \begin{cases} c_2 \rightarrow c_3 \\ c_4 \diamond \end{cases}$
>   **state**: $c_1 c_4$

Since c_4 has no child, its successor is considered by *US&R* to be an alternative child of its parent, c_2 in this case. (A command's successor is needed for when the user submits **redo**.) In general, each node in the script may have more than two children, then the user would have to make an explicit choice between the alternatives—*US&R* helps by ordering the choices in a most-recently-submitted order. Other orders are possible (for example, alphabetic or most-frequently-used), but there is a good reason for most-recently-used (Section 12.4.1).

If the user next submits `redo redo`, the commands c_2 and c_3 are redone in turn:

> **history:** $c_1c_2c_3$ undo undo c_4 redo redo
>
> **script:** $c_1 \rightarrow \begin{cases} c_2 \rightarrow c_3 \diamond \\ c_4 \end{cases}$
>
> **state:** $c_1c_4c_2c_3$

Now we are at the stage where the user wishes to undo back to the state c_1c_2. The user first undoes c_3 and c_2. This retraces the previous route through the script—this does not return the system to the state c_1 immediately, but to c_1c_4:

> **history:** $c_1c_2c_3$ undo undo c_4 redo redo undo undo
>
> **script:** $c_1 \rightarrow \begin{cases} c_2 \rightarrow c_3 \\ c_4 \diamond \end{cases}$
>
> **state:** c_1c_4

Then he undoes c_4,

> **history:** $c_1c_2c_3$ undo undo c_4 redo redo undo undo undo
>
> **script:** $c_1 \diamond \rightarrow \begin{cases} c_2 \rightarrow c_3 \\ c_4 \end{cases}$
>
> **state:** c_1

A redo at this point has two alternatives: redoing either child c_2 or c_4 would be possible. The system will enter into a subdialogue with the user, offering the alternatives (the most-recently-used being the default). The subdialogue is marked [?] in the history line in the diagram below. The user may choose to redo the c_2 child:

> **history:** $c_1c_2c_3$ undo undo c_4 redo redo undo undo undo
> redo [?]
>
> **script:** $c_1 \rightarrow \begin{cases} c_2 \diamond \rightarrow c_3 \\ c_4 \end{cases}$
>
> **state:** c_1c_2

And we have reached the state c_1c_2.

The example so far shows how the user may insert commands into the script, and submit undo and redo commands. The undo and redo commands are not inserted into the script, but instead navigate the user around the script, changing the current state. However, the model, as I have described it, is not yet general enough to delete or replace commands. Continuing with the example above, it is possible that the user wants to obtain the state c_1c_3. Since the commands may be arbitrarily complex, we assume the user needs to do this by submitting script commands alone: thus c_3 must be redone, not resubmitted. As we have described *US&R* so far, c_1 has only successors c_2 and c_4 and any new command the user chooses to submit at this point. c_3 is *not* a successor.

One further script command is required, skip. The user undoes back to state c_1, and then skips the command c_2 (the subdialogue establishing the choice between c_2 and c_4 would be structured as before). This may be represented thus:

$$\begin{aligned} &\textbf{history:} && c_1c_2c_3 \text{ undo undo } c_4 \text{ redo redo undo undo undo} \\ & && \text{redo [?] undo skip} \\ &\textbf{script:} && c_1 \rightarrow \begin{cases} \text{skip } c_2\diamond \rightarrow c_3 \\ c_4 \end{cases} \\ &\textbf{state:} && c_1 \end{aligned}$$

The commands skip c_2 together have no effect: skip 'skips' the following command. The next redo will offer no alternatives—there is only c_3 to choose—and the user will readily obtain the desired state c_1c_3 with little effort. Skip can later be used to skip skip and hence recover the state including c_2.

12.4.1 Properties of Undo, Skip and Redo

The precedence rules for sorting the choices open to the user are inertial: they arrange that the most recently redone part of the script will be the first choice for redo when the node is subsequently visited. This ensures that the first-choice (default) redo retraces the last undo at that note: in particular n undos followed by n default redos returns the system to the same state. This property is important because it means that users can readily recover from errors in their recoveries. If the system response is slow (feedback not synchronized) and undo is a single keystroke, for example, it would be very easy to undo too far, and the excessive undos would have to be redone.

Another important property, which is also an inertial property, is that redo choices do not disappear from the script. The script never shrinks.

12.4.2 Improving the Undo, Skip and Redo interface

The user must make a command selection (or skip a command) when making a redo choice. Unfortunately, the names of the choices at a node

---

Box 12.3   Undo as backtracking.

The user can be viewed as interacting with a system in order to establish a proof. Often, the proof will be an existence proof: the user wants to 'prove to himself' that he can construct a certain result.

More formally, we can suppose that the user has a certain goal, which can be formulated as a predicate, $P(x)$. P will be true of x if x is a satisfactory product of the interactive session. For example if x is an invoice addressed to the right consumer, and all the details are correct, then $P(x)$ will be true; but if the printed invoice has factual errors, or is addressed to a different person, then $P(x)$ will be false. For an *interaction*, the user wants a constructive proof of $\exists x\colon P(x)$. The user wants to know not only that there is some x that satisfies his goals represented by P, but also what x is or, actually, what any x satisfying P is.

When the user *acquires* an interactive system or commits himself to learning a new system, he wants a *non*-constructive proof that $\exists x\colon P(x)$. That is, the user wants to know that there is some way in principle of creating x, but he does not, at the moment, actually want an example x. (Chapter 13, following, formalizes this idea that 'there is a way in principle of creating ... ', by introducing so-called **strategies**.)

Just as Prolog constructs a proof by backtracking, it may be useful to consider mechanisms—of which undo is one—that support the user constructing proofs, that is, interacting. The facilities of Prolog (and other proof systems), then, have analogues as interactive commands.

---

do not fully specify the states obtainable from them. This is a standard navigational problem: the user may know where he wants to get to, but the information available at the current node is insufficient to choose a direction. As usual, the state space may be represented explicitly by a map, a concrete representation of the history tree and the state path. However, there is a tradeoff to be made: the *US&R* scheme permits a fairly efficient implementation, but representing the script as a map explicitly to the user might encourage the user to expect even more general possibilities for changing the script than are actually implemented.

12.5   The history assumption

We saw in Section 12.4 that the possibilities opened up by even a simple linear undo/redo system may be so confusing that a user might reasonably prefer to enter new commands rather than find out how to redo some previously submitted commands. We started this chapter by arguing that the user wants to be able to correct mistakes cheaply—indeed, this is a good reason for using interactive computer systems—but our discussion slowly slipped into discussion about what else we, as designers, could imagine doing once the script could be manipulated by the user. Undo is by no means the only operation that can be applied to a script: we saw, for instance, that skip and redo extend the capability of the interface. It sounds like creeping featurism (Section 7.5). We trade the power of the user interface against its ease of use.

We can justify creeping featurism easily, certainly given our technical orientation, and justify it very easily for undo features that help the user recover from errors: but, we would be ignoring the wider issues, for instance the purpose of the system. Even if we believe that undo is essential to recover from errors, there are some errors that the user would *not* want to recover from! Game playing is an example: it is cheating to take back a move: there are strong social conventions that would dissuade a user trying to undo any error! An artist might treat 'accidents' as an essential part of the creative process.

Almost all of the complexity of undo/redo mechanisms (more sophisticated than the simple truncate strategies) arises from the difference between the script and the state, and the reluctance to discard or tidy history. It is not clear that the user will want to redo previous commands often enough in order to provide the sort of confusing generality of *US&R* or other approaches.

Users may want to be helped by the system in more intelligent ways than merely repotting their history. Undo is something the *user* does—can't the *system* do something? For example, the system could use the history to predict the next most likely command to be submitted. Or the user might want to submit examples for the system to generalize in the future.

Saul Greenberg and Ian Witten (1987) have investigated the use of history mechanisms, and it seems that users do indeed resubmit a substantial proportion of previously submitted commands, thus the idea of providing redo commands is empirically well founded, and not merely a result of getting carried away with the technical possibilities. Of course, in these experiments, the proportion of redone commands may be as much an indicator of problems with the system (the commands may not have worked properly first time) as support for a redo scheme *in general*. When users do redo commands, they are likely to repeatedly redo the *same* commands; the inertial rules of *US&R* therefore appear uncontentious.

Systems like *US&R* provide a redo command: but, most likely, the user would be better off being able to reuse what he achieved with earlier commands, rather than have to redo the commands themselves. Text editors normally allow the user to reuse text rather than redo the commands that created it. And by reusing the result of commands, the difficulties of default parameters is greatly reduced: consider creating a line of text with relative motion commands; these commands may mean different things in different contexts, but the text created by their use is a constant with the same meaning wherever it is reused.

Box 12.4   Getting the user to undo.

Maybe life is too easy for the user if the computer can remember what commands to undo! A more educational approach may be to ask the user what needs undoing.

A geology teaching program provides commands to lay down sediments, to erode by water, to fault and to fold. There are various technicalities we need not go into; briefly, as each command is submitted, a graphical display builds up a picture of coloured strata, bending and shearing into characteristic rock formations.

After the user has tried out the range of possibilities, the computer might provide a typical cross-section and ask the user what geological operations brought about such a result.   Now the user has to run the program backwards. What does he think was the last thing that happened? The quiz for the user is to decide what commands have to be undone to return to the pristine state. With 'undo' he can do this one step at a time and see the geological processes 'unfold' on the screen.

(Such a program was seen at The Drumheller Museum of Paleontology, Canada in 1986.)

12.6   Non-historical undo

All of the undo mechanisms treated so far have taken as their basis that the user edits the script of commands, and thereby navigates and is enabled to modify the history of the session in some way. The *US&R* approach provides a uniform interface to contain the combinatorial explosion of alternative histories. There are two conceptual problems for the user:

▷   The history and script are not the same, and there may be no simple gueps to help understand their differences.

▷   The representation of the script can be awkward (because it is a complex graph), and the user may not understand the possible ways of navigating and changing it.

It happens that for some applications the state is very simply related to the commands of which it is a function. The assumption behind wanting an undo facility is that the state and script are not generally simply related; so the user may be able to achieve the state he wants most easily by explicitly manipulating the script (with **undo/skip/redo** commands) rather than by directly manipulating the current state. However, for suitable applications (text and picture editing being the most common examples) manipulating the state can be conceptually much easier than manipulating the script.

Box 12.5   The history paradox.

With undo, the history of interaction (or rather, the script) becomes a first-class value: the user can manipulate the history of his interaction. Paradoxically, as soon as history is available, it is no longer necessary to have it!

Histories arise because of a time ordering of command submission; yet as soon as the script can be arbitrarily modified, it does not matter in what order commands were submitted. For instance, a user can submit c_1 undo c_2 undo, then by judicious use of redo, it is possible to get to the state c_2c_1, even though the commands were originally submitted in the opposite order.

The same paradox arises in programming. If we start out writing programs in an imperative, that is history-sensitive style, it clearly matters in what order commands are performed. For instance, the classic 'swap two variables' (here a and b), temp := a; a := b; b := temp; only works in that order. If the assignments are executed in a different order, the variable values get duplicated rather than swapped. However, if we make the history explicit, perhaps by adding some timing information, it does not matter in what order things are done.

We could write a_t to mean the value of the variable a at time t. If each assignment takes a second or one unit of time, then the assignments to swap the values of the variables become more precisely:

temp$_1$:= a$_0$; a$_2$:= b$_0$; b$_3$:= temp$_1$;

Since each variable has a time 'tied to it' in its subscript, a given variable/time is not 'assigned to' in the usual sense, for it only ever has one value and is never changed—such a permanent association of a value with a name is called a **binding**. This means that what used to be a *sequence* of assignments has become a set of *simultaneous* equations. It is clearer if we replace the variable/time names with simple names:

tempone = azero; atwo = bzero; bthree = tempone;

Since tempone always has a value equal to azero, we can replace it, and simplify the equations to atwo = bzero; bthree = azero; We have swapped the values of the variables around correctly—and we would still have done so even if the order of the equations was permuted to, say,

atwo = bzero; bthree = tempone; tempone = azero;

In summary: by putting timing information into a sequence of commands, it ceases to matter what time those commands are performed. Scripts are used in a similar way: as soon as the user can manipulate a script (using undo), it ceases to matter (from the system's point of view) what time the user submits commands.

This insight is part of the basis of functional programming. Chapter 13, next, building on the idea of the 'meaning of a script' naturally proceeds to a functional analysis of interactive systems.

If the user types `abcdef` (that is, the sequence of commands, insert-a, insert-b ...) at a simple text editor, the state can be represented by the text so created, namely, `abcdef`. If the user moves the cursor (editing position) back, say, to just after `b`, then we could treat the script prefix `ab` as 'executed' and the script tail `cdef` as 'pending' (using the ACS model terms). In a normal text editor, nothing actually executes the text, so the distinction is purely notational.

The correspondence between script and state might be used productively for generating new design ideas. For example, suppose an editor provides a single-character truncate `undo`. Single-truncate undo corresponds to `delete-character` at any other point in the text. Therefore, if the design provides one, it should provide the other: the closure principle.

Only those commands that destroy information are a problem for undoing because to undo them requires knowing the lost information. Rather than provide inverses for such commands, it may be simpler to store the information elsewhere, so that it remains accessible to the user. It may be possible to present the saved information explicitly to the user; the user can then reuse it instead of undoing the destructive commands.

For an example of this, imagine a text editor that changes text to blue as it is deleted. Blue therefore indicates lost information. Undoing is now a matter of changing blue back to its original colour (white, say). If the user wants to see 'what he has got', this is only a matter of colouring the blue text black (so it disappears into the background colour), and perhaps reformatting. The advantage of this technique is that all deleted (blue) information is presented to the user, but suppressing the information about the time it was deleted. The order of the deleted information reflects the spatial ordering of the original text, rather than the time (or time-and-space) it was deleted, as with conventional undo.

Obviously, maintaining the lost information explicitly may be expensive, both from the implementation point of view and for the real estate available on the screen. Various methods can be used to compress the amount of information held: this would mean that the user may not be able to return to an arbitrary previous state directly, but he will be able to return to any previous state only by removing excess information. For example, the text editor need not keep track of information as it is lost per character, but it could keep track of information lost per line—then a single blue line would abstract over many individual deletions within a line. Most generally, a system would display computed **deltas**, that is, equivalent *short* sequences of commands to recover lost information, but not necessarily the inverses of the particular commands the user submitted. (In text editing, deltas are readily constructed by applying standard string-to-string correction algorithms.)

12.7 Conclusions

We started with the idea that users make mistakes and that by 'talking about what they are doing' (by using undo and other metacommands), they are given considerable power both to remedy mistakes and to explore the potential of the system with great ease. There are various problems with metacommands: although intended to provide greater flexibility, they may also make the system more confusing—remember the thesis of Chapter 6! Metacommands have problems with implicit information (for example, relative or absolute coordinates), but to some extent, a designer can circumvent these problems by providing task-oriented commands (for example, a good enough text editor might not need undo commands, because any error can be undone by further text, rather than command, edits).

We saw that our discussion of undo *became solutioneering for its own sake*—the discussion of Section 12.5 suggested that we ought to stop and check what empirical evidence there is to justify complex undo features.

After an entire chapter on one subject, we must remind ourselves of the phenomenological issues, specifically of blindness (Box 2.1). Some users, perhaps almost all users, do not require undo in their user interfaces: what they want is satisfaction in pursuing their goals. Undo is a function, not a goal—a means not an end—though under certain circumstances it may serve to facilitate the user reaching his goal more effectively. It will generally be the case that a user interface may be made more appropriate to the needs of the user if it can be designed so that it does *not* need undo. Undo is often (but not always) a merely technical solution to problems that we can think of no better way to avoid. In summary: by concentrating on undo, we necessarily become blind to other design issues. A wonderful implementation of undo in a bad system is probably better than a bad system without undo; but this does not mean that a quite different system might not have been altogether better, whether or not it has undo. The designer may be blind to such alternatives; it is also true that design progresses under resource limitations, and exploring alternatives may take too long. A good enough design, with or without undo, delivered on time is better than a perfect system still under development.

Chapter 13

A formal model
for interactive systems

The utmost abstractions are the true weapons with which to
control our thought of concrete fact.

Alfred North Whitehead

Without the requirement of mathematical aesthetics a great
many discoveries would not have been made.

Albert Einstein

The purpose of this chapter is to show that we can *reason* formally about
interactive systems, rather than merely *describe* them. The highlights of
the chapter will show that:

▷ Undo and modelessness are incompatible.

▷ Window managers have subtle mode problems.

This chapter is the most mathematically advanced in the book: so do not
suppose that the subsequent chapters are going to be worse!

The previous chapter, on undo, introduced us to the idea of the
script. The script of commands represents the complete history (from some
initial benchmark) of the user's interaction. Let us now formalize the idea
of interpreting the script and converting it into a state; that is, we shall
formalize properties of the user interface that are determined by the script.
We shall see that it is comparatively easy to specify certain gueps that script
interpretations can have. Very often seemingly reasonable properties will
conflict in one way or another: the major task for the designer will be to
obtain a balance between a truly trivial system (that satisfies—or, rather,
fails to flaunt—various properties) and a system that is useful as well.

There are, of course, many ways that user interface properties may be formalized. Different approaches would be taken depending on the particular concerns of the designer: for instance, the method illustrated here remains silent about such issues as response times. On the one hand, this is an advantage, for response time is 'just a detail' and we can assume the interactive system will be 'fast enough'. But computers are not arbitrarily fast and an analysis of time complexity will often be required.

The undo models of the last chapter used the term script for the sequence of the user's commands, but we shall now use the term **program**, which we will represent by P. P is simply a sequence of commands chosen from a set C. The user submits one command, then the next, and so on, the several commands taken together forming a 'program', which the system runs. The system executes the program P, interpreting it by an interpretation function I. The consequence of interpretation is to obtain an effect, E. This simple model is called the **PIE model** (Dix and Runciman, 1985).

13.1   Notation

The null program symbol $\emptyset$ is a notational device that allows us to denote the user submitting no command, or not having yet started submitting a program: there is no need for a system to actually implement a null command for the user to be able to do nothing. We will use $\emptyset$ when making precise arguments, so that we can make a noticeable mark on the paper to occupy the space that would otherwise have been taken up by nothing at all.

P is the set of command sequences that the user may submit. Strictly, the user submits commands not programs; we should equip P with an operation that supports the combination of commands into programs. Normally, the user does not really ask for commands to be combined together, this just happens automatically; the user has submitted a program, he now submits a command, and the program is extended. We shall represent this extension by the symbol $\smile$, called smile.

$\smile$ is not a command that the user can submit, it is a mathematical function: it takes the existing program that the user has already submitted, and the next command, and produces a new program. The new program is just the old program with the command appended. We can represent how $\smile$ works as a function of programs and commands, generating a new program by writing $\smile: P \times C \to P$, but since commands are a special case of programs (being programs of length one), we will find it more convenient to define $\smile$ by $P \times P \to P$. This notation is broadly equivalent to the Pascal `function extend(p1, p2: Program): Program`.[1]

---

[1] We call the Pascal function **extend** because this is mnemonic. **Smile** would have been more cheerful.

In some interactive systems there is then some potential for confusion with $\smile$ and enter. If we had a system with an enter command that was a newline then the user would submit

c_1

c_2

c_3

$\vdots$

typing newline after each command. This sequence would submit the program that we call $c_1 \smile c_2 \smile c_3 \ldots$ So it looks as if enter and $\smile$ serve the same purpose. But note that enter enter with no explicit intervening command may have some definite effect, for instance to submit a default command. Many systems would treat c_1 enter enter as equivalent to c_1 enter c_1 enter, repeating submission of c_1 by default. For some systems, then, $\emptyset \smile \emptyset \neq \emptyset$, and we would be best treating enter as an actual command and not as the representation of $\smile$. Nevertheless, we might want to design a system where enter merely served to separate commands and had no effect when it had no commands to separate, and then we could treat enter and $\smile$ equivalently. (The issue about how enter separates commands is reminiscent of our discussion of Pascal semicolons in Section 6.2.2.)

Note that enter may so effectively separate each command (in the mind of the implementation) that it also acts as a script committal. Once the user has entered newline or enter, the preceding lines might not be available for undo in a future edit activity.

13.2   An example PIE

The calculator described in Section 11.6.1, since we already understand it, is a good case to express as a PIE.

First, the command set of this user interface is defined by the buttons on the front of the calculator. There are probably direct manipulation commands on the back of the calculator to remove or replace the battery, but the effect of these 'commands' is adequately covered by the conventional ON and OFF commands—if the calculator had a calendar function that relied on continuous battery power, then modelling these normally-hidden features might be a good idea.

The command set, C, of the calculator is agreed to be the set:

$$C = \{\text{ON}, \text{OFF}, \text{C}, \text{AC}, +, -, =, \times, \div, ., 0, 1, 2, 3, 4, 5, 6, 7, 8, 9\}$$

The effect space, E, of the calculator is simply what can be seen on the display: a number, an error indication E, or (when the calculator is off) nothing at all, which is represented formally by $\emptyset$. We can represent these possibilities by writing, $E = \{\text{-99999999} \ldots \text{99999999}, \text{E}, \emptyset\}$. Notice that this apparently gives the precision of the calculator as eight digits, but gives no indication of the way decimals are handled; that is clearly an issue that should be addressed, though it need not concern us right now.

The user hits keys on the calculator, and we model this by defining an interpretation function I. All I does is convert sequences of commands—so-called programs—into their corresponding effects. Thus, $I(\emptyset) = \emptyset$, meaning that if the user has done nothing, not even submitted ON, the calculator shows nothing.

More interesting examples are:

$I(\text{ON}) = 0$ If the calculator has just been switched on, the display shows a zero.

$I(\text{ON 1}) = 1$ If the first keystroke after switching the calculator on is a digit 1, the display shows a 1.

$I(\text{ON 1 +}) = 1$ But submitting + has no effect on the current display.

$I(\text{ON 1 + 2}) = 2$ Now the display shows the second number, 2.

$I(\text{ON 1 + 2 =}) = 3$ Submitting = evaluates the preceding expression 1+2 and displays the value 3.

Concrete examples like this could of course be given endlessly, but nobody would learn anything about the underlying rules. Users need the rules in order to know how to interact with the system, and designers need to know the rules if only so that they can write a concise program to implement the system. Well, we would hope the designers also need the rules so that they can reason about how the user will reason about the system—and that is the purpose of gueps.

The first rule is the 'switch-off rule': $I(\ldots \text{OFF}) = \emptyset$. If OFF is the last command submitted, the calculator shows an empty display. In fact, the rule can be generalized to $I(\ldots \text{OFF } p) = \emptyset$ where p does not contain the command ON. We use p as essentially 'any program' and this allows us to talk about p explicitly by name (which can't be said for '...').

We might want to specify that the ON command does the same thing as the AC (all clear) command. It seems we can do this easily by $I(p \text{ ON}) = I(p \text{ AC})$, which means that whatever has been done so far, p, the effect of submitting ON or AC should be the same. In fact this only says that the *display* after submitting ON and AC will be the same: we also need to specify that the two commands have the same effect on any on-going calculation. This restriction is easily expressed as follows: $I(p \text{ ON } q) = I(p \text{ AC } q)$, for all p and q. What this means is that whatever the user does before (p) or after (q) submitting ON or AC, he cannot tell the difference—even if q was, say, +0= in an attempt to find out what the current calculation was. Thus, we have specified that the commands ON and AC are indistinguishable. We will encounter similar issues later in this chapter.

A more substantial rule is this: for any digits, d_1 and d_2, then $I(p\ d_1d_2) = 10 \times I(p\ d_1) + d_2$. In other words, if the user has just submitted two digits (d_1 then d_2), the result is whatever submitting d_1 got (namely, $I(p\ d_1)$) times ten, plus the value of the second digit. So, if $I(p\ 2) = 12$, because the p ends in +1 and $I(\ldots+12) = 12$, then $I(p\ 23) = 10 \times I(p\ 2) + 3 = 10 \times 12 + 3 = 123$. This is what we would expect from $I(\ldots+123) = 123$. However, this rule is not quite right, for the program p must exclude recent decimal points (the rule breaks down for, say, the 23 digits in 0·123), and for anything to happen at all the calculator must be switched on! Hence, more precisely

▷ $I(p\ d_1d_2) = 10 \times I(p\ d_1) + d_2$ where p must contain at least one ON, and at least one ON submitted after any OFF, and any decimal point in p is followed by any command that is not a digit.

Such rules and their constraints are exceedingly cumbersome! It is, however, very easy *for the designer* to side-step them, as follows.

We now define a new interpretation function I_{ON} which works exactly like I, except that we assume the calculator is on. Thus for any p, $I_{ON}(p) = I(\text{ON } p)$. The command set for I_{ON} is C_{ON}, which is simply C without OFF. We may or may not want C_{ON} to contain ON, depending on whether it does anything interesting to the effect E_{ON}. Note that E_{ON} is just like E, except that the display $\emptyset$ is not needed.

Now that I and I_{ON} have been separated, we can give rules for switching the calculator on and off separately from its rules of normal use (when the calculator is presumed switched on all the time). We can do the same thing with decimal points, defining an interpretation function I_N, say, which assumes that the rules of numbers are understood; we might also have abstracted away the C (clear entry) command by this device, because it only affects entering the current number, and the point of I_N is that we are only interested in the number itself, not the details of how the user submitted it.

Now we can write rules like, $I_N(n_1+n_2=) = n_1 + n_2 \ldots$ except we can now easily see that this rule is only correct if the result is in the range of numerical results catered for by E! There might be an overflow, if $n_1 + n_2$ is too big. Again, we can define a new I, and push problems of overflow to yet another subsidiary function. Then we can concentrate on the *real* (?) rules of interaction, for example, whether $I(n_1\text{-}+n_2=) = n_1 - n_2$ or perhaps $-n_1 + n_2$? One makes sense if we want to think of -+ as subtracting the number $+n_2$ from n_1; the alternative makes sense if we think of -+ as negating n_1, followed by adding n_2. If we can't make our minds up for this case, it won't be at all obvious to the user, and perhaps it should be required that $I(\ldots\ \text{-+}) = E$ to avoid confusion.

In conclusion then, we have shown that the PIE model is sufficient for describing the rules of behaviour of simple user interfaces: here we used it for the calculator described earlier in Chapter 11. The PIE model is quite adequate to describe all the relevant interaction features, and it can be used to express groups of related features by relatively simple rules. Furthermore, the PIE model can be used at different levels, for instance, to describe the behaviour of the calculator assuming it is on, or taking for granted the rules of number entry. In this way, the PIE model can be used to reason through the interactive features of arbitrarily complex systems. Although the designer, in order to reason more easily about the interface, can devise arbitrary functions (like I_{ON}), it is still an intriguing question how the user may (or may not) abstract such 'functions' and reason about their properties. If the designer finds or designs certain functions with useful properties, then it is incumbent on him to tell the user something like, 'If you think of the system in this way . . . , then it works nicely like this . . . '

Some people may complain that the PIE model is less suitable than, say, Pascal for describing user interfaces. This is partly true—else every interactive program would be 'written' in PIEs and not in Pascal or whatever. But here are two responses to this criticism:

▷ If, as suggested above, the user is urged to 'think of the system in *this* way', he will not require a three year training in Pascal programming to appreciate it.

▷ The structure provided by PIEs helps designers reason about interaction rules, including which interface features they need to abstract away before those rules are apparent.

The next chapter will take up this line of argumentation again, exploring the case that mathematics (which is what PIEs are) has intrinsic advantages that are not so obviously found in programming languages like Pascal.

13.3   Simple properties

13.3.1   Restartability and quantifiers

As the first interactive systems property to formalize in the PIE model, take **restartability**. A restartable system is one that has commands that can be used to bring it back to its starting state, for example a calculator may have a `clear` button—which actually has the same effect as restarting, switching the calculator off and on again.

We can express the property formally as follows:

restartable $\equiv \forall p \, \exists q \colon I(p \smile q) = I(\emptyset)$

This means that a restartable PIE has the property that whatever has been done (represented by p), there is something q that can be submitted so that the overall effect of p followed by q is the starting effect, $I(\emptyset)$. Notice that the $\forall p$ means that we want to be able to restart after *every* possible command sequence p, and the $\exists q$ says that for each p there *exists* some q.

The order of the quantifiers $\forall$ and $\exists$ is crucial. The restartability property we have just defined only says that the PIE is restartable with some command sequence for each p. A stronger property would be:

$$\text{uniform-restartable} \equiv \exists q \, \forall p \colon I(p \smile q) = I(\emptyset)$$

The quantifiers $\exists q$ and $\forall p$ have been swapped around. Now there exists a q for *all* programs p. This means that the same q will restart whatever p it follows.

We may want a system restartable with a single command, rather than having the user submitting some possibly long sequence of commands. We can specify this merely by being more precise about q:

$$\text{quick-restartable} \equiv \exists q \in C \colon \forall p \colon I(p \smile q) = I(\emptyset)$$

Here we say that q must be chosen from the set of commands C. It is probably a button like escape. However we still understand that p is chosen from all possible programs, including $\emptyset$ itself. For a PIE satisfying this property, then, escape always brings the system back to its initial state, even when escape is the only command submitted. Many systems treat escape escape as a means of escaping from the system altogether, rather than restarting it, but such a system would not be quick-restartable by our definition. (Why?)

The difference between uniform-restartable and quick-restartable depends on whether $q \in P$ or $q \in C$. A system is restartable if some sequence of commands $q \in P$ will restart it, but it is quick-restartable if only one command $q \in C$ will restart it. Since there is this difference, from now on we will always be explicit, and write $\in C$ or whatever as appropriate.

13.3.2 Equivalences

In many of the properties that follow we will want to say that the effects of two command sequences p, q are equivalent. This is expressed by $I(p) = I(q)$, that is, the interpretation of p is equal to the effect resulting from interpreting q.

However it is possible for the effects of two command sequences to be the same now, but not later because of the different modes that may have been introduced by them, and subsequently influence the interpretation of further commands. Thus, we may have $I(p) = I(q)$ now, but there may be some mode-sensitive program, r say, such that $I(p \smile r) \neq I(q \smile r)$. For instance, p might result in the system being in insert-mode, and q might be identical except that the system ends up in overwrite-mode. The effect immediately after p and q may be identical if the system does not say which mode it is in, but the user need only submit a single character $r = \mathbf{x}$ to get a different effect.

To specify that two command sequences p, q not only have the same effect now, but leave the system in the same mode we will write $p \sim q$. Put colloquially, if the user goes for a cup of tea, and when he comes back he cannot remember whether he did p or q, it will not matter if $p \sim q$; for if $p \sim q$, there will be nothing that he can do in the future that will distinguish one possibility from the other. Thus $p \sim q$ (programs p and q are $\sim$–equivalent) only if the interpretation of p followed by anything, r, is the same as the interpretation of q followed by the same thing. We define $p \sim q$ by:

$$p \sim q \equiv \forall r \in P : I(p \smile r) = I(q \smile r)$$

Note that the $\forall r$ includes the special case that $r = \emptyset$, since $\emptyset$ is a member of P; that is, that $I(p) = I(q)$ is implied by $p \sim q$.

The $\sim$ formulation will be used as a shorthand notation in the discussion that follows. However it is often useful to define a stronger equivalence, namely one independent of the initial state. The simple $p \sim q$ assumes that p and q are the *entire* command sequences since the system was switched on; often we may not want to think so far back. We define $\approx$ to apply to an isolated command sequence, when we do not know the previous history s:

$$\begin{aligned} p \approx q \quad &\equiv \quad \forall s \in P : s \smile p \sim s \smile q \\ &\equiv \quad \forall r, s \in P : I(s \smile p \smile r) = I(s \smile q \smile r) \end{aligned}$$

$\approx$–equivalence may be used to specify that command sequences have equivalent interpretations under *all* circumstances, whatever s the user had submitted beforehand. For example, using $\approx$, we may write $\mathsf{L} \approx \mathsf{1}$ indicating that the case of the $\mathsf{1}$ command is insignificant. But $\mathsf{1} \sim \mathsf{L}$ would only indicate that the case was insignificant when the command was submitted as the very *first* command.

As an exercise, you may like to show that $\approx$ and $\sim$ are indeed equivalence relations. (Use the fact that equality is reflexive, symmetric and transitive; it is itself an equivalence relation.)

It is now possible to define **state** formally. A state is a $\sim$–equivalence class of programs. Suppose we write down all possible programs, p_1, p_2, $p_3 \ldots$ We would find that, say, $p_3 \sim p_{11}$ and $p_{203} \sim p_{1\,045} \sim p_{4\,294}$, and maybe that there is no other program $\sim p_2$. The states of the system are just such classes of equivalent programs. If the user submits the program p_3 the system will end up in exactly the same state as if he had submitted p_{11}.

13.3.3 Observability

At any moment let us suppose that the user can see the full effect $E = I(p)$ of all commands p submitted to the system. In fact, because of the user interface bottleneck, most systems are *unable* to show the entire effect at any given moment. If the effect is considered to be the contents of computer memory at any moment, the effect space E may be many megabytes. Only some of this information can be displayed at the user interface, say, on a screen of 25 lines of 80 characters—only 2k bytes.

It is not necessarily the case that merely by knowing the effect, the user knows what state the system is in. For instance, consider the two programs $p \smile$ clear-screen and $q \smile$ clear-screen. The interpretation of both programs is a blank screen, $I(p \smile$ clear-screen$) = I(q \smile$ clear-screen$)$, yet what the user can do next is generally determined by p or q so it is possible that $p \not\sim q$.

Observability principles attack the 'gone for a cup of tea' problem. When you come back, you may have forgotten exactly where you were and where you were going; the screen may be blank. Does observation of the current effect provide enough information to decide how to continue? In this cleared-screen example, there is only enough information to decide how to continue if a blank screen always means the system is in the same state.

An effect is **ambiguous** if it can be produced in more than one state.

Suppose the command sequence p brings the system to a particular state. The effect visible to the user will be $I(p)$. Another, different, sequence of commands, q, may cause the same effect. We express this by $I(p) = I(q)$. The sequence q may or may not leave the system in the same state as p. This only matters to the user if it affects how subsequent commands are interpreted. If the user subsequently enters some commands r, the effect obtained will be either $I(p \smile r)$ or $I(q \smile r)$. If the effect $e = I(p)$ is ambiguous, then there will be some command sequences r such that $I(p \smile r) \neq I(q \smile r)$. In other words, an effect e is ambiguous if $e = I(p) = I(q)$, but not $p \sim q$. Put formally,

$$\text{ambiguous}(e) \equiv \exists p, q \in P: I(p) = e = I(q) \wedge p \not\sim q$$

If no effect is ambiguous then every effect that looks the same represents the same system state. Everything the user can see tells him what state the system is in: this is another form of WYSIWYG, if what you can see is the effect and what you have got is the state. If there are any differences in internal system state, the user has *no* way of discovering them—and therefore they can't matter. A PIE with this property is called **monotone**:

$$\text{monotone} \equiv \forall p, q \in P: I(p) = I(q) \Rightarrow p \sim q$$

alternatively,

$$\text{monotone} \equiv \neg \exists e \in E: \text{ambiguous}(e)$$

This is a very restrictive property—somewhat similar to modelessness. It is normally incompatible with providing an undo command: even if the current states are the same represented by $I(p) = I(q)$, an undo command would be able to 'reach back' into p or q to see if they were exactly the same. If we distinguish the class of metacommands that can examine the past and the other, normal commands, we might want to define a variant of monotonicity:

$$\text{normally-monotone} \equiv \forall p, q \in P: I(p) = I(q) \Rightarrow p \overset{\text{normal}}{\sim} q$$

where,

$$p \overset{\text{normal}}{\sim} q \equiv \forall r \in P_{\text{normal}}: I(p \smile r) = I(q \smile r)$$

In other words, in a normally-monotone system, states that look the same *are* the same unless the user looks too closely with special commands. And we can tell the user which commands, such as undo, would let him 'look too closely'.

13.3.4   Completeness

Are there some effects that the user cannot achieve? Completeness is the property that requires that all effects may be obtained by suitable programs: that there are no unobtainable effects.

$$\text{complete} \equiv \forall e \in E: \exists p \in P: e = I(p)$$

Mathematically, a complete PIE is one where I is surjective; in practice an incomplete PIE could only arise if we made spurious claims about I or E. Of course, the user might be thinking of an e' which he believed ought to be in E, but in fact isn't.

13.3.5   Reachability

Even in a complete system it is not necessarily the case that the user would be able to obtain any effect after making a mistake. There is the possibility that any errors could not be rectified; some effects might be unreachable from some states. To avoid the joke, 'if I were going there, I would not start from here', we require **reachability**, rather than mere completeness:

$$\text{reachable} \equiv \forall e \in E: \forall p \in P: \exists r \in P: I(p \smile r) = e$$

If the PIE is complete, the following is equivalent:

$$\text{reachable} \equiv \forall p, q \in P: \exists r \in P: I(p \smile r) = I(q)$$

In words, whatever the user did p can be converted to the same effect
as an intended submission q, by correcting p with r. Thus, not only can
you get anywhere (completeness) but you can get anywhere from anywhere
(reachability). In a text editor, reachability would ensure that any text
document could be edited into any other document—there are some text
editors where a user cannot create a zero-length document once he has
submitted any command: the zero-length effect cannot be reached from
anywhere.

Reachability remains silent about the complexity of r, and how hard
it is for the user to work it out. The user may in theory reach anywhere
from anywhere, but the effort involved might be prohibitive or the recovery
sequence r might be so intricate that the user may need to recover from
mistakes made in submitting *that*. A 'you can get anywhere from anywhere'
text editor might be one that has only commands to insert arbitrary text
and a *single* command to delete *all* text—not much use!

In a non-monotone PIE, a particular effect may represent different
states, but the reachability property above merely requires that the user
can always do something (called r in the definition) to get the system to
a particular *effect*, $I(q)$, not a particular *state*. We may therefore want a
stronger property that would require that a system allow the user to obtain
the effect in a given state. This requirement is called **mega-reachability**:

$$\text{mega-reachable} \equiv \forall p, q \in P\colon \exists r \in P\colon p \smile r \sim q$$

In words, whatever state the system is in (achieved by submitting the
arbitrary program p), there exists something the user may do, namely r,
such that however the user proceeds in the future, the effect is the same
as if the system were already in some arbitrary state (the equivalence class
containing q). The difference between reachability and mega-reachability is
that the former property says that the user can obtain a particular effect;
the second property, that the user can both obtain a particular effect and
determine the subsequent behaviour of the system. A monotone PIE that is
reachable is mega-reachable, since a monotone PIE is essentially modeless,
obtaining a particular effect determines the current mode uniquely, and
hence determines the future interpretation of commands.

The reachability properties are obviously useful for systems such as
text editors. 'Real-world' systems, certainly systems which have an idea of
real-world time, cannot be fully reachable; systems with 'start-up banners'
which are shown briefly when the system is booted may never be reached
again by normal means. To reason about such systems we abstract away
those details, in effect saying if you ignore certain details (like the time) the
system is reachable.

13.4 Expressing undo properties

If a system is reachable, then the user may undo any error, for any desired effect can be reached from anywhere, in particular after an error. However, the reachability properties do not directly help the user correct the mistake straightforwardly. Once the user has submitted p when he meant q, he may have no idea what r to submit, such that $p \smile r \sim q$, even though he knows that some such r exists. Understanding the reachability guep would only frustrate the user further!

We may require that there exists a function $\mathcal{U}$, a 'purely notional' mathematical function, not necessarily corresponding to any implemented system function, that tells the user how to undo an error caused by some incorrect commands q. Where this function is implemented is a question we need not ask immediately, but we might imagine that the system's manual explains the system well enough for the user (or for somebody else, a local expert perhaps) to be able to operate $\mathcal{U}$.

We can imagine the following scenario: The user makes (and recognizes) some mistake. Suppose that he has accidentally or incorrectly issued the commands q. He rings up his local expert, 'I typed the commands q by mistake. Oh! What can I do to get back to where I was?' The expert listens attentively, applies the function $\mathcal{U}$ to q and gets the answer, $a = \mathcal{U}(q)$. He tells the user to do a. Put more formally,

$$\exists \mathcal{U} \in (P \to P) : \forall p, q \in P : p \smile q \smile \mathcal{U}(q) \sim p$$

or, more briefly, $q \smile \mathcal{U}(q) \approx \emptyset$.

Thus the command sequence $\mathcal{U}(q)$ would undo q. Obviously we could propose different formulations for $\mathcal{U}$; the one illustrated has the advantage that it is a function only of what is to be undone, not on the preceding program p. Thus we are assuming, to the user's advantage, either that the system has some powerful recovery commands or that it is modeless so that p does not matter.

The trouble with this simple undo requirement is that $\mathcal{U}(q)$ might have to be different for each command sequence q. For instance, we might have $\mathcal{U}(\texttt{left}) = \texttt{right}$ but $\mathcal{U}(\texttt{up}) = \texttt{down}$.[2] The fact that is it possible to undo any error and, indeed, only knowing the mistake, and not what preceded it, is of little comfort if it is not easy to remember nor use $\mathcal{U}$. Remembering $\mathcal{U}$ means knowing how to undo a command; using $\mathcal{U}$ means being able to work out what to do in any particular case.

It would be nice for the user if $\mathcal{U}$ had a simple compositional property: $\mathcal{U}(a \smile b) \approx \mathcal{U}(b) \smile \mathcal{U}(a)$. Namely, to undo a sequence of commands, you merely undo each one in reverse order to the order they were submitted.

---

[2] Consider a system that used U to mean up, and N to mean next (or newline), to go down. Many users would have expected D to mean down, but it meant delete—an effect that could certainly not be undone by going up!

This is more intuitive than it looks when it is spelt out in detail! The user still has to know what the undo of each command is, for instance, to undo a `left` move he should submit `right`.[3] We'll soon see some technical problems.

Of course, there is no reason for the user to remember $\mathcal{U}$ if the system can! If there is a fixed function $\mathcal{U}$ that gives the undo of any command, then we could invent a command (call it `undo`) that instructs the computer to apply $\mathcal{U}$ to the last command, and submit the result of the application. This way the user does not have to know $\mathcal{U}$ intimately, only what it is called. To make the system easier to use maybe we could afford a keyboard with `undo` as a specially labelled key.

Whenever the user makes a mistake, he can ring up the local expert, and the expert will say, 'Have you tried `undo` ...?' This looks very appealing.

As the computer can implement the work of $\mathcal{U}$, and can cause it to be used when the user submits `undo`, then, for the user, $\forall c \in C : \mathcal{U}(c)$ is a constant, namely `undo`. Unfortunately, put like this, the idea contains an elementary flaw: the original function $\mathcal{U}$ existed over the set of commands C, and we then supposed it to be a fixed function. If the user is given access to $\mathcal{U}$ as a command, then the augmented user interface should retain the *same* desirable property: namely, that there is a simple, fixed way of undoing any error. Unfortunately, the command set is now different. The formula above, $\forall c \in C : \mathcal{U}(c)$ that we claimed was a constant, is incorrect. It should have been $\forall c \in (C \cup \{\text{undo}\}) : \mathcal{U}(c)$, because `undo` is one of the possible commands.

`Undo` either undoes itself or it does not undo itself. If it does undo itself, then the composition property is lost; if it does not undo itself, the user is stuck if he mistakenly undoes a command—for that undo cannot be undone. Losing the composition property is serious, because it means that the user has no easy way of undoing back more than one command—in fact, because `undo` undoes itself, the user has no way *at all* of undoing more than *one* command. This is what we called flip-undo in the previous chapter.

A system with flip-undo is ambiguous, not monotone. The critical issue is that `undo` undoes itself: monotonicity is lost because the user cannot predict what an `undo` will do—sometimes it undoes the last command, and sometimes it redoes a just-undone command. It is instructive to give the proof to demonstrate that PIEs facilitate clear reasoning about interactive properties.

---

[3] I have ignored **exceptions** throughout this chapter. What should `left right` mean if the `left` raises an error (for example, we are already as far left as we can go), and does nothing: should `right` also do nothing, to preserve the notion that `left right` is always an identity? A more sensible approach may be to introduce exceptions as an *explicit concept*. User interface properties can then all be of the form: 'unless there was an exception then [normal principle]' and 'exceptions can be recognized by [making a sound] and have the following general effect of [undoing the last command]'.

Let $C' = C \setminus \{\text{undo}\}$, that is, C' is the set of all commands except undo. Then by definition of undo, for all commands $c, d \in C'$: $I(q \smile c \smile d \smile \text{undo}) = I(q \smile c)$ whatever the preceding program q. Since two command sequences producing the same effect in a monotone system are $\sim$-equivalent by definition, $q \smile c \smile d \smile \text{undo} \sim q \smile c$. In full,

$$\forall q, r \in P: \forall c, d \in C': I(q \smile c \smile d \smile \text{undo} \smile r) = I(q \smile c \smile r)$$

We need only choose $r = \text{undo}$ to get

$$I(q \smile c \smile d \smile \text{undo} \smile \text{undo}) = I(q \smile c \smile \text{undo})$$

which simplifies to $I(q \smile c) = I(q)$, or to $I(q \smile c \smile d) = I(q)$, either of which is a contradiction since c is an arbitrary command, and because we have not restricted I to be a constant, to the trivial system where all commands have no effect (that is, all programs have the same effect). Thus, apart from silly systems—bugged or absolutely trivial—it is not possible to combine undo and monotonicity.

13.5   Predictability and strategies

The user interface property that we require a function $\mathcal{U}$ to exist (which might be used by a local expert or by the system itself) to help the user achieve his goals is a special case of a general class of functions called **strategies**.

If the user wants to do something, does there exist a strategy that will tell him what to do? We would hope so, but often there will be no computable strategy available.

A system has an undo strategy (of a certain kind) if there is a fixed way of determining the correction $\mathcal{U}(q)$ from the erroneous command sequence q. We wrote

$$\exists \mathcal{U} \in (P \to P): \forall p, q \in P: p \smile q \smile \mathcal{U}(q) \sim p$$

So $\mathcal{U}$ is a particular strategy for the user: given some information (in this case, the program q that is to be undone), it tells the user what to do to undo it.

More generally, the user will be interested not only in getting back to points in the past, but also in getting to goals set in the future.

For instance, a user wants to achieve a certain effect e, and he has already submitted a few commands p. What should he do next? He must clearly choose a command sequence that gets him from where he is now to where he wants to go to. The user might ring up the local expert and say, 'I have submitted the commands p, I want to achieve the effect e. What should I do?' You can imagine the expert he phones will apply a strategy function $\mathcal{S}$, and from the result be able to tell the user what to do, thus

$$\exists S \in (P \times E \to P): \forall p \in P, e \in E: I(p \smile S(p, e)) = e$$

This S is 'unwieldy': to use it, the local expert needs to know the entire history of the user's submissions (that is, p) and then has to tell the user a possibly long answer. It might be more practical to have a strategy for answering questions like, 'I am here, I want to do this, what do I do next?'

$$\exists S \in (E \times E \to C): \forall p \in P: \exists r \in P:$$
$$I(p \smile S(I(p), e) \smile r) = e$$

Which means that given where the user is now $I(p)$, and where the user wants to get to e, the command $S(I(p), e)$ followed by as yet unknown commands r, gets the user towards the goal effect e. Notice that this strategy caters for the 'gone for a cup of tea' problem: the user does not need to know what he has already submitted, he only needs to know the current effect $I(p)$.

We ought to be a bit more fussy, to avoid jokey suggestions from the local expert—if the system is mega-reachable, then submitting *any* command whatsoever will not stop the user getting 'towards' his goal! We should require the strategy to be sensible, in that the remaining commands r should be shorter:

$$\exists S \in (E \times E \to C): \forall p \in P: \exists r \in P:$$
$$I(p \smile S(I(p), e) \smile r) = e$$
$$\text{and } \forall m \in P: |r| < |m| \text{ where } I(p \smile m) = e$$

This formulation requires that if there is a sequence of commands that obtains the desired effect e, then the strategy S will provide a minimal route to it.[4] It may not be the easiest to comprehend, but it will be one of the shortest. The '$|r|$' notation normally means the length of r, which is easily established by counting the number of commands in r; we could 'cheat' and define it to be some more relevant norm, such as a comprehensibility metric, an error probability, or a time-to-submit—but we would likely not know how to measure it! And we note, while worrying about complexity, that the existence of a strategy function, even if it produces easy to use command sequences, itself may not be easy to use. The definitions above do not even require S to be computable!

13.6   Lazy evaluation strategies for strategies

The existence of the last strategy mentioned in the previous section suggests that if the user has achieved an effect e_1, and he wants to obtain an effect e_2 then he would be advised to submit $S(e_1, e_2)$ as his *next* command. We notice that one might be able to compute S without fully knowing e_1 and e_2.

---

[4] Actually, not if we are already there! (The formula needs modifying to cater for this case.)

The expert at the other end of the telephone (or, equivalently, the part of the user's brain that understands the strategy—it doesn't have to be someone else) may use an eager or lazy or some other evaluation method for evaluating the strategy. Conventionally, we might think that an eager approach would be taken: but this may cause a bottleneck crisis, as the following imaginary dialogue suggests:

User: 'I'm stuck. Can you tell me what to do next?'

Expert: 'What is going on at the moment, and what do you want to achieve in the end? Tell me that, and I can work out (from my strategy function S) what you should do next.'

User: 'Well. The screen shows the following ... and the next screen shows this ... and the next screen shows this ... have I told you enough? ... screen 234 (I think) shows this ... and ...'

Expert: 'Good; *now* you must tell me what effect you want. Now take it slowly...'

The problem is that the expert eagerly consumes the information the user provides. *All* of the current effect must be stated, then *all* of the desired effect must be stated, then the strategy function is applied to the fully ground data. In a real dialogue between a user and an expert, the data will be more flexibly evaluated. The strategy function S will be **lazy**: the thing that matters *first* is the output of the strategy function, not what it is told. The expert asks questions directed at giving the user an answer as soon as possible—that is, to get output from S by asking as few questions as possible.

If the strategy function can be evaluated lazily, the conversation (again with theatrical licence) might go somewhat as follows:

User: 'I'm stuck. Can you tell me what to do next?'

Expert: 'I can work out (from my strategy function S) what you should do next. First, tell me is the green light on at the moment?'

User: 'The green light is off.'

Expert: 'Tell me no more! What ever you want to do you have to switch it on. There is a button at the back ...'

13.7   Addressing the user interface bottleneck

The PIE model misses much of the important structure of non-trivial user interfaces. It is now time to address the following issues:

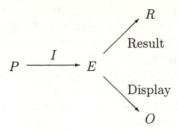

Figure 13.1   Refining PIEs.

▷   The user may not be able to observe the current effect in its entirety. For instance, the system may have a small screen that cannot show all of the information in the current effect (Section 2.1).

▷   The user may not want a particular final effect *using* the system, so much as a final result he can 'take away' (a picture on paper, perhaps). The user may want to achieve a certain goal (for instance, to print a certain document), and all other components of the final effect are irrelevant (for instance, what mode the system is left in).

▷   There may not be a simple relation between what the user can see and what result he will obtain (Section 11.6.3).

This wider view of the effect than the display is termed the **observable effect**, O. A function Display maps the effect onto the observable display, and a function Result maps the effect onto whatever final result the user obtains, such as the document (if an editor) or the machined object (if a numerically controlled milling machine). The result space could also be taken as certain configurations of neuronal activity in the user's head. The advantage of the simple view of result is that the function Result: $E \to R$ is not only computable given E (which we know having implemented I!), but if the system works we have an explicit program to compute it and we should know all its formal properties. Figure 13.1 makes the relations clearer.

With this simple structure, we can define the property **honest** (and the corresponding virtue, honesty): if a command sequence x changes the effect detectable in any circumstances y, then this is in principle obvious from the display after submitting x:

$$\text{honest} \equiv \forall x, y \in P: \quad I(p \smallsmile x \smallsmile y) \neq I(p \smallsmile y)$$
$$\Rightarrow \text{Display}(I(p \smallsmile x)) \neq \text{Display}(I(p))$$

The user is presumably most concerned with the final result, R. We therefore expect a computable map from the observable effect to the result. If no such function exists, then it would not be possible to determine the result from what the user could observe. We might require this map to be very simple ('what you see *is* what you get'). If we further required that the user could observe everything pertinent about the system, then there has to be an inverse map from the observable effect back to the full effect E. Display would be bijective.

We would like to say that a system is predictable if, in principle, the user could discover (by embarking on some activity such as scrolling the display) what the effect of future commands would be. With the simple PIE models, a system was predictable merely on the basis of the effect E, which we tacitly assumed could be seen (or otherwise known) by the user; now we want a more sophisticated notion of predictability. How can a system be predictable if the user does not know all about it because of the information lost by the display projection? We define **display predictability**: if two displays look the same then the system is in equivalent states:

$$\text{display-predictable} \equiv \quad \forall p, q \in P:$$
$$\text{Display}(I(p)) = \text{Display}(I(q)) \Rightarrow p \sim q$$

This may help the user, but it is a very restrictive property for the system! More generally we want the user to be able to follow a strategy to reveal the effect so that he can use this knowledge to predict the behaviour of the system in the future. Such a strategy must not upset the overall result the user is trying to achieve. There must be restrictions placed on what are considered 'reasonable' strategies. For example, an observation strategy that destroyed information (for example, go to first line, read it, then delete it ... until you reach end) would certainly put the user in a position to make trivial predictions about the interpretation of future commands! Another strategy we would want to proscribe would be 'lock the keyboard'. This permits the user to predict all future effects and results—there won't be any!

We can distinguish between two classes of command, **passive** and **active**. A passive command permits observation but does not change the result; it may change the state of the system, so long as the effects of subsequent commands (q in the definition below) on the result will be unaffected.

$$\text{passive}(c) \equiv \forall p, q \in P: \text{Result}(I(p \smile q)) = \text{Result}(I(p \smile c \smile q))$$

Thus results, now and in the future, after a passive command are unchanged, even if the user changes the display and internal states such as command defaults, the position of the cursor, and so on. In contrast, an active command is employed in order to change the result. An active command is not passive: $\text{active}(c) \equiv \neg\text{passive}(c)$.

A new definition of predictability may now be defined. We want a passive strategy to permit the user to observe enough of the effect space in order to be able to predict the effects of future commands. It would be over-zealous to write out a formal definition—though it would make it clear how much arbitrariness there is in deciding exactly what we mean by predictable! Suffice it to say that we would require, for example:

▷ The existence of a function $f: O^k \rightarrow E$, which given the information collected from k observable displays, can compute the effect in E.

▷ The existence of a strategy $s: O \rightarrow C$, which given a display informs the user of a passive command that will get him closer to *another* display in the set required by f. We might be more relaxed, and allow there to be two strategies, one for initializing (getting to the beginning of the set of k displays) and the other for working systematically through the displays. In a word processor, the initial strategy might be 'get to line 1' and the other is 'get to next line'.

Another possibility for us to consider is that the user might be able to get access to *all* of the result—perhaps he could print it out on paper, or perhaps he has a good mental image of it constructed partly from displays, partly from result artefacts and partly from long-term memory. This result could be used to supply some of the information about the effect, and the user might not need such a complex strategy. A subtle point is that the result may contain repetitions; the user may not be able to determine the position (more generally, the co-image) of the display O in the effect E: thus part of the explicitly displayed information should be the position of the display (for example, a line and column number for the cursor in a word processor).

Of course the physical copy of the result R would get out of date as active commands were submitted; but it might be nice to require the existence of the $O \times R \rightarrow E$ function since it imputes a reality to the final result: it means that the final result (which the user wishes to obtain) is a significant concept for the purposes of interaction as well. The user may develop a mental model of the result; as long as his model is synchronized with the actual result, he can in principle determine the current effect from his model and the display alone.

13.8 Window manager properties

A window manager enables the user to handle separate dialogues in separate regions of the screen called **windows**. Conventionally the windows will be rectangular regions of the screen, each representing a view on to a local interaction. The window manager enables the user to attach both his input devices (keyboard, mouse, and so on) and output devices (generally the display) to a selected window. Often, attaching the output device (the user's display) to a window may require some reorganization of the display if the selected window was partly covered by other windows or otherwise not already fully visible. Window managers generally provide analogous and varied features for programs as well as users, but we need not be concerned with the programmer's interface to window managers here.

In order to attach the user (user's IO devices) to a window, the window manager will suspend attachment to all other windows. This enables the user to pursue a dialogue with each window independently and deterministically. We can model a window manager as a PIE controlling a set of PIEs, each representing the system running in each window. In the course of a session, the user interleaves dialogues with separate windows and with the window manager itself.

The user interface is treated as a composition of the window manager PIE, PIE_{wm}, and each of the individual window PIEs, PIE_i for $i \in \{1 \ldots n\}$, n being the number of windows.

What will interest us is whether PIE_{wm} can have nice user interface properties if each window PIE_i has. Does the fallacy of composition (Section 7.6) apply?

First of all, for simplicity, let us assume that all of the PIE_i have a common set of commands C. C is the union of all C_i, the command sets of the individual PIE_i. It is a simple matter of adding null or error commands to any deficient PIE_i to ensure it is complete. It would actually be surprising if the PIE_i did not have an identical command set, for this would mean that the user could submit certain commands (for example, by pressing certain buttons on the keyboard) that are interpreted in some windows but are unimplemented in others—this would be a bug.

Define the command set for the window manager PIE_{wm} as simply $C \cup \{\texttt{select}(i)\}$. Thus our window manager is very simple: it supports a single command $\texttt{select}(i)$ that enables the user to attach to window i. Any other command (from C) goes 'straight through' to the currently selected window. Generally $\texttt{select}(i)$ would be submitted by the user using direct manipulation—there are obviously various ways in which the user might be able to specify i.

The effect space of the window manager is $E_{wm} = E_1 \times E_2 \cdots \times E_n$ which may be written more concisely as $E_{wm} = E^n$ if we assume the effect spaces are identical. For the present, we are assuming that the effect space is the cross–product of the individual effect spaces, and there is no component due to the window manager itself, nor are things confused by shared memory, overlapping window displays, hiding, and so on.

The interpretation function for the window manager, I_{wm}, is defined most easily as a composition of two functions, I' and I''. I' will interpret the $\texttt{select}$ command, and I'' the other commands, which it will do by employing the relevant I_i for the respective PIE_i.

The result of I' has to be a structure, from which I'' can determine the current window, and the programs for each of the PIE_i. It could be a number representing the current window and a list of the individual programs for the PIE_i, namely, $I': P \to (N \times P^n)$.

At any stage, $I'(p)$ gives a value we can write as $i \times \langle p_1, p_2, \ldots, p_n \rangle$. The i component of the value is the currently selected window, and the

$p_1, \ldots, p_n$ are the programs directed to each window, $1, \ldots, n$. We can readily define the interpretation of a single command c, given that a particular window i has already been selected:

$$I'(p \smallsmile c) = i \times \langle p_1, \ldots, (p_i \smallsmile c), \ldots, p_n \rangle \text{ where } i = \text{current } I'(p)$$

where current gets the window number. The command c is appended to the currently selected window's program.

If prog is the program part, we can now define the behaviour of select: $I'(p \smallsmile \text{select}(i)) = i \times \text{prog}\,(I'(p))$. For the initial case, our window manager defaults to selecting window number 1,

$$I'(\emptyset) = 1 \times \langle \emptyset, \emptyset, \ldots, \emptyset \rangle$$

I'' simply applies each of the I_i, the interpretation function of each PIE_i, to their respective programs: $I'': P^n \to E_{\text{wm}}$.

$$I''(\langle p_1, p_2, \ldots, p_n \rangle) = \langle I_1(p_1), I_2(p_2), \ldots, I_n(p_n) \rangle$$

Given I' and I'', then the interpretation function of the window manager, I_{wm}, may be defined straightforwardly:

$$\forall p\colon I_{\text{wm}}(p) = I''(\text{prog}\,(I'(p))$$

or more concisely, $I_{\text{wm}} = I'' \text{ prog } I'$.

We shall now show that PIE_{wm} is not monotone, *even if* all the PIE_i are, assuming that at least two PIE_i are involved (that $n \geq 2$)—it would not be very interesting otherwise! The proof is easy and hinges on demonstrating that the mode represented by the choice of current window is not in the effect of PIE_{wm}; this happens precisely because I'' discards the current component.

For brevity, let 1 be the name of the single command select(1) and 2 be the single command select(2). Now if 1 or 2 is the first command submitted, then it selects the current window (1 or 2), but the overall effect E_{wm} will be identical: $I_{\text{wm}}(1) = I_{\text{wm}}(2) = \langle \emptyset, \emptyset, \ldots, \emptyset \rangle$.

If the user submits the window selection command 1, then an arbitrary non-select command c: we would have $I_{\text{wm}}(1 \smallsmile c) = \langle c, \emptyset, \emptyset, \ldots, \emptyset \rangle$, but had the user submitted the same command after selecting window 2, $I_{\text{wm}}(2 \smallsmile c) = \langle \emptyset, c, \emptyset, \ldots, \emptyset \rangle$. Hence even though the interpretation of 1 and 2 is the same, the interpretation of $1 \smallsmile c$ and $2 \smallsmile c$ differs.

Recall that a PIE is monotone iff $I(p) = I(q) \Rightarrow p \sim q$. We have just shown that $I_{\text{wm}}(1) = I_{\text{wm}}(2)$ is true but that $1 \sim 2$ is false; therefore PIE_{wm} is not monotone for $n \geq 2$.

This is not really a very deep result: it simply affirms that a window manager that does not make it clear which window is currently selected may be difficult to use. Note, though, that it is the window manager *itself* that has to indicate which window is current, not the current window because a window might impersonate the selected window—perhaps a short step from being a Trojan Horse, a deliberate, malicious impersonation. We might modify the PIE_{wm} design so that the current window choice is explicitly part of the effect space, for instance $E_{wm} = N \times E^n$ and modifying I_{wm} accordingly. It can then be shown that PIE_{wm} is monotone if all PIE_i are monotone.

13.9   Modifying interpretations

Chapter 12 motivated the idea that the user might like to treat his interaction as a first class value, so that he could manipulate and display it like any other value available to him. Hence undo, skip, redo and other commands for modifying, navigating and displaying the script. Of course, the purpose of interaction is to obtain an effect, and the effect is a function not only of the script (or the program of the PIE model) but also of the interpretation placed upon it by the system. Thus, another generalization of interaction is suggested: the user may wish to modify the interpretation of the script, as well as (or instead of) the script itself. The notion is simple: the interpretation function I simply becomes a value accessible to the user.

The problem is that some changes to I will cause catastrophe: for the user might be able to produce interpretation functions that are not just modey, but have quite undesirable properties: for instance, that all definable effects are unreachable *and I* becomes fixed! Clearly, most users will want some constraint on the scope for change. The easiest to implement, and the easiest method to constrain the possible changes on I to be sensible, is to provide a small number of known options, or alternative features. There will be so few options that they can be fully defined by the designer; also the options can be arranged to be largely independent—this ensures that the formal analysis of the design is straightforward, and ensures that the implementation does not need to be particularly clever when the user selects certain combinations of option (for example, to avoid choices like green text on a green screen; such errors are relatively easy to anticipate at the design state).

The designer does not need to know the choice of options when the system is first designed. For example, the purpose of a conventional operating system is to permit the user to select between alternative I functions—by running different programs or subsystems. In general, such interactive systems are called **shells** (this allows us to reserve the term **operating system** for the resource multiplexer that underpins the implementation of all user interfaces). Some of the subsystems can be developed after the original shell. If the user wants to edit a file, he can tell the shell to change the user interface from $I = $ 'shell' to $I = $ 'editor'. The window manager we considered in Section 13.8 was a simple example of a system that allowed the user to select I from amongst the n interpretations I_i.

Many features have a range of values, rather than mere presence or absence. For instance, the key repeat rate can be varied; the time interval between mouse clicks for two clicks to count as an atomic double-click; or the control/display ratio (how much feedback the user gets for how much action, for example, how far the cursor moves in relation to the mouse movement) can be adjusted. Typically, changing such quantitative features will not change any essential property of the system.

13.9.1   Modifying interpretations by programming

The problem with anticipated features (whether optional or continuously variable) is that, of course, the designer cannot anticipate everything that the user might want to be able to do. The designer and user might not have the time to devote to spelling out a design in such detail: the user may want to start drawing the benefits of the system as soon as possible. And even if he had the time to draw up the requirements, the implementation of so many features might be too time consuming, particularly irritating if the probability of the use of some features is very low—but their implementation delays delivery of the system.

There are three options: (1) the designer can use an iterative design method (supply some features now, others later as and when they are deemed to be necessary); (2) the designer can provide **programmable features**;[5] or, instead, (3) the designer can be obstinate—there are times when a simple system may be best (it can be delivered earlier, and will be easier to learn and use).

The tradeoff is not simple. The advantages of fixed features are: the designer and user know (or should know) exactly what they have got; and the system can be implemented very efficiently. Being relatively few in number, the features can also be described clearly in documentation. The disadvantage of a few fixed features is their limited scope, whereas the clear advantage of programmable features is the great flexibility offered to the user, at the cost of inefficiency (balanced against the difficulty of learning how to program—generally efficient languages are harder to learn). The disadvantage of programmable features is exactly the same as their advantage: because they are general, the user can do anything—though quite possibly not what he intended!

The following points usually sway the argument: designing a good language is not easy; and many users may be quite satisfied with a limited range of options. Thus almost all interactive system designs either provide

---

[5] 'Programmable feature' is often hype for optional or variable feature. Here, by programmable feature, we mean a feature that can be composed out of other features, using sequence, iteration, conditionals, recursion, etc. Mathematically, a programmable feature in our stricter sense is a user-defined function rather than a variable.

non-programmable features, or employ an *existing* programming language (such as LISP) and require their users to become programmers. The advantage for the user of this result is that, *if* they want to program their system, there are only a few languages to learn (for example, they just acquire a Pascal compiler for their system), rather than one language per system.

There are three reasons for modifying the user interface by programs:

▷ The user anticipates wanting to repeat some actions several times in the future, however, the actions (and their interrelatedness), being idiosyncratic to the user, either could not have been anticipated by the designer, or, if they could have been anticipated, could not have been named conveniently.

▷ The user wants to control the behaviour of the system (particularly for *exceptional* circumstances, again which the designer could not have anticipated).

▷ The user wants to make efficient use of his time; he can write a program (taking a few minutes, say) and let it run (taking a few hours of computer time, say).

13.9.2   Modifying interpretations by adaption

Why make the user modify the interface? Programming is clearly a skilled business, and by increasing the intricacy of interaction, programmable user interfaces would offer even greater potential for mistakes, and much more obscure mistakes! Why not arrange for the system itself to perform the modifications?

If a system adapts to the user (for instance noticing that the user frequently undertakes a certain task after performing certain feature settings, then subsequently performing those settings itself), the user not only has to learn 'the' system, but also relearn the parts of the system that change. The effort of learning to use a system is now spread out and starts to encroach use. It is perhaps trite to point out that adaptive interfaces are in fact very common: they are used in computer games *to make them progressively harder as the user becomes more skilful*! So a benefit of adaptive interfaces, games aside, can be to maintain vigilance. Clearly, adaptive systems can make themselves difficult to use, and that difficulty may help maintain their users' attention and job satisfaction. This is ease of use one level removed.

The advocates of adaptive systems emphasize the advantage that a user can learn less before starting to use a system. The idea is that the system starts off by being 'easy to use' and increasingly becomes more sophisticated, keeping up with the user's growing fluency with the system. The detractors of the idea point out that if the user is continually learning

---

Box 13.1   Are people adaptive?

Our inspiration for adaptive systems comes from the obvious adaptability of people. You have a conversation with someone and somehow he seems to adapt to the style and level of conversation you want to have. But actually, people are remarkably unadaptive and stubborn. Go up to a shop assistant and ask what the lending rate is, and you are unlikely to get the assistant to adapt from his model of you, 'naïve shopper' to 'financially sophisticated shopper' mode! This is no indictment of shop assistants: the constraints of their job preclude major adaption. The few people who have really adapted to us are our spouses and children: and how long did they take? (I'm still working on my children, even after 42 man-years of user 'adaption'.)

   We also note that there aren't that many ways of adapting programs anyway. You can control how verbose a user interface is, whether it allows abbreviations, confirmations, and so on. But these are all trivial. It is all very well thinking that a sophisticated AI program could make useful adaptions. But we do not even know how to design interactive systems well enough for a well-defined and fixed sort of user!

---

how to use the adapting system, then there are two mutually adapting systems, and it is not immediately clear that the result will be stable. For instance, the user may at first appear to be expert, so the system becomes more advanced; the user then makes a mistake (perhaps the user had not really understood the change); the system then down-grades—but by which time the user is relying on the advanced features. The problem is that there is not enough bandwidth in the user interface both for the user to pursue a task *and* for adaption (user–system and system–user adaption).

   We can classify systems according to their complexity: some systems are not very complex; others are exceedingly complex. If a system is to be able to adapt itself to the user, it requires a sufficiently rich source of information about its use and it must also be a sufficiently complex system for adaption to be worth while. But the more complex it is, the weaker the patterns in the user's operation of it, and hence the harder it is to adapt productively.

   A database enquiry system is quite a good illustration of the dilemma. Adaption might be some form of database reorganization to make access to useful data easier. Of course, the computer has no idea what 'useful data' is supposed to be, and it will have to make do with frequently accessed data, and assume frequency indicates relevance and usefulness to the user (it could use some other sensible statistic instead of frequency). Now imagine an enormous database: the user is unlikely to access many items with sufficient relative frequency for reorganization to have much of an impact on the user's work. At the other extreme, imagine a very small database of perhaps half a dozen items. Now the user can be expected to become very familiar with those items, however they are organized—and the less the computer tries to modify their organization (unless it is initially very bad!), the more comprehensible the user will find them.

The question is, do the sets of self-adaptive and high complexity systems overlap? The answer that will satisfy everyone is that *parts* of complex systems are surely simple enough to be self-adaptive and complex enough to make adaption worth while, and the database example suggested that there is a continuous spectrum (in that case, based on database size) from possible–useless to impossible–useful. There is surely an optimal database size, where for some users there are enough benefits.

Quite likely, there are some techniques, parts of systems (for example, menu selection),[6] that are appropriate for adaptive techniques; their ubiquity ensures that even minor improvement from trivial adaptive techniques would have multiplied beneficial effect.

The preceding arguments made an artificially simplified assumption: that an adaptive interface changes the user interface in a way that the user can readily perceive. Superficially, it was assumed that adaption is only worth while if there is a perceptible benefit for the user, and if there is, the change itself may cause problems for the user adapting to the system. But, it is possible to change a system subtly to improve the user's performance without the user necessarily being aware of (or interested in) the changes. For example, a database may be so large, or the user's access to it so infrequent, that restructuring it to shorten frequent enquiries can be attempted with some confidence. Knowing that the enquiry dialogue satisfies properties like commutativity (to be discussed in Section 14.3.4) will allow certain adaptions (for instance, reordering of command prompts or menu entries) to be made without affecting any *system* meanings (such properties would not ensure that the user was not affected if he was partial to the old structure, for example, through satisficing).

13.10   Conclusions

Undo introduced the idea of the history being a first class value, and the state of the system being a function of this value. This observation led to the PIE model, one of many ways to formalize interactive system properties. The PIE model consists of a program, interpretation function,

---

[6] See Greenberg and Witten (1985) for an adaptive menu structuring example. This system continually reorganized a menu hierarchy so that length of search tended to be minimized. There is a simple relation between user's behaviour and the appropriate adaptive strategy, and there is a good theory about the time to search decision trees such as menu hierarchies. The system was very successful. Nevertheless, this sort of adaptivity did not change the style of the user interface, and the structure of the menu hierarchy was not an intrinsic part of the problem. It did not matter much to users that it continually changed in detail.

and an effect. These three categories helped suggest that metacommands need not be restricted to modifying the program, but could also modify the interpretation function; of course, modifying the effect is what text editors and similar systems do routinely.

The last two chapters started with a user interface issue, and then formalized it. We might, equally, have written them in reverse. We could have started with a formal model; reminded ourselves of the standard/non-standard model distinction (Section 6.4) and the virtue of standard models; then promoted the hidden history to a standard first class entity. That would have given the user undo. The general idea can be summarized in a metaprinciple or design heuristic:

> ▷ *Make models real or modify the models.* Formal models (for the designer) and explanations (for the user) are better the greater the correspondence between them. If you like, formal models are an interface of the system to the designer; why not permit them (in suitable form) to interface to the user?

We already met this idea in Section 9.4.4 as avoidance of essentialism.

Chapter 14

Mathematics

The language of the brain is not the language of mathematics.
John von Neumann

This chapter argues that mathematics can be used *constructively* in design. I shall not use advanced mathematics, but just enough to show that nice mathematical user interface properties are nice for users. Less contentiously, I shall demonstrate that striving for nice mathematical properties is certainly a profitable design heuristic. There will be many little examples on the way.

The purpose of this chapter, as seen within the plan of the book, is to use the relevance of simple mathematical properties in further support of the guep idea of Chapter 10. The intention is that the ideas presented in this chapter may be used to advantage by almost any designer, even one without a sophisticated mathematical background, beyond school algebra and set theory. By restricting the present chapter to elementary concepts there is the possibility that some of the ideas might very easily be put under experimental scrutiny.

14.1   Why might mathematics be relevant?

It is not totally clear that as interactive systems are used by fickle people that rigorous mathematics is a suitable tool to help make systems easier to use.

Bertrand Russell said that, 'mathematics is the subject in which we never know what we are talking about, nor whether what we are saying is true'. It is a great advantage 'not to know what we are talking about'—meaning that our mathematical efforts can be applied to *anything*; it is, of course, a problem that we do not know *a priori* whether the mathematics we choose applies truthfully to the particular system we have in mind! At least mathematics has the advantage that we can write down and criticize precise ideas: the first step towards the scientific approach. Mathematics may not tell us when we are right, but it will certainly tell us when we are wrong. We can expect no more, of course, since the users, not bits of paper, decide whether a system is well designed.

Consider the following fact. Notations for arithmetic have evolved over millennia and, presumably, the elementary algebraic properties we now recognize arose from implicit processes. These simple properties and conventions somehow make arithmetic easier to use. This chapter claims that considering properties, even of such low complexity, can be used to help designers examine alternatives and improvements in the designs of systems for people to use. It should be pointed out that much psychological work with user interfaces assumes a similar position, but with respect to the evolution and use of natural language (and other psychological currency) rather than mathematics. It would be unconventional to invoke the Sapir–Whorf Hypothesis in the present context but it would be no less appropriate.

Mathematics has evolved a common notation; thus Japanese, Finnish and Brazilian mathematicians can communicate in a common written language. Yet no conversational—natural or contrived—language has become a common tongue, despite the efforts represented by Esperanto. Perhaps partisan interests in languages are more important to their users than cross-cultural communication—just as in user interface design! We might conclude that mathematically based notations are probably a better choice of language for communicating with computer systems.

A more persuasive argument is that using mathematics reduces the cost of the design process. Mathematical notations are very economical, particularly in comparison with programming notations: economical not only because mathematicians command lower salaries than programmers, but because mathematics is concise when compared with programming notations. This means that *if* some design evaluation can be performed at a mathematical level, the designer is saved the expensive and time-consuming activity of actually programming a system and finding users for it. Mathematical design questions can often be answered by computers (acting as calculators, proof or simulation systems), but design questions about implemented systems can only be answered by behavioural experiments (with various procedural difficulties).

The point at issue is that mathematics is a *precise*, *concise* and *abstract* way of reasoning. A mathematician can see ways of relating several systems together, showing correspondences and hence pinpointing missed opportunities in each system. Interactive systems, when without any formal basis, have to be experienced—and experience is difficult to describe, raises emotions to criticize, and is particular to each system, and very often a significant feat of memory. Unlike mathematics, experience is expensive to obtain and the investment of obtaining it cannot be amortized over several systems. When mathematics allows various systems to be related, we gain the Russelian advantage of theft over honest toil—'stealing' the insights of one system for the other.

Mathematics is *supposed* to be criticized. There are wrong ways and sloppy ways of doing mathematics: if designs are expressed mathematically, there is considerable pressure to criticize them. This can only be beneficial, and is a good way to attack design bugs. In contrast, an implemented system is tempting to *use*, and few programmers come from a cultural background where criticism of a year's work would be well taken. If iterative design is a good idea, mathematically motivated iterative design is an even better idea: you can iterate faster, more cheaply.

Mathematics makes things clear. A very simple example will help. Suppose I say, 'a system with undo is easy to use'. This is ambiguous, a fact that becomes apparent when we try and formalize it. It may mean: $\forall X: \text{undo}(X) \Rightarrow \text{easy}(X)$, or it may mean $\exists X: \text{undo}(X) \wedge \text{easy}(X)$. In fact, the latter is probably true in most people's experience, from which they unreliably generalize to the former.

Mathematical methods may be necessary, but they are certainly not sufficient to design good user interfaces, for they remain silent about many crucial issues, mostly of an ergonomic and representational nature. Although mathematical criticism might avoid pathetic semantics, the normal design route is to palliate poor semantics with impressive user interfaces. This means that psychological or artistic considerations appear to be more important to designers than perhaps they really are. Certainly users are first aware of superficial aspects of a system and only later discover its semantics. Mathematics is a tool to make arguments, to perform calculations, to express facts. Its priority is to do this reliably: this means that it *must* be easy to use, for awkward mathematics will contribute to human error, to obfuscated arguments and to inexactitude. Thus mathematicians will always be seeking better—that is easier—ways of doing things.

14.2   What is algebra and why is it relevant?

Algebra is the study of those system properties that do not change when the representation of the system is changed. It is about how things work, without worrying about what we call those things or what they look like. Algebra is therefore the branch of mathematics that we can use most honestly during the early stages of user interface design, since it describes fundamental properties of interaction independently of how we may later decide to represent them.

A typical sort of concern from an algebraic point of view would be whether doing A then B is the same as doing B then A. We would not be concerned about what exactly A and B might mean, or how they were represented, how the user submitted or could see them. A and B might be single operations like pressing mouse buttons when a menu is displayed, or they might be long operations taking the user through several stages of detailed interaction, such as A being a product purchase, B being a product sale.

All algebraic rules have the form 'doing this' is equivalent to 'doing that'. How many times has someone told you a better way of doing something? He is relying on algebraic equivalences. Depending on what we want to talk about (the screen, the behaviour of the numerically controlled lathe, a word-processed document, a spreadsheet) we can choose the equivalences at different levels. Thus doing A then B, or doing B then A may produce exactly the same word-processed document results, but the picture on the screen might be different.[1] Such laws serve as gueps: they are principles for the user and can readily be taken into the software engineering side of design.

Algebra is important mathematically because a few algebraic properties can tell one a great deal about the entire system. Many algebraic structures have been found to occur again and again; a lot is known about their properties. You may be familiar with many simple properties, like associativity and commutativity laws, from your school days of doing arithmetic.

Relatively few algebraic laws are enough to specify completely every valid operation you can perform in arithmetic, how you can simplify $3 \times 4 + 3 \times 6$ to $3 \times (4 + 6)$, and so on. All systems with the same algebraic properties are to all intents and purposes the same up to our choice of representations. Thus, if we find that pebbles on the beach have the same algebraic properties as the natural numbers, then we can use arithmetic to reason about pebbles. This is a rather obvious example (for we learned the equivalence at an early age), but it is clear that adding 10 000 pebbles to 10 000 pebbles is easier to do with numbers than with pebbles! Everything we know about numbers becomes true of pebbles. This is a profound observation.

A user of an interactive system has commands (an **algebraic carrier**) which can be combined in certain ways to achieve various effects. Algebra, then, is concerned with the rules governing how the commands can

---

[1] Hence one more advantage of a WYSIWYG word processor. The screen algebra is complementary to the physical world, printed result algebra: commands that have equivalent results on paper must have equivalent results on the screen.

be combined, and the circumstances under which different combinations of commands have the same effect. The user can choose whichever is best, and as we saw with the example of pebbles (on the beach) and numbers (on paper), the improvement may be dramatic.

14.3 Examples

The following subsections illustrate the relevance of elementary algebraic principles to user interface design. Each subsection will define various properties formally, and give examples of how they affect usability of a selection of interactive features. (Of course, the principles are more or less relevant to particular applications and depend on all sorts of assumptions which we will discuss more fully in Section 14.4 below.)

We shall see that some algebraic properties (for example, distributivity) *encourage* modiness, and some (for example, commutativity) *discourage* modiness. The role of mathematical analysis is not necessarily to impose regulations but to suggest possibilities.

14.3.1 Distributivity

Distributivity is not the simplest algebraic property to start with, but it has some quite interesting user interface consequences, so it is a good, motivating, place to start if we are concerned with the user.

If a user interface supports distributivity (which it need not all the time: it may apply for different commands in different modes) then it assures the dual:

(i)   difficult command sequences can be split into simpler forms; and

(ii)   accomplished users can combine commands into more powerful forms

The significance to the user of these assurances obviously depends on the generality of the property, which command sequences and modes distributivity applies to. Almost everything distributes sometimes or somewhere; the question is, can the user rely on distribution?

Imagine a simple command-based interface. There is a command 'print *file*' that prints a file. The user can submit any number of print commands by separating them: for instance, 'print file1 enter print file2 enter print file3...' Perhaps ; would be used instead of a enter—but since we are talking algebra, this representational detail does not matter in the least.

Clearly, it might be convenient if several files could be printed all at once, by submitting a command like, 'print file1 file2 file3...'—it would save a bit of typing. If, indeed, this were possible, and the meanings of the two command sequences were equivalent (the files got printed in the same order, and every one got printed even if some file names were repeated), then we would say that `print` **distributed** over the `enter` (or semicolon).

This simple `print` example shows the promised results (i) and (ii) given above: (i) because printing several files at once can be done by printing them individually; (ii) because consecutive print commands can be combined into a single print command.

Expressed formally for two operations $\otimes$ and $\oplus$ and arbitrary objects a, b and c, distributivity means,

$$\left.\begin{array}{l} a \otimes (b \oplus c) = a \otimes b \oplus a \otimes c \\ (b \oplus c) \otimes a = b \otimes a \oplus c \otimes a \end{array}\right\} \text{left and right distributive laws}$$

You can understand these laws easily if you imagine a, b and c to be numbers and $\oplus$ addition, and $\otimes$ multiplication. Left and right distributivity is then just an elementary fact of arithmetic, and nothing mysterious. The first equation shows **left distribution**, the second **right distribution**. If, as the case may be, the operation $\otimes$ commutes (see Section 14.3.4), then the left and right laws are equivalent because $a \otimes (b \oplus c) = (b \oplus c) \otimes a$.

For an interactive systems interpretation, imagine that $\oplus$ means sequential composition, like `enter`, and $\otimes$ means `print`. Actually, the form of distribution specified here treats $\otimes$ as a **binary** operation, taking two arguments rather than `print`'s one. To fix this simply write $a\otimes$ as `print`.

Left and right distribution should be considered separately. Left distribution of a command introduces a mode: after submitting it, all members of the following group are affected by the 'mode' it introduces. Right distribution also requires a grouping mechanism, but as grouping starts to occur before the command has been submitted, the group cannot be identified with a particular mode, except that its first evaluation probably has to be delayed until the command is submitted.

Power deletion

As another example of distributivity consider a typical desktop manager (window manager): file deletion can right distribute over selection to provide a short cut as a so-called **power feature** for **power users** who want to delete more than one file at a time.

Suppose the user indeed wishes to delete several files. The long-winded way to do this is to select each file in turn and then delete it. That is: '`select delete select delete...`' if we abstract out which files are being selected and deleted. With deletion distributing, there is a briefer equivalent '`(select select...) delete`'. The single `delete` command deletes all the selected files.

In concrete terms, the bracketing can be supplied by another key. For example, if a selection is made while the `shift` key is held down, then the previous selection is not lost.

Partial compilation

Partial compilation, which is generally a good thing, is all about distribution. A program split between several files `f1.c`, `f2.c`... can be compiled by `compile f1.c f2.c`... but if it is possible to distribute the `compile` through its file arguments, `compile' f1.c; compile' f2.c; compile' f3.c`... will do.

The significant advantage for the user is that other commands can be interleaved between the individual stages of the separate compilation: particularly editing (and probably lots of unsuccessful compilations). In practice, this saves the user a lot of time because unedited files do not need to be recompiled again and again. Such advantages are not restricted to compiling programs, any other suitable operation—many of them interactive—such as printing, text formatting, rendering, and so on are candidates.

Operator priorities

If brackets are available to the user by modes, shift keys or control keys, the priorities of operators can be chosen arbitrarily. For whatever priorities are chosen by the implementation, the user can submit fully-bracketed commands. Thus $3 + (4 \times 5)$ has the same meaning, 23, whatever priorities are assigned to '+' and '×'. Nevertheless, it is conventional to assign a higher priority to multiplication than addition, so that brackets can be omitted some of the time, as they could be in the sum above. This convention arises because multiplication distributes over addition: $(a + b) \times c = (a \times c) + (b \times c)$ can be written more briefly $a \times c + b \times c$.

Note that distributivity is a *semantic* property, yet it leads to a *syntactic* convention. If the semantics do not give a clear choice about distributivity, then our desire to permit partial or incremental evaluation of the user's commands (see the discussion above about partial compilation) may give guidance. Thus algebraic considerations will give the designer hints about how best to represent certain operations.

14.3.2 Identities

Written formally, an **identity** command c_I has the effect that, for any command c, $cc_I \equiv c$. We can write $\forall c \in C : c \smile c_I \equiv c$ using the more precise notation of Chapter 13. The identity command leaves the system in an identical state. Note that the identity command is the same for all commands c, as opposed to an **inverse** command, which may be different for each command it undoes. Thus `left` and `right` are mutual inverses, but neither is an identity. For an arithmetic example consider multiplying x by 1: it does not produce a value other than x; thus, 1 is an identity for arithmetic multiplication but not for addition, since $x + 1 \neq x$. Now what use could identities be in interactive systems?

Users often perform tasks peripheral (in their view) to their main task. The commands of such tasks should have no effect on the main stream of commands: they should be identities (or, more generally, compose to identities). Strictly there would be no point at all in submitting a command that is an identity, because an identity by definition does not change the current state. That, of course, is exactly what you want if you ask for help!

However, we have abstracted away from temporal issues: identities can be used in interactive systems to synchronize events without changing the meaning of those events. Thus the user submits a command to delete some files; an identity command can then be submitted to synchronize the deletion of those files with the user's confirmed desire to delete them. It is possible that the user submitted a deletion command without the desire to delete particular files (the whole command might have been a slip): the identity provides an opportunity to check this. Treating the subdialogue as an identity allows us to abstract away from its details, yet assert that its normal completion does not affect the meaning of the interaction.

Referring back to the same sort of desktop manager mentioned in Section 14.3.1: if many files are to be deleted—a potentially risky operation—there should be a subdialogue to check that the selected files are indeed the ones to be deleted. On some bad systems a subdialogue appears in window form (a so-called **dialogue box**) but this pre-empts the user, forcing him to respond to *that* question and do nothing else. The way many systems implement it, the dialogue box even obscures information that would help answer its query! The user cannot move the window or perform any other window-type operations on it to reveal the information necessary to answer the query. If the user cautiously replies no, then the set of files is deselected and the information is no longer available. This design fault may be thought of as the user's response to the subdialogue not being a right identity. The law, `select` `delete` *subdialogue* `no` $\equiv$ `select` (more generally, `select` *action subdialogue* `no` $\equiv$ `select`) should hold: if the user denies, he does not want to have the selection affected.

In the *absence* of distributivity of deletion over selection only one thing can be deleted at a time, so the problem is less severe: human short term memory would not normally be overloaded by the *necessarily* single item in a selection.

The distribution of `delete` through `select` was not documented, and now we see that it interferes with the convention for subdialogues, which may have made sense in an earlier design when the user could only delete a single file. Could the designers have anticipated these extensions had they used a little algebra?

14.3.3 Idempotence

Idempotence is not as commonly talked about as associativity and the other properties we shall discuss here: it appears too simple a property to need a name at an elementary level!

Taking the absolute value of a number (making it non-negative; the absolute value of -3 is 3) is an example of an idempotent operation: taking the absolute value a second time has no further effect. In general, if c is an idempotent operation, then $cc = c$. From this you can conclude that $ccc = c$ and, in general for any sequence of n commands c the effect is the same as just submitting one, which we may write: $c^n = c$ for $n \geq 1$.

Idempotent operations are important for the user in many circumstances, for example:

▷ Following the 'eyes-shut' principle (Section 11.7.1), there should be commands like `escape` that put the system in certain modes (for example, the home menu). In which case, a second `escape` has no further effect, since the system is already in the desired mode. In other words, `escape` is idempotent since `escape escape = escape`.

▷ Deleting a file should be idempotent: the first time the file is deleted, it really disappears; if the file is deleted a second time, nothing further should happen for it has already gone. It would be a disaster for the user if the delete file command *always* deleted a file, even if the named file had already been deleted. If the delete file command need not take an explicit parameter, but by default deleted the most recently created file (say), then it would not be idempotent.

▷ Editors sometimes provide the three editing functions, `cut`, `copy` and `paste`. A selected region of text, or whatever is being edited, can be cut and removed to a 'cut-and-paste' buffer; copied to a buffer; or the buffer can be used to replace (paste-over) the selected region. It is important to minimize the consequences of errors. Thus, `cut` is idempotent: it not only cuts out the selected region, but makes the selection area of zero size; thus, a further `cut` will have no effect, and the buffer will remain intact. `Copy`, too, can be idempotent: repeated submission simply makes more copies of the same region, each copy leaving the buffer the same. `Paste` can be idempotent: if the material just pasted in at the selection is left selected, a subsequent `paste` will replace it with the same again. However it is more usual to make `paste` move the selection to the end of the pasted material: to ensure that a sequence of `pastes` continues to extend by the contents of the buffer—here the user's assumed needs override idempotent niceties.

▷ If the system keeps a log of user activities (see Section 12.1.4), it is essential that replaying the log is an idempotent operation. The purpose of replaying the log is to reinstate the world after some disaster, and we want the restoration to be the same even if we have to replay the log several times before success. (It might be that the system crashes before a complete restoration from the log has been possible.)

▷ Sometimes the computer system may be running slowly; the user submits a command. Nothing happens. Does this mean that the user made a mistake submitting the command (perhaps he did not hit the keys hard enough), or is the computer just being slow? If the command is idempotent, then the user could submit it again, 'just to make sure', and be certain nothing untoward would happen.

As an example of this last possibility, consider a multiprocessing system. Typically, a single keystroke like control-D (the ISO code for End of Text—what else?) is used as a terminator for all sorts of interaction. Submit control-D to the command processor, and the user is logged out. For the sake of 'consistency' (taking precedence over other considerations), it is often arranged that submitting control-D to almost any program will cause it to terminate, returning to the command processor which will then accept another command.[2] Now, suppose the user wants to finish running a command; he will submit control-D to finish it and so return back to the command processor. As often happens on a multiprocessing system, there is a delay. The user is now in a dilemma:

▷ If he really *did* submit control-D, then the system is being slow. Conclusion: do nothing and just wait, do not submit another control-D (for that would log the user off the system).

▷ If he *did not* submit control-D (perhaps the key was not hit hard enough, or he typed just D by mistake), then the system is still waiting for the user to do something. Conclusion: type control-D to leave the command and return to the command processor.

Now suppose another minute has passed, and still nothing has happened. This evidence increasingly tends to support the second alternative: the user will probably decide to hit control-D just to make sure that the system is not waiting for it. Perversely, as it happens, the system was just being slow—the first control-D was successful and had left the command; the system was just getting around to putting out a new command processor prompt. So the second control-D is unfortunately interpreted by the command processor, and the user is peremptorily logged off the system.

The problem is that control-D is not idempotent. If control-D *was* idempotent, then submitting it twice, which the example imagined the user doing in error, would have had no further effect. To make control-D idempotent is easy: the command processor should use some other method to log out, for instance, a specific command, logout, say. A weaker

---

[2] There is little consistency from the user's point of view, however: control-D appears to be used to *enter* the command processor (by terminating a program) yet also used to *leave* the command processor (by terminating it).

Box 14.1 Word motion.

Many text editors provide features to help the user move around in any direction faster than in single steps. Here we shall look at some design issues for atomic commands for word motion: let's call them L and R, which move the cursor left or right by one word. The questions are: what is a word, and what properties might we and the user want these word motion commands to have?

Alternative definitions used by many editors are: a word is anything between blanks, or a word is any sequence of alphabetic characters. They differ in that one definition includes punctuation, and therefore makes 'words' larger. The motion commands move the cursor right to the end of a word, or left to the start of a word. Some editors distinguish between words and word gaps, so that there are twice as many stopping places for the cursor.

With any of these definitions we would not have LRL = LLR = L nor RRL = RLR = R. In other words, an accidental overshoot, for instance, the user, trying to move right, but accidentally typing one too many R, cannot be corrected by reverse motion, by L in this case. In fact, these laws provide for accidental correction: if the user moves right, apparently too far and supposedly corrects by moving left, he can correct the supposed correction by moving right, and he is where he was before the mistaken correction. Such overshooting arises very readily when system feedback gets delayed: the user can no longer be sure of where the cursor is, and he may type ahead too much before he realizes that the system has not processed all of his input. Fast autorepeating keys, slow computers or dumb terminals used at low baud rates (for example, over telephone lines) are all easy ways for this to happen (Thimbleby, 1981).

These laws have wider application than to word movement. Whenever the user is certain that he wants to issue at least one command, this property assures him that submitting the command too many times is quite safe. A design issue is whether a pair of commands with this property is better or worse than one command plus an undo. If you need both commands (for example, in the word motion case, you can never move left from a starting position by right and undo alone), then the property is certainly useful. Direct manipulation systems with hysteresis would benefit from it.

design possibility would be for the command processor to ignore any spare control-D typed before its prompt had appeared; the prompt indicates that the system is waiting for the user.

Note that this example highlights a standard problem of consistency! *Whose* consistency? The interface has quite consistently used control-D to exit programs, including the command processor itself. The hidden inconsistency is that some exits are different and more costly for the user than other exits. This sort of consistency is bad; it is an *implementation* not a *user* consistency.

Box 14.2   Dr Spooner and commutativity.

At a dinner party that man of metaphasis fame, Dr Spooner, spilt some salt on the table; he then reached for some claret, which he carefully poured on top of the salt. The net result was a mound of purple salt, as if he had first spilt claret and had then tried to absorb it with salt. There is a sort-of sense: *if* claret and salt congealed into a salt-cake, it might have been easy to pick up the spilt salt as a damp lump. Of course, not in the world, but in user interfaces, the designer *can* create laws where really useful things happen.

The story of Spooner is also an anecdote that illustrates that commutativity does not restrict the intermediate meanings of commands for the end result is the same: 'pour salt; pour claret' ≡ 'pour claret; pour salt', yet 'pour salt' is not equivalent to 'pour claret'!

14.3.4   Commutativity

Commutativity means that doing commands in any order has an equivalent effect. Formally, $a \oplus b = b \oplus a$ is the commutative law expressed for the operator $\oplus$. Addition of numbers commutes: $3 + 4$ is equal to $4 + 3$.

Many commands appear to the user to be unrelated. The order in which they are submitted to the system should perhaps therefore have no effect on their interpretation, that is, they should commute.

If, part way through a multiple file selection (using the same window manager as in Section 14.3.1), it becomes necessary to scroll the window (perhaps not all icons are simultaneously visible), the mouse must be dragged on a scroll bar. However, clicking the mouse deselects all files. There seems to be no way around this problem for the user—that scrolling and selecting operations do not commute, that is, scroll select $\neq$ select scroll—though the *advantage* is that it is not possible to keep icons selected when they cannot be seen.

An interesting example of lack of commutativity is in the way many display editors interpret cursor control keys. The naïve user naturally expects cursor control (motion in up, down, left and right directions) to commute, perhaps with exceptions at the boundaries of the screen or window. A user interface will often provide aural indication that boundaries have been hit, and the standard interpretation of the cursor control key has failed.

If we really want commutativity, then boundary problems must be addressed. For instance, suppose the cursor is at the left boundary of the screen. Then, left right will not be the same as right left. The first moves the cursor right, and the second leaves it in the same position. The boundaries introduce modes. Invoking the 'you can use it with your eyes

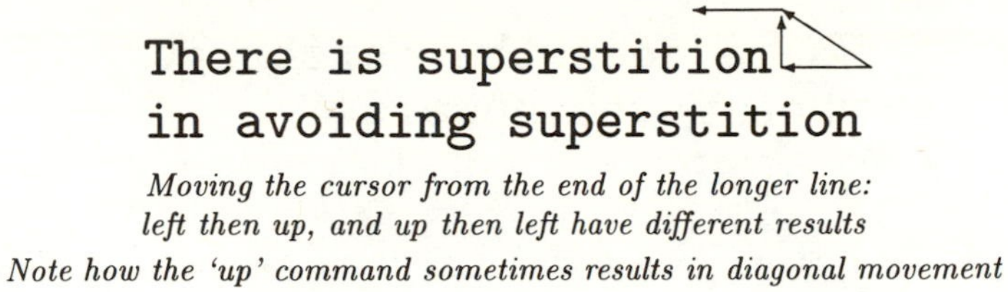

There is superstition⌐◺

in avoiding superstition

Moving the cursor from the end of the longer line:
left then up, and up then left have different results
Note how the 'up' command sometimes results in diagonal movement

Figure 14.1   Non-commuting editor.

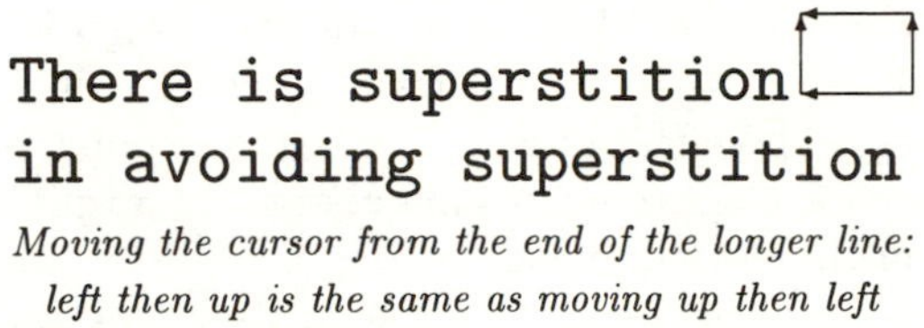

There is superstition⌐□

in avoiding superstition

Moving the cursor from the end of the longer line:
left then up is the same as moving up then left

Figure 14.2   Commuting editor.

shut' principle suggests: making an audible diagnostic when cursor keys have no effect—beep when `left` does nothing; or, the system could keep track of a virtual cursor position, so that there are no effective boundaries. The problem in the latter solution is that it introduces another mode: the cursor is either at a real coordinate, or is at a virtual coordinate—what happens if the user tries editing at a virtual coordinate (perhaps the origin of the document should be shifted)? The virtual coordinate idea seems a little weird, but it would mean that editing was symmetric at left and right extremes—many editors can extend documents to the right, but I do not know what use it would be extending leftwards, nor whether symmetry would simplify the user's task, given that no conventional text is bilaterally symmetric. Thus, at the end of this little analysis, we would suggest: commute everywhere, except at the left boundary, where a noise should be made to indicate breakdown in the rule (as suggested by the metarule of Section 10.8). The top boundary is handled by the same argument.

Many display editors actually edit text rather than a screen image. This means that the user is unable to position the cursor on 'blanks' to the right of a textual end of line. It is quite conceivable in such an editor that `right up` is sometimes equivalent to up, and not to `up right`. Figure 14.1, using a quote from Francis Bacon, shows the problem at its simplest. The cursor is moved up and left, or left and up, from a longer line onto a shorter line above. The cursor can end up in either of the two positions shown.

In contrast, Figure 14.2 shows the possibilities of a commuting editor design. In the route up then left, the cursor is momentarily at a position that has no ISO code (ASCII) representation—but what is that technicality to the user?

Where does the cursor go
when moved upwards?
◇

Figure 14.3   Ambiguity caused by modes in the non-commuting editor.

Some editors make the problem worse: being at the right-hand end (and, depending on the design, trying to move further right) of a line enters a mode where the cursor is 'attached' to 'end of line' until it is explicitly moved left. In this mode, move the cursor vertically and it will jump from end of line to end of line. The effect of `right up` at this point is indeterminate, and may then be equivalent to `up right right ... right` or even `up left left ... left` in the normal mode.

Editors are easier to use if `up/down/left/right` commute: but this requirement has direct consequences on the user interface. The user must be able to edit any blank part of the screen, rather than only be able to edit those bits of the screen that directly correspond to the text. Rather than make an artificial distinction between 'really blank' and 'written blankwritten space'—as some editors do—it is far simpler to reduce output modes, invoke WYSIWYG, and say that if a blank in one place means there really is a space there, then a blank anywhere else means there is a space there. Even beyond the end of the line.

That non-commutativity implies modes in the non-commuting editor is illustrated in Figure 14.3. The cursor, represented as usual by the symbol ◇, was moved down from somewhere on the line 'when moved upwards?' and is now immediately below it (it would do just as well if it had been moved up from a line below). Now, the effect of moving up from its present position depends on where the cursor started from: the cursor need not move vertically![3]

If some commands do not commute, then the user may submit them (or their arguments) the wrong way round. A file copy command allows the user to copy a named file[4] from one place to another. Clearly `copy a b`, which makes a copy of a called b, is not equivalent to `copy b a`, which makes a copy of b called a.

The special case `copy` a_{here} a_{there} occurs when the user wants to copy a file called a from here to another place, for instance to serve as a backup, or conversely, to restore a file from a previously backed-up version. Most

---

[3] That we need three figures in this chapter and a substantial part of Chapter 11 to describe a design feature so common and yet so patently silly *and unnecessary* illustrates what happens when design is led by implementation, unguided by principles.

[4] As usual, the file need not be named by typing its name; it may be pointed at by a cursor and clicked; it may be glanced at—eye contact might be enough to 'name' it.

copy commands are designed so that this special case can be abbreviated, for example, copy a *there*. This can be done naturally by direct manipulation: the user clicks on the file a and, keeping the mouse button down, moves the file to another location *there*; the system then copies the file to the destination.

There is a problem if a file of the same name already exists in both places, one of the versions will get replaced by the copy. Some systems intervene at this point and ask the user if he wants to 'replace items with the same names with the selected items'. At this stage the user may easily have forgotten which ones are which—and on a windowing system, the question probably obscures the information the user needs to answer the question!

Now copy can be modified so that it commutes in these circumstances. Simply arrange for copy a_{here} a_{there} to replace the older version of a. The command is then equivalent to copy a_{there} a_{here}. Now the user *cannot* make the mistake: copy will only replace a file with the more recent version whichever version the user tries to 'copy'.

Having modified the conventional copy command so that it commutes for the special case of same-named files in different places, and thereby reducing the chances of user error, we should continue exploring the design. It would be useful to provide the converse command—to restore a file from a backup, and it might be better to provide the command as postfix. The user might specify the file and its two locations and, if the file exists in both places, the system could ask if the user wants to update or backdate.

Connections with lazy evaluation

If commands commute, the user can choose the laziest—easiest—way to perform his task, knowing that the end result will be the same. Likewise, computers can exploit lazy evaluation just when the user cannot tell in which order commands are evaluated. See also Section 4.3.

14.3.5 Associativity

Associative laws simply state that bracketing is irrelevant, since the final meaning of some sequence of operations is independent of the order in which they were evaluated. For instance, the ordinary arithmetic + is associative, which means that in the sum $4 + 5 + 6$ we can either work out $4 + 5$ first or $5+6$, and then add the rest. Some elementary operations are not associative, for instance, subtraction must be done in the right order: consider $4 - 5 - 6$ which has the value -7. If we first worked out $5 - 6$, we would erroneously conclude the result 5. Brackets are normally used to specify an order for doing sums when operators are non-associative, when the order matters. In the last example, we could write either $(4-5)-6$ or $4-(5-6)$. In general, $a \oplus (b \oplus c) = (a \oplus b) \oplus c$ is the associative law for the operator $\oplus$.

Associativity is a useful property, for it permits the user—the person supplying the sums or solving them—to choose an order that suits him best. For instance, $123 + 500 + 500$ is slightly easier to work out as $123 + 1\,000$ rather than as $623 + 500$. (Addition also commutes, so there are even more possibilities that the user could try to make sums easier.) If associativity makes arithmetic operators easier to use, how can it be realized in user interfaces?

Associativity is basically a posh way of saying modeless. Consider an ordinary (modeless or modey) user interface. The user initially submits command c_1. The system goes into some state, which we can represent by c_1. Next, the user submits c_2, and the system goes into a state (c_1c_2). After submitting c_3, the system will be in state $(c_1c_2)c_3$; and after c_4 it will be in state $((c_1c_2)c_3)c_4$. And so on. In other words, the meaning of each command depends on the collective meaning of all the previous commands. That is what the brackets mean: work out what c_1c_2 means, *then* work out what that followed by c_3 means, and so on. If this is the only way of knowing what commands mean, then the system must be modey, for the meaning of submitting c_4 for instance, depends on the earlier effect of c_1. If, on the other hand, command composition associates, the brackets are unnecessary, and we can work out what the sequence of four commands means in any way.

The flip-undo problem exposed in Section 13.4 is a lack of associativity: $(c \smile \text{undo}) \smile \text{undo} \neq c \smile (\text{undo} \smile \text{undo})$.

Finally, consider a user interface for doing arithmetic calculations. Normally, the user must supply the sum in the order he types it! Which means there is no opportunity to take advantage of associativity. There are two ways around this problem: either the user can use an editor to construct the sum (thus, cursor motion means the sum can be constructed in any order, left to right or right to left), or he can use **equal opportunity** so that the system can evaluate parts of the sum as if the user had submitted it—but this is anticipating Chapter 15.

14.3.6 Cancellation

Cancellation laws allow users an easy way to reason about interactive systems or mathematical expressions. Thus, if you know $x \times 4 = 12 \times 4$, you can cancel the 4's and immediately obtain $x = 12$. Cancellation laws generally need exceptions: for instance, had the equation been $x \times 0 = 12 \times 0$ you could not conclude anything very useful about x.

Suppose there is a cancellation law applicable to the command **status**, such that if $c_1 \smile \text{status} = c_2 \smile \text{status}$, then the user knows that $c_1 = c_2$. In other words, the command status tells the user everything he needs to know about the state of the system. But a command like clear-screen would be a zero, making the result the same (a blank screen) but not implying anything about the preceding commands submitted by the user.

Cancellation laws can be written: $a \oplus c = b \oplus c \Rightarrow a = b$, or, in a typical form excluding $c = 0$ (where $\otimes$ is a multiplicative operation) as $a \otimes c = b \otimes c \Rightarrow a = b \vee c = 0$.

14.3.7 Substitutivity

Lastly we consider substitutivity, such a basic property that it is perhaps easy to overlook. Substitutivity requires that equivalent values can be substituted for each other. Thus, if $x = 4$ then we can substitute for x in $x + 1$ and obtain $4 + 1$, and in turn substitute 5 for $4 + 1$. All the time, the formula (here, $x + 1$) has the same value. (Though mostly a straightforward concept, substitutivity has certain profound aspects— issues of referential transparency—when expressions can refer to themselves, arising, for instance, in macro processors with quoting mechanisms.)

Section 11.6.2 gave an example of lack of substitutivity: the user interface requires a number, but does not allow the user to submit an expression. If a user could submit an expression, say 5/6, this would save him calculating the number himself, avoiding both errors and effort; indeed, the expression 5/6 is more mnemonic ('I want it 5 cm when it was 6 cm') than 0·833—or should it be 0·833 333?

Countless other examples could be given of the advantages of substitutivity in user interfaces. More persuasive, however, is the general argument: when a user can substitute alternative forms of input, he can choose whichever form best suits the needs of the moment. Conversely, there are advantages if the user can control the output forms used by the computer. This, indeed, was precisely the starting point for looking at algebra in this chapter.

14.4 Which properties are relevant and when?

When doing sums we often rely on the cancellation properties of addition and multiplication. For instance, if we have $x \times 2 = 4 \times 2$, we may cancel 2 and infer $x = 4$. But in set theory, if we used cancellation to 'infer' $A = \{\text{pear}\}$ from $A \cup \{\text{apple}\} = \{\text{pear}\} \cup \{\text{apple}\}$ we would be mistaken. Or again, we expect and rely on multiplication commuting, that $AB = BA$. For example, commutativity would be useful to help solve $5 \times 237 \times 2$; since we know multiplication commutes and associates, and that $5 \times 2 = 10$

we can simplify the expression to 237×10, and then employ the rule for multiplying by ten, to obtain $2\,370$. If we did not use commutativity, we would have to perform 5×237 or 237×2. But when we are working with some values, such as matrices, multiplication does not commute (though it remains associative), and indeed in general not both of AB and BA will be defined—we have already seen in Box 14.1 that LR $\neq$ RL for word motion.

We see simple algebraic properties sometimes apply and sometimes do not. Generally, when a property applies, the 'user' can take direct advantage of it, especially for simplifying his problems. Like any assumption, taking advantage of algebraic properties will not be without problems. Recall the mistake Spooner made with the salt and claret. Because pouring salt and claret commutes, Spooner was encouraged to solve a spurious problem, the offending pile of salt. Obviously Spooner had an inclination for this particular sort of mistake, but nobody is completely immune from error.

But too many 'good' properties may be a bad thing. The equations above (distributivity, associativity, commutativity, cancellation) are simple algebraic properties—satisfied by arithmetic—but if to this set we add an **absorption property** (a characteristic property of a Boolean algebra, for example, $A \cup (A \cap B) = A$) although it sounds reasonable, there is now no *useful* system satisfying the properties collectively. In computer science terms, we may build a system and claim that it satisfies certain design requirements (read, algebraic properties), which, when taken separately sound perfectly reasonable. But if, in fact, it is impossible to satisfy (at least non-trivially) such properties at once, the system *must* be bug-ridden, and the user has, correspondingly, no reliable way in which to use it—except by costly experience. We already met this problem when combining undo and predictability properties in Chapter 13. The issue is that at first adding helpful properties apparently makes a system easier to use, but at some point it becomes apparent that the properties we want are collectively too strong, they conflict and cease to have any value.

In general, it is not clear how to weaken properties, nor how to choose suitable candidates for weakening. My present view is that in general a few strong basic properties will be more helpful for the user than a lot of approximate properties.

There is in fact an advantage in not having **categorical** properties (that is, having effectively only one design solution), not least because completeness would result in an inflexible design. If instead the designer deliberately selects an incomplete set of properties this would mean that the 'psychological variables' would have a well-defined role: incompleteness in the properties could be exploited to improve usability. Presumably prototyping tools could be devised so that the human factors could indeed be factored out, and hence manipulated in an efficient fashion under experimental control. At present, of course, manipulating human factors often means complete revisions of the software and this is generally too expensive to contemplate.

All computer systems are finite, so we cannot expect them to be faithful to the algebraic properties of any theoretically infinite system (such as the real number system). All computer systems have finite boundaries (for instance, in the size or precision of objects they can represent, in screen viewing size, and so on): so most algebraic properties will be ideals that are compromised when these limits are encountered. We can sometimes make these boundaries so generous that a user cannot reach them in the time available (assuming he has no accelerators, see Section 16.9.2); presumably my bank account has some finite limit on the amount of money it can represent, but I suppose I shall never discover it. It is possible to devise finite algebraic structures with 'useful' properties (for example, permutation groups), but it will often be the case that finite structures result in curious user interface characteristics. Consider a text editor, where we might require the motion operations **up**, **down**, **left**, **right** are paired inverses (so that **up down** and **left right** do nothing). This seems reasonable: movement in real space has this property. But it will not work at the edges of the screen (or text being edited): since **up** may not actually move up. Solving this problem (which we brought on ourselves!) would require us to make the text file spherical (or toroidal, or worse), so that it had no edges, and the commands worked everywhere without exception. Presumably this would be harder to use—as the user could get lost far more easily!

See also Section 10.8 about metagueps: when the designer cannot tell whether a principle applies, but nevertheless thinks it is a 'good thing', it may be possible to ensure that the user has a way of telling when the guep is applicable and when it is not. The system's sound synthesizer synthesizers might be connected to various functions or predicates in the implementation. This way, the designer, rather than worrying about vagueness and probabilities, has shifted to a higher level view of the interactive system design. It may be that if the user can ask questions (or whatever, depending on how the metagueps are supported) about the behaviour of the system he will be better off than had the designer provided a thoroughly consistent system, with strict (and possibly restrictive) properties applying everywhere and at all times.

14.4.1 Assumptions about representation

Now a warning about assumptions about representation. Certainly algebra allows the designer to transcend considering details of user interface representation, but choice of representation may still be crucial. We have already seen (Section 14.3.1) the connection between syntactic choices over bracketing and distributivity, but some assumptions run quite deep.

Earlier we said that we were not interested whether the interface used ; or **enter** or anything else. This is true at one level of abstraction, but note that **enter** as newline would scroll the screen more than a semicolon (or comma, or any equivalent character). Newline would certainly reduce screen clutter (on a display screen), since only the last 20 or so commands could be seen, and there would only be one command per line. On the other hand, the user would have to rely on LTM or some system feature if he wanted to know what he did more than 20 commands back. Contrariwise, command separation by a semicolon would contribute to a cluttered screen. The user might have some visual difficulty searching for a command 20 steps back, and perhaps be the more frustrated because he knows the command is there somewhere. Semicolons or newlines? It is not an easy design decision if you stop to think about it.

Most earlier sections made the tacit assumption that operators were represented as **infix** (for example, plus is infix when written *between* the numbers it is adding). Had prefix or postfix operators been considered, priorities and brackets would not have been necessary at all.

Certain principles may interfere with desirable representational principles, even before we bring in ergonomic considerations. For example, WYSIWYG requires a simple relation between what the user can see and what he has got. This precludes, amongst many other things, the liberal use of abstraction. If something is abstracted, the user cannot *see* it—which is half the point of abstraction, because it avoids unnecessary clutter! Thus, a resolution of the principle of abstraction and WYSIWYG would require: (*a*) a visual convention to indicate abstractions (some things will not stand for themselves, as required by strict WYSIWYG, but stand for their definition text or objects); (*b*) obviously, an announcement in the documentation and perhaps on the screen disclosing the convention.

Abstract methods only work reliably in the 'hard sciences' by definition. Thus the trajectory of a missile does not depend on its colour, cost, phase of the moon, but only on its initial physical conditions (mass, centre of mass, velocity, surface) which can be specified numerically. And we know what sort of approximation results from ignoring, for instance, air resistance, or variation of gravity. But with user interfaces it is hard, if not impossible, before a system is used, to separate the superficial representation (corresponding to the missile colour and phase of the moon) from the essential abstract concepts (corresponding to the missile mass and velocity). User interface design, then, is hard only in the everyday sense.

14.5   Weakest pre-specifications

Some sorts of usability depend on certain sorts of algebraic properties. In other words, at a very abstract level, before many commitments have been made to a design, the designer can satisfy himself that the user can employ certain sorts of effective problem-solving strategies while using the system.

We will imagine the user has a goal in mind, and somehow has to transform his goal into a sequence of commands that achieve the desired goal. The user may be given (or be able to find out) various strategies (Section 13.5), and in turn be able to prove that they are effective. Of course, most users would not so much prove, as convince themselves with more-or-less precise arguments.

In order to formalize the idea of the user's goal, call the set of all possible command sequences that could possibly satisfy the **specification**. 'All' the user has to do is to decide on a specification, then choose a member from the set, then submit it; the system will achieve the user's goal.

The problem is that the specification will rarely be known **extensionally**, that is, explicitly. The user will have a description of the set, but may not have a useful description of any of its members. Of course, in some cases, the user might define the specification in a way that would immediately determine its members: the goal *might* be, 'I want to use the up command to go up'. More likely, the user will only recognize members of the specification when they satisfy the goal.

In set notation, the specification will generally look like $\{x|\mathcal{G}(x)\}$, where x is a sequence of commands and $\mathcal{G}(x)$ is some predicate that means that x achieves the stated goal $\mathcal{G}$. The specification may be oblique, for example: $\{x|x$ is a program that does what I want$\}$. As we saw, in very simple cases, the user may have an explicit specification, practically of the form, $\{$up, down, left, right$\}$, if that is what he wants to do, which would be an extensional form of $\{x|$moves-the-cursor-one-step$(x)\}$.

Suppose the user has a specification S of what is to be done. We suppose there is a sequence of commands (that is, a **program**, using Chapter 13 terminology) p that satisfies the user's specification. Since the specification is the set of all possible programs that satisfies it, $p \in S$. We will not impose any requirement on the form that S should take. A system will be usable if a user can determine a member of S, in other words, solve $p \in S$ for p. This determination has to be computable (Sections 5.2 and 5.6).

This problem is exactly analogous to the program development model: transforming specifications to programs, achieving the goals of the programmer. We are in fact looking at so-called **weakest prespecifications** (Hoare and He, 1987), which can be motivated by plausible user interface assumptions. Their general application requires certain algebraic properties.

Given a specification S in whatever form, the user has to find p from $p \in S$. This just means that p must be one of the possibly many sequences of commands that satisfy the goal represented by S. The immediate problem for the user is to find a solution to the equation $p \in S$. Given a solution p, he will know a sequence of commands to submit to achieve his goal. After we have worked through this idea, we will show that there is a generally easier approach for the user: he need only discover the first command of p in order to know what to do immediately next.

Of course, only exceptional users would actually solve *this* equation; what happens is that the user thinks in some mysterious way and, hopefully, ends up with a solution for the equation. Our discussion will ignore what actual method the user employs, for it will be sufficient to assume he almost solves the equation by ordinary, non-mysterious mathematical means. The following analogy may help the sceptical: if you go to a shop and buy something for less than the money you offer, the shop keeper may give you change by using an algorithm that only relies on adding. He may solve the problem of how much change to give you by an iterative method (for example, first give you the small change in coins, then the big change in paper notes). He could correctly be said to be solving a subtractive equation, *change = money − cost* by adding. How people do things (here, by adding) may be very different from how we want to interpret them (here, as subtracting). We shall return to this point below; for the moment it will be clearest if we see what we can achieve if we assume the user really does solve the equations mathematically *or anything equivalent*.

It may be difficult to solve $p \in S$ directly. But like the shop keeper, the user almost certainly uses an iterative algorithm. Think of the first command to submit, do that, then see what else needs to be done. Suppose the user can think of a plausible first command to submit; call it c_1. Now the user has to solve the equation, $c_1 \smile p_2 \in S$ for p_2, given c_1 and S. We need the existence of an inverse to composition so the equation could then be rearranged[5] to $p_2 \in S \frown c_1$.

The operator $\frown$ is not necessarily easy to use (the symbol is even called *frown*!)—division of numbers is bad enough and they are structurally simpler than programs and specifications. But even if the user can only derive a simpler specification S_2 by solving $S_2 \subseteq (S \frown c_1)$, which should be easier than completely solving for p_2, his task would be simplified. Finding a subset is no harder than finding a member. Each time the user submits a command, the complexity of the specification of the task remaining decreases. It should get easier and easier.

For example, assume the user's goal is to print a file. Let $S = \{x | x \text{ prints a certain file}\}$. The user may start by submitting the mnemonically named `print` command; this is the command c_1. Now the user wants to know what to do next! He must now solve the equation:

$$\texttt{print} \smile p_2 \in \{x | x \text{ prints a certain file}\}$$

To do this, he rearranges to solve,

$$p_2 \in \{x | x \text{ prints a certain file}\} \frown \texttt{print}$$

This should suggest providing a file name next, since

$$\{x | x \text{ prints a certain file}\} \frown \texttt{print}$$

---

[5] To solve $2 \times x = 4$ we use the inverse of $\times$, namely $\div$, and rearrange to get $x = 4 \div 2$. For $\times$ and $\div$ read $\smile$ and $\frown$.

simplifies to $\{x|x$ is a certain file$\}$. Thus, $p_2 \in \{x|x$ is a certain file$\}$, and if the user knows what the file is, p_2 can easily be found.

This is a simple example; in general usability will depend on the operator $\frown$ existing. It is important to prove that it exists, otherwise the rearrangement of the equation may be no more than a sleight-of-hand. As a numerical example, consider rearranging $0 \times x = 7$ to $x = 7 \div 0$, and supposing thereby to have found a way of calculating x. For our present purposes, however, such proofs will be too technical.

It probably seems rather implausible that the user has to 'dream up' the first command c_1, `print` in the example, to submit. More generally, the user can find two sub-specifications, S_1 and S_2, such that $(S_1 \smile S_2) \subseteq S$. The user may now solve $p_1 \in S_1$ first, then solve $p_2 \in S_2$. This is an important problem-solving strategy called **decomposition**. It is applicable just when the problem-solving strategy, call it $\mathcal{S}$, distributes through $\smile$: it relies on the identity $\mathcal{S}(S_1 \smile S_2) = \mathcal{S}(S_1) \smile \mathcal{S}(S_2)$.

It would often help the user if he could solve such equations in any order. In this case, p_2 might be easier to determine, and knowing that, the user could subsequently obtain p_1 more easily. If all commands commuted, the user would not need to rely on STM or other memory for p_2: if he worked it out first he could submit it first. Text editors and form-filling dialogues are the prime examples of systems that permit users to solve problems (writing documents and filling in forms) in an order that best suits them and not some arbitrary imperative program sequence.

If S_1 and S_2 are still too complex, the way that S was decomposed into S_1 and S_2 can be repeated to decompose S_1 and S_2 in turn to simpler specifications: $(S_{1,1} \smile S_{1,2}) \subseteq S_1$ and $(S_{2,1} \smile S_{2,2}) \subseteq S_2$. Ultimately, the user will reach simple-enough specifications to handle directly. Consider the complex initial specification, $\{$tidies my desktop$\}$. The user may start to decompose this specification into $S_1 = \{$tidies any icon$\}$. Clearly $S_2 = \{$tidies other icons$\}$, where $S_2 \subseteq (\{$tidies my desktop$\} \frown S_1)$.

Instead of commutativity to give the user flexibility in choosing an order for command submission, an alternative is to enable decomposition to be carried out in any order. This would require both left and right inverses for composition to exist. In general, the user should be enabled to employ powerful problem-solving heuristics, such as divide and conquer and dynamic programming (not that he needs to recognize problem-solving strategies as such). In fact, the simple 'think of a sensible prefix' used in the example to print a file employed the so-called greedy method.

Users do not *explicitly* solve set-theoretic equations in their heads unless they are mathematicians! Instead, our argument relies on the Church–Turing Thesis: if there was no computable way of solving the equations, then the user would find the interface very difficult to use. If we can show that there is an inverse operator of the sort we have been discussing, we know that in principle the user has a computable method to convert his goals into actions to achieve these goals. We have not made a psychological statement about *how* users may actually go about doing this: we have merely shown one way of ensuring that it is easier than it might otherwise have been.

14.6   Some evaluation methods

If a system has been formally defined, then the designers know what it is *supposed* to do. Conversely, if a system has not been formally designed, there is little point evaluating it, because you have no idea what it was really supposed to do, nor do you really know how to improve it. Evaluation is no easy matter, whether you try to be rigorous or superficial. At least a formal design method permits evaluation to be as rigorous as you are prepared to make it—and to have some idea of the consequences of various approximations you may make in the course of the studies.

This section briefly describes two interesting statistical evaluation methods that can be based on formally specified designs. It should not be forgotten, however, that formal methods can only help make a formal assessment of a system: in the end, evaluation should help the user (or the user's employer, and so on) decide whether the system is fit for its intended use.[6] The importance of a formal evaluation method is that it can be employed early on in the design process (and therefore quite cheaply), and it avoids involving actual users and invoking the long list of risks outlined in Section 3.3—Hawthorne Effect, homeostasis, cognitive dissonance, and so on.

14.6.1   Witnesses

The purpose of this section is to show how mathematical ideas may help directly with evaluating interactive systems. The main problem with evaluation is that real systems are *far* too complex for them to be tested to see if they maintain some property *everywhere*. Instead, we normally model an abstraction of it, and then we want to test the felicity of the implementation with respect to the formal abstraction we have of it.

Consider that the set of states in a simple text editor includes every possible document text as a component, and for a possible 1 Mb document this represents about $2^{10\,000\,000}$ states—and for each of those states, there

---

[6] It is useful to distinguish between **evaluation** (which designers or their colleagues do) and **acceptance** (which users or their employers do). A user may be prepared to accept a system on practical criteria; whereas a designer evaluates a system with a view to improving it, making it better fit the users' needs. The distinction gets confused because users are often directly involved in evaluative studies, and the results of evaluation may contractually influence acceptance.

will be 10^6 cursor positions, several modes, and so on. A more manageable, abstract, model of a text editor would probably consider about ten states (corresponding, for instance, to the main modes), abstracting out many details—the different documents and cursor positions.

It is clear that the algebraic approach cannot be used empirically at the user interface except for very simple systems—where we were probably not in much doubt as to whether they were usable. For more complex systems we can take inspiration from human experts who tend to try out tests that are likely to fail. We have already seen this before—in Section 6.2 where experts try things like division by zero, and in Section 9.4 where scientists try experiments that obtain negative results. There is a similar problem in number theory, and it is interesting to make comparisons with user interface evaluation.

To see if a number N is prime, we have to see if any numbers divide exactly into it. If any do, then N is composite and not prime. We can easily see that 17 is prime, by trying out all putative divisors from 2 upwards. In fact there are a few optimizations that can be tried: there is no point trying divisors that are multiples of divisors already tried: if 2 is not a divisor, then $4, 6, 8 \ldots$ cannot be either. The procedure seems quick and feasible, until we come to consider very big numbers. And, of course, almost all numbers are very big—just as almost all interactive computer systems have very big state descriptions.

The problem is that if we wanted to see if a large number is prime, it could take a *very* long time to find out. Suppose we want to know whether $N = 2^{400} - 593$ is prime. It would take far longer than the known age of the universe just to find primes less than $\sqrt{N}$, which would be a necessary part of checking. Even then we would be assuming that the computer does not break down in all that time. We would have died and everybody else would have long since forgotten the question when the computer finally gave the answer.

Rather than use an algorithm that tries every possible divisor we could use a **probabilistic algorithm**. The idea is that if a number N is composite, there are some numbers, called **witnesses**, that satisfy certain technical conditions. If a number N is prime, there will be no witnesses to 'say' N is composite. Conversely, if N is not prime there will be witnesses. As in real life, the evidence has to be weighed, for the witnesses may be mistaken.[7] A probabilistic algorithm based on this idea simply keeps on asking different witnesses until the combined probability of all of them being wrong is small enough to be acceptable. If randomly chosen witnesses are wrong with probability 1/2, and 100 assert that N is prime, then you know with a probability of just one part in 2^{100} of being wrong that N is prime. *That* is being pretty certain.

---

[7] Their attention might have been divided.

It turns out that the conditions (that is, the questions you ask the witnesses) are quite simple and can be performed very fast. It took one minute of computer time for Rabin and a co-worker to find that $2^{400} - 593$ was indeed prime, with a probability of being wrong of just one part in 2^{100}. They point out that a standard algorithm, which would have taken an astronomical time, would have to have been run on unrealistically reliable machinery to give such certainty in its answer (Rabin, 1976).

Now to return to testing interactive computer systems: first, we have to suppose that there is a property (akin to primeness) for which we want to test by witnesses. We might look for simple conditions and then try and invent a guep that corresponds to those conditions. There is also the problem of deciding what 'random' means in the state-space of the user interface and, indeed, how to submit a 'random' command. Of course, if we cannot make truly random command submissions, then there is no concept of probability.

Despite the difficulties of a theoretically-based approach to probabilistic testing by witnesses, there is some support for the method from the way in which experts tend to test systems, as we have already noted. It may be possible to devise artificial tests (for example, press 'x' for an hour)—if the system cannot cope with lots of x's, then it surely cannot cope with something more realistic! And corresponding to these tests will be (probably embarrassingly trivial) engineering principles. Another approach would be to design the system specifically so that it could be tested by probabilistic methods.

14.6.2 Mutants

If a witness is a funny user who tries to find out whether a system is faulty, a **mutant** is a funny system that tries to masquerade undetected as a normal system.

Instead of checking a single program with probabilistic methods, as in the witness method, the converse approach is to test random variations on the design (see Spafford, 1990). These variations are called mutants. Mutant designs can be used to help provide a statistical basis for evaluation methods.

Suppose you check an interactive system and find no faults. Is that because your test was not thorough enough, or because there really are no faults to discover? The idea of the **mutation testing** method is that if your testing can detect one of the random faults deliberately introduced into a mutant design, you can work out the probability that there were no faults in the original.

The problem with mutation testing, as with witness evaluation, is to decide what a 'random' mutation would be. A random mutation of the program source code implementing the user interface would with some probability introduce a syntax error, and the program would not run at all: presumably even a superficial test would detect that error! The advantage of mutation testing is that the method relies on lots of systems, not lots of users; indeed, parallel hardware (or linked systems) can be used straightforwardly to accelerate the method.

14.7 Mathematics in design

Consider the statement 'The computer crashed'. Technically this implies the statement, 'The computer crashed or the user made it crash' (since $a \Rightarrow a \vee b$, whatever b). But the first statement is not about the user at all, so how can it imply that user might have made it crash? More intriguing is the counterfactual, 'If I had a theory of design then I could design good interactive systems', which is logically equivalent to 'If I had a theory of design then I could *not* design good interactive systems'—because the antecedent, my having a theory of design, is false, and false $\Rightarrow b$, whatever b.

If mathematics so easily comes up with such causal absurdities, there seems to be little basis to believe it can be helpful in design. If there is no reason to believe mathematics is profoundly true, there is certainly no reason to involve it in user interface design. Of course, there are other reasons for using mathematics, not only for employing mathematicians, but to help implement a given design, prove it correct, and help optimize it. But these conventional uses of mathematics are *transformational*, rather than *creative* design.

Yet I have been claiming that mathematics is a good foundation for designing and understanding user interfaces, rather than being a mere tool for the designer alone. The claim is that a 'mathematical' interface is a better interface than a 'non-mathematical' interface: for mathematics expresses consistencies, rules, and so on, and these are seemingly necessary for the interface to be usable. In some sense it could be claimed that mathematics captures something about the world and our interaction with it, and that it is a good idea to carry over this 'something' into the design of user interfaces. Clearly mathematics *does* capture things about the real world in our *normal* use of it, but would mathematically guided design capture useful things about the world? What happens when the design is completely novel?

There is an important point in this enquiry. Imagine that the designer has a discussion with the user about the requirements he would like to see satisfied in the system. The user explains what he wants. After a pause, the designer says, 'but you are inconsistent!' I argued earlier (in Section 3) that everyone is inconsistent, but is it not arrogant to think that mathematics can make a judgement about human wishes? Why are we so certain that if, mathematically, someone's desires are inconsistent, that *he* is inconsistent? Why should mathematics say anything relevant about the working of the human mind, which surely has free will, and can do what it likes; which might include *not* obeying mathematical laws.

This discussion relates back to user interface design in several respects.

▷ **Intellectual sacrifice** (Section 3.3.1): Using a particular user interface causes people to become committed to it. It becomes 'right', and apparently better than competing systems even if they *would have* been right had they been used first. The users simply make a choice of axioms (and reasoning methods), then use them, then become irrevocably committed to their original choice—and it also becomes almost impossible to disabuse them of 'incorrect' aspects of the user interface design.

▷ **Intellectual sophistication** (Section 8.1): Designers are tempted (particularly by commercial pressures) to make strong claims about their systems. They may appeal to theories and experiments as a basis for their authority. Now we see such arrogant claims should be relativized. Consistent as mathematics may be, it does not mean that a mathematically based design is consistent with anything else, let alone the user.

▷ **Metacircularity** (Box 4.2): Mathematical meaning is no more and no less than what we are able to describe. This leaves almost everything undefined because of metacircularity. The 'metacircular illusion' is a quite general phenomenon and precisely the same problem is rampant in user interface design: it causes people to have fixed ideas about what is good for them and others.[8]

Simple properties are **predicates**: meaning, they are either true or false. They either hold generally, or they do not apply at all. Yet real life is full of compromises; we might like to say that 'almost all' commands of an interactive system have an inverse (that their actions can be undone), or that some technique 'usually works'. In any event, once our nice design starts interacting with the world of other systems, perhaps through international networks (themselves badly designed!), we may no longer be able to *guarantee* any particularly useful properties at all. Thus predicates will often be found a bit naïve for the issues of real design. Recall the thinking/feeling distinction—a thinking type of person evaluates things as true/false or right/wrong, whereas the feeling type of person would evaluate a system on how acceptable a system felt: something might be 'wrong', but he will go along with it because it feels all right (see Section 8.5).

---

[8] The issues discussed here can be treated more formally, see Smullyan (1988). Löb's Theorem is the place to pick up some of the issues.

Predicated principles for user interface design have to be presented as 'if appropriate, then inviolate'. Of course, the designer may wish to violate a principle because it is too restrictive or conflicts with others, and besides (one hopes) the probability that a user encounters the exception is small. This approach is justifiable, if only because human users are inconsistent, as we saw in Chapter 3. Mental inconsistency is legitimate because the computational cost of establishing inconsistency could be prohibitive—and so you never find out. Likewise, it may be safe for a system design to be inconsistent, so long as encountering this inconsistency is prohibitive for a real user, if not for the designer. Then again, encountering inconsistency is quite different from recognizing it—a system may be able to have certain sorts of visible faults which its users do not recognize.

The immediate problem for the designer is that he has no precise idea of what the user will do with the system; if the designer is cautious he will not even estimate the probabilities that the user will do one thing or another. It is not safe to permit bugs to pass the design stage, for the designer doesn't know how likely the user will be to encounter them under actual conditions of use: thus, a design should be 'correct' (that is, satisfy certain given principles *completely*). Once a system has been tried out on users, it may be possible to distinguish between obscure bugs that the user is unlikely to encounter and the 'real killers' that will frequently upset the user—particularly the naïve user who may not be able to recover from their untoward effects.

14.8   Conclusions

Formality is a good thing. It helps designers make better use of their design experience: things learned on one system can be carried over into other systems. It is also the best and most concise way to communicate designs and design issues with other designers. Using formal methods accelerates the scientific process.

There are many sophisticated ideas than can be expressed in algebra. Mathematics may be used as an aid to the designer, to help him consider various possibilities, though he must also employ other considerations such as computability and practicality—and human factors, for it rapidly becomes an issue whether algebraic ideas are of benefit more for the designer alone, or the designer *and* user. Put briefly:

▷ We can describe a lot even by elementary mathematics.

▷ We can raise design issues very simply, and explore their consequences cheaply—mathematics has a Socratic role in design.

▷ We can relate design problems to known structures and solutions.

▷ We can talk about the issues using standard terminology.

Francis Bacon claimed that truth emerges more from noting error than from being in confusion, that is, we are better knowingly compromising formal principles than never considering them in the first place. It is sad that many people are frightened of mathematics in user interface design: it is a good way of noting errors and staying out of confusion. In all other engineering disciplines, like bridge building, mathematics is a normal and essential part of design—it looks like mathematics has a useful place in user interface design too.

Chapter 15

Equal opportunity

> Remember, in most places, equal opportunity is not just a good
> idea, it's the law.
> *Bob Floyd*

Equal opportunity is a heuristic for designing user interfaces (Runciman
and Thimbleby, 1986). The basic idea is that interactive systems can treat
their input and output with 'equal opportunity'. Thus, it would often be
nice for the user if something displayed by the computer (for example, the
date) could later be supplied by him as part of some input: using output
as input is one way of realizing equal opportunity. An equal opportunity
system will perform the chores, such as inputting the date, that the user is
often asked to do on other systems. We shall see some more examples in
this chapter. A number of existing and successful interactive system styles
can be viewed as the outcome of employing equal opportunity. By using
equal opportunity explicitly in a design, the aspects of the successful styles
of these systems can be systematically sought.

One view of interactive computer systems is that the user has
problems to solve. The user submits the 'givens' of these problems to
the machine, which in response supplies as output the 'unknowns'. For
example, the given might be my name, and the unknown might be how
much I have in my bank account. A time-honoured heuristic for problem
solving is to reassign or discard these labels 'given' and 'unknown'. This is
the so-called **working backwards** heuristic (Pólya, 1948b)—see Box 15.1.
Equal opportunity can be viewed as a specific application of this heuristic
in user interfaces.

Before defining equal opportunity more closely, it will be useful to
motivate the idea by a few brief arguments.

345

Box 15.1   Working backwards.

You are asked to place a suit of cards down on a table in order, A♠, 2♠, ... J♠, Q♠, K♠. To do this, take any of the 13 cards and put it down in what will be its final position, for instance the 2:

$$\underline{\quad}\;\;\overset{2}{\underline{\quad}}\;\;\underline{\quad}\;\;\underline{\quad}\;\;\underline{\quad}\;\;\underline{\quad}\;\;\underline{\quad}\;\;\underline{\quad}\;\;\underline{\quad}\;\;\underline{\quad}\;\;\underline{\quad}\;\;\underline{\quad}\;\;\underline{\quad}$$

A   2   3   4   5   6   7   8   9   10   J   Q   K

To continue you must take cards one at a time, at all times keeping a continuous line without any gaps: your next card would have to be the ace or the 3. If you choose ace, then the rest of your choices are fixed: you can only take 3, 4, and so on in order. The problem is: how many different ways are there for laying down the cards?

Working forwards, you can first choose any of 13. What you can do at any later stage depends on whether you have already chosen the ace or king. Once the end of the line is down, there is no more choice left. These boundary conditions make the calculation rather difficult.

Alternatively, imagine that all 13 cards are down. How many choices would you have working backwards, picking cards up? You can take a card from either end. At any stage, working backwards, there are always two choices, and you can exercise your choice right down to the last-but-one card. There are 2^{12} different ways.

▷ When several real-world events appear to be **instantaneous**,[1] an observer may not be able, or may not wish, to distinguish between causes and effects. For example, naïve students of computer science often fail to appreciate the subtleties of character echoing when characters appear to be echoed on a display *at the same time* as they are typed. A perceptible delay in echoing increases the acceptability of a cause-and-effect explanation. Similarly, users often fail to distinguish between moving a cursor (on a screen) and moving the mouse (which is the input which the program interprets to make the display outputs to move the cursor icon). Users frequently talk in terms of moving the *cursor*, rather than the mouse (or, indeed, their hand). What is strictly feedback is viewed as the user's direct input. In general, people seem to prefer explanations without input/output distinctions for fast interactive systems: this is not surprising, since if the system is fast enough, the user would have no way to perceive the distinctions to help follow an explanation.

▷ A telephone can be used for two-way 'instant' communication and it therefore appears to be equal opportunity. If a perceptible delay is introduced in the feedback loop (perhaps by using a satellite link),

---

[1] Instantaneous is a technical term meaning *perceived* as instantaneous. For a human, an instant is about 1/16 of a second, though the duration of instants depends on which sensory modality is used (touch and smell are slower; hearing faster).

coherent speech becomes difficult. The effective exercise of certain skills (speech in this example) requires that the illusion of equal opportunity is well maintained.

▷ Human problem solving is rarely confined to a linear chain of thought from given to unknown. The vast majority of mental links are undirected—they do not serve as one-way streets of cognition; rather they *relate* information in a general manner. If a person can translate (say) French to English, it is reasonable to assume he can also translate English to French and, indeed, elaborate on the relation between French and English in a general way. In whatever way the mechanism of human translation really works, it does not seem to involve fixed assumptions about what is given and what is unknown.

▷ Educationalists sometimes distinguish rote learning from deeper understanding by using exercises varying the kind of information given. If you *understand* addition you can complete '6 + $\Box$ = 3'; if you *understand* quadratic equations, you can find not only roots of given equations, but also construct equations from roots, check roots, and so on (see Section 15.2.1).

▷ Improving the mere speed of systems that embody fixed distinctions between input and output often contributes little towards ease of use and understanding—it may only serve to emphasize a frustrating mechanical dumbness and inflexibility. If a computer system embodies a fixed classification of pieces of information that may be communicated during interactive use—causes and effects, givens and unknowns, inputs and outputs—that system will very likely present an unnatural appearance of frustrating dumbness to its users. Whereas, following equal opportunity, if a system has no predisposition to a particular assignment of roles to pieces of information, or if it is fast enough so that distinctions are imperceptible, it will appear to its user as flexible and cooperative.

▷ At a less 'philosophical' level, if the form of system input and output are the same, then the user has his learning burden halved! Where it is possible, output should be easier to interpret when it is presented in exactly the same form as the user himself would have written it for input to the system. Achieving this level of closure generally necessitates some radical rethinking of the user interface; this may or may not improve the design, depending on the circumstances, but it is certain to lead the designer to new ideas.

In summary, the motivation for this chapter is the observation that it is both practical and useful to build interactive systems which do not, presumptively, impose a fixed mode of cognition, cause and effect, input and output, upon their users. We will show that reassigning the labels given/input and unknown/output can be fruitfully applied to the design of interactive systems. This is the **equal opportunity heuristic**.

15.1   Equal opportunity defined

Conventionally, programs *do* distinguish strongly between inputs and outputs: programs are expected to take certain input data as 'given'; corresponding output data are 'unknowns', to be obtained.

Take an elementary programming exercise as an example, typical of what students might be asked to program. The idea is to write a program that, given the coefficients of a quadratic equation, calculates the roots of that equation. The computer asks the user for a, b and c in turn and solves $ax^2 + bx + c = 0$, printing out the roots. The usual emphasis on this programming project is to cope with various tricky programming conditions, such as the user providing coefficients that give a double root, or complex roots. The user might supply input that cannot be parsed as numbers—he might ask the program for help.

You can imagine a user hearing about the quadratic solver: coming up to it, wanting to find out what quadratic corresponds to roots at 3 and -1. This is a quadratic equation solver, after all. But even though it is possible to obtain coefficients of a quadratic with given roots, in fact it is much easier, the quadratic equation program is unable to do so. It obtains roots from coefficients and not the other way around.

A better quadratic solver would treat input and output more equally. The user of an equal opportunity quadratic equation program could supply both coefficients and roots and have their correspondence checked. Or he might give some coefficients and some roots, in which case the response of the machine will be possible values for the others. Even giving neither coefficients nor roots is a possibility. We will see how to provide this sort of interface in the next chapter.

The exchange of input and output roles is only one of many possibilities. In what we shall call an **equal opportunity** system, all that can be supplied or demanded by the machine can also be supplied or demanded by the user. Equivalently, each item of information passed across the user interface can pass in either direction. In this way, there is a form of parity between the human and computer participants. This is the ideal, in practice *some* restrictions will be an inevitable consequence of overall design aims.

Chapter 13 developed a functional model of interactive systems: for inputs p you get an output $e = I(p)$, the *PIE* model. The output, or effect, of a system was considered a function of the user's input, the program. All equal opportunity is doing is suggesting that the functional relationship I is generalized to a relation.

15.2   Equal opportunity illustrated

We now want to show briefly that several well-established styles of user interface design that you may have regarded as quite separate have, to varying degrees, involved some equalization of opportunity in the sense just described. Indeed, we should like to go further and suggest that this is of the essence in each case, although it takes different forms in the different kinds of system. The coverage is by no means exhaustive, but will give some idea of the pervasiveness of incipient and actual equal opportunity in many interactive systems.

15.2.1 Quadratic equation solvers

The quadratic equation solver is one of the first interactive programming exercises a programmer faces in training. The usual emphasis of the exercise is implementing a robust program that, for instance, does not crash when asked to solve an equation involving complex roots, or even trivial cases like $x - 1 = 0$.

In an equal opportunity quadratic equation solver, cells on a display screen can be used to contain either user input or system output. Some text, representing the agreed task of solving quadratics, has to be fixed and hence is displayed in a distinguishing font or colour. If the user has submitted nothing, the display might be: $x^2 + \boxed{?}\,x + \boxed{?} = (x + \boxed{?})(x + \boxed{?})$; the question marks are the system's best attempt at solving such an under-determined problem. The user employs arrow keys to move between boxes.

As an example of the use of this equal opportunity quadratic solver, assume the user has defined the x coefficient to be -2 and set one root at $x = 6$. The display would show: $x^2 + \boxed{-2}\,x + \boxed{-24} = (x + \boxed{-6})(x + \boxed{4})$, where the user's input has been underlined. The system has been able to compute the other root, -4, and the constant -24. Notice how the fixed text $+$ forces an ungainly representation for negative values—a detail that can easily be solved.

15.2.2 Spreadsheets

The interface presented by a **spreadsheet** program is a rectangular grid of cells. Associated with each cell there is a rule (often expressed in a BASIC-like programming language) that governs what value is to be displayed there. A rule may be very simple (for example, 'is 15·43') but will often involve the values displayed in other cells (for example, 'is total of other cells in this column').[2]

---

[2] Many spreadsheets make a distinction between rules and values. Since a rule can specify that a constant value is displayed, this distinction may introduce complexity in the user interface. On the other hand, some users may want to work with preprogrammed spreadsheets and have nothing to do with the actual rules involved. In this case, it may be sensible to make a clear-cut distinction between data and program (see also Section 11.9.1). The user would be allowed to modify data, but not program (at least in the 'evaluate' mode), and the system would *appear* to be simpler.

There is no predetermined concept of 'input cells' or 'output cells'; the user simply sets rules in whatever cells he pleases and the system adjusts values displayed in whatever other cells are necessary, so that all display rules are obeyed. At one moment the user may inspect a cell to view an 'unknown', at the next he may redefine the display rule for this same cell, thereby introducing a new 'given' with potential 'unknown' effects on other cells.

In use, spreadsheets are not always used to calculate a result from given data. Instead they are often used backwards. The user may know what profit margin his company division will have, now he wants to fiddle with the parameters so that he can optimize his resources. The program in the spreadsheet allows him to adjust various cells, and the more equal opportunity the more easily the user will get a deep understanding of the model being manipulated.

15.2.3   Programming by Example

In **Programming by Example** the user provides what would normally be considered the output of a program in order to define the program itself. In other words, the user provides the system with an example of what he would like it to do; the system records the user's actions and can perform them again. The system organizes the program so the user can later generalize and parametrize what he did.

Peridot is an example (Myers, 1988). The user uses a mouse to draw boxes (and other objects) on the screen. When a box is positioned, the system constructs a piece of program, that if run draws that box. If the user draws a box inside the first, the system constructs the extra fragment of program, but also asks the user what the relation between the two boxes is supposed to be: is the inner box supposed to be centred or is it really supposed to be 2 cm off-centre? Is it 1 cm smaller, or 90% smaller? Or is it just coincidence that the box is inside: maybe the user wants it at that position on the screen, wherever the outer box happens to be. The program then constructs the program as indicated. The overall effect is that the user can very easily write programs to draw complex pictures.

15.2.4   Query by Example

Query by Example (abbreviated **QBE**) is a language and associated interactive system for manipulating the information in a relational database (Zloof, 1975).

Suppose a system maintains a database of people, their names, sex, age, and birthday. If the database was small enough to fit on a single screen, we might wonder whether a computer was the appropriate medium—but for typical applications of database systems, the database is huge, and will certainly not all fit on a computer screen. Handling the user interface bottleneck is now an issue. The user will typically want some information about one or more of the database entries. Rather than submitting a query in a command language, it may be easier for the user to construct an 'example' of the information that he wants.

Suppose the screen is initially blank apart from the top header line, which is in the same format as the database fields:

name	sex	age	birthday

The user can employ a mouse or cursor keys to move from column to column. Perhaps the user wants to know about everyone aged 10. The cursor is moved to the age column, and *10* entered. The system responds by filling in the rest of the details. The figure below shows the result.

name	sex	age	birthday
Will	M	*10*	30/12/80
Emma	F	10	18/12/80
⋮	⋮	⋮	⋮

Notice that the information on the screen contains both information output by the system and information input by the user, here the first line of the age column. If the user wants to see a more specific group of people, perhaps those that are both 10 and female, the cursor can be moved left, and an *F* submitted. In our example, the top line would disappear (and the F and 10 would be shown distinguished as input).

This is clearly a simple equal opportunity database query system. The user gives information as specific as he wishes, and the computer responds with all (or up to a screenful of) those records matching what the user has specified. Once the user sees some of the information, this may remind him or give him cues that will help formulate more specific queries.

Notice some important properties of simple QBE as described. First, the system's initial display gives the user a very good idea of the sort of information available in the database; as if the system were saying, 'This is what I know; just tell me what you want in the same way'. Second, the user interface is **declarative**. The screen display is the same *however* the user filled in the initial examples. If the user first fills in an age, then the sex; or first the sex, then an age; the final display will be the same. The system does not over-determine the user's order of thinking.

The scheme can be extended in various ways, for instance, in the case that the user's examples are not very restrictive the computer might show which fields would be most sensitive, and hence most worth filling in. QBE in fact provides variables and other language features.

15.2.5 Prolog

In Prolog, and other logic programming languages, it is normal to define procedures for which the input/output roles of parameters are flexible (**polymodal** is the programming term). A standard introductory example is concat. concat(A, B, C) means 'if possible make substitutions so that A and B concatenated together are the same as C'. It may be defined as follows:

concat([], X, X).	The first clause states that the concatenation of the empty list with any list X is just X.
concat([H|T], X, [H|TX]) :- concat(T, X, TX).	The second clause states that the concatenation of a list with first item H and remaining items T with any list X is H followed by the concatenation of T and X.

Prolog procedures like concat can be used in a variety of ways, depending on which parameters are input (data) and which are output (results computed by the procedure). Here are a few possibilities (note that in the last case, Prolog finds each of several valid solutions):

Call	Effect
concat([1,2], [3,4], Q)	Q = [1,2,3,4]
concat([1,2], Q, [1,2,3,4])	Q = [3,4]
concat(Q, [3,4], [1,2,3,4])	Q = [1,2]
	P = [], Q = [A,B]
concat(P, Q, [A, B])	or P = [A], Q = [B]
	or P = [A,B], Q = []

Contrast Prolog's flexibility with Pascal's. We could define a Pascal function concat that takes two lists A and B and returns their concatenation; but this function only solves problems of the first kind shown in the table above. An ingenious programmer might arrange A, B and C as var parameters, but Pascal provides no way to establish whether they are inputs or outputs to the function. Obviously the desired effect can be simulated, but only by fighting: in Prolog equal opportunity is free—it is part of Prolog's programming paradigm.

In the Prolog dialect micro-Prolog, the freedom of argument roles extends to arithmetic primitives. An expression such as 'F = 32+C×9/5' may be used to check that F and C have the desired relation, for denoting temperature in Fahrenheit and Celsius units. In this case both C and F are given. If, however, only C is given, micro-Prolog will determine F as output. This is not too difficult, but micro-Prolog is unusual in that if F alone is known precisely the same expression will determine C, by 'working backwards'. When *both* F and C are unknown there needs to be some additional information such as 'F between (0 500)', from which an F–C conversion table can be constructed.

In practice it is unusual for the user of an application written in Prolog to be able to benefit directly from equal opportunity procedures in the underlying implementation. Typically in large Prolog programs the variation of argument roles is slight. It seems that most Prolog programmers (having been first accustomed to programming in, say, LISP or Pascal) are unaccustomed to this kind of flexibility and fail to exploit its potential, and certainly fail to pass on the benefits to the user.

15.2.6   Smalltalk

Smalltalk enables a user to select any text, whether typed by the user or output by the system, and submit it to the system for execution. This is a very general and powerful interaction technique. It is of value not only in programming environments, but also in more mundane applications like word processing, where 'selecting and submitting' (copy- or cut-and-paste) may save the user remembering and retyping a piece of text.

The user can type and edit text in any suitable text editing window and, like any reasonable text editor, the system makes no distinction between new text the user types and any previously existing text that happens to be there. Furthermore, the user can select any region of text—which is therefore either new text, typed and edited by the user, or previously existing text—and request that it be run as program input.[3] Perhaps the user selects the text *2 * 3*. The output from running the fragment of program, which in this case would be 6, will be inserted into the text just after the user's selection, as if the user had typed it there. The screen would show something like *2 * 3* 6. This new output is automatically selected, and can be used exactly as if the user had just input it. It can be used as the next input, to be run, or as the subject of an editor operation (for example, to move it, copy it or delete it).

Such equal opportunity in Smalltalk makes for a pleasant user interface, with a pleasing flexibility. But it also encourages a powerful sort of documentation for both user and programmer:

---

[3] A region of text is selected, for instance, by moving the cursor to one end, then sweeping over it to the other end while simultaneously holding a 'select-button' down. The region will be highlighted (for example, displayed in inverse video) to indicate its extent.

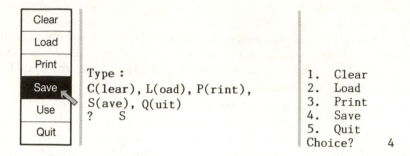

Figure 15.1   Three menu systems: the user has selected save in each.

▷ The text that the user edits and runs can be actual user manuals. The user can take advantage of the editor to navigate around the manual, for instance to search for a certain topic. But the manual can also provide real examples which the user can run *directly*, merely by selecting them.

▷ Ordinary programs contain comments that can be selected and run to illustrate what they are supposed to do, or to help test whether they work properly.

Smalltalk's style of equal opportunity is not confined to such fancy hardware. **Mux** (Pike, 1988) is a system that can run on old character-mapped terminals without a mouse. All text on the screen can be edited, whether the user typed it or the system output it. Any text, again whether originally the user's or the system's, can be edited and resubmitted to the system. This generality of equal opportunity guided other design decisions within Mux. Thus there is a command to determine the value of a variable, and it displays the variable's value in an assignment statement. If t is a variable, its value would be displayed as t = /usr/harold/cx/main.c. *Exactly* the same text could be resubmitted to the system to assign this value to t (though the user may want to edit it some way first).

15.2.7   Menus

Menus may be viewed as a specialization of the 'select and submit' technique. Instead of permitting the user to select *any* text, the user is restricted to certain predetermined choices. However, since the choices are predetermined, the act of selection can be greatly simplified. With menus, the system knows exactly what can be selected: a selection therefore need require no more than a single action of the user. Menus are particularly advantageous when the user would have difficulty inputting the item himself by hand—it might be a picture or symbol.

In Figures 15.1 and 15.2, the underlying semantics of the command-based and menu systems are the same, though the command-based system

```
?  help
   Possible commands are:
   clear, help, load, print, save, use or quit
?  save
```

Figure 15.2   Equivalent command-based system (with help).

does not display the command set unless the user submits the command `help`. The `help` command provides the same information as the menu, but the output cannot be reused by the user. In the menu system the output or menu entries are effectively submitted by the system when the user merely selects them.

It is worth emphasizing how relevant equal opportunity is to the menu concept. In a menu, the menu entries, as output by the system, *are exactly* what the user can submit as input. Menus provide the obvious abbreviation mechanism: if the menu entry already shows exactly what the user can do, there is no need for the user to retype it himself—it need only be confirmed (for example, by a single keystroke).[4] In a command-based system, however, any text the system provides (for instance, helpful command summaries) has to be read and understood by the user; then it cannot be used directly.

15.2.8   Cameras

Modern cameras contain computers to set the aperture and shutter speed. Light sensors measure the light intensity over regions in the picture, consider the film speed, look up the lighting pattern in a database of expert opinion, and then adjust the optics of the camera. Yet computer control is too rigid for some photographers: almost every camera has a user interface to allow the user to submit his own requirements to override the camera's taste.

If the user wants to photograph a fast moving object, a racing car perhaps, he would like to be able to control the shutter speed. Even though it is a rainy day for a race, cloudy and dim, the user wants a fast exposure so the car is not blurred on the film. The computer should calculate the correct aperture, and activate the flash if it is not possible to widen it enough (or there are other considerations, such as the loss of depth of field). This mode of camera use is called **shutter priority**.

For another photograph, perhaps of railway lines disappearing into the distance, the photographer wants an unusually stopped-down aperture

---

[4] Many menu systems are easier to use if they are **inertial**, whereby the default selection is the most recently submitted choice from that menu. Alternative strategies would be to select the most frequently used, but without further knowledge about the application, it is probably best to choose either the first or the safest (if different). Similarly, better use of the user interface bottleneck is achieved by employing a 'known' model for laying out the choices.

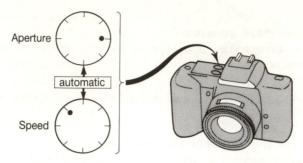

Figure 15.3 Equal opportunity camera dials.

to get the necessary depth of field. Now the camera should compute a slower shutter speed, and perhaps invoke the flash to get more illumination. This mode of camera use is called **aperture priority**.

As described, such cameras are equal opportunity. If the user specifies an aperture, the camera calculates the shutter speed; if the user specifies a shutter speed, the camera calculates the aperture; for standard use the camera can be left to calculate both, based on its own interpretation of the lighting conditions. Finally, in **manual**, the user can specify both aperture and shutter speed—typically, the user will specify deviations from the automatic settings, for instance to get a certain amount of over-exposure, so that he does not have to input absolute exposures.

Sophisticated cameras also allow the user to input other parameters which would normally be output by the camera's program, such as the desired depth of field, and whether flash is to be used, and what sort of flash synchronization is to be used.

Cameras naturally have various styles of user interface. One sort, shown in Figure 15.3, provides two dials: for aperture and for shutter speed. Each dial can either be set to `automatic` or to a specific value chosen by the user. If both dials are at `automatic`, the camera is fully automatic; if one is set to `automatic`, the camera calculates a suitable value for it; if neither is set to `automatic`, the camera is fully manual. In any case, the user should be given feedback in the viewfinder whether the camera itself considers that the photographic conditions are difficult or impossible, if the exposure will be grossly wrong, or that the shutter speed is so slow that a tripod is essential. A flashing light in the viewfinder is adequate for this, and also happens to be where the user will be looking.

15.2.9 Graphics applications

A graphics system lets the user draw shapes. Typically, the system does not know whether the user wants the shape to 'look right' visually or to be measured out.

An equal opportunity graphics system will let the user stretch a line by direct manipulation and will tell him how long it becomes—the drawing action is input, the length measurement is output. Conversely, submitting a length (preferably in the same place it would have been output) will change the length of the line accordingly—here, the measurement is input, the drawing output. In engineering drawings, the user may further require *both* line and length as output, say, to show, '⟵ 100 m ⟶'. In this case, the user could either stretch the arrow to change its length (and hence measure a distance on the drawing) or he could edit the number, and hence draw an arrow of a specific (scaled) length.

With appropriate variations, equal opportunity can be applied successfully to all other graphical dimensions: position, angle, skew, scale, colour, and so on.

15.3 The necessity and the dangers of some inequality

If a computer system *could* move a mouse it would in principle have a choice of valid responses when the user moved the mouse. In particular, rather than tracking the mouse with the cursor, the system could respond simply by moving the mouse back again, leaving the cursor where it was. Under this arrangement both mouse and cursor would be immovable! Hence the convention that the mouse is always an input device and the cursor an output.

The user of a constraint-based system might supply an equation to convert between Celsius and Fahrenheit. As the user sets and resets the Celsius value the system responds, always displaying the corresponding Fahrenheit temperature. Similarly if the user changes the Fahrenheit temperature the system alters the Celsius. But it would be unfortunate if equal opportunity extended to *all* values in the system: why then shouldn't the system instead alter the *equation* relating Fahrenheit and Celsius so that it becomes true? The convention is, of course, that the equations are never considered valid means of system output.

As these examples illustrate, some inequality of opportunity is invariably and quite properly introduced at some point in a system design. The danger is that it can be introduced by hidden and unquestioned assumptions rather than as the result of an explicitly reasoned design step. Once such assumptions have been incorporated into a design it can be extremely difficult to reorganize the system to permit greater variation of input/output roles or greater equality of opportunity in interaction.

Because of this, I believe that many of the standard Human Factors success stories of iterative design (for example, rationalizing screen layout after user participation) are entirely fortuitous. It is easy to imagine a program design based upon a computational model for which it is impossible to redesign a screen layout without redesigning the entire implementation.

15.4   Designing design principles

Having discussed the general principle of equal opportunity, we now use it as a guide to derive more specific design ideas.

We have been worried about from where designers can get new principles. In response, we will show that equal opportunity interaction is a promising heuristic for developing principles. Designers can be more certain than usual that the principles *they design themselves* are applied appropriately.

15.4.1   WYSIWYG

We discussed WYSIWYG at length in Chapter 11 (Section 11.7.4); we saw that the principle could be seen as a consequence of assuring the user that what he saw was the same as what he could get *out* of a system or, for the stricter form, the same as what he thought he had *in* the system. We shall now derive a simple version of WYSIWYG by starting from equal opportunity.

Suppose a word processor provides an editor E which operates on text T. The word processor includes a formatter F which formats the current text and causes it to be printed. Initially we suppose the word processor is not of the WYSIWYG genre, so that the text probably contains all sorts of incantations to a text formatter ('centre this text', 'underline this' and so on). We can view E as a set of functions $E_i: T \rightarrow T$, each E_i being a command that transforms the text. F is a single function $F: T \rightarrow P$, where P is the set of printed results.

We start with text t_1, which can be printed to get printed copy p_1. The user submits a command, E_i, which, perhaps by inserting or deleting something, changes the text from t_1 to t_2. This may be printed off to obtain printed copy p_2. The problem is that the interface forces the user to perform operations in T when he would rather think in terms of P. The directions of the arrows in the diagram make plain the assumptions about input/output roles for data involved in the editing and formatting operations:

$$
\begin{array}{ccc}
t_1 & \xrightarrow{\;E_i\;} & t_2 \\
F \downarrow & & \downarrow F \\
p_1 & & p_2
\end{array}
$$

Apply the ideas of equal opportunity to F by trying to discard its fixed assumptions about input and output roles of T and P. That is, we want to replace the two arrows labelled F by undirected links. The main obstacle in the way of this plan is that, for all conventional formatting systems, F is severely many–1. So it seems we must force either non-determinism, or arbitrariness or irritating choices on the user.

But this problem has a standard solution: we conceal unwanted distinctions between equivalent members of T by making T an internal representation and only retaining quotients of it (the obvious choice being P) in the external specification. The concealment is indicated by boxes in the diagram below. The result is an abstract interpretation of WYSIWYG.

$$\boxed{t_1} \xrightarrow{E_i} \boxed{t_2}$$

$$F \downarrow \qquad\qquad \downarrow F$$

$$p_1 \qquad\qquad p_2$$

15.4.2 If you can see it you can use it

Any output displayed on a screen should be able to be reused and provided as input for other functions. This gives the user 'pronoun reference': the user can say to the system *this* expression or *that* value. This greatly increases the system's effective input bandwidth available to the user. Some systems permit textual output to be selected, edited and then resubmitted as new input to the system—Section 15.2.6.

There is considerable potential in editing the output of commands.[5] For example, a generalized editor may permit the user to edit file properties, by effectively editing the output of some file enquiry, then the user can change those properties. A debugger is a core-image editor; an electronic mail system is a mail editor and so on.

The issues of equal opportunity arise because once the 'unknowns' (outputs) of these commands (file lister, debugger, mail system, and so on) are edited the user will then wish to treat them as new 'givens'. A high degree of interface uniformity can be attained by making as many as possible state-changes achievable by the same editing mechanisms.

15.4.3 Commensurate effort

The relative computational costs of tasks carried out by the system should be reflected in the relative amount of work the user must do to invoke the necessary computations. A user must not be able to destroy data significantly faster than he can create it: this may seem restrictive, but it

---

[5] This is the design idea. The designer may have to radically revise the commands so that editing the commands' output causes the corresponding changes to take place. Section 15.2.9 gave a graphical example.

may also be seen to encourage the provision of accelerated ways of creating information in the first place!

Note that an estimate of the time taken to create information ought to include the time for the user not only to submit it, but also to devise it. For example, a BASIC system may inform the user that there is an error in statement 2 350. If the user types 2350 by mistake, instead of LIST 2350, the entire statement will be deleted: the user now has to recall the statement (perhaps by looking through an old listing if he made one), under the emotional burden that what he remembers is wrong anyhow! Would it not have been more sensible if deleting a statement was at least as difficult as listing it? Another possibility suggested by equal opportunity would be that the statement number output in the diagnostic could be directly input by the user: indeed, the error message might be phrased in a form like, 'LIST 2350: REM error' where the user can submit enter to execute this command, which immediately lists line 2 350.

The principle of commensurate effort works to minimize **regret**. When a user misses a chance to gain reward, he regrets his behaviour (if, of course, he understands the system well enough to recognize the missed opportunity for reward). The greater the regret, the more a user will be motivated to try again. Regret is proportional to the loss of reward, but inversely proportional to the magnitude of the slip that lost it. Thus, if some activity is very difficult, but you fail, this does not lead to much regret. But if some activity is very easy and you still fail to obtain reward, that causes far more regret. The more the regret, the more the user would like to redo the last commands and get it right.

15.4.4   Sense of progress

In 'the old days' computers often had a loudspeaker that was connected to the computer's program counter. As each instruction was executed, a pip was sent to the speaker; thus, the faster a program went, the higher the pitch. There are many variations on the idea, but the effect is that the user can easily learn what the computer is doing. For instance, if the noise made is of unchanging pitch, maybe the computer has got stuck in a loop. Users quickly learn to recognize the sounds associated with their programs making 'good progress'. Many systems today are silent (exacerbating mode problems), and give the user no clue to their progress.

Typically, the user submits a command, and the computer responds, next? (or equivalently). If the user submits a null command (just enter) the computer responds next?; if the user destroys half-an-hour's work with an injudicious command, the computer responds next?. There is no **sense of progress**. Everything is uniformly bland.

Clearly, providing the user with a sense of progress is a corollary of the commensurate effort, itself a corollary of equal opportunity. It may be worth the system letting the user know how difficult *it* finds things; it may be worth while if the user is clearly informed about the amount of information processing being performed on his behalf. The experience with the old fashioned—and simplistic—sound feedback suggests that users gain a great deal, both practically (for example, recognizing faults) and emotionally (for example, being able to adapt the use of their time to the progress of the computer), from a direct sense of the computer's progress.

15.4.5 Non-pre-emption

Non-pre-emption (or non-modality) can be seen as a corollary of equal opportunity. A computer system should not demand input from the user, refusing to continue or provide any output until the user supplies the required input. A pre-emptive system corners the user, forcing him to supply input before proceeding. This can be very disruptive.

15.4.6 Self-demonstrability

The provision of help and guidance is another aspect of equal opportunity: the system output is intentionally selected as descriptive of potential input.

The prejudice that a system cannot be easy to use if the user needs help with it presumably arises because graphical systems (that can draw pictures of themselves) lend themselves directly to self-demonstration, and non-graphical non-self-demonstrable systems are manifestly harder to use. It is a truism that a system that *really needs* help cannot be one that is easy to use. But does this mean that a system should be so simple that a user can easily use it; or does it mean that a system should be so metaphorically true to life that its usability capitalizes on the user's existing world knowledge? In the latter case, the system is not intrinsically easy to use, for the world knowledge and skills on which its use relies depend on at least a few years of real-world training which is necessary to unravel the metacircularity problem of self-demonstrating systems.

15.4.7 Closure under equal opportunity

If the output of the computer can be treated as input by the user, then closure would mean that *all* output is acceptable input and vice versa. Equal opportunity closure is a very strict property: it would forbid almost all help, for instance, except in a natural language interface!

Even if strict closure is impractical, at least it gives us design ideas. If a database system informs the user that some data is incorrect, then there should be a command to locate that information (and, indeed, to correct it).

If a BASIC system tells the user that a certain expression caused numerical overflow (say, $x/0$), then there should be some way for the user to find that expression. The user wants to know what input caused that ouput.

15.5   Conclusions

Removing assumptions about what is given and what is unknown first appeared as a heuristic for problem solving. It is used in education to distinguish understanding from rote learning. In some sense, demonstrating ability to accommodate variation in input and output demonstrates intelligence or at least a certain advantageous and cooperative flexibility in approach. Humans appear to prefer equal opportunity explanations when these are not weakened by noticeable delays. Technically trained people tend to overlook the value of potential equal opportunity explanations because of their bias towards cause and effect distinctions.

For interactive computer systems, we have adopted the equal opportunity slogan to advocate a corresponding removal of assumptions about which side of the interface, computer or user, must supply a particular piece of information. Equal opportunity is only one of many heuristics for design. At another level this chapter promotes the general idea of using heuristics in user interface design, and, in fact, equal opportunity comes from a large repertoire of problem-solving ideas which the designer may wish to draw on. Like any other heuristic, equal opportunity is not guaranteed to work—in fact, there are many cases where its full employment in a system is intractable: but, at worst, considering equal opportunity will help the designer think of new ways of looking at the design issues. At best equal opportunity will suggest radical improvements to designs, greatly increasing their usability and flexibility.

When designing a new system, ask:

▷ *What does the computer do for the user?*

▷ *What does the user do for the computer?*

▷ *Why is there inequality?*

▷ *What ideas could make the design more equal?*

A large number of successful interactive system styles incorporate equal opportunity to varying degrees. It appears that placing equal opportunity interaction as an ideal can usefully guide user interface design, and even when innovative styles do not emerge we would contend that useful insights will still be obtained by the designer who adopts this problem-solving heuristic.

Whether users have the capacity or inclination to exploit equal opportunity effectively remains to be explored in complex cases. It will certainly depend on the purpose of the user's particular interactive session.

The user's performance in a 'creative' session may be degraded by the explosion of choices open to him, whereas a 'problem-solving' session may be facilitated by the greater adaption by the system to the user's framework. Of course, the user's perception of his performance and his preference for equal opportunity will be determined by many factors other than his actual performance. The cost of implementing full equal opportunity may be prohibitive; consistent restrictions of the ideal—which the user readily comprehends—may be difficult to determine. A system that is almost equal opportunity might have more surprises for its user than one that has no such pretensions.

It should be noted that increasing equal opportunity, which may be good for users, often increases the computer's execution costs. There is consequently an important tradeoff between equal opportunity and its benefits for users and machine efficiency. In the future, a software tool to help in design could be constructed to facilitate making such design tradeoffs, and note that efficiency tradeoffs may be easier for equal opportunity than for some other properties (such as predictability, which is a user-referenced property, so design tradeoffs against predictability cannot be made until 'predictability' is defined, or the user interface is running and can be evaluated). Equal opportunity is a systemic property; its design tradeoffs can be made at any stage in the design process.

It seems like an inversion of all good user interface practice but equal opportunity suggests that, as well as a user using a computer, a computer ought to be able to use a user! Equal opportunity reminds us that if the user interface is to work, not only does the computer have to be programmed, but so also must the user. Normally we leave programming the user entirely up to that person: he has to read manuals, and so on, to program himself. Designers ought to consider the complexity of 'programming' the human user as part of user interface design.

Chapter 16

An example design

> **Principle**: Never dismiss as obvious any fundamental principle,
> for it is only through *conscious application* of such principles
> that success will be achieved.
>
> *David Gries*

The last chapter introduced and advocated the notion of equal opportunity
in interactive systems. We will now explore the use of equal opportunity as
a design heuristic by reappraising the conventional four-function calculator.
Of course, equal opportunity is but one of many properties to which a
user interface design might aspire; the calculator interface described here
arose by a serious attempt to close under equal opportunity. Examples
of other properties which might have been illustrated are modelessness,
WYSIWYG, undoability. In fact, the interface we develop will have all of
these properties.

Here we will describe the design itself, but later, in Chapter 17, we
will emphasize the general approach taken. The calculator is a novel and
interesting design; but the general method employed will work for more
sophisticated applications that cannot be covered in detail in this chapter.

16.1   Why design a calculator?

One reason for taking a calculator is that they have evolved to an almost
standard user interface, and perhaps this makes it harder to be creative.
What do we expect to achieve? What user interface problems do we hope
to overcome by redesigning a calculator?

▷ Although a typical sum may involve a lengthy sequence of key presses, the only display is typically a single eight-figure number. This shows either the current number being entered, or the result of the last calculation. Thus, the calculator gives the user no help remembering what he is doing. If there are mistakes, such as miskeying + instead of -, the only effect is a different result.

▷ Errors are handled by calculators in a very coarse fashion. If a number is miskeyed, then the only option is to clear the entire number and start again. Starting again increases the chances of yet another error! Of course, if there is only a single numeric display, partial correction would be more confusing—especially when you consider that 'correction' might itself be accidental and cause further errors!

▷ Calculators typically distinguish between `Clear` and `Clear Entry`. One clears the entire calculation, resetting the calculator. The other merely clears the last number entered, in case of a minor mistake. The effect of `Clear Entry` immediately after an operator is not so obvious. Confusion with clear functions is increased with those calculators that double-up keys so that the `On` button also functions as `clear`.[1]

▷ Cheap calculators have no brackets, and no idea of operator associativity. Thus teaching these concepts in school is bound to be confounded! Furthermore, some calculators treat doubled-up operators (for example, doing `--` or `++`) as doing funny things with numbers stored in memory. For example, on one quite typical calculator, `--` does not add the next number entered to the running calculation (as it would do on paper, for example, 3--4=7), but subtracts the current number from memory. More advanced calculators have bizarre concepts like stacks, Polish notation, radians and exponential notation: we need not consider them further in the present context.

▷ Many calculators provide percentage and memory operations that can be extremely confusing; these are the keys usually labelled `MR`, `M+`, and so on. To understand the effect of these operations, the user has to know about numbers stored inside the calculator. What numbers are stored inside? Few calculators provide the obvious facility to ask what numbers are in the memory without disturbing the current calculation.

▷ When there is overflow or some other error, calculators display some cryptic symbol, like `EEEEEEEE`. Usually the calculator also locks-up and is inoperable until `Clear` is pressed. Very often such error messages appear to be inexplicable: it is no use taking a calculator

---

[1] I'm confused too! In earlier chapters I used the names '`all clear`' and '`clear`' respectively.

to a teacher to ask exactly what went wrong because the EEEEEEEE is the only evidence left!

▷ For children particularly, calculators tend to reinforce the incorrect notion that = is asymmetric, that the answer should always follow it. Symbols like + come to have a meaning like 'do an addition', rather than as a flexibly applied relationship between values.

▷ Although exercises can be contrived, a most fundamental limitation of a conventional calculator is that the sum has to be rearranged in the user's head or on paper so that the answer comes last. Thus, if you want to calculate what to add to 4 to make 10, you have to rearrange to suit the calculator and ask '10 minus 4 is what'? Put in other words, any question has to be rearranged so that 'is what' comes last.

It is only fair to point out that these problems can be understood as opportunities for learning. Thus a fill-in-the-blank exercise like '4 + □ = 10' has to be converted to 10 − 4 = (or even 10 4 − on a Polish notation calculator) to be run on a calculator; this is useful symbol manipulation, and a child gains something by acquiring such skills essential for handling calculators. Certainly calculators are ubiquitous and no harm, apart from lost time, will arise from learning to use them effectively! Yet few people who need to use numbers in the course of their adult employment will have much problem learning how to use calculators, though they may make mistakes exacerbated by the problems listed above.

Handheld calculator design was initially constrained by the cost and complexity of electronics, particularly the cost of the display. Sensible engineering decisions then guided what is now the standard design. Computers, of course, have very different, more relaxed, engineering limits: they have much larger screens; software complexity is much more easily managed than the electronics complexity of early calculators; a large keyboard is available as standard.

We must be able to do better by starting again.

16.2 Design by naturalism

The first way to design a user interface might be to do a task analysis (find out what the user currently does) and then emulate it as closely as possible. Present display technology means that it is very often possible to make a satisfactory visual rendition of the user's pre-computer task. There are twin advantages to this approach: the user has practically nothing new to learn, and the designer's job is merely one of copying.

Assuming desk-top calculators do the user's job well enough, then an obvious user interface will be a visual representation of a typical desk-top calculator. As convention dictates, it would have buttons and a single display. It can be quite fun—both for user and designer—to carry realism as far as possible: some calculators even show shadows behind the keys. The keys can appear to be pressed into the screen. There is obviously a place for this sort of convincing photographic 'naturalism', certainly if it reduces the user's anxiety about the novelty of full-scale computer interfaces. Naturalism means that the technology can be the designer's scapegoat: if a user interface is not natural enough, this fault can be blamed on the hardware—the computer is too slow, or the display resolution inadequate.

Often naturalism has serious problems: there are some features that naturalism dictates should be included, but good sense would not include. Some calculators have an auto power-off feature, for instance. If the user does not do a sum in a given time the calculator switches itself off—a watchdog (see Section 4.2.14) that discards the present calculation to save the user in the long run from having a dead battery. In a computer a watchdog ought to *save* the user's work on disk in case the user (or power company) switches the computer off—just the reverse, in fact!

I admire those cartoonists who can draw highly suggestive pictures with a few strokes. I need not show you my drawing of a dog. To improve my drawing, I add details, such as whiskers, collar, a few hairs, and so on. In brief, I have to try to correct my initial design by adding resolution and features, when any cartoonist would have scrapped the initial design and started again! My drawings look worse and worse the harder I try to make them more realistic. Isn't this how most people design interactive programs? By adding more hairs! Perhaps design should be shaved by Occam's Razor.

Perhaps the designer will appraise direct manipulation. The pressable calculator buttons were a step in this direction, but a moment's reflection suggests better user interfaces to exploit direct manipulation. What about an abacus, with movable stones? What about a slide rule, with movable cursor and bar?[2]

Clearly the success of naturalism is that direct manipulation depends crucially on what style of design is being emulated. Computers have the potential for completely novel user interfaces, and we should be careful to exhaust innovative solutions before copying existing solutions that were inevitably compromised by limitations in technology. This is a harder, and less certain approach to design—and sometimes it will not be appropriate because a good-enough design is needed rapidly, or because the users specifically require backwards compatible interfaces. Empirical evidence ought to be analysed to support either approach if any effort is to be invested—'effort' might be the designer's or the user's effort, though over

---

[2] The slide rule idea is promising precisely because it is equal opportunity. The user submits a ratio or product, and can then read off all equal ratios. There is no fixed sense in which one ratio is the input and all the others the output. Slide rules often confuse users because of this very flexibility and the daunting quantity of numeric information displayed. Experts learn to filter the information.

its lifetime, many users will collectively waste more effort than the few designers involved.

So, in summary, design by naturalism is not for calculators. Putting that less contentiously: the design issues in making a calculator realistic are not sufficiently interesting for the rest of this chapter.

> I conclude that there are two ways of constructing a software design: One way is to make it so simple that there are *obviously* no deficiencies and the other way is to make it so complicated that there are no *obvious* deficiencies.   *Tony Hoare*

16.3   Design by principle

Conventional calculators have an unequal opportunity user interface. For a typical infix notation calculator, the user has to provide an equation (the input), and press = or `enter` to obtain the result (the output). In a typical command-based system, the computer may not provide any response (other than echoing) until *both* = and `enter` are submitted. A typical interaction with such a system, illustrated below, emphasizes the inequality of interaction:

        4 + 5 × 2 = ↵
        14

The user types the seven characters 4, +, 5, ×, 2, =, `enter`. This provides the input from which the computer obtains (straightforwardly) the result 14 which it prints as output.

Some calculators provide the user with the opportunity to use the system output value as part of his next submission. Simply, the system output is printed on the next line and may form part of the user's next expression. The following example shows how the system is used to evaluate 4 + 5 × 2 to 14, which the user then multiplies by two. The user has not had to submit the 14 itself.

        4 + 5 × 2 ↵
        14 × 2 ↵
        28

Notice how equal opportunity has aided the user break down the calculation into manageable steps. Without equal opportunity, the user would need either paper (or other extra memory) or extra knowledge, in this case about bracketing to do $(4+5\times2)\times2$. With more complex applications than four-function calculators we would expect the gains to be more impressive—this is the Smalltalk style described in Section 15.2.6.

In summary, design by principle (here illustrated by some trivial equal opportunity) is creative and opens up new possibilities for use.

16.4   An equal opportunity calculator: Design I

If we wish, we may view the = or enter operator as a symbol separating the input, supplied by the user, from the output, supplied by the computer. The user's equations must always be conceived, as it were, in a form '4+5×2 = x; what is x?' The unknown x comes *last*, because it has to appear after enter.

To close the design under equal opportunity the user must be able to demand contributions from the computer on the left-hand side of the = sign: to be able to ask questions like, '4 + 5x = 14; what is x?' If the user had had in mind such a question for the original calculator, he would have had to reformulate it as, '$(14 - 4)/5 = x$; what is x?' and have taken due regard for overflow and numerical accuracy. For equal opportunity he should also be able to provide the entire equation, including the answer, to be able to ask questions equivalent to '4 + 5 × 2 = 14; is this correct?' Such questions would have had to be reformulated for the original calculator perhaps as, '4 + 5 × 2 − 14 = x; is x zero?'

It is easy to implement an equal opportunity calculator directly supporting the style of interaction suggested by these considerations. When the user wishes to provide the computer with an opportunity for output he can introduce variable names (such as x) as 'place holders' in the input. The user can then ask the questions outlined above. The system's output will be the set of values to be associated with those names. The calculator would ensure that the equation the user input is numerically correct, given the name and value bindings output by the system; otherwise it will have to say 'no this is not a valid equation'—that would answer the last sort of question posed above.

To explore these ideas quickly I wrote a simple Prolog program of about 90 lines. The following is a selection of excerpts from a dialogue with the prototype. Standard Prolog will not allow us to prototype the final representation of the user interface, but it is a convenient way to explore the semantics.

First, we might ask the original question *directly* ('▷' is a prompt):

```
▷    4 + 5 × 2 = x  ↩
     x = 14
```

The user has submitted an equation in x and the computer has printed a solution. Of course the extra facility has meant that the user has had to type '= x', which would not have been necessary with a conventional calculator. But the extra flexibility allows the second question, that is, the first unconventional question, to be asked directly as well:

```
▷    4 + 5 × x = 14  ↩
     x = 2
```

Role integrity suggests that *if* we can put one variable in an equation, why not more—for the keyboard certainly has more than an x key! So we are

---

Box 16.1   The implied task domain problem.

Design I calculator was prototyped so that we could get an idea of the possibilities for *interaction*. It does not handle general equations, yet its user interface suggests it can—this is a role integrity problem. The user might submit a × a = 16, which should be solved by outputting a = ±4, but the prototype treats it as $a_1 \times a_2$ = 16: the system then asks for an equation for a_1 and the user may define any value—not necessarily 4! This role integrity problem is typical of many user interfaces: that the 'obvious' (that is, simple or unrestricted) user's conceptual model requires a more comprehensive implementation than that actually provided.

In our case it would be tempting to introduce an exponentiation operator (then a × a could be written a^2 or a↑2, so the name a is not repeated). However this merely increases the feature-count of the interface without attacking the cause of the problem—the fallacy of composition. The user could still submit insoluble equations. It is an unnecessary burden for the user to have to read the fine print of the documentation in order to avoid violating the system's misfeatures. We shall see how this problem can be avoided in calculator Design II (Section 16.5).

---

led to formulate more general questions. But more general questions may not have numeric answers, so our prototype requests more information from the user, as the following example shows:

```
▷   fahrenheit = 32 + celsius × 9 / 5 ←
    to help solve fahrenheit=32+celsius×9/5 give
    another equation for celsius or say 'no'
▷   celsius + 2 = 20 ←
    fahrenheit = 64·4
```

The reason for the 'no' option is that the user might want to give an equation for the Fahrenheit value instead. The prototype does not make this choice very clear! This is an aspect of the design we would want to reconsider and polish up later, and which we will do in Section 16.5.

A redo feature will be very useful. This is particularly true for an equal opportunity calculator, for a single equation can be used in a great variety of ways. So, **again** is to be used as an abbreviation to facilitate reuse of the last equation. We continue with the same dialogue:

```
▷   again ←
    to help solve fahrenheit=32+celsius×9/5 give
    another equation for celsius or say 'no'
▷   no ←
    to help solve fahrenheit=32+celsius×9/5 give
    another equation for fahrenheit or say 'no'
▷   fahrenheit = 32 ←
    celsius = 0
```

The design here over-determines the user.   After the first question the user either defines `celsius` or answers `no`.   A more sophisticated system could easily spot that a definition of `fahrenheit` straight away was a refusal to define `celsius`, and hence save pestering the user with two questions.   Such developments, however, presuppose a more sophisticated numerical equation solver underlying the user interface (as does the example in Box 16.1).

16.5   An equal opportunity calculator: Design II

At one level we have obtained equal opportunity with the Design I calculator by introducing names, though with more flexibility than is usual for a handheld calculator.   If we wanted to pursue Design I, there are some numerical problems that need to be put right.   We will put aside such issues, and aim first to resolve problems by developing the user interface, not by enhancing the underlying machinery for solving equations; rather than *solve* the numerical problems, we will *dissolve* them by changing the user interface.

Our original goal was to attain equal opportunity interaction, but we have merely shifted our ground.   The user submits an equation with identifiers representing unknowns; but this is just more complex *input*.   The essential inequality of the dialogue is emphasized by the continued presence of ← symbols which the user *has* to press in order to prompt the computer into revealing the results.   Is it possible to eliminate this inequality?

With the style of dialogue previously discussed, inequality arises since once the user has provided certain data as input it has to remain as *fixed* input; there is never any going back.   When the computer provides output, that too has to remain as output associated forever with the previous input. The user is unable to change the system's output and the system is unable to change the user's input.   The leap in calculator design is to *use* a display screen, rather than be conceptually stuck in the continuous-sheet-of-paper style of interaction.   With a display, each character cell on the display may change role from input or output as necessary.

Hypothetically, the idea is that if the user typed $4 + 5 \times x = 14$, then the system could itself change the *input* x to *output* the answer 2 directly. The character cell first filled by the user with the unknown *x* as input, changes role to output its value. There are naturally some problems with this idea that we need to resolve.

First, what output or feedback, if any, should be provided when the expression the user is still typing is incomplete or is otherwise syntactically incorrect? Secondly, is it wise for the computer to erase the user's input? Consider what would happen if the user submitted, x `delete`, but the computer had already changed the x to 6342: what should the `delete` delete?

These problems, and the role integrity (see Box 16.1) needed for the general equation solving implied by Design I's Prolog prototype above may be solved as follows. First, the computer may error-correct incomplete or incorrect expressions. Secondly, the error-correcting text *itself* can serve to display the solution of the equation.

With error correction, we no longer need identifier names. Instead of submitting a name, the user simply omits giving any operand at all: the computer error-corrects and inserts a suitable value to balance the equation. Since no identifier names are involved the user has no way to submit those equations that we had problems solving with the earlier design. No non-linear polynomials can be expressed, and no systems of simultaneous equations, and we have regained role integrity.

It is hard to represent a dialogue as it unfolds on a screen in a static presentation medium like this book. Unfortunately the rather cluttered style of presentation necessary for clarity gives an unfavourable and spurious impression of verbosity. In the excerpts below, the left-hand column shows each key typed by the user; and the right-hand column shows *successive* displays. Individual lines from the right-hand column are all the user would normally see. For our exposition in this chapter, the computer's contribution to the display output has been shown in boxes, $\boxed{\text{thus}}$, but an interactive system would use a different colour or some other clear and easily noticed method, perhaps inverse video. For the first few examples only, we show the cursor explicitly by the symbol ◇; on a computer display it will probably be represented less intrusively but more obviously, for example, by the character to its left flashing.

The system starts in an initially error-corrected state, having corrected *nothing* submitted by the user, represented by $\boxed{0 = 0}$. This means that, so far, the system has output $0 = 0$ and the user has input nothing. We start by asking the original question, '$4 + 5 \times 2 =$ what?' The sceptical reader is invited to construct a similarly detailed blow-by-blow account of a conventional four function calculator for fair comparison. Some of the sums demonstrated on the equal opportunity calculator will be impossible on a conventional calculator.

The user submits, 4, +, ..., and the display changes accordingly:

input	display
	$\diamond\boxed{0 = 0}$
4	$4\diamond\boxed{= 4}$
+	$4 + \diamond\boxed{0 = 4}$
5	$4 + 5\diamond\boxed{= 9}$
×	$4 + 5 \times \diamond\boxed{1 = 9}$
2	$4 + 5 \times 2\diamond\boxed{= 14}$

A pleasing property is that we could have asked, 'what is ...' just by submitting the = first rather than last. The next dialogue, corresponding to the old question '$4 + 5x = 14$; what is x?' goes as follows:

input	display
	$\diamond\boxed{0 = 0}$
4	$4\diamond\boxed{= 4}$
+	$4 + \diamond\boxed{0 = 4}$
5	$4 + 5\diamond\boxed{= 9}$
×	$4 + 5 \times \diamond\boxed{1 = 9}$
=	$4 + 5 \times \boxed{1} = \diamond\boxed{9}$
1	$4 + 5 \times \boxed{-0{\cdot}6} = 1\diamond$
4	$4 + 5 \times \boxed{2} = 14\diamond$

I arranged, as can be seen in the examples, that the user's typing *seems* to overwrite system output. Actually it inserts non-destructively between user input. The user interface for the editing commands treats system output *precisely* as if it is not there. This behaviour is made clear in the following example, where the 2 overwrites the system's 0, but the 4 inserts before the user's 2:

input	display
	$\diamond\boxed{0 = 0}$
2	$2\diamond\boxed{= 2}$
←	$\diamond 2\boxed{= 2}$
4	$4\diamond 2\boxed{= 42}$

A free feature of the screen-based style of editing interface is that the user may move the cursor and easily make corrections or other adjustments to the equation. For instance, the user may submit **delete** as a single key press, to delete characters already part of the equation. Conventionally **delete** would erase any character immediately to the left of the cursor; in our case, it has to delete the rightmost user-typed character to the left of the cursor—it makes no sense to delete a system-output character, since syntax correction would simply reinstate it immediately!

Editing permits the reuse of equations without retyping them from scratch; but with this calculator the scope of reuse is much enlarged. Reuse helps the user experiment with a problem to find an effective solution. Consider the task of converting centimetres to inches. The conversion factor is 2·54; a choice of different conversion factors would generalize this example to many tasks, such as currency conversion. If the user types **2·54 × =**, the system will error-repair this and display $2 \cdot 54 \times \boxed{1} = \boxed{2 \cdot 54}$. If the user now enters **100**, representing one metre, the system can error-repair the expression to display $2 \cdot 54 \times \boxed{39 \cdot 37} = 100$. We might now suppose the user is interested in how many feet one metre is. To do this, the user can enter **×12** on the left-hand side of the equation (for example, by using text-editing commands, to move left and insert text): this obtains the display $2 \cdot 54 \times 12 \times \boxed{3 \cdot 28} = 100$. So, one metre is 3·28 feet. To obtain the conversion into feet and inches, the user could submit or modify the existing input to **2·54× (12×+=100**, where there are two slots for the system to compute feet and inches. Note that the user is taking advantage of the error repair by omitting the closing bracket. The system need not choose an integral number of feet, of course! So we can imagine that the user, once he has discovered that a metre is just over 3 feet, edits the expression so that it appears in error-repaired form as $2 \cdot 54 \times (12 \times 3 + \boxed{3 \cdot 37}) = 100$; thus, one metre is 3 feet, 3·37 inches, to this precision.

Reuse allows the user to solve related problems with different data economically. Once the user has entered an equation such as, $32 + \boxed{1} \times 9/5 = \boxed{33 \cdot 8}$ it may be edited to examine *any* Fahrenheit/Celsius or Celsius/Fahrenheit conversion or, indeed, for verifying the relation of two given temperatures.

From the examples it can be seen that if the user enters a syntactically correct equation which numerically does not balance, or an incorrect one which cannot be (such as '$0 \times = 1$'), the system makes some adjustment, for example, having typed **4 = 3** the display would show $4 = 3 \boxed{+1}$. Multiple equations are corrected in a similar fashion, for example, if the user types **4 = 5 = 7** then $4 \boxed{+3} = 5 \boxed{+2} = 7$ would be displayed. This is not the only way to do it; the rationale for this particular correction strategy is discussed below, but after we give some more interesting examples of the calculator in use.

16.5.1 Recreational mathematics

In choosing the following two examples of the calculator 'at work', we are not assuming that the user *has* to be sophisticated but, rather, we want to show how the simple user interface can be exploited for tasks beyond ordinary calculators. If complex tasks are easy, ordinary tasks should be easier still.

The Golden Ratio

The Golden Ratio can be expressed as a continued fraction $1 + 1/(1 + 1/(1 + 1/(1 + 1/ \cdots$ and this can be typed *directly* to the calculator in this form. Indeed, at this stage the calculator would display $1 + 1/(1 + 1/(1 + 1/(1 + 1/\boxed{1)))} = 1{\cdot}6$.

Since the calculator continually corrects the equation by supplying the right number of closing brackets and performing the calculation, the user can easily see how the fraction converges without worrying about the brackets balancing. An important point is that *at every moment* the sum displayed is correct: there is no chance that the user will read an out-of-date result simply because he forgot to hit the = button.

In fact, this fraction converges *very* slowly to the value 1·618... If this value is already known it is interesting to fix it and see what happens. Thus, typing = 1·618 will immediately obtain $1 + 1/(1 + 1/(1 + 1/(1 + 1/\boxed{1{\cdot}616\,44)))} = 1{\cdot}618$. Perhaps 1·618 is not precise enough and more decimal places should be supplied; for instance, submitting 1·618 034 will get the calculator to supply 1·618 034 5. The exact details will depend on the sort of computer the calculator is running on.

Such experimentation helps clarify why the fraction converges to the Golden Ratio. The Golden Ratio, ϕ, has the property that $1 + 1/\phi = \phi$, hence $1 + 1/(1 + 1/(\ldots 1/\phi \ldots)) = \phi$. The more the fraction $1 + 1/(1 + 1/(1 \ldots))$ is extended, the less the difference between 1, written as the right-most denominator, and the exact value $\phi = 1{\cdot}618\ldots$ matters.

There are surprisingly elegant continued fractions that converge to π, e, $\sqrt{e}$, and so on, so the equal opportunity calculator comes into its own supporting simple experiments.

Ramanujan's 1 729 problem

A final example: 1 729 can be expressed as the sum of two integer cubes in two different ways (Ramanujan's 1 729 problem). How can the calculator be used to help solve such recreational problems?

The calculator provides no direct support for problem solving: such features might be expected in an artificial intelligence program, but not in a four-function calculator! However, the editing features facilitate the systematic search for a solution.

We start out by submitting $1\,729 = 1 \times 1 \times 1 + 1 \times 1 \times 1$, and of course the computer corrects this to $1\,729 = 1 \times 1 \times 1 + 1 \times 1 \times 1\boxed{+ 1\,727}$. The sum of $1^3 + 1^3$ is clearly far too small. So we guess and increase one term to 11 cubed (easily done by typing 1 three times in the appropriate

places), and obtain this result: $1\,729 = 11 \times 11 \times 11 + 1 \times 1 \times 1 \boxed{+\,397}$.
This is clearly still too small, so we try $1\,729 = 12 \times 12 \times 12 + 1 \times 1 \times 1$.
The computer supplies no correction, so we have established one solution,
perhaps with luck on our side. We now search for the other.

At this stage, the computer's relaxed approach to syntax is useful,
for we can leave the solution we have just found on the screen. We just
type a second $=$ and start looking for the next solution. At this point the
display will look something like: $1\,729 = 12 \times 12 \times 12 + 1 \times 1 \times 1 = \boxed{1\,729}$.

We know that the first term must be 11 cubed or less: $1\,729 =$
$11 \times 11 \times 11 \boxed{+\,398}$. Is 398 a cube? It isn't, but we may as well
check, by trying 5 cubed (correction $\boxed{273}$), 6 cubed (correction $\boxed{182}$), 7
cubed (correction $\boxed{55}$), 8 cubed (correction $\boxed{-114}$). We have overshot,
so reduce the 11^3 to 10^3. The calculator immediately shows: $1\,729 =$
$12 \times 12 \times 12 + 1 \times 1 \times 1 = 10 \times 10 \times 10 + 8 \times 8 \times 8 \boxed{+\,217}$. Eight
cubed is too small, so we try changing the $8 \times 8 \times 8$ to 9s. We get
$1\,729 = 12 \times 12 \times 12 + 1 \times 1 \times 1 = 10 \times 10 \times 10 + 9 \times 9 \times 9$. No correction:
success!

A slower way would have been to delete the $8 \times 8 \times 8$ and start from
scratch with 10^3. The correction would be $\boxed{729}$, so the task then would be
to see if we can find a cube root of 729. $1^3 = 1$ is obviously far too small;
we could try $2^3, 3^3, 4^3 \ldots$ tediously one by one. Better still, we might notice
that $10^3 = 1\,000$ will be just a bit too big, and so try 9^3 straightaway.

16.6 Handling non-determinism

Consider the following interaction with Design II, where the user establishes
the not surprising $5 = 46 - 41$:

input	display
	$\diamond \boxed{0 = 0}$
5	$5 \diamond \boxed{= 0}$
=	$5 = \diamond \boxed{5}$
4	$5 = 4 \diamond \boxed{+1}$
6	$5 \boxed{+41} = 46 \diamond$
−	$5 = 46 - \diamond \boxed{41}$
4	$5 \boxed{+37} = 46 - 4 \diamond$
1	$5 = 46 - 41 \diamond$

Notice how the system's correction, successively, $\boxed{+1}$ on the right-hand side,
$\boxed{+41}$ on the left, $\boxed{41}$ on the right, $\boxed{+37}$ on the left, swaps from side to
side: there is no **display inertia**. It would have been possible to constrain
numerical corrections entirely to the right-hand side (in this case to, $\boxed{+1}$,

$\boxed{-41}$, $\boxed{41}$, $\boxed{-37}$) creating a far more stable inertial display. But if the user attempted to show $46 - 41 = 5$—the same equation but with the left and right sides exchanged—the system would have output different intermediate corrections.

The choice we took is that if the user submits an equation equating the expressions x and y but numerically $x \neq y$, then the equation is to be corrected by increasing the least side. If $x < y$, then '**x = y**' is corrected to display $x\boxed{+ N} = y$, where $N = y - x$; and the same equation with left and right sides exchanged is corrected with the *same* value: $y = x\boxed{+ N}$. This tactic makes = symmetric and the corrections $\boxed{+N}$ positive, at the expense of display inertia. This is a choice in favour of semantic inertia rather than display (representation) inertia. In retrospect, this was probably a bad, but easily rectified, decision: users seem to prefer display inertia—although the users who expressed the opinion were probably less sympathetically inclined to the underlying mathematics than I was (see Section 7.2).

Ignoring useless system corrections (such as, multiply by zero), there are a variety of valid responses which the system may output. For example, if the user inputs just =, the system could correct it by $\boxed{0} = \boxed{0}$ or $\boxed{1} = \boxed{1}$, or indeed by any equality. The system output is **non-deterministic**. Handling non-determinism is a major issue in user interface design (see Section 2.5) and this calculator provides a well-contained illustration.

A user might submit '$1728 = \times\times$' hoping to find cube roots. Rules *could* be devised to handle such specialized task requirements, but they would be complex and the user may be uncertain of their correct application for any but the predetermined tasks. For example, if one rule was that typing $\times$ over a system-computed number would instead find its square root (a quite plausible rule); the chances are that typing it twice would *not* help the user find a cube root, but would find the square root and two fourth roots: typing the second $\times$ over one of the originally computed square roots would find *that* root's root. The implied task domain problem again.

The present design handles these indeterminate cases by a simple rule: as a first guess on a value, try the right identity of the relevant operator. It may then be possible to balance the equation. Identities are zero for additive operands (including the decimal point), one for multiplicative operands. This rule is perhaps not as useful for profound tasks as it might be, but it usefully inhibits the user from inferring a more sophisticated rule which has not been implemented.

The choice of right identity increases display inertia assuming the user types from left to right (the right operand is the one usually being error-corrected); besides, $-$ and $/$ do not have left identities. For example, if the user has typed 3·14, typing any operator ($\times$, $+$, and so on) does not change the computed result: the display 3·14$\boxed{= 3\cdot 14}$ changes to 3·14 $\times \boxed{1 = 3\cdot 14}$ as the $\times$ is submitted.

Another view of the right identity correction is that it automatically chooses an 'interesting' example value. Thus, if zero had been chosen to correct for a missing multiplication operand, the user would know less about the equation.

I have found that some of my children enjoy using the calculator, but some are still at the stage that the numeral 11 can be confused for the expression $1 + 1$. If numbers were displayed as counters (for example, ::::::.) the confusion would be less likely to arise. Now, if × had a prime factoring rule, this would permit the user to experiment with so-called 'rectangle' numbers (non-primes which can be represented as $n \times m$ rectangles of counters) very easily. The present system, following the right identity rule, provides a much less interesting factorization, $12 = \boxed{12} \times \boxed{1} \times \boxed{1}$!

Non-determinism arises not just from error correction and alternative strategies for solving the equation, but also from numerical errors arising in computations. Lack of precision in the internal representation for numbers results in the unfortunate inequality that if the system computes x from a user input y (say, in an equation $x = 1/y$), it is unlikely to compute precisely y had the user input x. The four-function calculator *could* be exact if it worked internally in rationals, displayed where possible as integers or decimal fractions. This would be deterministic, but pedantic, and unfortunately would not be an appropriate solution if we enhanced the calculator with operations such as square root, exponentiation, trigonometric functions—for which rationals are not a model.

Rationals however suggest a useful approach, with equal opportunity for input and output, for overflow and division by zero: overflow can be represented by 0/0 and infinity by 1/0. Whether rationals are used internally or not, the calculator would then need no new notation (which would have to be explained to the user) for any overflow conditions.

Another approach to handling overflow is to error-correct the user's input more intrusively than we have so far been considering. For example, if the user submitted 1/0, it might be corrected by displaying $1/\boxed{(\!(0\boxed{+1})}$. Simpler for the designer, but harder for the user, would be to prohibit any input that could not be solved exactly: for instance, any arithmetic error results in the last character being deleted from the input—a rash idea that needs a guep to constrain its consequences.

In order to ensure that, for a particular expression, *however typed* there is precisely one display, to avoid the error correction, rounding errors and so on depending on the way in which the user built up the equation— to eliminate temporal non-determinism—analysis of the expression always starts from the user-typed characters *alone*. The previous error-correcting system output is discarded before the equation is processed. This provides the assurance: **delete** not only deletes a character but also undoes the *effect* of the deleted character. This law may be spelt out formally:

$$\forall \sigma \in \{+, -, \times, /, \cdot, =, 0, 1, 2, \ldots 9\}: \sigma \smile \text{delete has no effect.}$$

In PIE terms, the law can be expressed as $\forall x \in C': x \smile \text{delete} \sim \emptyset$, where C' is the set of commands C, less any editing commands; that is, $C' = C \setminus \{\leftarrow, \rightarrow, \texttt{delete}\}$. It is readily proved by induction (with the above property as basis) that n characters may be deleted by n `deletes`. A generalization of this property covers $\leftarrow$ and $\rightarrow$ commands, and demonstrates a very general undo capability.

16.7   Problems with the minus sign

Pascal had his problems with negative numbers (Section 6.1) and now we do too! The minus sign is a problem in the error-correcting calculator: the same symbol '$-$' means 'minus' (as in -3) and 'subtract' (as in $4 - 3$). As 'minus', the operator is unary; as 'subtract' the operator is binary; the error correction should be different in the two cases. If the user simply typed, say, -3, there is no way to infer whether he meant minus three or subtract three *from something*. In one case the system should supply a value (for example, to find 5 as a correction to 2 = - 3), in the other case it would try to force a correction at some other error point in the expression.

A realistic example will show that the minus/subtract sign is not a purely theoretical problem. Consider the classic Fahrenheit/Celsius conversion. Suppose that the error correction for - assumes it is minus (unary), and perhaps the user wants to obtain a conversion to degrees Kelvin. The user would be forced into typing a 'spurious' addition sign so that = + - 273·15 can be corrected appropriately: the addition is necessarily binary, and guides the error correction to treat +- as binary subtract. It would take a quite sophisticated user to realize this—indeed users do struggle at the seeming impasse when the calculator refuses to treat - as a binary subtract! They have to be taught the idiom that +- is binary subtract if they want the minuend calculated for them.

As usual, we see that the bandwidth to the computer is not great enough to disambiguate what the user is really trying to do. If the computer could listen to the user it would probably be able to hear him saying, 'but I meant ...' We could increase the bandwidth very easily by changing the representations, so that minus and subtract had different symbols: this would be providing a name for the curious convention +-. The problem is now transferred from use to training.

16.8   Generalizations of Design II

The previous section discussed the problems of the arbitrary system choices that can be made to eliminate non-determinism. The designer's choices are almost inevitably compromises. Instead, we might require the user, rather than the designer, to propose the choices to the system. This is equal opportunity again: we propose that the user should be able to input constraints on the strategy for handling non-determinism.

Box 16.2   Equal opportunity in other interfaces.

An entire chapter on the user interface to four-function calculators! Surely we could do something more interesting? Yes, *any* command-based interface that requires parsing might be improved by the techniques being explored in this chapter. Arithmetic just happens to have a simple grammar and we can explore the user interface issues very thoroughly.

Chess, for example, has a standard notation of the form ⟨*piece*⟩ ⟨*square*⟩ ⟨*to*⟩ ⟨*square*⟩ ⟨*details*⟩, where ⟨*piece*⟩ is one of K, Q, B, N, R or empty for a pawn; ⟨*square*⟩ is the coordinate of a square, such as d4; ⟨*to*⟩ is either − for a move or × for a capture; and ⟨*details*⟩ are comments, mostly to indicate mate or castling. This is even simpler than arithmetic, but (following chess conventions) we want the system to supply as much of the move details as possible. Thus the system could easily correct a1-b to $\boxed{\text{N}}$a1-b$\boxed{3}$; under certain circumstances it could also provide the 1, and when the user has no other alternative, it could provide the entire move which could be taken by the user as a default.

The same idea is a powerful way to develop syntax-directed editors. Syntax-directed editors are text editors that know the syntax of the text the user is submitting. Syntax-directed editors are generally intended for helping students write correct programs in Pascal or whatever syntax they are set up with. However useful it may be to remind the student of correct syntax, or whatever advantages there are in not wasting time making syntax errors, it is certainly the case that syntax-directed editors over-determine their users. Very often users want to develop programs that, for a large part of the time, are not syntactically correct but rather 'place holders' for pieces of correct program that the user has still to devise.

An equal opportunity syntax-directed editor designed along the lines of the equal opportunity calculator would first of all allow the user to submit any text, since in the worst case 'place holders' can always be commented out by the system to ensure that what remains is syntactically correct. More usefully, declarations of appropriate type might appear when the user introduces a new variable. Here is an example: `var i: integer;` for i := 1 `to` 10 `do` write`(`i`)`. This looks promising (especially if you imagine the colours!) and it would be a challenge to implement an interface that was fast enough to be usable (though note that many corrections, such as declarations, would initially be 'off screen', so could be computed lazily). Providing spaces and indentation—symbols of no great syntactic significance—is another possibility, and we then have the system prettyprinting dynamically.

Suppose the user has submitted '2 + ='. We have assumed the system will 'happen' to choose to correct with zero, and that for fairly tenuous reasons, which may or may not be helpful for the user's particular task in hand. More generally, imagine that the system is somehow able to display *all* valid corrections: the screen (being finite) would show some view on to this enumeration. By analogy with text editing, the user might be able to scroll to locate ranges of values that interest him, and to select a scaling factor as a way of concealing or folding unnecessary detail. In effect, the calculator becomes a generalized slide rule!

The user has to be able to specify an origin and a step-size or equivalent information, such as origin and scale, assuming a given screen size, for any system-computed value. If this information is specified by a command, then the calculator would recquire a mode; instead the pair might be represented by {*origin : scale*} or as an explicit set (for example, $\{3, 5, 7, 11, 13\}$). The existing error-correction mechanisms may be used as before ... now with recursive problems of non-determinism!

With this extension it is no longer always possible to perform the error-correction in the same line as the user's input. Instead we may imagine the user typing on the bottom line of the screen. If the user does not employ any of the new features, the calculator works precisely as before (**transparent power**). However, when the user enters a set or range of values, the upper region of the screen is filled with error-corrected expressions with system-computed output. Obviously, this requires a much more sophisticated implementation—for example, consider the user requesting a view of *natural number* Celsius/Fahrenheit conversions (by $32 + 9/5 \times \{1 : 1\} = \{1 : 1\}$).

The dialogue style used in the equal opportunity calculator is appropriate for a wide range of applications (see Box 16.2). The use of colour (or of typographical font) and the overwriting of error-correcting system-output is a useful style to consider for command processors and syntax-directed editors. The usual arguments for and against syntax-directed editing apply also to Design II: naïve users may be greatly helped, but expert users may find the error-correction distracting. It should be noted, however, that the error-correction is not prescriptive and can be in a different colour: it is less distracting than in conventional syntax-directed systems. Indeed, an experienced user might customize his interface so that the error-correction was displayed in background colour so it would not be visible—his user interface would be otherwise unaffected and would appear like a conventional editor.

16.9   Alternative approaches

Consider the user working on imperial/metric conversions. For converting between inches and centimetres, the relevant factor is $2 \cdot 54$. Suppose the user has submitted $2 \cdot 54 \times = $. The two 'slots' allow the user to convert inches to centimetres, or to convert centimetres to inches. The equation can be reused in a variety of ways (see also the Fahrenheit/Celsius examples above), and this is one of the powerful spin-offs of the equal opportunity design. In practical terms it means that the user can experiment, and come to feel 'at home' with whatever equation he is using. But we ought to briefly examine alternative approaches for command reuse, to see whether this advantage could have been gained by a route with other spin-offs that we might have found more desirable.

16.9.1 Undo and redo

Command redo obviously provides a powerful and general mechanism for reuse. The advantage of redo is that it is integrated into a view of interaction (for example, *US&R*) that can be provided with a great variety of user interfaces. It is non-specific and allows users to redo the history of their submissions, when what they probably want is to be able to redo the equations. Redo was described fully in Chapter 12 and needs no further space here.

16.9.2 Macro expansion

If a particular equation is to be reused several times, the user is likely to chunk it. So the interface ought to provide a mechanism to directly support the chunking. **Macro processing** is the most common approach.

Any expression submitted by the user can be named. Thereafter, the user can just submit the name. The name denotes a **macro**, and the system **expands** the macro into its **body**, the text (or other command sequence) provided in the definition.

The pleasant thing about macro processors over redo is that the user can select the macro name to suit his requirements, for instance, to forge a mnemonic association between the name and the body. As a simple example, suppose the keyboard has a **#** symbol. A user might want to define this as subtract to overcome a silly problem in the user interface. This is easily done: the basic sequence would be 'define # as + - end', though details vary from system to system.

The symbols **define**, **as**, **end** may be single keystrokes, they may be spelt out (as here) so that they can be seen more readily, or they may be actions taken with a menu-based interface. In fact, the symbol **as** is superfluous if the macro processor only permits the definition of single keys, so-called **soft keys**.

Macro processors are prime examples of **interface accelerators**: techniques that extend the information bandwidth of the user interface and therefore make systems easier to use. Suppose the user wants to send a certain message several times to the computer. Either the designer can anticipate this, and supply some easy means for submitting the message when it is relevant in the course of a dialogue (for example, it might be a single keystroke), or the designer is unable to anticipate it. This is the more conservative case: if the designer cannot anticipate the message, then when the user submits it, it carries *more* information. The macro language now comes into its own, for it allows the user to anticipate the messages *he* will most frequently want to use in the future. He can choose messages without reference to the designer.

Macro processing presents the same tradeoff as redo: it is a general-purpose mechanism, applicable almost everywhere and therefore not *specially* applicable to equation reuse (or reusing whatever, when we look further than calculators). This non-specificity of macro processing is its greatest problem:

▷ Errors and other output may occur inside the body of a macro. How should the equal opportunity calculator handle macros with bodies like '=2×('?

▷ Macros can affect the syntax and algebraic laws of the user interface. If we define x as $3+4$ then funny things happen if we write x × 2. Should it be taken as 11 or 14, or as an error? This problem can be avoided by evaluating macro bodies as soon as they are defined, and then treating macro names syntactically like numbers—but this destroys the normal application independence of macro processing, which is the macro processor's main attraction for the designer.

So there is a question when the application should evaluate the bodies of macros. If the macro processor is recursive (so that macro bodies can contain macro names), then there is also a question when the macro processor itself should evaluate the bodies of macros and their parameters. Lazy and eager evaluation are but two possibilities, and both are really too obscure for interactive applications of macro processors. Macro processors usually come with **quotation** mechanisms that delay evaluation one or more stages. Quotation is a *very* complex issue: it is important to design quotation mechanisms well.

In summary, macro processors are easy to implement, they can easily be made to satisfy the design principle 'easy to do simple things, yet make complex things possible' (with recursion and conditionals they are Turing Complete)—yet they contain all sorts of pitfalls and can be the source of endless confusion. Macro processors are of special interest because they are particularly easy to implement and very general, yet they introduce all manner of obscure syntactic and quotation problems of their own.

16.9.3   Predictive calculators

If the designer can anticipate the detailed requirements of the user, then particular features can be built in. If not, then a macro processor can be provided for the user to customize his own features. This simple dichotomy leaves the computer out.

Suppose an intelligent helper is looking over the user's shoulder as problems are submitted to the calculator. If the user is doing anything at all repetitive, the helper will soon be able to predict what the user is going to do next, and could even type to save the user the trouble, leaving anything that the helper cannot predict to be typed by the user. Now all we have to suppose is that the helper is an integral part of the calculator's user interface. This is the standard ruse, introduced in Chapter 1, of designing abstractly.

Here is an example of a predictive calculator being used to calculate values of xe^{1-x} for x equal to $1, 2, 3, \ldots$ (the example is adapted from Witten and Cleary, 1986). The user first calculates xe^{1-x} for $x = 1$. The way this calculator works, we submit 1 first, clear the memory (MC), then add 1 to the memory (M+=). Then we change the sign of x (+/- key), then add one, then press =. This calculates the exponent $1 - x$. Press exp to calculate e^{1-x}. Next press × to multiply by the stored value of x, recovered by the MR key. Finally, pressing = completes the calculation: in all, 1 MC M+= +/- + 1 exp × MR =.

For $x = 2$, the user *starts* to submit '2 MC M+= +/- + 1 exp × MR =', but after a few keystrokes the predictive calculator guesses what is coming, shown here boxed: 2 MC M+= $\boxed{\text{+/- +}}$ 1 $\boxed{\text{exp × MR =}}$.

So the user can calculate $2e^{1-2}$ in only four keystrokes instead of ten. If now the user calculates $3e^{1-3}$, the calculator will not be thrown by the 3 being different from 2, but will catch on that the 1 is a constant: 3 $\boxed{\text{MC M+= +/- + 1 exp × MR =}}$.

Subsequently, the user just types 4, 5, and so on, calculating successive values of the formula. A more powerful system could soon recognize that 1, 2, 3, 4, were predictable.

At first, the calculator may make bad predictions. Two features are essential to ameliorate this: there must be an undo command, to take back a prediction, and there must be a single-step mode, whereby the calculator's predictions are worked through slowly enough so that the user can convince himself that the right thing is going on. Once the user is satisfied that the calculator has the right behaviour, it can be changed to a quick mode to perform all the predictive steps at once. The calculator will then only stop to request new input values.

It may seem that the predictive calculator is more complex than a macro processor extension to a calculator (though the undo and single-stepping features would be useful for a macro processor too). The comparison is not that simple, however, since even the prediction shown here permitted parameters (for example, to allow the 1 in xe^{1-x} to be varied). Macro parameter mechanisms are a matter of quotation: a topic far more complex (see Section 16.9.2) than we are prepared to broach!

Box 16.3   Did You Know?

David Owen (1986) has suggested a system called **Did You Know**, (**DYK**). The gist of the idea is for the system to come up with helpful remarks like, 'Did you know that typing 'xp' transposes characters?' Even though Owen's system comes up with such remarks at random, users find it helpful.

Now, how do you arrange for the DYK system to tell the user something he did *not* know?

One possibility would be for the DYK system to compare several users. It might be able to come up with remarks like, 'Most people use 'xp' but you don't. It transposes characters. If you want to know more, why not ask Isaac, he uses it most.'

Another possibility would be to build a predictive model of all users (for example, a Markov model). Then the DYK system could come up with remarks like, 'You've just typed 'thier'. Most people would now do 'xp'.' Seen like this, DYK is a generalization of the reactive keyboard described in Section 16.9.4.

We normally think of system evaluation being used to help the designer, for instance, to guide iterative design: in the idea discussed here the user has a feature to help evaluate his own performance, in this case with respect to 'standard' behaviour. Evaluation can be used to help users directly. Other forms of self-evaluation (for example, typing speed scores) may help motivate the user to improve his skills.

16.9.4   General predictive systems

The predictive calculator and our equal opportunity calculator (which can be thought of as a syntax-driven predictive calculator: it predicts—and ensures—that the user will submit a well-formed arithmetic expression) both know about the user's problem domain. It is also possible to build predictive user interfaces that have no prior domain-specific knowledge. Their advantage is that the designer does not have to worry about specific details of the task: the designer can attack more abstract (and presumably more fundamental) design issues to do with prediction generally without being diverted with features to solve very specific, and possibly specious, problems. On the other hand, without specific details of the task built in by the designer (like syntactical or semantic constraints), there will be some 'obvious' things that the user expects the system to predict which it has not yet learnt, and perhaps will never be able to. We will look at more tradeoffs after giving an example.

One such general predictive user interface is the **reactive keyboard** (Darragh, 1988). As the user types, the system builds a Markov model of the text being typed. This model is used to predict probable continuations on from where the user has got to.

If I was just typing this sentence, and had got to *here*, the computer might display the following (note that the predictions need not be single words):

```
...   and had got to here  │ is a
                           │ are
                           │ the
                           │ must
                           │ so
                           │ ⋮
```

The user could move the cursor to some item, `is a`, `are` ... and select it. Alternatively, if the cursor was placed *within* an item, say, on the r of `are`, the computer would insert the prefix ('ar' in this case, so the user could continue typing *ose* or whatever).

To be successful such a system should be built on two principles:

▷ The user can operate the interface as if the predictor was not there.

▷ If necessary, the interface can be operated from the predictor alone.

The first principle requires that the prediction is discretionary—the user may always ignore it, and just continue typing. The menu must certainly be movable so that the user can 'see under it'. The second principle requires this interface to make at least one prediction per character of the alphabet. If there are going to be many predictions (at least 60 or so), then steps should be taken to control the visible complexity of the interface, such as only displaying the five most probable predictions, and revealing the others if the user starts to search for them (perhaps by using a scrollable menu).

Although such interfaces can save a considerable amount of user input, especially for routine highly structured tasks like writing thankyou letters, they do have their problems:

▷ The predictions (of course!) can only be based on the past analysis of the user's work. The predictions are therefore likely to be unimaginative: a predictive interface may not be very useful for authors writing a novel or working on some other essentially imaginative task.

▷ The screen gets cluttered, yet the user may need to view the screen properly to help make a sensible choice. The menu (or whatever interaction technique is used) must be movable or speech based.

▷ The system is only as useful as the specificity of its predictions (otherwise you may as well use a 100 000 word dictionary!) but this means that the prediction set must be continually changing. There is a conflict, then, with the principle of display inertia, that if the screen does *not* change the user can internalize some of it and hence use the system more easily without relying on continual re-reading.

▷ There is a difficult tradeoff between adaptive systems, that continually update their model so as to make the 'best' predictions, against non-adaptive systems that have a fixed model. Fixed models may make obsolete predictions, but the user has a fair chance of memorizing their predictive strategy. That is, a simple non-adaptive model can be internalized by the user, and perhaps can be used without too detailed attention to the screen. In contrast, an adaptive model generally makes different predictions in superficially the same circumstances, and the user would always have to read the screen carefully.

▷ Although a predictor has potentially greatest benefit for a handicapped typist, the decision whether to continue typing or to select a prediction may interfere with the user keeping in mind what to type. If it takes an entire day to type five words, remembering what you are going to type for 12 hours is hard enough without having to make additional decisions required by the predictor.

▷ Like all supportive systems, a decision must be made about the tradeoff between supporting the user at a particular level of development, and facilitating the user's personal development to go beyond that level. A predictive system that had been trained on an English dictionary would not much help its user learn how to spell, though it might encourage him to write better stories. The user may be better motivated to learn letter formation and word spelling having first very easily completed stories using a predictive word processor (without computers, things have to be done in the other order)—the tradeoffs are very complex.

Notice how predictive systems are necessarily equal opportunity. The system's prediction (its output) is intended to be selected by the user for the user's next input.

16.10   Conclusions

In many ways, the new calculator is rather like a teacher looking over the user's shoulder, continually making the best possible correction to the user's sums. The user can manipulate sums in any way whatsoever without restriction. Nothing is ever 'wrong' but can always be rescued to make an interesting and valid sum. It is ideal for teaching children, and perhaps makes a contribution to the contentious debate about calculators in schoolrooms. The computer is seen to be a little less intrusive and critical than a human teacher. Perhaps this is the best possible sort of calculator?

The equal opportunity calculator is interesting because the user's conceptual model is **declarative**: what is displayed is *always* a correct equation (a guep that can be told the user). The user may enter equations or fragments of equations using the standard keys, and may edit them at will; always the display will show a correct result, and for the same equation, the same result. However, for the user to have an operational ('how it works') understanding of the calculator is almost prohibited by the sheer complexity of it. This is in contrast to conventional calculators (infix or otherwise) which, by their operational simplicity, encourage the user to devise an operational interpretation (or **conceptual model**): if the user's understanding is incomplete, confusion, error or inefficient use may ensue. Maybe no opportunity for such confusion can arise with Design II? Clearly there is scope for empirical studies.

The calculator illustrates several gueps in a user interface. The design is modeless and WYSIWYG.

Chapter 17

Good by design

The rule is, "Simple things should be simple; complex things should be possible". One of the ways to design a simple user interface that can really do things is to take the hardest tasks imaginable and try to create convincing scenarios of how they might be done at all. Then the simplest tasks must be considered in the light of the structures postulated for the most complex. The simplest must rule! Force the interaction structures to do *both* without making the simplest and most-done tasks suffer.

Alan Kay

Design requires first an inventive or creative step, followed by filtering—so that the invention is polished into something that is feasible. The frameworks we have examined up to this point allow designers to criticize, and may indirectly suggest new ideas (for example, equal opportunity; principle of correspondence; and so on), but now it is time to try to be more systematic about the creative side of design.

Almost all existing methods for the design of computer systems presuppose people know what they want, and often that what they want is an unchanging constant. If the programmer knows exactly what he is supposed to be programming, there are various methods that enable him to produce a program, or to know he is unable to progress to a working system—because of the inconsistency or complexity of the problem or of limitations in the resources (including his own brain) available to him. The bulk of this book has tried to make this part of interactive systems design more open to deliberate analysis and more scientific appraisal.

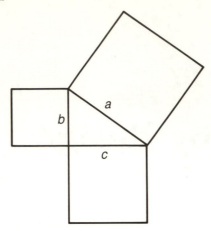

Figure 17.1   Theorem of Pythagoras.

17.1   Generalize, specialize, explain

The design method used for the calculator (Chapter 16) can be summarized by a three-step process: generalize, specialize, explain. This is a very productive approach, which will be first illustrated by departing entirely from interactive systems to a proof of the Theorem of Pythagoras. Apart from the story about Sam in Chapter 6 there is no relevance to user interface design in geometry *per se*. That is the point: the generalize, specialize, explain approach is *very general*.

The problem is to 'design' a proof for Pythagoras, to show that the square on the hypotenuse of a right-angled triangle has area equal to the sum of the areas of the squares on the other two sides. We may express the problem in algebra: if the squares have sides a, b, c, we want to find a proof that $a^2 = b^2 + c^2$. Figure 17.1 shows the standard problem.

The first step is to see if we can *generalize* the problem.[1] Indeed we can. We might choose some shape other than a right triangle. Figure 17.2 has used shark fins. However, we know that the areas of similar figures are proportional to the squares of given sides or dimensions, a fact proved in Euclid's Elements. With this knowledge, an obvious generalization is to consider the proof that the area of a figure on the hypotenuse is equal to the area of similar figures constructed on the other two sides. It is clear that a proof of this more general theorem will satisfy our requirement for a proof of Pythagoras as a special case. In algebraic terms, we have changed our problem to finding a proof for $\lambda a^2 = \lambda b^2 + \lambda c^2$, where λ is determined by our choice of figure.

---

[1] The rather elegant proof is due to Naber, a Dutch maths teacher who lived at the turn of the century. It relies on the method Hippocrates employed to perform quadrature of a lunule (see Chapter 6) used in Euclid's Elements. The interesting form of presentation given here is due to Pólya (1948a).

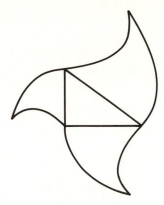

Figure 17.2   Generalized Theorem of Pythagoras.

But we have surely got ourselves a far more complex problem! The next step is to search for a specialization of our generalized problem. Can we think of a particular figure that will make our task easier? Again, in this case, we can. A heuristic we may use at this point is to try to eliminate spurious information that we have introduced: the general figure has introduced an extra degree of freedom into the proof. We can *specialize* our proof by fixing this freedom. Our diagram has two shapes: a right triangle, and three similar figures. Since their shape is arbitrary— in consequence of the deliberate generalization—we can specialize them, in particular, to be similar to the original right triangle. The effect of this is to fix a particular value for λ, now depending only on an angle in the right triangle.

So, construct similar right triangles on their hypotenuse on the three sides of the given triangle, which is a straightforward exercise. Now the area of the triangle so constructed on the hypotenuse is equal to the area of the given triangle, in fact, they are congruent. We would normally have constructed the triangles on the *outside* of the given triangle: if instead we construct the triangles internally it is clear that their combined area is equal to the given triangle (Figure 17.3).

We have now finished the proof and its explanation. Note that constructing the triangles *internally* is simply a matter of dropping a perpendicular to the hypotenuse; indeed we might have chosen similar triangles on the basis that they would be the easiest examples to construct!

In summary, we have a problem (concerning the area of certain squares), which we generalized (to areas of arbitrary shape). We were then free to fix this shape to simplify the rest of the design (of the proof).

Review

We started this book by describing the advantages of abstraction. We were going to use the words, *user*, *computer* and *designer* abstractly. That is,

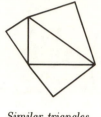

Similar triangles,   *Similar triangles,*
constructed externally   *constructed internally*

Figure 17.3   Specialized Theorem of Pythagoras.

these words were being used in as general a way as possible—the rest of the book then specialized them for particular purposes, to bring out certain features that we wanted to explain.

We talked about science in the most general way (Chapter 9), then specialized to user interface design principles (Chapter 10) and then specialized again to specific principles (for example, Chapter 11). Or again (in Chapter 12) undo started out as a special purpose feature—to undo the last command—but ended up as a way of discussing far more general issues such as adaptive and programmable user interfaces. Chapter 13 was able to formalize the most general idea that arose from undo, the idea of history as being a tangible, first-class thing.

Equal opportunity (Chapter 15) is an excellent example of using generalization as a deliberate design heuristic. Interactive systems are often designed by *first* deciding on the nature of their required inputs and outputs. Of course this is making a specialization—and one that is possibly premature, particularly for highly interactive systems. It is generally necessary to distinguish between the user's input to the computer and the computer's output to the user, but the point is that designers often make these distinctions too early in the design process and therefore fail to perceive various reasonable, and often powerful, possibilities. Equal opportunity suggests doing the specialization to input/output commitments *second*.

In the calculator example (of Chapter 16), we generalized from conventional calculator interfaces guided by equal opportunity, then specialized to eliminate the variables and other complexities introduced in the generalization stage.

There are three steps: generalize, specialize *and* explain. In all our examples the explanation has been part of the process. This book contains various tangled routes of generalization $\Longrightarrow$ specialization, and is itself the explanation. In interactive systems design—rather than in books about it— the explanation can take several forms. It may be material solely for the

Box 17.1   Generalizing hardware.

The view a computer has of its user is of a one-fingered typist (and with a finger that is either pressing or not pressing—no analogue input), with a narrow field of vision with poor acuity, and ears that can only detect the crudest of monophonic beeps. But we really know that humans are much more capable than this! Why not generalize user interfaces to, for instance, allow users to exploit both hands? Why not have two mice? Why not allow users to exert pressure to get different effects, like musicians do routinely? Even cars make use of analogue input from feet and hands.

Why not make more exciting sounds in stereo? What sort of sounds could be devised so that a blind user could use a WIMP system? Different sounds could be made (coming from different directions) as the cursor is moved from region to region. And several sounds can be made simultaneously for overlapping regions; or a sound for menus, with supplementary sounds as the mouse moves over various menu items. If you can devise that for blind people, why not provide the sound for sighted people too? Maybe the extra redundancy would reduce error; it would certainly facilitate many tasks such as copy typing where the user cannot watch the screen all the time.

internal use of the design team; it may be explanation negotiated with the users; there must be explanation[2] for the user—the explanation is necessary, but it need not be supplied explicitly.

All three parties, user, computer and designer need explanation. The user needs explanation so that he knows how to use the system. The computer needs explanation—usually called program—so that it knows how to 'use' the user. The designer needs explanation so that he can think clearly.

The next three sections look at each of the steps (G $\Rightarrow$ S $\Rightarrow$ E) of the method in turn.

17.2   Generalizing designs

In user interface design we are faced with rapidly changing technological options to fit rapidly changing user needs; we also have the most plastic of all technologies to hand. An interesting point is that generalizing in non-programmable technologies often leads to complexity (consider, for instance, swing-wing aircraft) that may contribute to failure, whereas in computer

---

[2] Recall Section 1.2: **explanation** can mean any way to inform the user: it may be written documentation, on-line help, weekend training courses, or it may be explanation based on the user's world knowledge.

science generalizing may lead to simplifications. Turing Complete systems can be very simple (and in a sense, nothing can be more general!), as witness Turing Machines themselves.

Generalization is an initial heuristic for design. On the one hand it is a pervasive but implicit technique—'programmable' is almost synonymous—and hardly merits discussion. But once recognized it may be systematically and explicitly exploited.

Generalization is about spotting design features that share aspects in common, and replacing them with that common feature. (If the features are in the machine and virtual machine, then generality leads to metacircularity.) The generalized feature can be used in different ways, providing each of the original features as special cases. Successful generalization will provide new features. In programming, the most obvious way to implement a generalization is to think of a suitable procedure that can be used in different parts of a program. Different parameters to the procedure get it to do different things, and what it does is more general than any of them. That's the idea, but there are clearly good and bad ways of going about it.

A generalization of a complete system will contain several functions, themselves generalizations of various features. Drawing from Gerrit von Blaauw's design principles for the IBM/360 architecture, good generalizations should be:

▷ **Consistent**: A good generalization is consistent.

▷ **Orthogonal**: Component functions of a generalization are independent.

▷ **Appropriate**: Only essential functions are provided.

▷ **Parsimonious**: Each function has a single form.

▷ **Transparent**: The way the generalization works should not be visible to the user.

▷ **Powerful**: Each function (despite the limitations given above) should do as much as possible.

▷ **Open-ended**: Freedom should be provided to implement new functions; there should be ways to combine functions. Whether the freedom can be appreciated by designer or user is another question, and depends on the level of generalization—is it a generalization of the user interface customization facilities?

▷ **Complete**: The generalizations provided should do the job.

The Russian Dmitri Ivanovich Mendeleev discovered the Periodic Table by trying to explain chemical patterns to children. He had made a card game he called Patience. Each card represented an element and so the cards could be arranged in families, rather like the suits of a conventional pack of cards but just more of them. But there were gaps in the table, for in the 1870s not all the elements were known. Mendeleev had considerable insight to recognize that the problem, gaps in his game, was caused by as-yet undiscovered elements! He became famous for predicting the properties of several elements with great precision many years before they were discovered. Here we have the nice analogy: Mendeleev takes the known elements (*qua* functions) and tries to generalize them, into families that share chemical properties. His generalization then exposed holes in what was known about the 'design' of nature. From the perspective of the generalize, specialize, explain scheme it is very interesting, too, that Mendeleev made his breakthrough because he was trying to explain chemistry to children.

Mendeleev's Periodic Table splits elements sharing the same general properties into columns, that is, the columns represent certain chemical functionality. Similarly a good way to analyse and generalize from an interactive systems design is to construct a matrix of features and their interaction with each other. Gaps indicate omissions, and patterns of connections possibly indicate common features that can be factored out.

17.2.1 Generalized commitment

If we take the 'synthetic science = design' analogy (Section 9.1), we might consider each design as an experiment, indeed, set up to be falsified by empirical evidence in its use. That is not satisfactory for designs that really have to be used, rather than designs made in the course of a research programme and not intended for immediate use. Thus design as synthetic science suggests the designer should be committed to the *means* by which he designs; whereas pressurized, real design suggests the designer should be committed rather to the *end* result. There are, in fact, three basic sorts of design commitments:

▷ **Precommitment**: Design for the real world is too complex. It is not possible to consider every option, even if we assumed we knew all the facts and relationships between them and could be perfectly rational. In precommitment, the designer simplifies his problem by arbitrarily fixing some parts of the design: what is left over he is more likely to be able to plan around optimally. Precommitment is a very general concept: although we can assume a designer can program, he will precommit to a given programming system, simply because that saves him the trouble of designing it himself—he wants to concentrate on other issues, even though he might have been able to do a better job, given enough time, if the entire programming system were rewritten to suit his project better.

▷ **Delaying commitment**: Designs are never quite right, so it would be wrong to have design ideas fixed too soon. Delaying commitments means leaving design decisions as late as possible, perhaps even providing features for the user to customize the system for himself. Programmable systems, of course, enable much design commitment to be delayed indefinitely: but then the difficulties of programming may be insurmountable for those users who would rather have adopted a design based on a precommitment strategy. (Delaying commitment was discussed more fully in Section 8.6.)

▷ **Postcommitment**: Designing computer systems is so difficult that the designer is never quite sure what sort of product he will end up with. With postcommitment to design, the designer builds the best system he can, and *then* finds out who wants to use it and for what. Postcommitment is probably the most common approach to design: a designer solves a narrowly defined problem (perhaps modifying the initial problem against implementation constraints) and then advertises his solution (see Box 8.4).

Each strategy may be used on the *small scale*, for isolated aspects of a design; or on the *large scale*, as the overall approach to a design. Importantly, the strategies may be applied once-off or iteratively. As usual the same feature may be viewed from different perspectives as an example of any strategy. Thus a macro processor provides the user with features for precommitment: users can anticipate what they want to do in the future, and commit certain macros for pursuing these goals; or the designer provides a macro processor so that he need not commit the design to a particular command structure; or, a general-purpose macro processor is developed independently and may be adopted by a user for helping with his particular tasks. This equivalence between the strategies can be explained by treating each as an alternative computational approach to running design 'programs'. The output of each program is a design, but the way the program was conceived was different in each case. Precommitment corresponds to eager evaluation; delaying commitment to lazy evaluation; and postcommitment to non-deterministic evaluation (oracle-driven). And since each strategy is a general-purpose computational strategy it may be employed by people: indeed each strategy corresponds with a personality trait (Section 8.5).

17.3 Specializing designs

Butler Lampson advises, 'Don't generalize; generalizations are usually wrong'. That is the point: we generalize our *ideas* as much as possible, but because we cannot implement what we think in its most general form, we next must specialize to something that is feasible and can be done properly.

Specialization is the outcome of a decision, a commitment, to target a generalized idea towards a more particular or achievable goal. Designers

---

Box 17.2   The Inventor's Paradox.

Designing for the general case may often be easier than designing for specific cases. There is a paradox here: Pólya's **Inventor's Paradox** (Pólya, 1948b) that deliberate attempts to generalize may have more chance of success. For example, try showing that $1+2+3+\cdots+10\,000 = 50\,005\,000$ by doing the arithmetic. It is much easier to prove the parametric $1 + 2 + 3 + \cdots + k = k(k + 1)/2$ and then specialize it by setting $k = 10\,000$. This method, which requires solving a more general problem, is easier than doing 9 999 sums! Experience is needed to choose a parametrization appropriate to the problem. In this case it would have been counter-productive to parametrize by the exponent $(1^k + 2^k + 3^k + \cdots + 10\,000^k)$ or by operator. Similar difficult choices arise when parametrizing programs and user interfaces.

---

almost always make specializations from imperfect information and often too early in the design cycle. The earlier specializations are made the easier the rest of the design will be, because it is more focused and its problems are more closely defined. When design commitments are more accidental than deliberate, the chances of easy software development, of iterative design, at a later stage are greatly reduced. Wherever possible, then, we wish to postpone specialization as long as is practical, in case it becomes too specialized and therefore too difficult to generalize.

> Perfection is reached, not when there is no longer anything to add, but when there is no longer anything to take away.
>
> *Antoine de Saint-Exupéry*

17.3.1   Why are designs over-specialized?

Generalization is a basically mental activity: if the generalization is really general it will be too hard to implement! There is a temptation to specialize too soon, or to specialize too much. Premature specialization reduces opportunities for iterative design, and generally results in an investment in design that cannot be revoked. The designer quickly confuses *specialization*, which is merely a method, with *commitment* which is an attitude as well. We can always revoke a premature specialization in principle, but the undoing of the commitments it represents may not be so easy.

The most common 'technique' for failing to delay specialization is deciding what functions to provide in a system by deciding how we want to express those functions. If it turns out that the chosen notation

---

Box 17.3   What is design?

Design is a process of discovering and transforming what has to be done into something that does it. We do not need to think that the description or specification remains fixed throughout this process, unaffected by insights that arise throughout the design process: certainly this would not be typical in interactive systems design. In user interface design the result is invariably a computer program, but the fact that we may eventually need a program should not blind us to design methods that seem far away from programming. Some people warn, 'separate design from implementation'. Probably they are concentrating too much on the final program. This warning seems to forget the rich ideas that computing science can input to the generalization stage of design (see, for instance, Chapter 4).

We can view the design process as searching for an acceptable design in an indefinitely large design space. There are three problems in searching for a good design:

▷ we may not search very effectively;

▷ we may not recognize a good design when one is found;

▷ we may mistakenly take a bad design for a better one.

The first problem is caused in part by data and resource limitations: the lack of information about the structure of the design space, its size (the sheer clerical and mental overhead of keeping track of decisions that may have to be revised) and psychological issues—particularly the designer's natural tendency to prefer fixing 'reasonable' design decisions as early as possible so that he can accelerate depth-first search (and concentrate on specific rather than abstract design problems). Also the more effort that is expended after any design decision has been made the more likely the designer will become fixated on it, even when he is able to keep track of its alternatives.

(command language, programming language, and so on) cannot express certain functions, then of course the implementation need not provide any support for those functions. Thus when a change to the design is required later (for example, adding a certain operation that had been omitted) it will come as a complete surprise; it will be awkward to implement because the syntax (or lexical vocabulary) is too inflexible.

A very common example is where system functions are mapped onto single-letter names (or equivalently, we could say, onto menu entries); later, the commitment to this lexical form leads to embarrassment when the system is further extended and function names conflict or become overloaded. Many terminals and printing devices suffer from the same problem: their designs provide for (are committed to) a fixed set of features, such as selecting certain display styles, moving the printing position, and so on. If an application requires something slightly different from the designer's anticipated device, nothing may be possible. This is an acute problem with terminals: they provide so many features, but there is no way of combining the features to make new features. Hence micro-computers are supplanting terminals because they can be programmed; yet old habits die hard—many more modern windowing systems emulate early display terminals!

Social, managerial and commercial pressures are perhaps the most common cause of premature specialization and avoidable commitments. If a project has to be completed to a tight schedule, careful design may be sacrificed for manifest short-term productivity. What should have been prototypes are committed and sold as products.

17.3.2 Good specialization

Some of the best examples of good specialization can be seen in the design of certain programming languages. Niklaus Wirth's G $\Rightarrow$ S $\Rightarrow$ E sequence ending in Pascal,

$$\text{Algol 60} \quad \overset{generalize}{\Longrightarrow} \quad \text{Algol 68} \quad \overset{specialize}{\Longrightarrow} \quad \text{Pascal}$$

for example, started with the recognition of the contrast between the success of Algol 60 and its take-up. It was a neat language, but not widely adopted. A committee met to design its successor, and (to cut a long story very short), culminated in Algol 68, a rather complex language. Algol 68 represented the outcome of the generalization phase, indeed it was too complex for immediate implementation. Wirth developed a specialization, developing from the good ideas of Algol 68 but restricted to something that could be implemented by students. The result was Pascal. Pascal has been enormously successful, precisely because it is not too complex (its manual is clear and brief), and lends itself to efficient implementations. Pascal, too, has more recently been generalized and specialized to Modula, Modula-2 and Oberon—languages that can be seen as specialized generalizations of Pascal to multiprogramming.

It is interesting to note that Algol 68 was designed by a team, whereas Pascal—an extremely successful language—was the work of one man. If a single designer controls the G $\Rightarrow$ S $\Rightarrow$ E process, this forces tradeoffs. The result is never too complex to do properly. Another explanation of the complexity of Algol 68 and other committee designs is that committees, perhaps more easily than individuals, confuse many features for generality. Also note the timescale: *years* covered in the 'iterative design' cycle ending in Pascal.

Many further examples can be taken from programming language design. For example: the use of a specialized form of unification in Prolog; the development of Scheme from LISP; the generality of Apl; the development of UNIX from Multics; the development of Cedar from Mesa. Programming languages are however far simpler than most user interfaces!

Box 17.4   Hacking designs.

Hacking is hard to define: hacked systems generally work sooner but perhaps are not so easily generalized. 'Hacking' is not a pejorative term— it is often very important to find particular solutions rapidly, to satisfice in design. A user interface may be hacked simply as a valid means to get a job done, and where getting the task completed overrides any worries about future maintenance of the system or aesthetic worries on the way in which the job is performed. We would not expect a user to find a hacked interface particularly reliable or easy to use: but *having* something that can be used to do a good-enough job may be sufficient.

It is profound that many apparently simple ideas turn out to be extremely hard to implement properly, especially when their implementation is based on or uses existing software. Very often existing software makes distinctions that are incompatible with the new ideas, or it does not make distinctions that the new ideas require. Rather than rebuild the existing system (which means discarding a large investment) the original idea ends up being only partly implemented, that is hacked, because it is just too expensive and time consuming to fix the assumptions throughout the existing software.

We will end this section on specialization by considering just two interactive systems examples.

Menus

Pop-up menus are menus that appear where the cursor is. If a menu entry in turn brings up another menu in the hierarchy, that too 'pops up' adjacent to the entry (in fact, where the cursor is if it is used to select menu entries). This is a nice, general idea. The problem is that as the user moves the cursor about on the screen, the system needs to change the display so that it shows the corresponding menus *and* all the menus from the top-level selection. This is quite a tricky design task, and can be difficult to use. It is perhaps easier to specialize to a **pull-down** menu style. Here the top-level menu is permanently displayed in a **menu bar**, usually along the top of the screen, and sub-menus are 'pulled down' from it. This specialization will have problems with many levels of menus, but if the interface only needs two or three levels, we have a specialization that can be implemented much more thoroughly and will be easier to use than a pop-up menu. See Figure 17.4, which shows both pop-up and pull-down menus being used to select the address style for use with headed note paper.

Figure 17.4 does not show how the styles of menu behave as the user moves the cursor; both are quite difficult to describe in a book! Briefly, the selected entry in pop-up menus moves in two dimensions as the cursor is

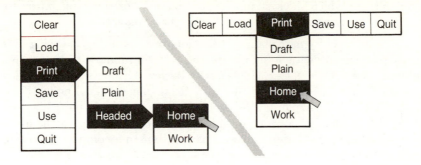

Figure 17.4   Pop-up and pull-down menus compared.

moved; in the pull-down menu it only moves vertically. Note that the pop-up menu can be 'popped up' anywhere on the screen, but the pull-down menu bar is always displayed at the top of the screen (thus always showing the user what is currently possible). The pull-down menu is much simpler, but more restricted in the amount of functionality it can reasonably support. (Various combinations are possible, for example, a pull-down menu with pop-up entries.)

Undo

We want undo to be able to undo anything: this is the general case. As this is frequently too difficult to implement, we can specialize to flip-undo or, better, to truncate* strategies (see Chapter 12). The user will almost always be better off with a correctly implemented and well-explained specialized form of undo, than a poorly implemented 'general' undo with *ad hoc* exceptions.

17.4   Explaining designs

To recapitulate: a design (whether a design on paper or a working prototype) must be scrutinized, and potential principles identified. A generalized design is then considered that closes these principles. The generalized design has been generalized so that there are no or very few exceptions. Naturally, a perfectly generalized system might be impossible to implement! So the generalized design is specialized to something more realistic. The process of specialization takes account both of the possibility of actually building such a system, and of describing its limitations to a user.

The way to take account of these issues is to explain them. In summary, in order to explain a system you need to extract the general principles on which the system design is based. For the explanation to be truthful, the system must be closed under its explanation.

The difficulty of explaining (documenting, lecturing, devising on-line help) provides us with a simple measure of the quality of the proposed design. The simpler its explanation the better. Of course, we are allowed to explain our design in more specialized languages than English if we so wish. Since we are exploring the problem space, we would most likely use a stylized English, with various technical words or formulae. In the extreme we may explain the design, not to a person, but to a computer—of course, we would then use a programming language, and with luck our 'explanation' will be manageable enough for the computer to run! Nevertheless if we are unable to express our design concisely in simple English, this should give us grounds for suspicion. Another design might be more readily explained?

> Thus, I came to the conclusion that the designer of a new system must not only be the implementor and first large-scale user; the designer should also write the first user manual. The separation of any of these four components would have hurt TEX [a big system Knuth wrote] significantly. If I had not participated fully in all these activities, literally hundreds of improvements would never have been made, because I would never have thought of them or perceived why they were important.
>
> But a system cannot be successful if it is too strongly influenced by a single person. Once the initial design is complete and fairly robust, the real test begins as people with many different viewpoints undertake their own experiments.
>
> *Donald Knuth*

Some might say that Knuth is an exceptional person and perhaps combines more skills as designer, implementor, document writer and user than most of us can muster—and he must have a lot of time to spend doing it! Indeed, isn't it better when a good programmer programs, a good expositor writes, and a good evaluator evaluates? No! The advantage Knuth writes about arises precisely when the designer takes on all the tasks together, and makes tradeoffs between them. If different people do the work it will become separated; opportunities for improvements will get missed. If the documenter *only* has to document, perhaps he will not so often ask for the design to be improved to make documentation easier. (Of course, Knuth's systems were large and similarly scaled projects or larger will normally be undertaken by a design team: but so then should the entire job, design, documentation and initial use, be undertaken by the same team.)

Box 17.5   Users explaining design to designers.

It can be a bit pompous for designers to ask users what they want; then develop a system; then tell the users about the completely different thing that has been designed.

That may be polemic (designers are trained to have design insight; users are paid to do as they are told), but it hints that users have a lot to give designers in the design process. Certainly users know more about what they are doing than designers. Only users know why they are puzzled, only users know what they wanted to do, only users know what they *thought* was happening.

A very simple technique, the **think-aloud method**, is a powerful and cheap way of evaluating user interfaces. Simply, a designer sits down with a user who is encouraged to say whatever comes into his head as he tries to use the system.

The advantage of sitting with the user and encouraging him to think aloud as he works is that many things would quickly be forgotten. Giving the user a questionnaire afterwards may be too late. In fact a new user may not know whether he is making mistakes, but the watchful designer can make a note of the problem.

A few simple rules need to be observed. First, the user must be encouraged to feel at ease thinking aloud. The designer should make it quite clear that this is a test of the system, and not a test of the user! Thus every problem the user has is valuable to hear about. Secondly, think aloud is an artificial situation: the designer has to be there, but he must not give special help to the user even if he is asked for it. This may seem rude, and the designer should explain and apologize in advance. The designer should explain that he needs to see how the user sorts out problems for himself. Nevertheless there will be times when the designer needs to intervene and provide hints: this will be when the difficulty has been noted, and it is apparent that the next design can fix the problem. It is however useful to remember that being helpful is a temptation— especially because you as designer know far more about the system! The more help that is given, the less useful the think-aloud work will be about the *current* design being tested.

Think aloud can be used not only for helping to debug the computer system, but can also help with the design of documentation, and to help discover discrepancies between the documentation structure and the way people use the system to perform their tasks.

Think aloud is so effective in leading to design improvements that an n person design team will often be better split up as an $n - 1$ member team, with the 'lost' person doing something else. When the system is almost ready, the 'lost' designer returns to be the 'user' for think-aloud debugging. Because he has not seen the system, *and has not been party to the reasons—or excuses—why the system has turned out the way it has*, he will have what seem like startlingly good insights into the user interface design! The end result will be far better, and can be done with fewer man-months' work.

17.4.1   Literate programming

Programming is a difficult enough part of design without also having to document your work. Inclination—technically trained programmers probably don't like writing prose—and good sense, namely separation of concerns, lead the documentation process to be isolated from the programming process. In the end the originally sensible strategy of separation of concerns, and of postponing investment in writing up what is for most of its time a moving target, leads to complete isolation: there is then very little correspondence between the documentation and the implemented system. Users suffer, but so too do designers: with no reliable documentation designers lose common ground to discuss their design, and they lose the insights they might have got if they had taken the trouble to explain carefully what they were designing.

The separation of documentation and programming is artificial, largely inherited from the days when computers could provide support for one or the other, but not both at once. A very simple scheme for combining documentation and program is called **literate programming** (Knuth, 1984), and we shall briefly describe it here. Literate programming is for *internal* (how it works) documentation, but we will see below that the idea can be generalized to *external* (how to use it) documentation.

Literate programming is a system of combining program and internal documentation, so that both may be developed closely together with ease. Various automatic aids to readability are provided, such as substantial cross-referencing and indexing, pretty printing, and so on. Special macro processing allows the program to be written in any order to improve and simplify the exposition; macros are automatically numbered so that their usage is easily cross-referenced.

An important point is that a literate programming system converts the documentation and code into beautifully typeset material with no additional effort by the programmer. All features combine to simplify and encourage the documentation process and to keep it in very close correspondence with the actual program.

We will illustrate literate programming using Pascal, although the idea of combining different types of text to make them easier to maintain together is quite general. Another obvious application is the combination of formal specification with conventional program.

The example shown in Figure 17.5 shows the use and definition of a macro called `<Insert $v$ in the array>`. (Macros are a reasonable feature to support Pascal programming, but there is no intrinsic reason to use macros as the abstraction mechanism in literate programming.) Note also that macro names may be abbreviated (for example, `<Insert...>`), to encourage programmers to use longer, mnemonic names. The $ symbols tell the literate programming system to typeset and cross-reference certain text as code rather than as commentary.

Extract from the source of a literate program—illustrating interleaving of code, macros and documentation.

```
    ⋮
Insert sort
This is the standard insert
sort algorithm.  Assumes a
sentinel at $a[0]$.
@for i := 2 to N do
begin v := a[i]; j := i;
<Insert...>
end
@<Insert $v$ in the array>=
while a[j-1]>v do
begin a[j] := a[j-1]; j := j-1 end;
a[j] := v
    ⋮
```

Figure 17.5 Input to a literate programming system.

```
    ⋮
for i:=2 to N do
begin v:=a[i];j:=i;
while a[j-1]>v do
begin a[j]:=a[j-1];j:=j-1 end;
a[j]:=v
end
    ⋮
```

Figure 17.6 Output from a literate programming system: generated code.

Efficient means are provided to extract the program code from the literate program so that it may be compiled or processed in the usual ways. The result of processing this example fragment is shown in Figures 17.6 and 17.7. The crucial point is that literate programming is paradigmatic (Section 4.4)—you get this support *for free*.

Such a small example as we can show in these figures hardly gives a good impression of literate programming. Literate programming comes into its own when programs grow to conventional sizes, because this encourages the amount of documentation to remain in proportion to the amount of program!

⋮

31. Insert sort. This is the standard insert sort algorithm. Assumes a sentinel at $a[0]$.

   for $i := 2$ **to** N **do**
   begin
     $v := a[i];$ $j := i;$
     ⟨Insert v in the array. 32⟩
   end

32. ⟨Insert v in the array. 32⟩≡

   while $a[j-1] > v$ **do**
   begin $a[j] := a[j-1];$ $j := j - 1$ **end**;
   $a[j] := v$

Used in section 31.

⋮

Extract does not show automatically generated table of contents, index, and so on.

Figure 17.7   Output from a literate programming system: typeset program.

17.4.2 Literate using

There is no need for literate programming to be confined to batch programming languages and conventional documentation. The symbolic mathematics system **Mathematica** (Wolfram, 1988) uses a form of literate programming in its 'notebooks': it allows mathematical articles to be written mixing text with mathematics. Mathematica evaluates the mathematics, just as a Pascal system evaluates programs, producing numbers, graphs or equations. As in literate programming, in Mathematica the very close proximity of explanation (the mathematical paper) and the 'program' (the mathematics itself) helps to ensure their mutual correspondence.

    In general, literate programming need not be confined to non-interactive languages such as Pascal (or mathematics, for that matter). Instead it can be used to explain the *use* of a system. Imagine a typical user manual for an interactive system. It will contain examples of how to use the system: 'do this, then this will happen'—and it shows you. In almost all manuals, those illustrations, textual or pictorial, are *made up*. There is no guarantee that they are correct; there is no guarantee that the manual writers remembered to update them when the system was modified. Clearly we have a candidate for automation: and this is **literate using** (the name suggests the history of the idea rather than its potential)—though calling it 'self-documenting' would be more suggestive.

It is easiest to illustrate the idea with the very system used for writing this book. The manual says that if you write \dag you get the symbol '†' printed. Because I do not have a literate using system, I had to construct the example in the previous sentence by hand, and it is fallible. There is no reason why it should be correct; certainly, a simple mistyping results in: 'The manual says that if you write \dag you get the symbol '‡' printed.' This is quite wrong and is the sort of error that would be difficult to spot in a long document. It would have been better if I could have written something like:

```
The manual says that if you write @INPUT(\dag)
you get the symbol '@OUTPUT' printed.
```

That way, the output would always correspond to whatever I described. Handling output for non-textual interactive systems is more complex—but there is no reason why a literate using system itself cannot be interactive and use to the full the features it is helping to explain.[3] In addition, when the system is modified, the literate using system can check that none of the examples in the manual has been modified. If they have been modified, say '†' has become '‡' in Version 2, then the manual writer should be informed automatically and the manual should be brought up to date.

Literate programming and literate using make documentation a cheap part of the design process, and they encourage a close correspondence between the program (either its text or its execution) and its explanation. Such tools, then, discourage the unfortunate separation of documentation from normal design. It is interesting to compare the success of hypertext systems, for they do exactly the same: by making authors easily access graphics, semantics and content all at once. Before hypertext systems, interactive systems designers found graphics so hard that its design had to be a separate stage; they found programming so hard that it too had to be separated; and the content of a system was provided at the end when everything worked. Good hypertext systems provide the support that allows a designer to interleave these three stages, and therefore keep them more coherent. Literate programming and hypertext also share, as major features, cross-referencing and linking.

The effectiveness of both literate programming and literate using underlines the important observation: *computer support for design enables design to be undertaken in new ways.* Design is surely a complex task, and doing it tends to compartmentalize effort. In particular, documentation gets separated off, postponed or lost (*surely* the system works *without* documentation!)—literate methods attack this specific issue. More generally, the needs of the user get pushed aside by the immediate

---

[3] I hope you can see many ways to generalize this idea! For example, input and output pairs might be named and need not come in order (for example, @OUTPUT(dagger) ... @INPUT(dagger, \dag). Or you may want all output and input to appear in a distinguished way so that the manual writer cannot fake examples.

Box 17.6   On good notation.

User interface design is about designing new notations. Admittedly the notations are more ephemeral than the conventional notations of pen and paper. Most teaching, even up to graduate level, concerns itself with instilling better facility with *given* notations. There is a serious gap in both computer science curricula and user interface course content when problem solving and designing new notations are omitted.

> ... We don't try to teach how to invent notations that are efficient in view of one's manipulative needs. And that is amazing, for it seems much less ambitious than, say, trying to teach explicitly how to think effectively.
>
> *Edsger Dijkstra*

Interfaces are often extended without regard for their notation, or language. If an interface uses a good notation, then that ought to be a useful guide as to what the interface should be designed to do, not the other way around. A good notation is more important than what the system might be able to do by arbitrary extension. Good notations are easier to explain and understand.

---

technological pressure of just programming. Computer-supported design systems help bring these apparently separate concerns closer.

17.5   Faking the design process

Throughout this book we have been looking at ways of doing design. We have seen that there are systemic problems: designers are not clever enough in principle; the world is far too complex; and everything keeps changing— to mention just three points! Yet there are systematic ways to tackle design: we can follow the standards set out in *Science* (Chapter 9) or this chapter, or use standard top-down, structured or whatever methods. But too often being systematic and being creative do not seem to go together.

David Parnas and Paul Clements (1986) have some good news and some bad news for us. The bad news is that indeed we cannot do design properly. The good news, however, is that we can *pretend* to do design properly. That is, if we **fake design**—which is of course easiest if we actually do the design in part properly!—we can at least explain the result in clear fashion. Thus, issues like maintenance and documentation are eased when the design *appears* to have been done properly—whether or not it really was.

We used the idea of faking powerfully in Section 9.4 (*What is good science?*) Nobody does good science, yet it is useful to study what science would be like if only people did it properly! That is a faked reconstruction of ideal science. When we diverge from the ideal, we need to admit and allow for the divergence. In programming terms, it is not always possible to design in the best possible way, we must ensure that the *ad hoc* bits of design—the bits that need faking in their reconstruction—include watchdogs or other guards. Or, the user interface might provide customizability so that the user can program around design faults. At least the parts of the design faked over must have corresponding warnings in the manual. A coherent 'fake' explanation of a design with exceptions is better than an incoherent design with no concept of exceptions!

> The things that are difficult to fake are usually also hard
> to learn.   *Jon Elster*

An extreme form of faking the design process is to make it up completely! Suppose we are confronted with a finished system, perhaps even one where we had no part in its original design. As retrospective designers—as imaginative historians—we might learn a great deal. We may also be able to improve the design and its documentation together with its training materials, if we now imaginatively reconstruct it. That is, a **rational reconstruction** is a historical reconstruction of a design as it 'ought to have been done'. Cynically, rational reconstruction is merely converting the current system into a prototype for another one that is more rational. Less cynically, it is a respectable method for improving designs that *should have been* discarded as prototypes.

Rational reconstruction may come too late to fake a design, because the intention was never there in the first place to do design explicitly (because too much ground breaking had to be done to do rational design as well) but rational reconstruction may achieve some insights into the system design. Incipient principles may be discovered, and perhaps ways in which their application could be closed. At worst, rational reconstruction will help future designers improve on the system—*long-term* iterative design. Rational reconstruction should also be a tool in the user interface researcher's toolkit: it is an ideal way to reappraise existing system designs in the light of new perspectives.

17.6   Conclusions

This chapter proposed a simple sequence for design: generalize, specialize, explain. The more effort put into making a 'good' design decision, the harder it is to change one's mind later. Therefore put as much effort as possible into making the most general plan. Then, later, specialize it to something that is feasible. Devising explanation is not only essential for enabling the user, but itself is a good way to gain further insights into the design. Anything that is awkward to explain is a candidate for revision. This is true whether we are explaining to the computer (programming), explaining to the user (documenting) or explaining to the designer (thinking). In Chapter 10, we suggested generative user-engineering principles as dual explanations of user interface properties, serving both formal and explanatory roles. The computer has to know how to behave, and the user has to know how to use the computer: the designer can shift his stance as he thinks from either perspective. To quote Don Knuth again, 'As I said above [quoted in Section 17.4], manual writing provides an ideal incentive for system improvements, because you discover and remove glitches that you can't justify in print'.

Much of this book has been promoting formal methods, from the scientific approach through to mathematical formalisms for capturing and reasoning about interactive behaviour. How then do formal methods fit in with the generalize, specialize, explain scheme? With formal methods you *automatically* (paradigmatically, in the terms of Chapter 4) generalize, and by being formal you should know exactly what you are doing, so honest explanation is direct.

Lastly, don't give up. Whatever you design, it is worth describing as you really wanted it to be. Fake it! ... then quickly put it right, so that you remain truthful.

Chapter 18

Epilogue: What of the future?

All of us, professionals as well as laymen, must consciously
break the habits we bring to thinking about the computer [...]
It is hard to think about computers of the future without
projecting onto them the properties and limitations of those we
think we know today [...]
                                                Seymour Papert

A common misconception about computers is that they will become
invisible, rather like motors are today. Motors are everywhere, in clocks
and washing machines, yet none of them intrudes into everyday life except
in educational toys. Likewise, modern telephones rely on computers for
routeing calls, yet those computers are not visible: all the user sees is
a telephone and the computer is hidden. From such observations people
generalize and suggest that all computers will be hidden: hence their user
interfaces will be an issue purely of ergonomics, sociology and other human
sciences. The view of the future suggests that the best interactive systems
designs should by-and-large imitate natural objects or ordinary machines.
A washing machine is a washing machine even though the dials on it are a
user interface to an intricate little computer system. Who cares if it has a
computer in it, so long as it gets the clothes clean? The desktop metaphor—
the computer screen simulating an office desk—is another example. If the
desktop metaphor is carried out well, then the user does not need to think
of his screen 'desk' as a computer at all.

This book has looked at more profound parts of computing. There are
cases where people want to use computers *as* computers. Expert systems,
programming languages, and many interactive tools are useful to the extent

that the computer is explicit. Concepts such as programming can help people solve real problems—their *own* problems. Thus the user interface designer of the future will still have to be a computer scientist at heart!

18.1   Interactive applications in the future

A few years ago the pervading style of interaction was for users to first know the language for interaction, what they should do, and then type their carefully chosen commands at the computer. They had to remember the commands and their syntax. This symbolic style largely gave way to the more immediate and visual see and point style. Instead of remembering commands, the user could look at a menu, and point at the desired choice of command. Actually, the user still had to remember many commands, but they were now single keystrokes and had immediate effect which could be seen. This greatly speeded learning and exploratory use. The most salient operation on data became 'cut and paste'. Information that can be seen can be pointed at, and then cut, maybe copied, then pasted somewhere else. This style of interaction is successful because the cognitive load is low, yet many everyday actions are directly supported. Almost all human–human *trans*actions are copying and moving information around. When the operations available require the user to see the data being affected, so much the better for usability. Cut and paste do this naturally: you cannot cut something that is not displayed, and you cannot paste to a location that is not visible.

But very few human–human *inter*actions are merely copying and moving chunks of information. Information is created by talking about it and by using it. New information is created by linking, processing and mixing existing information, by questioning it and re-representing it.

Today's computers *move* information; soon, perhaps encouraged by write-once storage media, we shall see more *linking* of information. Information can stay in its original context and still be used in new ways. Hypertext is one way to link information in new ways, perhaps dynamically as the user explores and extends it. We do not yet know what the 'sensible' operations for linking information are: so far, people seem to get lost far too easily in what are theoretically rather simple linkages. But then present systems make practically no use of sound (even in stereo), no use of the user's gestures (other than pecking at a keyboard), no use of three dimensions or visual depth cues, no use of animation, and no use of those underplayed senses—smell, touch, taste. There is clearly enormous potential here even before we start implanting computers into human bodies. (That is an important area already: there are some people who control their various bodily functions by electronics.)

From a formal perspective we are immediately led to ask what operations one might perform on links. How are they composed? How are they computed—if the computer determines links, you can have *lots* of them, perhaps so that they form an almost continuous weave, or a topological transformation? Are links computed lazily? None of these questions has been attacked at the time of writing, and nobody has any idea how best to interact with systems that provided such deep features, or about the applications that could be supported.

The last generation of computers were big, expensive and shared between many users. The users were given timeshared environments that simulated 'personal computers'. Today personal computers are a reality, and can physically sit on a desktop, some even on your lap or wrist. Simultaneously with this miniaturization, the services provided have fragmented: a user may have a computer on his desk, but his work is not closely connected with other users. Today's users are independent, having moved away from a period of technological subservience to shared, expensive computing resources. Once we measured computer performance by response times (one second was considered good); today we use MIPS (10 million instructions per second is considered reasonable); but it does not matter how fast my machine goes if it does not do what I want, or is not where I need it. Note how performance was once related to the user's task but now is entirely technical!

In the future computers will be able to facilitate collaboration. More powerful ways of communicating than merely exchanging chunks of information, cutting and pasting—which is all electronic mail is—will be developed. Information can itself take part in the interaction, keeping track of how it is used, and what commitments for the future its use entails. In other words, computers will be able to talk *about* interaction and how to improve it.

18.2   User interfaces in the future

The computer is understood by its user to the extent that it adheres to a model, usually a metaphor based on the real world. Thus early word processors were based on the typewriter metaphor, which gave way to the more powerful WYSIWYG principle. Direct manipulation systems display objects on the screen which the user can move around almost as if they were real objects: the screen is a metaphor of the real world. Even if we change the laws of physics to suit our application (which may be to teach physics!), the fact is that:

▷ The user interface gets better the more invisible the computer. Use metaphors!

▷ When invisible, the computer is not being exploited *as a computer*. Realism may involve a lot of computation, but it is not under the user's control.

▷ Most present interactive systems have not decided which to be: invisible or visible.

So the future holds a division between two sorts of user interface. Some will tend to be realistic: in these the computer will disappear, just as the electric motor has. Others will use the computer as a computer: to think in new ways, to reason with an intelligent partner. We want to do things that would not be possible with human partners. Almost all work in user interface design has concentrated on the first option, and rather assumes that a good computer is an invisible computer. I think that a good computer is one that does powerful things: and for that one needs abstraction, and interesting rules of behaviour. This book has made a start at exploring the new issues that arise.

So often developments in technology direct new applications. 'Computers can now do this, so let's do it!' At present, the difficulties of implementing some ideas makes designers hesitate, but in the not too distant future, designers will be able to build systems with the aid of computers that even they do not fully understand in principle. If they can do almost anything easily, it is essential that a more thoughtful attitude takes a grip of design.

18.3   Formal methods in the future

The style of reasoning elaborated in this book is mechanical and may soon be overshadowed: Euclid has given way to nature's fractal geometry; precision (in principle) has given way to unavoidable chaos. Perhaps the sorts of things that can be thought about by conventional means are not at all the sorts of things that users will be interacting with in the future. Today's computers are 'sealed off' from their environment; unlike animals they rely on brute force thinking rather than reacting to their changing environment. They rely, as it were, on interacting with people to translate the world into simple terms. The way we interact with computers of the future will change dramatically when computers can gather information and participate *in* information for themselves.

Computing has discovered that building programs that are both correct and efficient is rather difficult, and in fact is infeasible even for modest sized programs. Ideally, automated theorem provers can be used to show a high level description has the required properties, and optimizers are used to transform the description into an efficient program. So both processes, making correct and making efficient, can be automated—or will be given the attention of more research.

Formal methods do not tell you anything new (in the Kantian sense they are analytic). Worse, using formal methods requires a decision to decide what to formalize and having the expertise to carry it through.

Having made this decision, you are blind to all those things that were not formalized, those things that have been abstracted out. What is powerful about formal methods is that trying to apply them gives the designer insight into his problems, ways to innovate by drawing on abstractly similar designs. That is one view, the other is that formal methods recruit standards to design. Some things are correct, others not correct. In the broadest sense, using formal methods protects against bugs, which is the topic with which we started this book, and with which we now shall finish it.

18.4 Bugs

Now for a final argument why we need both better design methods and attitudes.

Almost all work in user interface design is about 'second order' effects: effects of marginal difference to the user. This book has vacillated between 'this is crucial' and 'the user can get used to anything'! But there is one user interface feature that makes all the difference to usability. Bugs. Users cannot get used to a system that does not work, or worse, destroys their livelihood.

If your best ideas in user interface design result in doubling productivity, halving error rates, increasing job satisfaction—then when the inevitable bug hits, the user will just lose far more than he would have done in a slower, pedestrian, system. Undo is clearly essential to recover from the *computer's* mistakes, but there is more to bugs than this.

Although individual programmers are often responsible for bugs, various forces within the computing industry, including mistrust of users, drive software manufacturers to strategies that exacerbate the problem. Such methods as software manufacturers adopt 'in defence' not only work against users but also undermine scientific work, which in turn retards the advancement of user interface design generally. Amazingly many bugs are known about and accepted before software is released to users. Many bugs could have been corrected if there had been any motivation to do so.

On Friday 19 May 1989 I sat down at my home computer to write a letter. I started to use a standard, long-established word processor; it crashed and took with it 64 Mb out of my 100 Mb disk, including all of this book. The disk recovery program, designed to rescue users from such disasters could not cope and suggested the disk was reinitialized. My last backup was on the previous Monday (naturally it was a partial backup), though I had fortunately saved a few files on individual floppies. It took me *all* Saturday to get back to where I was, more or less, plus the rest of the weekend to recover emotionally!

Why is software so bug ridden? Why is my word processor so complex that its designers overlook major flaws? Why is the computer's disk structure so lacking in redundancy that the recovery program had nothing left to go on? Why is the machine's basic architecture so unprotected that a user program can go so badly wrong?

You could say that a few bugs are inevitable given the complexity that users demand—or is forced on them by manufacturers providing more features in their software than their competitors. All bugs could charitably be dismissed as accidents, of which I was an unfortunate victim. I do not believe they were accidents. They are not the only examples that could be mentioned from recent experience. I believe that the entire industry is set up to exploit users, and that what I described above is typical and symptomatic of a deep malaise. I believe the industry's dismissive attitude to bugs is the most serious problem facing computing today.

18.5   The scope of the problem

If you buy a car or a washing machine, and it does not work, then you can take it back and get a refund or a replacement. Computer programs are different. I am talking about computer programs costing between one pound and several thousand pounds—these are issues that affect all computer users, from home enthusiasts to large companies.

Computer programs come in sealed plastic bags. On the bag will be a legal warning: once the bag is opened, then you are deemed to have accepted the software. Once you open the package, you cannot return the program even if it is defective or totally inappropriate for your uses. (One reason manufacturers don't want the software back is that you might have infected it with a virus. See later in this chapter.)

Manufacturers of programs will argue that they also supply documentation, instructions and manuals. You can read those before breaking the seal. But is this reasonable? Do you read the manual of a car before driving it? The driver's manual actually gives you very little idea of how the car works or what it will feel like to drive. It is the same with programs: program manuals are very often not the place to start if you want to know what the program does. Furthermore, the manual will have a legal statement that the program is supplied 'as is'. You've bought what you've got, that is. Typically the manufacturer will expressly disclaim, in suitable legal jargon, anything and everything that the manual says. The risks are all yours. The manufacturers want to protect themselves from mistakes in the manual or the program, so they say that the manual does not constitute a warranty or implication of the way the program works. And opening the program to find out what it does implies an acceptance of it.

With computer programs, then, manufacturers put their customers in a Catch-22 situation. The program cannot be tried until you have irrevocably broken a seal, and until you break that seal you have no idea what the program does. Once you break the seal, you cannot return the program as unfit. Actually the situation with computer programs is even worse than I have so far made out. There are three more facts:

▷ Computer programs are *terribly* complex. It is not unusual for manuals to run to 1000 dense pages. Cars are trivial in comparison! It is therefore quite unreasonable to expect a purchaser to understand a program merely from the manual without trying the program out.

▷ Computer programs are *secret*. For commercial reasons, manufacturers are reluctant to disclose the code of their systems. If it were released, then competitors would benefit from the original manufacturer's development investment. In contrast, conventional industries such as car manufacture require considerable investment to tool up for a particular production; copying a computer program is no harder than copying files and having a suitable compiler available—which in turn might easily be bootlegged. (Computer programs are also 'secret' in the sense that many are so complex that they are effectively unknowable.)

▷ Computer programs have bugs. The programs do not do the right thing in the right way. They go wrong. In particular there will be bugs *in the manuals*, in the sense that the program does not do what its manual says it does, or it does things the manual says it does not. It may even do completely bizarre things. It is something rather like having a car that loses a wheel only when overtaken on the inside by a 1976 yellow car doing 59·3 mph. Of course the manual doesn't tell you that! The word processor bug I mentioned earlier was more like the wheel dropping off without warning, just driving normally. Presumably because of a major design flaw.

The manual for the word processor I mentioned earlier that crashed warns, 'You can't cut more than 100 paragraphs at a time'. That statement in the manual means the designers must have known about this simple bug *before* the program was sold; they must have been content to leave it in (and it isn't the only one they left in). We argued in Section 1.1 that this problem could have been solved.[1] Another example in a programmer's manual warns in several places,

> Failure to restore the video environment may cause the machine to 'lock up' when another program is run.

But the system knows exactly when the video environment is changed, and it knows when another program is run: so why doesn't it restore the video environment (unless the program asks for it not to be restored)? Or take

---

[1] The example was used in Chapter 1 to motivate the idea of using computability as a standard for user interface design. Here we are just moaning about the low standards that permit bugs.

the UNIX manual that warns that switching the computer off when the system is doing a disk update (which it does once every 30 seconds or so) may cause the disks to be corrupted! And the manual even suggests what program changes to make in order to fix the bug—so the designers knew both the bug and its fix! Sadly such explicit comments are rather easy to find in almost every user manual. Of course, it is good that the user is warned at all, but wouldn't it have been better to have fixed the bug if it was known about? These are just a few examples!

Not long ago UNIX was an exciting but unreliable system. It had security loopholes; applications programs could crash the system; filestores could easily get corrupted. But the source code of the UNIX kernel was available to academics. That meant that bugs were fixed, and it also meant that many people read the code and improved it in various ways. Bulletin boards are routinely used for sharing bug fixes around the world. The effect is that the community of programmers worked, and still work, together to improve UNIX. Of course, there were risks: there are now many versions of UNIX, all slightly different from each other (Section 7.12). Nevertheless it is undoubtedly true that all of these versions are improvements on reliability and security of the original. Now compare the open approach of UNIX with the standard closed approach of proprietary systems. Manufacturers with very few exceptions keep their code as secret as possible, partly to stave off clone manufacturers. When an upgrade is announced it is sold, and therefore has to be designed, on its new features. You don't get yourself a positive market image by admitting you have fixed appalling bugs! So new versions of proprietary software come with new features and new bugs.

The aim of much practical research into programming presently going on is to make programming *even* easier that it already is, that is, to find easy ways to make changes to complex programs. Even if we make the distinction between exploratory programming as against serious programming, it is clear that the emphasis is on making systems more powerful rather than more reliable. Why don't interactive computer systems have an extra process (a watchdog, Section 4.2.14) checking that certain invariants are maintained at all times? This at least would detect many bugs before they got out of hand. The reason is that it is an expensive route, and anyway there are all sorts of features that could be implemented if we did not use so many resources for checking. Yet many industries (railways, military, process control) demand such security and reliability, and get it. Office workers, and users of interactive systems more generally, are suffering from unnecessarily poor standards at the user interface.

There are marketing reasons to add features on each software release, but another powerful factor is the manufacturer's attempt to stay ahead of software pirates who would otherwise be copying their software. It is to a manufacturer's short-term advantage to make his software as intricate as possible. The more features there are, the easier it may be to uphold a prosecution in the law courts when a competitor is found to have copied ideas. And we know, the more features—especially ones added for such reasons—the more bugs and the worse off the user. Richard Stallman (1985) has argued forcibly that our legal ideas of copyright, based on authorship, book and printing technology, are inappropriate for computer programs. That means enforcing conventional copyright, whether by legal or computing means, imposes obsolete strictures on commercial computing. This will narrow the horizons of society in the long run.

To return to bugs; bugs in themselves are interesting, but more interesting is why manufacturers brazenly sell programs full of bugs and refuse to take any responsibility for them. In fact they actively disown bugs: they admit their manuals and programs may be wrong, but it is not their responsibility. Look at this 'warranty' paraphrased from the user manuals of some popular interactive systems:

> The software is provided 'as is' without warranty of any kind, whether expressed or implied including without limitation any implied warranties of merchantability of fitness for a particular purpose all of which are expressly disclaimed. The authors, their distributors and dealers shall in no event be liable for any direct, incidental, or consequential damages, whether resulting from defects in the disks, or from any defect in the software itself or documentation thereof. The entire risk as to the results and performance of the software and materials is assumed by you. If the software is defective, you and not the authors their distributors or dealers, assume the entire cost of all necessary servicing, repair or correction. This warranty provides you with specific legal rights.

Not only do your 'specific legal rights' seem rather weak, but most manufacturers go on to ask for more money to 'upgrade', or to have a 'servicing agreement', that is, to fix problems in programs that should never have been sold. It is a profitable business to trap users on an upgrade path.

There are several reasons why consumers are complacent about bugs. As we saw in Box 7.1, there just aren't the words to talk about bugs to get excited about them. Programs, even ones with bugs, are terribly useful and many people would find it hard to think of them being much improved. I can do things with a computer that I could not do without one. I put up with its quirks: yes, sometimes it goes wrong and wastes time, but mostly it is worth it. A more subtle reason is cognitive dissonance, which basically says that if you do something silly often enough, you make up a very good reason for doing it—otherwise you'd go mad (Section 3.3.1). That is why *bad* programs are popular. If you regularly use a bad, nasty program, you have to make up a good reason for doing so. Typically you set yourself up as an expert. Now everyone looks to you for advice about this silly program. So you turn a potentially bad purchase into an opportunity to get esteem!

Box 18.1   Computer viruses.

Viruses are bugs that are installed by malicious programmers: they hide within innocuous programs. (So-called **virus construction kits** enable anyone, not just highly motivated people, to do it.)   As soon as an 'infected' program is run, the virus copies itself to some other convenient host. Thus the virus spreads. You give a disk to a friend, and it carries the virus with it. At some stage in its life, the virus decides to do something nasty, such as destroying your data. By this time you have unwittingly copied the virus all over the place—and all of the copies are waiting to spring more surprises on you.

You can get virus detection programs to help protect your information (some of which themselves carry devious infections). A virus detection program searches your work for recognized bugs and attempts to save you from their effects. Most copy protection schemes work by doing devious things indistinguishable from virus infection—many viruses have copied the copy protection mechanisms for their own devious uses. If you run a virus detector, you run the risk of it wrecking your expensive copy-protected software. So what does the user do?

So far as the user is concerned, viruses are indistinguishable from bugs: both cause chaos. While respectable manufacturers refuse to provide reasonable warranties on their software, while programmers take no liability for their work, there will be no effective way to control deliberately malicious programmers. Indeed, some viruses have already appeared with 'warranties' with clauses that could have been copied directly from 'real' software warranties!

If some of the worst programs around were improved, had their bugs fixed, whole professions and career structures would be destroyed! Of course, it would have been better if the bugs and low standards of programming had never been accepted in the first place. Users are just making the best of a very bad situation: the manufacturers are squarely to blame for the problem, and possibly for taking advantage of the trap they get advisory services into. Consumers become committed to bad systems because they are bad: it takes so long to understand a program that you do not want to waste that investment by getting a 'better' program. It is now quite common for computer systems to be sold on the strength of their *faults*, that is, that they have the *same* faults (and possibly a few more). It's often called 'compatibility'—an example was given in Section 7.12.

Some 'pseudo' bugs are in programs to enforce certain policies. The bank may take several days to clear cheques; the library cannot say what books a reader has out. A complaint elicits the answer that the computer is programmed that way: to make life easier for the management or to better exploit the computer users. This exploitation can be achieved while everyone accepts severe limitations and bugs as inevitable.

At the beginning of this book we contrasted the problems of the computer when it encounters a bug with the problems its user faces. When a computer divides by zero, it is in trouble. There has been some mistake in its program. Now when a program has that sort of bug, the *computer* complains, usually it stops working and crashes. The programmer recognizes this sort of problem—it is one he has been taught to try and avoid. The program will be fixed, because the computer cannot continue until it is. Why is it a bug to divide by zero, but not to delete the user's data? Why are complaining users told to do things differently, but programs are redesigned when computers have problems? Why is it neat to write short programs for computers, but it is of no interest to give users an easy time? Aren't these interesting contrasts? If a computer finds a bug, then the bug is *serious*. But if a human discovers a bug, then that is the human's fault. He shouldn't have been doing that anyway! Humans are too flexible and adaptive, they can cope.

In short, *computers get a better deal than humans, their users*. And this should not be so. Computers impose strict standards with which manufacturers cannot fail to comply. Humans can be exploited, by large manufacturers hiding behind the law and by some programmers hiding behind their immaturity and lack of social conscience. Immaturity (or whatever it is) isn't always the programmers' fault. One reason why programmers deliberately and so complacently leave bugs *they know about* in programs is that they are not taught well enough. Some of the problem starts at school. Isn't it a good idea to teach children computing at school? To write their own programs? Then they can get hi-tech jobs in information technology.

Actually, no.

An analogy will help: Isn't it a good idea to teach children building at school? To build their own houses? Then they can get craftsman jobs in the building trade.

The problem is you teach children using building blocks and imagination; yet you build houses out of bricks, gas pipes, glass, girders and rules. Not many skills learnt about building blocks in the playroom help build real buildings. The trouble with school computing, indeed *all our attitudes about computing*, is that we think it is *easy*. It is very easy to write a program, and if it goes wrong it is very easy to fix it—almost so easy it's trivial and isn't worth the bother. That is what children learn at school, that is what university graduates think. But it is only true in the building block world of the playroom. (Another analogy drawn from the building blocks world was discussed in Section 7.9.)

Real programs are far more complex—and their user interface code is often the most arbitrary and intricate part. Cavalier attitudes to programming result in badly designed programs, built out of ill-conceived building blocks. Real programs are therefore full of accidental bugs which arose because their designers simply did not understand the way large programs must be put together to be safe.

Our analogy between building and computing runs deeper still. If you want to build a house, you have to satisfy various planning authorities that the building is adequate, safe and acceptable for the neighbourhood. If the living room has an unsupported wall running over it on the first floor, there must be some engineering calculations that the joists can support the load. Such calculations are quite technical and they are absolutely necessary.

Many programmers cannot do mathematics. Many programmers cannot do simple algebra—that is probably why they chose (or were advised) to be programmers rather than engineers! Engineering disciplines have professional standards: if a car or a washing machine has an engineering fault, you can send it back. Professional engineers are insured, and are required to take responsibility for any faults in their designs: a stark contrast to the 'liability' implied by the software warranty quoted earlier! It is time that computing had similar professional standards, and it is time some of these standards became regulations. It is time that manufacturers stopped treating computers like toys, and stopped abusing the law, treating computer users like children.

18.6   Prospects for the future

Not long ago computer systems were shared between large groups of users, and the users would be represented by a central computing service. Any complaints about software could be addressed to manufacturers through the more powerful representation of the service. Today most users work with personal computers. Even if they work in a department, they are required to pay fees for their software: essentially manufacturers want to relate to users on an individual, separated basis. As separate individuals, users are powerless against the relative might of unscrupulous manufacturers. We've seen that few manufacturers would think of their behaviour as unscrupulous: everybody does it. Because of the Free Rider Paradox (Section 7.11), it will always seem to any individual manufacturer that excessively protective attitudes to their software is advantageous if not actually necessary; then, with every manufacturer thinking similarly, standards are inevitably dragged down.

Manufacturers forbid users to share software (when previously software *had* to be shared because the machine it ran on was shared): this can be seen as another part of their strategy to divide and conquer users. Shareware, users sharing their own home-grown software, is a trend against this. Viruses are worrying in this regard: they make users frightened of each other (of each other's disks, bulletin boards and shareware) and frightened to cooperate in computer-supported activities. We need quite a few technical advances, particularly in secure computer hardware, before users can safely share their work without significant risk of viral or other infection. If such technology becomes available, the present generation of personal computers will rapidly become obsolete—written off by its sensitivity to virus epidemics.

Users must unite, they must be represented and they must become aware that such concerted action would improve computer systems to everyone's benefit. We have all been brainwashed that bugs are inevitable. Bugs are only inevitable if we accept over-complex systems, secrecy, non-accountability. Professional bodies, such as the British Computer Society, the Institution of Electrical Engineers, the ACM, the Institute of Electrical and Electronic Engineers and their equivalents are well placed to initiate and coordinate such action.

In the early days of electrical engineering, every village probably had its own cable and switch-gear manufacturer. Today, every village has its own software manufacturer. But the little electrical companies gave way to major manufacturers who could adhere to the relevant standards. Nobody misses the little companies, because nobody wants to buy their unreliable, unsafe products. One prospect for the future is that programmers will be similarly regulated (this regulation—perhaps supported by hardware authentication—will also help address the virus problem).

Literate programming (see Section 17.4.1) is a technique for combining program code with its internal documentation ('how it works', rather than 'how to use it' documentation). Literate programming has been used to publish several large, successful programs. Never before have such large programs been published in their entirety for public scrutiny. One wonders whether software manufacturers would dare publish their programs! Nevertheless, techniques such as literate programming could be used internally within companies. Programs would then get better peer assessment. (Many commercial programs I have seen that were not intended for publication leave a lot to be desired: they are often obviously hastily thrown together, undocumented and impenetrable. If commercial software looks like this, then publishing it would only make users lose confidence! That might be a good thing, but it is another reason why software is kept secret.)

The Free Software Foundation (Stallman, 1985) is one group that has reacted against the conventional commercial approach to software development that has been criticized here. It develops software and distributes it in source form for a nominal distribution fee. Users are encouraged to report and fix bugs. Providing the software in source form for those who are interested is an effective way of fixing bugs before users encounter them when programs fail. More benefits of free software are discussed in Box 18.2.

Free and open software attacks bugs in a number of ways. Making the source code freely available makes it available for scrutiny and improvement;

Box 18.2   We need public user interfaces.

Algol 60 started a trend in programming languages: it was the first language to be well-defined. The immediate consequence of this was that many people were able to produce good compilers for it. Because there was a standard, all efforts to implement the language were, to a large extent, compatible. There was a *lingua franca* for the workers who developed or used Algol systems. More than Algol's popularity spread, the benefits of syntactic specification (in particular, BNF, Backus–Naur Form) spread. Today, it is expected that programming languages—Ada, C, Pascal, Smalltalk, and so on—are standardized. Thus, a program written in ISO Pascal will run on any ISO Pascal system. Manufacturers, who provide compilers, compete at the level of providing faster compilers, better optimized code, or better support tools, such as debuggers.

The situation in user interfaces is in complete contrast. It is practically the case that each interactive system is unique; users cannot go from one place to another without significant retraining. What runs on one machine is incompatible with what runs on another.

Programming languages, and hence programming language skills, may be portable, but because interactive systems designs are not, users and their skills are not portable either. Users become tied to particular brands of machine or program.

In short, *programmers get a better deal than users.* And—like the case that computers get a better deal (made in Section 18.5)—this should not be so. Very few interactive systems are standardized, let alone specified. Manufacturers supply proprietary user interfaces, of which they are very jealous. Very often user interfaces are supplied by the same makers of the machines on which they have to be run: this ties users to a particular brand of computer. Litigation, rather than healthy competition, is the norm in the user interface arena. Each manufacturer jealously guards its intellectual investment in—supposedly—helping the user have an easier life.

We need user interface notations so that user interface designs can be public, so that manufacturers can compete by providing better systems, instead of 'competing' by invoking exclusive rights to their designs. Without designs in public ownership, that is, without suitable notations (and the motivation), this will never happen.

A step in the right direction is to make the source code of interactive systems public: this is a positive step for the short term. (It is discussed in Section 18.6.) Let's hope that the problems of Section 7.12 (of counterfinality) do not overtake any popular solutions.

making programs freely available creates a large user base, which in turn is more likely to detect bugs. The freedom for anyone to fix these bugs, without going through the hassle of central updates, means that the software will improve faster than proprietary software. The danger, though, is the ever-present threat of malicious or merely careless programmers who introduce bugs into the software. There still need to be checks and some form of copyright. One effective way to distribute software at low cost and to retain copyright in a sensible non-oppressive way is to distribute it on write-once media, or from *bona fide* bulletin boards. Most people do not have the facilities to make CD-roms and this will help stop people introducing bugs; also, CD-rom disks are in a sense a 'conventional' medium that can be treated by the copyright laws—any social copyright conventions—in the usual way. A vast amount of software is already available on CD-rom, and it is pleasing to see that some distributors emphasize that the software has been as thoroughly tested for bugs and viruses as possible. It would also have been nice to see that the software had also been checked rigorously, but that is coming to our next point.

Perhaps one reason why nobody criticizes the current sad state of the software industry is that most software is not good enough to be worth criticizing. Users have their jobs to do. Programmers have a hard enough time just getting their programs together, let alone worrying about responding to criticism that probably demands complete rewrites! Clearly criticism must be available to designers much earlier in the design cycle. Formal methods are therefore a most promising approach. Formal methods occur at the beginning of design, before commitments and investments become irreversible; they are concise and comparatively cheap to alter in response to criticism; but they are mathematical. In fact, most formal development methods are too mathematical for widespread adoption in the industry. But mathematics has one very desirable feature: it is meant to be criticized. Mathematics as a discipline has chosen and developed a social obligation to *prove* its results. This is essentially what is lacking in programming; in programming there is not even a distinction between conjectures and theorems. Science, its values and benefits (Chapter 9) are inaccessible and unheeded.

It is to be hoped that, if not formal methods as mathematical activities, formal methods as high standards are rapidly adopted. Because formal methods *are* difficult, they encourage designers to change their minds! The advantages of flexible approaches to design were discussed in Section 8.6 (delaying commitment) and particularly in Chapter 17. We note that formal descriptions of systems do not reveal as much as source code: it may be possible to publish formal descriptions of systems without seriously compromising commercial interests. Publishing formal specifications would not only help to reduce bugs as the specifications go under public scrutiny (also the fear of having bugs exposed in this way would increase standards!), but it would also help users (or their advisors) to make an educated choice between systems with different specifications.

Thorough mathematical descriptions of even simple systems tend to be extremely lengthy. The obvious benefits of mathematics, that can be seen in small examples, seems elusive in realistically sized applications. Perhaps some of the ideas of Section 4.2 can help: giving formal descriptions of *differences* is a more concise way of describing systems. But this relies on some systems of sufficient complexity being well defined, that is, publicly defined without copyright, and we've already seen that there are pressures to keep commercially useful work as secret as possible.

We have not mentioned minor bugs, bugs of interface presentation. In themselves presentation bugs do not stop a user operating a system, they just make it unnecessarily harder. I believe that such bugs will be harder technically to handle than the catastrophic bugs that we have concentrated on here. We've almost finished the book and still only addressed a few dozen user interface bugs!

18.7   Conclusions

Whether motors are 'easy to use' is not an issue, for the motors of today are largely invisible. Thus we have clocks and washing machines, not motors. Similarly clocks and washing machines often contain computers, and the user does not need to be aware of them. Is this the ideal for the future? I believe that this vision is somewhat naïve because it forgets about computation: there are other uses for computers than being control systems. We often want users to be able to benefit from the wider possibilities offered by computers. If you like the 'invisible motor' analogy, it is rather like being reminded, on the contrary, that some motors, such as electric drills, that is motors-as-tools, are very useful just because they are *visible* motors.

But the 'invisible computer' vision has one merit: when your washing machine goes wrong, even when the fault is caused by the embedded computer's bugs, you can get it fixed. You have a right to get it fixed and a right to compensation for consequential damage. The sooner applications like word processors are designed as carefully as washing machines the better; the sooner users require—and get—similar protection from bugs the better.

Some bugs are obvious, but other things *seem* like bugs but are 'merely' deviations from what the user has been led to expect. If only interactive software was designed from principles then those deviations would be bugs too, and the user would have a right to expect higher standards. This book's contribution to user interface design is to raise standards, specifically by promoting designing-by-principle (conversely the ability to spot a *failed* principle, a bug), but also to make the designer's job of working with principles interesting, innovative and worth while, more likely and more successful.

Chapter 19

Carrying on

It has been said by many people in many ways that learning
should be active, not merely passive or receptive; merely by
reading books or listening to lectures or looking at moving
pictures without adding some action of your own mind you can
hardly learn anything and certainly you can not learn much.

George Pólya

This final chapter contains suggestions for carrying on: by reading and by
doing.

The literature in user interface design is diverse and comes under
the banner of many separate disciplines. Thus, user interface design can
be found spread out under the general headings of psychology, computing,
anthropology, linguistics and more specialist disciplines, like games theory.
Worse, the subject is developing rapidly. Overall, then, there is no one place
that you can monitor to stay abreast of developments.

I have selected a few major books in user interface design and closely
related areas: this provides detailed background material and context that
could not be covered in the present short book. I also give a list of major
periodicals and conferences: this provides the means to keep abreast of
developments in the field.

But reading is not enough: until you have practised user interface
design, many of the ideas will be academic—and you may give them
an unconditional authority that they do not deserve! The final part of
this chapter therefore makes a few suggestions to carry on by practical
involvement. Unfortunately, there is no space here to interrelate the

suggestions with the preceding chapters—but, of course, you *are* meant to take advantage of the ideas throughout this book, particularly those of Chapter 17.

19.1   General reading

The following books are all very good and easy reads, aimed at the 'general reader' of user interface design. I can highly recommend them.

▷   *Designing Integrated Systems for the Office Environment*, William M. Newman (McGraw-Hill, 1987). This book will be ideal if you are not very familiar with interactive computer systems. There are lots of illustrations and examples, making the text very clear. Newman gives a broad-ranging coverage of user interface design, emphasizing computer technology for office systems.

▷   *Gödel, Escher, Bach*, Douglas R. Hofstadter (Basic Books, 1979). Hofstadter's classic, wide-ranging discourse, covering computability in art, music, biology and computing.

▷   *Descartes' Dream*, Philip J. Davis and Reuben Hersh (Penguin, 1988). An exploration of the role of computers in mathematics, and of the place of mathematics (particularly as mediated by computers) in our lives. The same authors' *The Mathematical Experience*, also Penguin, is fun and reading it will be particularly good preparation for Chapter 14.

▷   The following two books are complementary: one about the realities of hardware design, the other about the realities—and common misunderstandings—of software and complex systems design. *The Soul of a New Machine*, Tracy Kidder (Penguin, 1982) tells the journalistic story of how a new machine was designed. It gives good insight into the sort of managerial pressures that impel design. To complement it, *The Mythical Man Month*, Fred P. Brooks (Addison-Wesley, 1982) is about software design, and is now a classic background book for all software engineers. The title refers to the myth that if a system takes so many man-months, then (supposedly) the more men who work on the project, the faster it can be completed—a variant of the fallacy of composition.

▷   *The Computer and the Mind*, Phil N. Johnson-Laird (Fontana, 1988). A useful introduction to psychology, providing a very good supplementary background to the needs of this book. Several important topics mentioned by Johnson-Laird (learning, grammar rules, vision) are not developed in the present book. Howard Gardner's *The Mind's New Science* (Basic Books, 1987) is a complementary history of cognitive psychology.

▷ Computing science is so popular that it is hard to recommend any particular book. Immediate availability may be a stronger influence on what you want to read. A very good (but long) book to introduce you to programming is Richard Bornat's, *Programming from First Principles* (Prentice-Hall, 1987). Other styles of programming are well covered (from within LISP) by Harold Abelson, Gerald Jay Sussman and Julie Sussman's *Structure and Interpretation of Computer Programs* (MIT Press, 1985). David Harel's *Algorithmics: The Spirit of Computing* (Addison-Wesley, 1987) covers the central ideas and results in computer science; his bibliography is very good.

▷ The first 20 years of the Turing Award Lectures are available as an anthology (Addison-Wesley, 1987). The Turing Award is an annual presentation to individuals who are judged to have made lasting contributions to computing science; many of these contributions are system designs, and the designers' lectures make valuable and informative reading—several have been cited in this book.

Now for more specific user interface books:

▷ Ben Shneiderman's *Designing the User Interface* (Addison-Wesley, 1987) is a good survey of human issues in user interface design. Raymond S. Nickerson's *Using Computers* (MIT Press, 1986) is an encyclopedic survey of the human factors of information systems. Brian R. Gaines and Mildred L. G. Shaw's *The Art of Computer Conversation* (Prentice-Hall, 1984) is a nice short book presenting a list of principles. Paul Booth's *An Introduction to Human–Computer Interaction* (Lawrence Erlbaum, 1989) is more recent, thorough, and has useful annotated bibliographies. The number of such books is growing rapidly, as is the range of target audiences and levels addressed.

▷ Ronald Baeker and William Buxton have edited a large collection of papers, *Readings in Human–Computer Interaction* (Morgan Kaufmann Publishers, 1987). The collection is made all the more useful as they include their own commentary and perspectives. I recommend the book for its broad coverage which will bring you up to 1987, though there is little that is formal in the collection.

▷ Robert W. Bailey, *Human Performance Engineering* (Prentice-Hall, 1982) covers psychology for interactive systems design. The main purpose of Bailey's book is to provide designers with knowledge of how people process information, as well as to give data, principles and methods that contribute towards good design. The book emphasizes human rather than technological skills in the design process. *User Centered System Design*, edited by Donald A. Norman and Stephen W. Draper (Lawrence Erlbaum, 1986) provides a cognitively oriented and more discursive view on user interface design.

▷ *The Psychology of Everyday Things*, Donald A. Norman (Basic Books, 1988). Why are doors designed so that we have no idea how to open them? Why are video recorders too complex to use to the full? This book *must* be read, especially if you wish to design any direct manipulation systems.

▷ Jim Foley and Andy van Dam, *Fundamentals of Interactive Computer Graphics* (Addison-Wesley, 1982) compensates for my avoidance of graphics in this book, and also has good chapters on graphical user interfaces, use of colour, and so on. *Man–Computer Interfaces: An Introduction to Software Design and Implementation* by R. B. Coates and I. Vlaeminke (Blackwell, 1987) is an introductory text that emphasizes implementation of dialogue techniques. It contains quite a lot of Pascal program code—which certainly serves to emphasize that user interface code is not particularly brief! Rather than copying their code, fortunate readers may be better served by gaining access to a system that comes with source code (for example, Smalltalk; many academically available systems, such as UNIX; or the Apple Macintosh with MacApp).

▷ Nan C. Shu's *Visual Programming* (van Nostrand Reinhold, 1988) is a tutorial and introduction to how visual interaction can be used for programming. Combined with direct manipulation, visual programming provides an alternative to text-based interaction.

▷ Apple Computer, Inc., *Human Interface Guidelines: The Apple Desktop Interface* (Addison-Wesley, 1988) describes the standards behind the Apple-style user interfaces. It includes ideas for designing for international markets and for handicapped users. Their *HyperCard Stack Design Guidelines* (Addison-Wesley, 1989) is probably the best brief description of how to design a user interface, targeted at developers of their own system: it stresses the surface features of the interface—the graphics, 'feel' and evaluation.

▷ Henry Ledgard, Andrew Singer and John Whiteside have written a book that includes its own commentary, *Directions in Human Factors for Interactive Systems* (Springer-Verlag, Lecture Notes in Computer Science, no. 103, 1981; series edited by G. Goos and J. Hartmanis). The book brings together a number of the authors' articles and serves as a balanced, though brief, survey of user interface design. A significant part of the book is devoted to annotating some specific designs and experiments of theirs. They describe many of the design decisions behind 'The Pascal Assistant' and an interesting annotated diary of the experiment underpinning their controversial paper 'The Natural Language of Interactive Systems'. This is not the sort of stuff that is normally revealed. The 'Natural Language' paper provoked an interesting range of responses in the Letters to the Editor column of the *Communications of the ACM* **24**(6), 403–6, 1981.

These last three groups provide technical background:

▷ Stuart Card, Tom Moran and Allen Newell's *The Psychology of Human–Computer Interaction* (Lawrence Erlbaum Associates, 1983) is an important landmark in applying psychology to user interface design. Their work has, however, come under some criticism for its reductionist stance: it has been criticized for being over-concerned with time, and performance of error-free users (Allen and Scerbo, 1983). Newell and Card (1985) responds to this criticism.

▷ Both Frank George's *Philosophical Foundations of Cybernetics* (Abacus, 1979) and Michael Arbib's *Brains, Machines and Mathematics* (Springer-Verlag, 2nd edn., 1987) carry many of the ideas of this book into a more formal framework, though neither are specifically concerned with interactive systems and user interfaces. Arbib's is the more mathematical, and has the advantage of being recently updated. *Formal Methods in Human–Computer Interaction*, edited by Michael Harrison and Harold Thimbleby (Cambridge University Press, 1990) is a varied collection illustrating several different approaches to formalizing user interface issues, taken from psychological, mathematical and programming perspectives. Heather Alexander's *Formally-based Tools and Techniques for Human Computer Dialogues* (Ellis Horwood, 1987) shows how formal methods can be used to help in particular with rapid prototyping.

▷ Recently there has been much criticism of the narrowness of conventional formal methods. Terry Winograd and Fernando Flores' *Understanding Computers and Cognition* (Ablex, 1986) is perhaps the most eloquent exposition of this phenomenalist view (and one with which I agree). Lucy Suchman, in *Plans and Situated Actions* (Cambridge University Press, 1987) balances Winograd and Flores with much interesting empirical work. Jon Barwise and John Perry's *Situations and Attitudes* (MIT Press, 1983) provides a theoretical framework within linguistics.

19.2 Keeping abreast: Reading

Merely reading items from the bibliography is not enough if you wish to progress up the levels of intellectual sophistication: you should see the discussions in the literature, and you have to get involved in design. Keeping up to date with this fast moving subject is a daunting exercise in itself. It may be easier to leave the choice of what to read to other people: go to your local university bookshop, and see what books are for sale. Presumably some of them will have been recommended for courses, or acquire up-to-date book catalogues from publishers and scan recent copies of journals (see below). Some universities and research centres specialize in HCI: once you have found a few interesting references to help your work, see if any of it is going on at a certain place, then write to them and ask for their most recent reports. Better still, visit them.

19.2.1   Journals

As of 1990, the most relevant periodicals are: *Human–Computer Interaction* (Lawrence Erlbaum); *Behaviour and Information Technology* (Taylor & Francis); *International Journal of Man–Machine Studies* (Academic Press)—particularly good for new (and sometimes idiosyncratic!) ways of approaching interaction; *IEEE Transactions on Systems, Man and Cybernetics* (IEEE)—also has a wide coverage of feedback and control systems; *Communications of the ACM* (ACM)—has particularly good conference listings and general articles from a computing perspective; *BYTE* (McGraw-Hill)—particularly good on small personal computers; *Interacting with Computers* (Butterworths)—an interdisciplinary journal emphasizing discussion and debate; *International Journal of Human–Computer Interaction* (Ablex) specializes more in the areas of ergonomics, cognition, social and health issues.

19.2.2   Conferences

The most relevant conferences are: *CHI* (pronounced χ), organized by the ACM, annually in the USA; *SIGGRAPH*, the annual conference organized by the ACM special interest group in graphics; *HCI*, organized by the British Computer Society, annually; and internationally, *INTERACT*, by the International Federation for Information Processing (IFIP). The British HCI conference proceedings are published by Cambridge University Press; the USA conferences by the ACM; the international by North-Holland.

19.2.3   Abstracting and database services

If all these books, journals, and conferences are too much to follow, consider looking at *HCI Abstracts* (Ergosyst Associates), which regularly publishes abstracts of HCI-related publications, including university and industrial research laboratory reports. Many good libraries provide on-line database facilities where you will be able to make specific enquiries.

19.3   Keeping abreast: Doing

The best way to keep abreast is really to design some of your own systems, and to discuss your ideas with other people in an active special interest or user group.

There are many ideas throughout the book that can (and should!) be tested or taken up in practical ways, including the following: Box 1.1 suggested writing programs to simulate the user; Box 9.1 briefly described a debate about the status of science in human–computer interaction work; Box 10.2 suggested trying to apply JOSS rubrics to various systems; Box 11.1 described the Johari Window and suggested putting it to use; and Section 10.9.1 suggested comparing the same features as provided in different parts of a system with a view to finding closure. You may want to follow up these ideas. Here are some more suggestions.

19.3.1   Design a system

Most people just forge ahead and build interactive systems. This project asks you to design (and possibly build and evaluate) a very simple interactive system. The intention is that the system is so simple that it will not be too daunting to explore alternative approaches to its user interface design. Yet there are so many possibilities even for such a simple system— in which case, one wonders how many interesting possibilities are ignored for more complex systems.

You are to design an interactive system for addressing mail (possibly electronic mail, but conventional mail addresses will do). There will be a database, containing entries like the following:

```
* Emma Charlotte Mary Thimbleby
Miss E. C. M. Thimbleby,
63, Dodsworth Avenue,
YORK, YO3 7TZ.
```

The first line (marked ⋆) has a person's full name, and subsequent lines give the full postal or email address. Addresses are separated by blank lines.

The user will know a person's name, and will want to find his or her address and have the mail suitably directed. The user knows a person's name, in this case Emma, and submits it to the program. The program should respond with the corresponding address.

Now for some of the problems the interface will have to handle: What if there are several Emmas? What if there are none—how does the program ask for more information? What if there is an address, but the user wants another address (perhaps Emma's work address, or perhaps the address of a different Emma)? What if the user mistypes the name (perhaps typing emma or even ema rather than Emma)? What if this is the first time the program has been used, and the database of addresses does not yet exist? What about showing the user all addresses, and then letting the user accept or reject each one? If there were many addresses, how would the number of questions be reduced to sensible proportions? What should happen if some system limit is about to be exceeded (for example, too many addresses are selected to cope with)? What should happen if the user goes off for a cup of tea in the middle, and some autocratic part of the system terminates the dialogue (a **timeout**)? How can the user get help, when typing `help` should get Help's address!? How should the program be extended to handle telephone numbers (perhaps the computer has an auto-dialler)?

On many systems, the address program will have to cater for non-pre-emption (Section 15.4.5)—for instance, the user may have started to run the program (and collected a few addresses), but now wants to browse on an old letter somewhere in a file (or even on another disk or computer) to remind himself of some person's name. Some systems (especially windowing managers) directly provide features to do this sort of thing, and the address program perhaps need not make any special concessions.

19.3.2   An interactive Turing Machine

The argument in Box 5.1, trying to make the case that a Turing Machine would be difficult to use is a bit tenuous. It glossed over the contrast between a 'batch' Turing Machine with its user interface. We already know that batch programs are not as easy to use as they might be, so the result possibly is neither surprising nor informative.

How would you modify a Turing Machine so that it was interactive: that is, what is the fundamental *interactive* computing machine? Could you still sustain the argument that using such an interactive machine (rather than trying to understand what it was doing) would be difficult?

19.3.3   An HCI demonstrator

The purpose of this project is to provide a well-engineered 'work bench' for research and teaching in HCI. The work bench will exhibit many interaction techniques, and support various techniques for design and evaluation such as Wizard of Oz. No such general system exists.

It is surprising that HCI, of all fields, has practically no readily available demonstrator programs. What programs illustrate HCI techniques, like defaults, direct manipulation, dialogue boxes? We intend our system to be an easily understood HCI technique demonstrator. We would include several techniques for the handicapped, speech and screen magnification being obvious features.

But a demonstrator would also be good for research. Much current work in HCI seems to have been based on very complex applications, and in many cases results from the research have to be carefully disentangled from artefacts due to the specific details of the application.

The first problem with a work bench is to choose an application. Programmable applications are discounted, since this is the interactive programming environment route and introduces too much complexity, too far removed from HCI issues. An application is needed where almost all potential users will be conversant with the task, yet there is still a range of skill level in the population. It is also essential that the application is simple enough to be implemented reliably.

This project will be based on chess, though you can substitute another application if you wish. Chess has the advantage that many users of all ages and skills are available who know it. The computational aspect of chess is well-enough understood for the implementation to be unproblematic. Also, there are many people who like the game and like trying to write programs to play it.

Chess provides a practical basis to explore many ideas in HCI. For example, undo and redo to take back and adjust ill-considered moves; direct manipulation to move pieces; adaption to adjust timing and skill level to motivate the user; task-specific help; user training identifying tactics and strategies of play; time-to-completion indicators (a normal requirement of chess); the interface can be designed to pace the user for suicide chess.

Novel user interface ideas include **literate using** (Section 17.4.2), where a chess program helps users write-up, annotate and check chess games. Literate using is not just an application, but can also be time-stamped and annotated by researchers, for more general research in HCI.

Chess is a good vehicle for demonstrating the use of speech and sound, to diagnose user errors and to announce moves, mate, and so on.

It is possible that users could be taught strategies by viewing, for example, end games animated at high speed. Equally researchers could replay interactions at high speed to identify salient features of interaction.

Chess can be played with a single user or with a group of users. Users may cooperate on a single game, or may play multiple games with a single computer. In either case, windowing techniques are appropriate

Chess has a choice of recognized 'command languages', and a chess program should recognize the common notations. Abbreviation mechanisms and so-called command completion are easy to exploit, though Box 16.2 gave other suggestions. An interesting problem is figurine algebraic notation: although it is international, how is it typed, and does it have any advantage as a command language over direct manipulation?

Unusually for such a simple application, chess also provides possibilities for abstraction. A user may want to play the Sicilian opening, or castle, or to chase the black king into the corner.

An HCI demonstrator should also include powerful features for instrumenting interaction, and for supporting intervention by experimenters. We would provide features so that two (or more) computers could be connected back to back. In a typical experiment, a user at one would not know whether he was interacting with a computer or a remote user. Multiple remote computers are a useful facility so that Wizard of Oz type help can be elicited from several humans, none of whom is aware of the overall task.

19.3.4   Assess a course

What are the really important insights you have got out of this book (or, better, what are the important insights you *should* have got out of a good book on user interface design)? How would you teach a course on user interface design so that you could best communicate the insights, skills and knowledge?

Once you have taught or planned a course, how would you assess your students' understanding? Would you have lots of practical things to do (takes a long time; what do you do about 'failure')? Would you set them essays or programs to write? Would you use unconventional teaching techniques, like peer assessment? Would you let your students actively contribute to the formulation of their assessment, so they will work at it far harder?

Setting an exam is itself a learning experience. You are likely to learn more by setting an exam than by sitting one! Certainly, setting *clear and direct* questions demands a great deal of careful thought: it is impossible to waffle. And, of course, the first step in design is to ask the right questions—not to come ready armed with answers!

It is questionable that a conventional closed exam is the best way to assess students on a user interface course. How would you use continuous assessment—would students do group projects evaluating or designing interactive systems? Remember that designing a complete interactive system would probably be too difficult, or too time-consuming, a project to undertake. Will you use peer assessment? Finally, you could ask your students to set a better exam and work out how to assess it—and learn from them.

Once you have set an exam, you have started to explore syllabus issues. You may have asked yourself why I wrote about some things and not about others in this book. What would you have wanted to cover in a course or book of your own? Would you imagine selling it to industry, giving expensive seminars to a few people, using lots of flashy visual aids and glossy notes? Would it be an intensive course, morning until evening for a week? Would you give it to a university class of sixty-plus students over a term? Would you give handouts, or expect the students to go off to the library and find things out for themselves? What about hands-on experience of computer systems, both good and bad (perhaps some designed by the students in other courses)? Promotional and research videos are readily available: these can make a valuable resource, particularly if you collect videos for competing products.

19.3.5   Implement a calculator

The calculator, Design II, described in Chapter 16 can be implemented as a 600-or-so line Pascal program. It requires some thought to implement, and this section briefly describes how it works. Almost all of the implementation of the calculator is providing the equal opportunity user interface; the arithmetic itself is fairly trivial. After reading this section, if you think implementing the calculator is complex, then consider how much *more* complex a typical interactive system ought to be.

The calculator keeps a line buffer and keeps track of where the cursor is within it. The user can move the cursor left or right by submitting ← or →; legal printing characters (digits and calculator commands like +) are inserted into the buffer at the cursor position, and characters to the right are shuffled up to make space. There is no 'overwrite' mode. The command `delete` (a single key) removes the character at the cursor position, moves the cursor left, and shuffles the characters to the right down over the deleted character. All this goes on without producing any output: the line buffer itself is not displayed.

Whenever the buffer is modified, it is parsed. A recursive descent parser can be used to build a tree representing the expression in the buffer. Instead of reporting syntax errors, dummy nodes are created in the tree. Nodes for missing operands default to the right identity of the operator, as described in Section 16.6. Nodes for missing operators can default to + for simplicity. For consistency, brackets are treated as pre- and postfix unary operators; bracket nodes may have to be inserted when = is parsed. Minus (-) is treated as binary subtract—unary subtract is handled by a simple trick described below. Numbers are treated uniformly as expressions (thus the decimal point is an operator).

As the tree is being built, it is convenient to evaluate the subexpressions and store their values in the nodes; the evaluation must also keep track of whether calculated values are actual or guessed. Note that special cases like division and multiplication by zero (the user having submitted, say, 0 / =) are handled by special rules.

At the end of parsing, then, a tree has been built with an actual or tentative value at every node. The leaves of the tree are either dummy nodes created during parsing, or characters in the line buffer. Now the tree must be displayed. Calculated error corrections are printed at the appropriate points as the tree itself is printed. The general technique for calculating the error corrections is called **constraint propagation**, and we have already completed forward propagation during the parsing. Backward propagation is performed as the tree is printed.

The approach is to have a procedure that can print the expression corresponding to a tree and, by judicious correction (if necessary), print the expression with a specified value. This procedure is used recursively to print the entire tree.

If the entire expression has a tentative value, we arbitrarily choose to print a tree with value 0, otherwise the value calculated from the user's expression is used. This value then propagates back down the tree, being split up appropriately at each node, as the subtrees are printed. Thus, if 20 is the value the node $\langle 2 \rangle + \langle 7? \rangle$ should be printed as having, the left subtree is printed to have value 2 and the right subtree printed to have value $20 - 2$, hence overriding the tentative $\langle 7? \rangle$. The subtree could have obtained the tentative value 7 if the user had submitted a subexpression $(7+)$, which would now be corrected by inserting $\boxed{18}$ in the missing operand position.

Note that a correction either propagates down the tree to be inserted at the point of a missing operand, or the expression has a fixed value, in which case it must be corrected immediately. A fixed expression must be adjusted, if necessary, by printing an appropriate operator and the calculated correction (nothing has to be done to the tree). This correction can only occur for the immediate operands of $=$.[1] Assuming $+$ and $-$ are the lowest priority operators and are left-associative, no brackets are required.

When the node is $=$, then a correction is calculated, and printed if it is non-zero. There is a difficult choice whether to print the correction on the left, on the right, or arrange for the correction to be positive (or, conversely, negative). In my design, I chose to print only positive corrections, but there are disadvantages to this strategy.

When a $-$ node is to be printed, if the left operand has a dummy value, then the user has in fact submitted a unary negate rather than a binary subtract operator. In this case, no left operand is printed if the expression is correct or if it can be adjusted: $-$ is printed, followed by the right subtree, which is forced to display the appropriate negative value. This heuristic works nicely, except if the user wants to calculate something like, '10 = what minus 3?' The user can apparently only submit 'what minus 3' by submitting *10=-3*, which appears to employ a unary minus. The expression would be corrected by whatever strategy the $=$ correction uses, perhaps obtaining the surprising result 10=-3 $\boxed{+13}$, rather than the expected 10= $\boxed{13}$ -3! The solution to this problem is discussed in Chapter 16.

When the tree-printing procedure actually displays a character, it chooses an appropriate colour (red or green; black or white; or whatever) so that user input and system output can easily be distinguished. Finally, the output routine positions the display cursor (a flashing mark, perhaps) just to the right of the character pointed to by the cursor in the line buffer. If you have a display device that cannot print the cursor at an arbitrary position, you can achieve the same sort of effect by printing the expression, outputting return, then moving the print head (or whatever it is) to the position where the cursor ought to be; alternatively, a gap or distinctive character can be left at the cursor position.

---

[1] Once an expression is corrected, all its subexpressions are necessarily correct and need no further adjustment.

Many improvements and optimizations are possible. There is no point reparsing the line buffer if the user has typed an unacceptable character or has merely moved the cursor left or right. There has to be a way to handle overflow (division by zero is only the simplest case to recognize). Round-off errors may produce results that are printed with spurious precision: it may be worth implementing the arithmetic with error margins and using these to indicate appropriate precisions to print results. Unless you have a fast machine, it will get noticeably slow with very long expressions: instead of parsing the entire line buffer every time a change is made to it, parts of the parse tree that are necessarily unchanged could be reused directly.

Extensions to the calculator could include providing operators like sqrt to calculate square roots. If the user submits **s4**, the parser would provide qrt(and) in five dummy nodes, and the result of printing would be s⟨qrt(⟨4⟩⟩. Other extensions were discussed in Chapter 16.

At the same time as working on the program, or once the calculator works, try developing a simulation to see how a hand-held calculator would work in practice. One of the problems that will need solving is that the display size may be smaller than the size of the expression that needs to be displayed. But the user has the commands ← and → and perhaps these can be used to scroll the display contents right and left: maybe the display should move past the cursor, rather than the cursor move along the display? (Notice that this solution means that ← would move the display left, hence moving the cursor rightwards across it.)

You should certainly evaluate your calculator with users. Children would be good users, and certainly have less disdain of a 'mere four function calculator' than adults: it would be interesting to put a prototype in a rugged box and try it out in classroom conditions.

References

Allen R. B. and Scerbo M. W. (1983). Details of command-language keystrokes. *ACM Trans. Office Information Systems*, **1**(2), 159–78.

Alm N., Newell A. F. and Arnott J. L. (1987). A communication aid which models conversational patterns. *Proc. Rehabilitation Engineers' Society of North America (RESNA) 10th. Annual Conference*, 127–29.

Archer J. E., Conway R. and Schneider F. B. (1984). User recovery and reversal in interactive systems. *ACM Trans. Programming Languages and Systems*, **6**(1), 1–19.

Axelrod R. (1984). *The Evolution of Cooperation*. New York: Basic Books.

Baker C. L. (1967). *JOSS: Rubrics*. Rand Corporation, P-3560.

Bevan N., Pobgee P. and Somerville S. (1981). MICKIE—A microcomputer for medical interviewing, *Int. J. Man–Machine Studies*, **14**, 39–47.

Bobrow D. (1968). *ACM SIGART Newsletter*, December.

Brown P. J. (1982). Tools for amateurs. In *Tools and Notions for Program Construction* (Néel D. ed.), 377–90. Cambridge: Cambridge University Press.

Bush V. (1945). As we may think. *Atlantic Monthly*, 101–8. July. Also in Bush V. (1988). *ACM History of Personal Workstations* (Goldberg A. ed.), 237–47. Reading, MA: Addison-Wesley.

Carroll J. M. (1982). The adventure of getting to know a computer. *IEEE Computer*, **15**(11), 49–58.

Carroll J. M. (1984). Minimalist design for active users, 39–44, *Proc. Human–Computer Interaction—INTERACT'84* (Shackel B. ed.), 661–66.

Carroll J. M. (1989). Taking artefacts seriously. *Proc. Software Eronomie'89: Aufgabenorientierte Systemgestaltung und Functionalitaet* (Maass S. and Oberquelle H. eds.), 36–50.

Carroll J. M. and Campbell R. L. (1986). Softening up hard science: reply to Newell and Card, *Human–Computer Interaction*, **2**(3), 227–49.

Chapanis A. (1981). Interactive human communication: Some lessons learned from laboratory experiments. In *Man–Computer Interaction: Human Factors Aspects of Computers and People* (Shackel B. ed.), 65–114, NATO ASI Series E, number 44.

Darragh J. J. (1988). *Adaptive predictive text generation and the reactive keyboard*. MSc. Thesis, Department of Computer Science, Calgary University.

Deutsch D. (1985). Quantum theory, the Church–Turing Principle and the universal quantum computer. *Proc. Roy. Soc.*, **A400**(1818), 97–117.

Dix A. J. and Runciman C. (1985). Abstract models of interactive systems. *Proc. British Computer Society Conf. People and Computers: Designing the Interface* (Johnson P. and Cook S. eds.), 13–22, Cambridge: Cambridge University Press.

Festinger L. (1957). *A Theory of Cognitive Dissonance*. Stanford, CA: Stanford University Press.

Gaines B. R. (1988). A conceptual framework for person–computer interaction in complex systems. *IEEE Trans. Systems, Man, and Cybernetics*, **18**(4), 532–41.

Glegg G. L. (1969). *The Design of Design*. Cambridge: Cambridge University Press.

Good M. D, Whiteside J. A, Wixon D. R. and Jones S. J. (1984). Building a user-derived interface. *Commun. ACM*, **27**(10), 1032–43.

Greenberg S. and Witten I. H. (1985). Adaptive personalized interfaces—A question of viability. *Behaviour and Information Technology*, **4**(1), 31–45.

Greenberg S. and Witten I. H. (1988). How users repeat their actions on computers: Principles for design of history mechanisms. *Proc. CHI'88*, 171–8, Washington, DC.

Hick W. E. (1952). On rate gain of information. *Q. J. Experimental Psychology*, **4**(11), 11–26.

Hoare C. A. R. and He J. (1987). The weakest prespecification. *Information Processing Lett.*, **24**(2), 127–32.

Hofstadter D. R. (1986). *Metamagical Themas*. Harmondsworth: Penguin.

Jefferson D. R. (1985). Virtual time. *ACM Trans. Programming Languages and Systems*, **7**(3), 404–25.

Jensen K. and Wirth N. (1985). *Pascal User Manual and Report (ISO Pascal Standard)*, 3rd. edn. Berlin: Springer-Verlag.

Johnson-Laird P. N. and Wason P. C. (1977). A theoretical analysis of insight into a reasoning task. In *Thinking: Readings in Cognitive Science* (Johnson-Laird P. N. and Wason P. C. eds.), 143–57. Cambridge: Cambridge University Press.

Knuth D. E. (1984). Literate programming. *Computer J.*, **27**(2), 97–111.

Kuhn T. S. (1970). *The Structure of Scientific Revolutions*. 2nd. edn. Chicago, IL: University of Chicago Press.

Luft J. (1963). *Group Processes: An Introduction to Group Dynamics*. National Press Books.

McGregor D. (1960). *The Human Side of Enterprise*. New York: McGraw-Hill.

Mayo E. (1933). *The Human Problems of an Industrial Civilisation*. Macmillan.

Myers B. (1988). *Creating User Interfaces by Demonstration*. Academic Press.

Myers I. B. and Myers P. B. (1980). *Gifts Differing*. Consulting Psychologists Press.

Newell A. and Card S. K. (1985). The prospects for psychological science in human–computer interaction. *Human–Computer Interaction*, **1**(3), 209–42.

Newell A. and Card S. K. (1986). Straightening out softening up: response to Carroll and Campbell. *Human–Computer Interaction*, **2**(3), 251–67.

Norman D. A. (1988). *The Psychology of Everyday Things*. Basic Books.

Owen D. (1986). Answers first, then questions. In *User Centered System Design* (Norman D. A. and Draper S. W. eds.), 361–75. Lawrence-Erlbaum.

Papert S. (1980). *Mindstorms: Children, Computers and Powerful Ideas*. Harvester Press.

Parnas D. L. and Clements P. C. (1986). A rational design process: How and why to fake it. *IEEE Trans. Software Eng.*, **SE-12**(2), 251–7.

Perry W. (1970). *Forms of Intellectual and Ethical Development in the College Years: A Scheme*. Holt, Reinhart and Winston.

Pike R. (1988). Window systems should be transparent. *Computing Systems*, **1**(3), 279–96.

Pólya G. (1948a). Generalization, specialization, analogy. *American Mathematical Monthly*, April, 241–47.

Pólya G. (1948b) *How to Solve It*. Princeton, NJ: Princeton University Press.

Pólya G. (1981). *Mathematical Discovery*. Combined edn. John Wiley.

Popper K. R. and Eccles J. C. (1977). *The Self and Its Brain*. Springer International.

Rabin M. O. (1976). Probabilistic algorithms. In *Algorithms and Complexity* (Traub J. F. ed.), Academic Press.

Rassmussen J. (1983). Skills, rules and knowledge; signals, signs and symbols, and other distinctions in human performance models. *IEEE Trans. Systems, Man, and Cybernetics*, **SMC-13**, 257–66.

Robinson A. (1966). *Non-Standard Analysis*. North-Holland.

Runciman C. and Thimbleby H. W. (1986). Equal opportunity interactive systems. *Int. J. Man–Machine Studies*, **25**(4), 439–51.

Searle J. (1984). *Minds, Brains and Programs*. The 1984 Reith Lectures, British Broadcasting Corporation. (Also Pelican Books, London, 1989.)

Smith S. L. and Mosier J. N. (1984). *Design Guidelines for User-System Interface Software*. Report ESD-TR-84-190, Mitre Corporation, Bedford, MA.

Smullyan R. (1988). *Forever Undecided: A Puzzle Guide to Gödel*. Oxford: Oxford University Press.

Spafford E. H. (1990). Extending mutation testing to find environmental bugs. *Software—Practice and Experience*, **20**(2), 181–9.

Stallman R. M. (1985). *The GNU Manifesto*. MA: Free Software Foundation.

Tennent R. D. (1981). *Principles of Programming Languages*. Prentice-Hall.

Tesler L. (1981). The Smalltalk environment. *BYTE*, August, 90–147.

Thimbleby H. W. (1980). Dialogue determination. *Int. J. Man–Machine Studies*, **13**(3), 295–304.

Thimbleby H. W. (1981). A word boundary algorithm. *Computer J.*, **24**(3), 249–55.

Thimbleby H. W. (1984). Generative user-engineering principles for user interface design. *Proc. Human–Computer Interaction—INTERACT'84* (Shackel B. ed.), 661–6.

Thompson K. (1987). Reflections on trusting trust. In *ACM Turing Award Lectures* (Ashenhurst R. L. and Graham S. eds.), 171–7. Reading, MA: Addison-Wesley.

Tufte E. R. (1983). *The Visual Display of Quantitative Information.* Connecticut: Graphics Press.

Turing A. M. (1950). Computing machinery and intelligence. *Mind*, **59**(236), 433–60.

Vitter J. S. (1984). *US&R*: A new framework for redoing. *IEEE Software*, **1**(4), 39–52.

Weizenbaum J. (1976). *Computer Power and Human Reason.* San Francisco, CA: W. H. Freeman.

Winograd T. and Flores F. (1986). *Understanding Computers and Cognition.* Norwood, NJ: Ablex.

Witten I. H. (1987). Computer (in)security: infiltrating open systems. *Abacus*, **4**(4), 7–25.

Witten I. H. and Cleary J. G. (1986). Foretelling the future by adaptive modelling. *Abacus*, **3**(3), 16–36 & 73.

Wolfram S. (1988). *Mathematica.* Reading, MA: Addison-Wesley.

Zloof M. M. (1975). Query by example. *Proc. AFIPS National Computer Conf.* **44**, 431–8. New Jersey: AFIPS Press.

Index